How to do Everything with

Everything

with

Microsoft Office

Excel® 2007

About the Author

Guy Hart-Davis is the author of more than 40 computer books on subjects as varied as Microsoft Office, Windows Vista, Mac OS X, Visual Basic for Applications, and the iPod. His most recent books include *CNET Do-It-Yourself iPod Projects,* and *How to Do Everything with Microsoft Office Word 2007.*

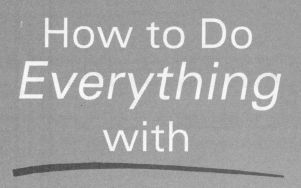

How to Do Everything with

Microsoft® Office Excel® 2007

Guy Hart-Davis

New York   Chicago   San Francisco   Lisbon
London   Madrid   Mexico City   Milan   New Delhi
San Juan   Seoul   Singapore   Sydney   Toronto

The McGraw·Hill Companies

McGraw-Hill books are available at special quantity discounts to use as premiums and sales promotions, or for use in corporate training programs. For more information, please write to the Director of Special Sales, Professional Publishing, McGraw-Hill, Two Penn Plaza, New York, NY 10121-2298. Or contact your local bookstore.

How to Do Everything with Microsoft® Office Excel® 2007

1234567890 CUS CUS 019876

ISBN-13:   978-0-07-226369-5
ISBN-10:   0-07-226369-5

Sponsoring Editor Roger Stewart	**Proofreader** Bev Wiler	**Art Director, Cover** Jeff Weeks
Editorial Supervisor Janet Walden	**Indexer** Kevin Broccoli	**Cover Designer** Pattie Lee
Project Manager Vasundhara Sawhney	**Production Supervisor** Jean Bodeaux	**Cover Illustration** Tom Willis
Acquisitions Coordinator Carly Stapleton	**Composition** International Typesetting and Composition	
Technical Editor Karen Weinstein	**Illustration** International Typesetting and Composition	
Copy Editor Sally Engelfried		

This book is dedicated to Rhonda and Teddy.

Contents at a Glance

Contents

PART II   Calculate, Manipulate, and Analyze Data

Acknowledgments

My thanks go to the following people for making this book happen:

- Roger Stewart for getting the project started and keeping it going
- Karen Weinstein for performing the technical review and providing helpful suggestions and encouragement
- Janet Walden, Jean Bodeaux, and Vasundhara Sawhney for coordinating the project
- Sally Engelfried for editing the text with care and a light touch
- International Typesetting and Composition for laying out the pages
- Bev Wiler for proofreading the book
- Kevin Broccoli for creating the index

Introduction

The most widely used spreadsheet application in the world, Excel is a key part of the Microsoft Office suite of applications. You can use Excel for anything from a small spreadsheet of household finances to monster tables of all your company's products, customers, and sales. You can use Excel either on its own or together with the other Office applications.

Excel 2007 builds on the many previous versions of Excel to deliver powerful functionality and many new features along with a slick and easy-to-use interface. If you're new to Excel, you've got a large amount to learn. If you're coming to Excel 2007 as an experienced user of earlier versions, you've still got plenty to learn, because Excel 2007 introduces major changes. But either way, this book will get you up to speed quickly.

Who Is This Book For?

This book is designed to help beginning and intermediate users get the most out of Excel 2007 in the shortest possible time. If you fall into either of those categories, you'll benefit from this book's comprehensive coverage, focused approach, and helpful advice. If you're an Excel expert seeking super-advanced coverage, look elsewhere.

What Does This Book Cover?

Here's what this book covers:

- Chapter 1, "Navigate the Excel Screen," shows you how to launch Excel in the many ways that Windows provides, how to control Excel using the Ribbon (the graphical component that replaces the menus and toolbars of previous versions), and how to navigate the main components of the Excel screen. You'll also learn what workbooks and worksheets are, how to select objects, and how to get help on using Excel.

- Chapter 2, "Configure Excel to Suit Your Working Needs," discusses how to improve your view of worksheets by splitting the view, displaying extra windows, hiding and redisplaying windows, zooming the view, and freezing particular rows and columns so they never move while everything else scrolls. You'll learn how to set the most important of Excel's many options to customize its behavior, how to load add-ins when you need the extra functionality they provide, and how to configure AutoCorrect to save you time and effort.

- Chapter 3, "Create Spreadsheets and Enter Data," starts by explaining how to create a new workbook in any of several convenient ways and how to save it, and then shows you how to create your own templates to use as the basis for future worksheets. You'll also find out how to enter data in your worksheets manually and by using Excel's AutoFill feature, how to use Excel's Find and Replace features, and how to recover your work if Excel crashes.

- Chapter 4, "Format Worksheets for Best Effect," discusses how to manipulate the worksheets in a workbook, and then moves on to cover formatting cells and ranges using the many types of formatting that Excel supports.

- Chapter 5, "Add Graphics and Drawings to Worksheets," shows you how to add visual impact to your worksheets by including pictures, shapes, diagrams, and other graphical objects. This chapter also explains how Excel's drawing layer handles graphical objects and how you can position, resize, and format objects.

- Chapter 6, "Check, Lay Out, and Print Worksheets," explains how to get your worksheets into shape for printing and how to print them. Topics covered include checking spelling, setting the print area, specifying the paper size and orientation, creating headers and footers, and using Print Preview to avoid wasting paper. You'll also learn to set and adjust page breaks and specify which extra items to include in the printout.

- Chapter 7, "Perform Calculations with Functions," covers what functions are and how you enter them in your worksheets. You'll also learn about the different categories of functions that Excel provides, with examples of some of the most useful functions in each category.

- Chapter 8, "Create Formulas to Perform Custom Calculations," starts by teaching you the basics of formulas in Excel and the components from which formulas are constructed. After that, you'll learn how Excel handles numbers, and how to create both regular formulas and array formulas. The end of the chapter shows you how to troubleshoot formulas when they don't work correctly.

- Chapter 9, "Organize Your Data with Excel Tables," shows you how to create Excel tables, enter data, and sort and filter the data to find the information you need. This chapter also covers how to link an Excel worksheet to an external database (for example, an Access database) so that you can extract data to an Excel worksheet and manipulate it there, and how to perform web queries to bring Web data into worksheets.

- Chapter 10, "Outline and Consolidate Worksheets," discusses how to outline a worksheet so that you can collapse it to show only the parts you need and how to consolidate multiple worksheets into a single worksheet. Both outlining and consolidation can save you welcome amounts of time.

- Chapter 11, "Analyze Data Using PivotTables and PivotCharts," explains how to use Excel's powerful PivotTables and dynamic PivotCharts to manipulate your data so that you can draw conclusions from it. You'll also learn how to create a conventional chart (one that is static rather than dynamic) from PivotTable data.

- Chapter 12, "Solve Problems by Performing What-If Analysis," discusses how to create data tables that enable you to assess what impact one or two variables have on a calculation. This chapter then describes how to use Excel's scenarios to explore the effects of alternative data sets within the same worksheet, how to solve one-variable problems using Goal Seek, and how to use the Solver to solve multi-variable problems.

- Chapter 13, "Create Effective Charts to Present Data Visually," covers how to use Excel's chart features to create compelling charts. You'll learn how to create charts quickly, how to choose the right type of chart for your data, and how to edit and format charts to give them the effect you need. You'll also learn how to copy formatting you've applied to one chart to another chart, how to unlink a chart from its data source, how to print your charts, and how to add custom chart types to Excel's existing types.

- Chapter 14, "Share Workbooks and Collaborate with Colleagues," explains the range of features that Excel provides for sharing workbooks, protecting them from types of changes you don't want others to make, and collecting and reviewing input from your colleagues to produce a final version of a workbook.

- Chapter 15, "Use Excel's Web Capabilities," describes Excel's key features for creating and working with Web data. You'll learn when to save files directly to intranet sites and Internet servers, how to save a worksheet or workbook as a Web page, and how to configure Excel's Web options. If your company uses XML for data exchange, you can also learn how to use Excel's powerful XML capabilities, including external schemas.

- Chapter 16, "Use Excel with the Other Office Applications," discusses how to transfer data smoothly and easily among Excel and the other Office applications (such as Word and PowerPoint). This chapter starts by discussing data transfer via the Clipboard, then covers embedding and linking, two different technologies for including a part of one document in another document. The end of the chapter explains how to insert Excel objects in Word documents and PowerPoint presentations, and how to insert Word objects and PowerPoint objects in worksheets.

- Chapter 17, "Customize Excel's Interface," describes how to customize the Quick Access Toolbar and the status bar to make the commands and features you need easy to reach. This chapter is short, but it can save you considerable time and effort, so it's worth a visit.

- Chapter 18, "Use Macros to Automate Tasks in Excel," explains how to use Office's built-in Macro Recorder feature to record macros (sequences of commands) so you can perform them automatically later. To use macros, you must configure Excel's macro virus–protection mechanism and Trust Center, so you'll learn about these features in this chapter as well.

- The Appendix lists the keyboard shortcuts you can use to make Excel do your bidding without touching the mouse.

Excel 2007 runs on Windows Vista and Windows XP. The illustrations in this book show how Excel looks with Windows Vista's Vista Basic user interface. If you're using the Vista Aero user interface, or if you're using Windows XP, your windows will look somewhat different, but everything should function the same.

Conventions Used in This Book

To make its meaning clear concisely, this book uses a number of conventions, three of which are worth mentioning here:

- The pipe character or vertical bar denotes choosing an item from the Ribbon. For example, "choose Page Layout | Page Setup | Orientation | Portrait" means that you should click the Page Layout tab on the Ribbon (displaying the tab's contents), go to the Page Setup group, click the Orientation button, and then choose Portrait from the panel that appears.

- Note, Tip, and Caution paragraphs highlight information you should pay extra attention to.

- Most check boxes have two states: *selected* (with a check mark in them) and *cleared* (without a check mark in them). This book tells you to *select* a check box or *clear* a check box rather than "click to place a check mark in the box" or "click to remove the check mark from the box." (Often, you'll be verifying the state of the check box, so it may already have the required setting—in which case, you don't need to click at all.) Some check boxes have a third state as well, in which they're selected but dimmed and unavailable. This state is usually used for options that apply to only part of the current situation.

This book assumes you're using Internet Explorer rather than another browser. Given that Internet Explorer currently still has the bulk of the web browser market, that's probably a reasonable assumption. But if you're using another browser, you'll see different behavior when you take an action that causes Excel to access your default browser.

Part I

Get Started with Excel

Chapter 1

Navigate the Excel Screen

How to...

- Start Excel manually or automatically
- Understand the components of the Excel screen
- Understand the basics of worksheets and workbooks
- Open an existing workbook
- Open other formats of spreadsheet file in Excel
- Navigate in workbooks and worksheets
- Select cells, ranges, and other objects
- Get help with Excel

Excel is a powerful spreadsheet application for organizing, calculating, summarizing, and presenting data. Coming to grips with Excel involves a learning curve, because Excel 2007 has a radically different user interface than earlier versions of Excel—and indeed different from almost all other Windows applications except for its sibling applications, Word 2007 and PowerPoint 2007. Even if you're experienced with Windows applications or with earlier versions of Excel, plan to spend several hours getting up to speed with this new user interface.

In this chapter, you'll see how to navigate the Excel screen and understand its components. You'll learn the basics of *worksheets* (the spreadsheet pages that Excel uses) and *workbooks* (files that contain worksheets), how to open existing workbooks, and how to navigate through them and select objects in them. At the end of the chapter, you'll learn how to use Excel's built-in help features to find information you need.

Start Excel

To start Excel, choose Start | All Programs | Microsoft Office | Microsoft Office Excel 2007. When it opens, Excel creates a new blank workbook containing three worksheets.

When you need to start Excel and open an existing workbook at the same time so that you can work in that workbook, start Excel in either of these ways:

- Choose Start | Recent Items, and then select the workbook from the Recent Items submenu. (In Windows XP, choose Start | My Recent Documents.)

NOTE *In Windows Vista, if the Recent Items list doesn't appear on your Start menu, right-click the Start button and choose Properties to display the Taskbar And Start Menu Properties dialog box. On the Start Menu tab, select the Store And Display A List Of Recently Opened Files check box, and then click the OK button. In Windows XP, if the My Recent Documents item doesn't appear on your Start menu, right-click the Start button and choose Properties to display the Taskbar And Start Menu Properties dialog box. Click the upper Customize button to display the Customize Start Menu dialog box. On the Advanced tab, select the List My Most Recently Opened Documents check box. Click the OK button to close each dialog box.*

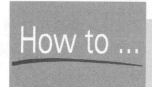

Set Up Officewide
Options at First Launch

The first time you launch one of the Office 2007 applications after installing them, the application prompts you to enter (or verify) your user name and initials, and then choose privacy options in the dialog box shown here.

These are your choices:

- **Get Online Help**   Select the Search Microsoft Office Online For Help Content When I'm Connected To The Internet check box if you want to use online help as well as the help files stored on your computer. Online help includes the latest information, so searching it is usually helpful—but if you have a slow Internet connection, you may prefer to search the help files on your computer instead.

- **Keep Your System Running**   Select the Download A File Periodically That Helps Determine System Problems check box if you want Office to automatically download a file that helps track system problems. This option is usually helpful.

- **Make Office Better**   Select the Sign Up For The Customer Experience Improvement Program check box if you want to let Office collect information about how you use the Office applications, your computer's configuration, and problems Office runs into. Office then connects to Microsoft via the Internet and uploads the information. The information is anonymous, but some people prefer not to provide it.

(continued)

After the Privacy options, Office displays the screen shown next, recommending that you sign up for Microsoft Update, which automatically downloads and installs new files for Office and Windows when Microsoft makes them available. If you want to let Windows keep itself and Office up-to-date, select the Download And Install Updates From Microsoft Update When Available option button, and then click the Sign Up button. Otherwise, select the I Don't Want To Use Microsoft Update option button, and then click the Finish button. (Windows changes the name of the button in the lower-right corner from Finish to Sign Up depending on which option button you select.)

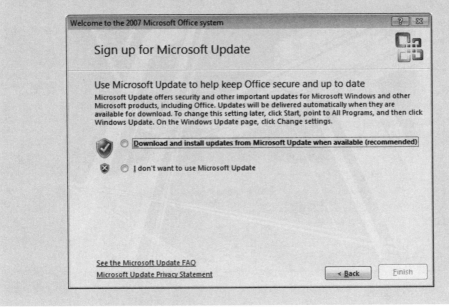

- Double-click the icon for an existing workbook in a Windows Explorer window or on your desktop.

NOTE *For instructions and illustrations, this book uses a standard installation of Windows Vista as the operating system on which Excel is running. If you're using Windows XP, the user interface will look a little different, but you should be able to follow the instructions easily enough.*

 **Start Excel Easily and Often**

If you start Excel more frequently than most other applications, Windows automatically places a shortcut to Excel on the most frequently used applications section of the Start menu, shown here. You can then start Excel by choosing Start | Microsoft Office Excel 2007.

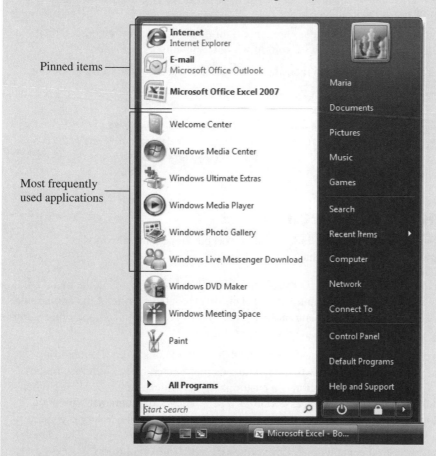

To make launching Excel even easier, *pin* Excel to the pinned items section of the Start menu, so that it always appears there, no matter which applications you launch most frequently. To pin Excel, choose Start | All Programs | Microsoft Office to display the Microsoft Office folder, right-click the Microsoft Office Excel 2007 item, and choose Pin To Start Menu from the shortcut menu. (If an Excel icon already appears on the most frequently used applications section of the Start menu, you can right-click that icon instead of displaying the Microsoft Office folder.)

(*continued*)

If you use Excel in every Windows session, configure Windows to launch Excel automatically each time you log on to Windows. The logon process then takes a few seconds longer, but you don't need to launch Excel manually.

To make Windows launch Excel automatically when you log on:

1. Choose Start | All Programs | Microsoft Office to display the Microsoft Office folder.

2. Right-click the Microsoft Office Excel 2007 item and choose Copy from the shortcut menu to copy it to the Clipboard.

3. On the Start menu's All Programs submenu, right-click the Startup folder, and then choose Open to open a Windows Explorer window showing its contents.

4. Right-click in the window, and then choose Paste Shortcut from the shortcut menu.

5. Click the Close button (the × button) to close the Startup window.

 *If you're using Windows in a corporate environment, an administrator may have prevented you from customizing your startup group. If this is the case, you'll need to have an administrator customize the startup group for you.*

Understand the Excel Screen

Figure 1-1 shows the Excel application window with a workbook open and a worksheet displayed. These are the main elements that you see:

■ **Office button menu** Where earlier versions of Excel had nine menus in the menu bar, Excel 2007 has only the Office button menu. This menu contains some of the commands that used to appear on the File menu in earlier versions of Excel. You can open this menu by clicking it or by pressing ALT and then F (ALT, F).

■ **Quick Access Toolbar** A new feature of Excel 2007, the Quick Access Toolbar is a toolbar that provides quick access to the commands represented by the buttons you put on it. (See Chapter 17 for instructions on customizing the Quick Access Toolbar.) When you first start Excel, the Quick Access Toolbar appears in its small version, which is positioned to the right of the Office button menu. You can also display a larger version of the Quick Access Toolbar below the Ribbon instead of the small version. The Quick Access Toolbar at first contains only three buttons: Save, Undo, and Redo.

■ **Ribbon** Another new feature of Excel 2007, the Ribbon is a tabbed bar across the top of the Excel window, appearing just below the window's title bar and to the right of the Office button and the Quick Access Toolbar (if you're using the small version of the Quick Access Toolbar). The Ribbon replaces all the remaining menus and most of the toolbars that previous versions of Excel used. Each tab of the Ribbon contains a different set of controls that are linked thematically. Only one tab can be visible at a time. To switch tab, you click the text label at the top: Home, Insert, Page Layout, Formulas, Data, Review, or View. (At first glance, users of earlier versions of Excel may take the tab labels to be menus,

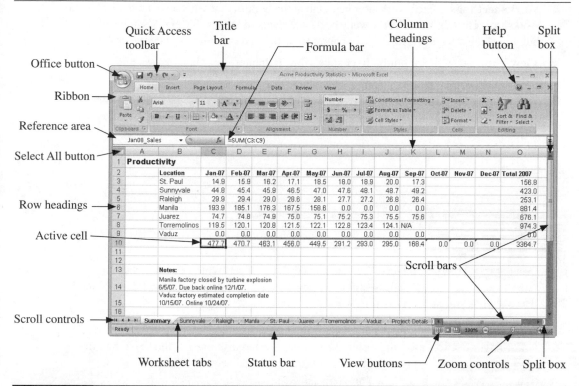

FIGURE 1-1   Excel application window with a workbook open and a worksheet displayed.

because they occupy the position that menus used to.) Figure 1-1 shows the Home tab of the Ribbon selected, as it is by default when you open a workbook.

TIP   *When you need as much space as possible on screen to view a worksheet, you can collapse (or "minimize") the Ribbon to just its labels by double-clicking the label of the tab you're currently using. While the Ribbon is minimized, you can click a tab to display the Ribbon so that you can issue command; once you've issued the command, the Ribbon minimized itself again. Double-click the tab again to expand the Ribbon back to its normal size when you want to have it displayed again.*

■ **Reference Area**   This area, at the left end of the row just below the Ribbon, shows the address of the active cell.

■ **Formula bar**   This area, to the right of the Reference Area, enables you to enter and edit data and formulas.

■ **Row headings and column headings**   The row headings are the numbers at the left side of the screen that identify each row by number. The column headings are the letters across the top of the worksheet grid that identify each column by one or more letters.

■ **Worksheet tabs** Each worksheet has a tab at the bottom that you can click to display the worksheet. The tabs in each new worksheet have standard names (Sheet1, Sheet2, and so on), but you can give the tabs descriptive names to help you easily identify your worksheets.

■ **View buttons** Click a button to change view. (Chapter 2 explains views and how to use them.)

■ **Zoom controls** The readout at the left end of the zoom controls shows the current zoom percentage. You can zoom by dragging the slider or by clicking the – (minus) and + (plus) buttons.

Work with Task Panes

Like Excel 2002 (which introduced task panes) and Excel 2003 (which continued them), Excel 2007 uses various task panes—but with major differences from Excel 2002 and Excel 2003. Here's what you need to know to work with task panes:

■ Excel 2007 no longer displays the Getting Started task pane when you launch Excel. For anyone who's used to closing the Getting Started task pane at the beginning of each Excel session, this is a relief.

■ Where Excel 2002 and Excel 2003 display only one task pane at a time but let you switch from one task pane to another by using the drop-down menu of whichever task pane is currently displayed, Excel 2007 displays multiple task panes as needed.

■ Most task panes appear in the default position, *docked* (attached) to the right side of the Excel window. You can drag any task pane by its title bar to any other edge of the window to dock it there if you prefer. Alternatively, you can display the task pane *undocked*, floating freely anywhere in the Excel window, by dragging it away from the side of the window to which it's currently docked.

■ You can close a task pane by clicking the Close button (the × button) at its upper-right corner.

■ When the task pane is docked, you can resize it by dragging the border on its open side to change its width or depth. When the task pane is floating free, you can resize it by dragging any side or corner.

■ Excel displays some task panes automatically in response to actions you take. You can display other task panes manually when you need them. Excel makes task panes available only when you can use them and doesn't allow you to display a task pane that's irrelevant to the task you're currently performing.

Most of the task panes are available for the majority of the time when you're working in a workbook in Excel, but some are available only for specific files. When a task pane isn't available, it appears dimmed in the list.

Here are examples of the task panes you'll use when working in Excel:

■ **Clip Art**   Enables you to search for graphics files organized by collection, file type, and location. You can display this task pane by clicking the Insert tab, going to the Illustrations group, and then clicking the Clip Art button.

■ **Research**   You can search specified encyclopedias, thesauruses, and translation tools for more information about selected words. You can display this task pane by clicking the Review tab, going to the Proofing group, and then clicking the Research button.

■ **Clipboard**   The Office Clipboard can hold up to 24 items copied or cut from any Office application. You can then paste these items elsewhere. You can display this task pane by clicking the Home tab, going to the Clipboard group, and then clicking the Clipboard button (the tiny button at the right end of the bar that says "Clipboard," the button with an arrow pointing down and to the right).

Understand Worksheets and Workbooks

Excel's basic unit is the *worksheet*, a grid of cells in which you enter data. Each worksheet consists of 16,384 columns and 1,048,576 rows, up from 256 columns and 65,536 rows in earlier versions of Excel. The intersection of each row and column is a cell, so each worksheet contains 17,179,869,184 cells, up from the 16,777,216 cells in earlier versions. You're not likely to fill a worksheet of this size, but it's great to have plenty of room for growth.

By default, Excel uses the A1 reference scheme to refer to columns, rows, and cells:

■ Columns are designated by letters: A to Z for the first 26 columns, AA to AZ for the next 26 columns, then BA to BZ, CA to CZ, and so on. After ZZ comes AAA, AAB, and so on to BAA, BAB, BAC. The last column is XFD.

■ Rows are numbered from 1 to 1048576.

■ Cells are designated by column and row. The first cell on a worksheet is cell A1, and the last cell is XFD1048576. This designation is called the *cell address*.

Instead of A1, Excel can also use the R1C1 reference format, which uses the letter *R* and a number to indicate the row and the letter *C* and a number to indicate the column. For example, cell B2 is R2C2 in R1C1 reference format. You can change to R1C1 format by clicking the Office button, choosing Excel Options, clicking the Formulas category, selecting the R1C1 Reference Style check box in the Working With Formulas area, and then clicking the OK button.

Excel saves worksheets in *workbook* files. These files use the Excel Workbook file format, which has the .xlsx file extension. Workbooks can contain one or more worksheets.

By default, new workbooks contain three worksheets and can contain up to 255 worksheets. The worksheets are named Sheet1, Sheet2, and so on. You can change these names as needed by right-clicking on the name of the worksheet and choosing rename from the menu.

Workbooks make it easy to keep related information on separate sheets that you can access quickly. For example, you might use a separate worksheet to track the sales results for each of your company's sales territories. Excel provides features for entering the same data on multiple worksheets simultaneously, so you can quickly create a group of worksheets that contain the same basic information—for example, the layout of those sales results and associated information. On the top sheet of the workbook, you might put a summary worksheet that presents an executive overview of the sales results. Excel lets you create formulas that link from one worksheet to another, so the sales-territory worksheets could automatically update the summary worksheet.

See the section "Divide Data Among Workbooks and Worksheets," in Chapter 3, for guidelines on how to divide your data.

Open an Existing Workbook

Excel offers a variety of ways to open an existing workbook—from the Office button menu, the Open dialog box, a Windows Explorer window, or the Desktop. Experiment with these ways of opening workbooks and learn which you find easiest for which purpose.

Open a Recently Used Workbook from the Office Button Menu

The Office button menu lists the workbooks you've used most recently. You can open one of these workbooks by displaying the menu (for example, click the Office button or press ALT, F) and choosing the appropriate entry. Figure 1-2 shows an example.

To keep a workbook on the recently-used list, you can *pin* it in place. To do so, click the pin at the right end of the workbook's entry on the Office button menu. Excel pushes in the pin, indicating that the workbook is held in place. (To unpin the workbook, click the pin again.)

By default, Excel lists your nine most recently used workbooks, but you can make the Microsoft Office Button menu show anywhere from none to 50. To change the number of workbooks listed, follow these steps:

1. Click the Office button, and then click the Excel Options button. Excel displays the Excel Options dialog box.

2. Click the Advanced category to display its contents.

3. In the Display area, change the Show This Number Of Recent Documents list setting.

4. Click the OK button. Excel closes the Excel Options dialog box.

Open a Workbook from the Open Dialog Box

If the workbook you want to open isn't listed on the Office button menu, use the Open dialog box:

1. Click the Office button and choose Open, or press CTRL-O. Excel displays the Open dialog box (see Figure 1-3).

FIGURE 1-2   If you've worked recently with the workbook you want to open, you can select it quickly from the listing on the Office button menu.

TIP   *You can enlarge the Open dialog box by dragging the dotted triangle in the lower-right corner down and to the right.*

2. Navigate to the folder that contains the workbook:

- Use the Recently Changed link in the Favorite Links panel on the left to display a list of your recently opened workbooks.

- Use the other links in the Favorite Links panel on the left to quickly access your desktop, Documents folder, Computer folder, or other frequently used folders as necessary.

- Click the Recent Pages drop-down button to display a list of folders you've accessed recently. Select a folder to go to that folder.

- Click one of the navigation buttons in the address box to display a list of folders in the folder that appears before the button. Select a folder to go to it.

Recent Pages
drop-down
button

Click one of these navigation buttons
to display a list of folders contained in
the folder before the button

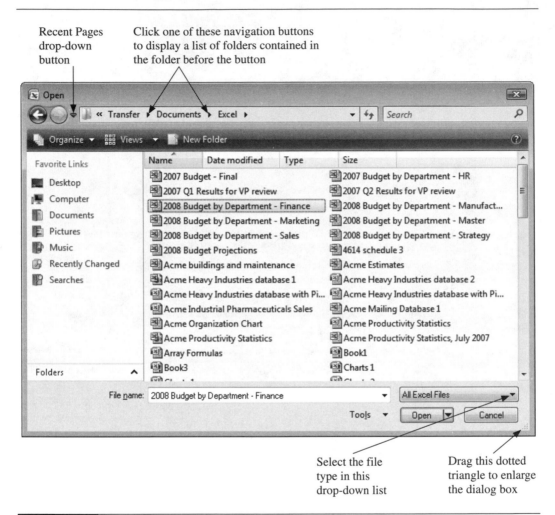

Select the file
type in this
drop-down list

Drag this dotted
triangle to enlarge
the dialog box

FIGURE 1-3   The Open dialog box lets you open workbooks that don't appear in the recently-used list on the Microsoft Office Button menu.

3. Select the workbook. If the Open dialog box doesn't show the workbook file, you may need to choose a different filter in the drop-down list above the Open and Cancel buttons. The default filter is All Excel Files, which displays all the file types that Excel can open (including files such as web pages, text files, add-ins, and toolbars).

4. Click the Open button. Excel closes the Open dialog box and opens the workbook.

Know When to Use the Alternate Open Commands

As well as opening the workbook for editing, the Open dialog box also enables you to open the workbook in the following ways by clicking the drop-down button on the Open button and choosing the action from the resulting menu, shown here:

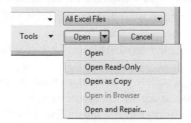

- **Open Read-Only**   Opens the workbook in a read-only format, which prevents you from saving changes to this copy of the file. You can save changes by using a Save As command to save the workbook under a different file name or path. Use this command when you need to ensure that you don't unthinkingly save changes to a workbook that you're not supposed to change. (If an administrator or another user decides to allow you to view their workbooks but not change them, Excel enforces the read-only status automatically when you try to open the workbook.)

- **Open As Copy**   Opens a copy of the workbook under the name Copy (1) of *filename*—for example, Copy (1) of Project Budget.xlsx. This command can be useful for quickly creating a copy of the workbook, but renaming the copy from its default name is cumbersome: even if you use a Save As command to save the copy under a different name, you'll need to subsequently delete the Copy (1) Of file so as not to leave it lying around.

- **Open In Browser**   Opens the file in your computer's default browser (for example, Internet Explorer). This command is available only for HTML files.

- **Open And Repair**   Opens the workbook and attempts to repair the damage it has sustained. Use this command only when Excel crashes on trying to open a particular file.

Open a Workbook from Windows Explorer or Your Desktop

You can open a workbook directly from a Windows Explorer window (or from your desktop) by double-clicking it. This technique is useful for files you've chosen to store on your desktop and when you've just used Windows Explorer to find, move, or copy a file. By opening the folder directly from Windows Explorer, you avoid having to navigate in the to the folder Open dialog box.

Another advantage is that when you open a workbook in this way, Excel doesn't change the working directory to the folder that contains the workbook. So the next time you display the Open dialog box, it still displays the folder from which you last opened a workbook using the dialog box.

 *You can also open a workbook from the Start | Recent Items menu (on Windows Vista) or the Start | My Recent Documents menu (on Windows XP), if this menu appears on your Start menu.*

Open Other Formats of Spreadsheet in Excel

If you've used another spreadsheet application before migrating to Excel, you may need to transfer data from your old spreadsheets to Excel. To help you do so, Excel includes filters for converting data from other formats, such as dBASE, earlier Excel formats (for example, Excel 97-2003 format), and XML.

Excel can also open text files in widely used formats, such as comma-separated values (CSV)—a format that uses commas to denote the divisions between data fields. To get data from applications such as address books or organizers into an Excel worksheet, you'll often need to export the data to a CSV file and then open that file in Excel. Similarly, if Excel doesn't have a converter for a spreadsheet file that you need to open, use the application that created the file to save a copy in CSV format, then open that copy in Excel.

To convert a file, open it via the Open dialog box as usual—for example, click the Office button, and then click Open. Use the Files Of Type drop-down list to specify the type of file you want to display in the main list box. If the type of file doesn't appear in the list, select the All Files item to display all files—but be warned that Excel probably won't be able to convert the file. If it can't, Excel may display a message claiming the file format is not valid.

"Not valid" almost always means that Excel doesn't have a converter for the file format. (You may sometimes find that the file has become corrupted and useless.) When this happens, open the file in the application that created it (or an application that does have a converter), export the data to a CSV file, and then import that file into Excel.

Deal with Security Warnings When You Open a Workbook

When you open a workbook, you may see a security warning appear on a new bar below the Ribbon. The following illustration shows an example. The message is "Security Warning: Automatic update of links has been disabled."

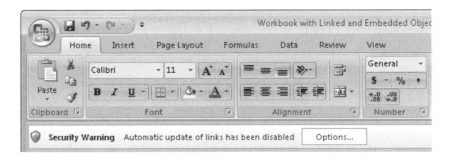

You'll learn how to work with links in Chapter 16. A *link* is a way of inserting content from one file into another file—for example, inserting a chart in a workbook—while keeping the inserted content connected to the original file. For example, you might insert a chart from another workbook into a worksheet. By keeping the chart linked to the workbook that contains it, you can update it automatically from within the worksheet that contains it. This is useful, but it raises security issues, and Excel objects to linked content whose original files are stored in a folder that Excel doesn't trust.

For now, if you need to have the linked content updated, click the Options button. Excel displays the Microsoft Office Security Options: Security Alert - Links dialog box (see Figure 1-4). Select the Enable This Content option button, and then click the OK button. If you don't need to have the linked content updated, click the Close button (the × button at the right end, not shown in the illustration) to close the Security Warning bar.

TIP   *Your choice in the Microsoft Office Security Options: Security Alert—Links dialog box will depend on how well you trust the source of the workbook file containing linked material and how important you judge the links to be to the workbook.*

See the section "Understand and Set Security Levels" in Chapter 18 for a detailed discussion of how Office's security mechanism works and how to configure it.

FIGURE 1-4   Choose whether to update links automatically or leave the linked content disabled.

Convert a Workbook to the Excel 2007 File Format

Excel 2007 introduces a new format for Excel workbooks. Confusingly, the new format is called "Excel Workbook," just as the previous format used to be; the previous format is now called "Excel 97-2003 Workbook." However, the new format uses the .xlsx file extension, rather than the .xls extension that earlier versions of Excel used, so you easily can tell the formats apart.

When you open a workbook created in an earlier version of Excel, Excel displays the words "[Compatibility Mode]" in the title bar after the workbook's name to remind you that the workbook isn't in Excel's preferred format. To update the workbook to the Excel 2007 format, follow these steps:

1. Click the Office button, and then choose Convert. A Microsoft Office Excel dialog box appears, as shown here.

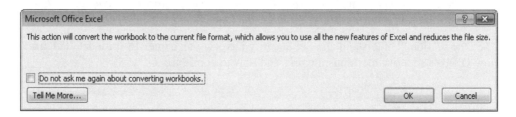

2. Select the Do Not Ask Me Again About Converting Workbooks check box if you don't want to see this dialog box again.

3. Click the OK button. Excel converts the workbook to the latest format, saves it using the .xlsx file extension, and then prompts you to close and reopen the workbook so that you can use the new features, as shown here.

4. If you want to remove the "[Compatibility Mode]" readout from the title bar, click the Yes button. Excel closes the workbook, and then reopens it. Otherwise, click the No button, and continue working in the workbook until you want to close it.

Navigate in Workbooks and Worksheets

After creating a new workbook or opening an existing workbook, you'll need to navigate to the worksheet on which you want to work. You'll then need to navigate on that worksheet to access the right cells or ranges.

Like almost all other Windows applications, Excel supports navigating with both the mouse and the keyboard. For most purposes, the mouse is quicker and faster than the keyboard.

Navigate to the Worksheet You Need

To move to another worksheet with the mouse, click its tab. If necessary, use the scroll buttons (shown with labels below) to make the tab appear in the list.

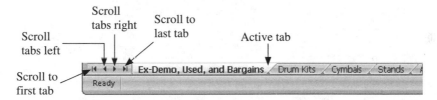

Excel offers these keyboard shortcuts for navigating among and selecting worksheets:

Action	Keyboard Shortcut
Move to the next worksheet	CTRL-PAGE DOWN
Move to the previous worksheet	CTRL-PAGE UP
Select the current and next worksheets	CTRL-SHIFT-PAGE DOWN
Select the current and previous worksheets	CTRL-SHIFT-PAGE UP

Navigate to Cells and Ranges in a Worksheet

Most people find the mouse the easiest way of navigating in worksheets:

- ■ Click a worksheet or cell to access it.

- ■ Use the horizontal and vertical scroll bars and scroll boxes to scroll to different areas of the worksheet.

You can also navigate easily by using the arrow keys ($\uparrow$, $\downarrow$, $\leftarrow$, and $\rightarrow$) and keyboard shortcuts. Keyboard shortcuts are especially effective when you're working in a large worksheet that requires extensive scrolling to navigate.

The following list shows the most useful keyboard shortcuts:

Action	Keyboard Shortcut
Move to the specified edge of the data region	CTRL-↑, CTRL-↓, CTRL-←, or CTRL-→
Move to the first cell in the row	HOME
Move to the first cell in the worksheet	CTRL-HOME
Move to the last cell ever used in the worksheet	CTRL-END
Move down one screen	PAGE DOWN
Move up one screen	PAGE UP
Move to the right by one screen	ALT-PAGE DOWN
Move to the left by one screen	ALT-PAGE UP
Scroll the workbook to display the active cell	CTRL-BACKSPAGE

You can move to a specific cell by typing its address in the Name box (lowercase is fine—you don't need to press SHIFT) and then pressing ENTER.

Select Objects

After navigating to the right area of the worksheet, you select objects (such as cells and ranges) so that you can work with them. You can select most objects with either the mouse or the keyboard.

Select Cells and Ranges of Cells

Much of your work in Excel will be with *ranges* of cells. Excel supports ranges of both contiguous and noncontiguous cells:

- A range of contiguous cells is a rectangle of cells defined by the starting and ending cell addresses, separated by a colon that indicates the addresses together form a range. For example, the range C3:E5 (shown on the left in Figure 1-5) consists of a block of nine cells.

 Technically, a range can consist of a single cell, but most people understand ranges to have two or more cells.

- A range of noncontiguous cells consists of a collection of cell addresses separated by commas. For example, a range consisting of the cells B3, B5, B7, and B9 (as shown on the right in Figure 1-5) would be represented as B3, B5:B7, B9. Ranges of noncontiguous cells can include ranges of contiguous cells—for example, B3, B5:B7, B9.

You can select objects in worksheets by using the mouse, the keyboard, or both. These are the basic techniques you need to know:

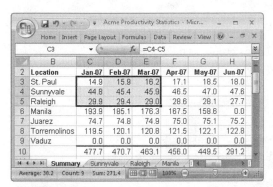 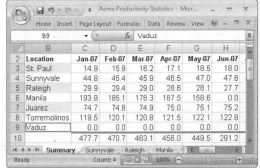

FIGURE 1-5   Ranges can be either contiguous (left) or noncontiguous (right).

- To select a cell, click it, or use the arrow keys to move the active cell outline to it.

- To select a row or column, click its heading. Press SHIFT-SPACE to select the row or CTRL-SPACE to select the column that the active cell is in.

- To select a contiguous range of cells, click the cell at one corner of the range and then drag to the other corner. You can drag in any direction—up, down, or diagonally. This technique works best when the full range of cells appears on screen. If you need to scroll the window to reach the end of the range, you may overrun the far corner of the range. In this case, use the next technique instead.

- To select a contiguous range of cells, click the cell at one corner of the range, scroll if necessary to display the far corner of the range, hold down SHIFT, and click. This technique works well for ranges that run beyond the current window.

- To make multiple selections, make the first selection, hold down CTRL, and then make the other selections.

To select all the cells in the active worksheet, click the Select All button, the unmarked button at the intersection of the column headings and row headings.

You can also select cells and ranges by using the names assigned to them and by using the Go To dialog box and the Go To Special dialog box. These techniques are discussed below.

Assign a Name to a Range

To make a range easier to access and identify quickly, you can assign a name to it. You can select the range easily by using the Name box's drop-down list or the Go To dialog box, and then you can quickly apply formatting to the range and use the range's name in calculations rather than having to specify their addresses.

To assign a name to a range, follow these steps:

1. Select the range.

2. Click the Formulas tab, go to the Defined Names group, and click the Define Name button. Excel displays the New Name dialog box (shown here).

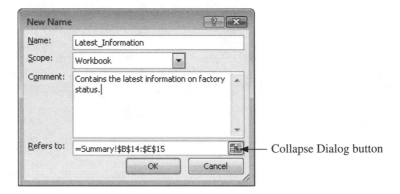

Collapse Dialog button

3. Type the name in the Name text box.

4. In the Scope drop-down list, choose the *scope* for the name—the part of the workbook to which you want the name to apply. Choose Workbook to make the name accessible from the whole workbook; this is the default setting and is usually the best choice. Sometimes, however, you may want the name to apply only to a particular worksheet—for example, so that you can use the same name on different sheets in the workbook. If so, select that worksheet in the Scope drop-down list. If you want to add a comment explaining what the named range refers to, type it in the Comment text box.

5. Verify that the Refers To box show shows the range you selected in step 1. If you need to change the range, click the Collapse Dialog button to shrink the New Name dialog box down to a minimal size, select the range in the worksheet, and then click the Collapse Dialog button again.

6. Click the OK button. Excel assigns the name to the range and closes the New Name dialog box.

To delete a range name from a workbook, follow these steps:

1. Click the Formulas tab, go to the Defined Names group, and then click the Name Manager button. Excel displays the Name Manager dialog box (see Figure 1-6).

2. Select the name in the list box.

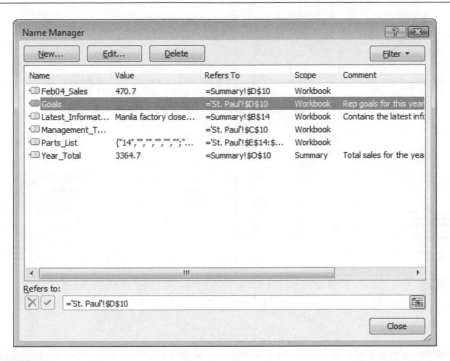

FIGURE 1-6   Use the Name Manager dialog box to delete an existing range name, change the range to which a range refers, or add a new name.

3. Click the Delete button. Excel displays a confirmation dialog box.

4. Click the OK button. Excel deletes the name.

5. Click the Close button. Excel closes the Name Manager dialog box.

TIP   *You can also name a range by selecting it, clicking in the Name box, typing the name for the range, and pressing ENTER. However, using the Name Manager dialog box lets you more easily see which other range names you've defined, which can help you implement an orderly naming scheme and avoid duplicating names.*

Select Ranges by Using the Go To Dialog Box and the Go To Special Dialog Box

For selecting ranges and cells with specific contents, Excel provides the Go To dialog box and the Go To Special dialog box. The Go To dialog box (shown on the left in Figure 1-7) largely duplicates the functionality of the Name box, but it also offers you quick access to unnamed ranges you've worked with recently—if you can identify them by their addresses. To display the Go To dialog box, press CTRL-G or choose Home | Editing | Find & Select | Go To—in other words, click the Home tab,

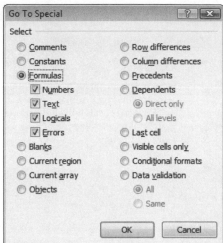

FIGURE 1-7   Use the Go To dialog box (left) to select named ranges or unnamed ranges you've recently worked with and the Go To Special dialog box (right) to select cells that match specific criteria.

go to the Editing group, click the Find & Select button, and then choose Go To from the panel. (For concision, from here on, this book uses this shortened form of notation for choosing Ribbon items.)

The Go To Special dialog box (shown on the right in Figure 1-7) tends to be more useful than the Go To dialog box, as it enables you to easily select cells that match specific criteria, such as containing comments, conditional formats, or data validation.

To display the Go To Special dialog box, click the Special button in the Go To dialog box. (You can also choose Home | Editing | Find & Select | Go To Special to display the Go To Special dialog box without going through the Go To dialog box.) Choose the appropriate options (described in Table 1-1), and then click the OK button to select the cells with those characteristics. You can then move through the range of cells selected by using ENTER, SHIFT-ENTER, TAB, and SHIFT-TAB.

Table 1-1 explains the options that the Go To Special dialog box offers.

Select Worksheets in a Workbook

You can select worksheets in a workbook as follows:

- Click a worksheet's tab to select it.
- SHIFT-click another worksheet's tab to select all the worksheets between the currently selected worksheet and the one you click.
- CTRL-click another worksheet's tab to add that worksheet to the selection, or CTRL-click a selected worksheet's tab to remove it from the selection.

Option	Explanation
Comments	Cells that contain comments.
Constants	Cells that contain constant data (text, numbers, or dates) rather than formulas. Select or clear the Numbers check box and Text check box under Formulas to specify whether to include numbers and text in the search.
Formulas	Cells that contain formulas rather than constant data. (In other words, the cell's contents begin with =.) Select or clear the Numbers check box, Text check box, Logicals check box, and Errors check box to specify whether to include numbers, text, logical values (TRUE or FALSE), and error values, respectively. For example, you might use this option button to check all your formulas or to quell errors.
Blanks	Cells that contain no data or formatting. Excel excludes cells after the last cell in the worksheet that contains data.
Current Region	The active cell and all cells around it up to the first blank row and blank column in each direction.
Current Array	The active cell and the array it's in.
Objects	Objects such as text boxes, charts, AutoShapes, and other objects (for example, sounds).
Row Differences	Cells within the selected range whose contents are different from the contents of the comparison cells you specify. Select the range to evaluate, click a cell in the comparison column to make it active, then select this option button in the Go To Special dialog box.
Column Differences	Cells within the selected range whose contents are different from the contents of the comparison cells you specify. Select the range to evaluate, click a cell in the comparison row to make it active, then select this option button in the Go To Special dialog box.
Precedents	Cells to which the active cell refers. Under the Dependents option button, select the Direct Only option button (the default) or the All Levels option button to specify whether to select direct references only, or indirect references as well.
Dependents	Cells that refer to the active cell. Select the Direct Only option button (the default) or the All Levels option button to specify whether to select direct references only or indirect references as well.
Last Cell	The last cell ever used in the active worksheet.
Visible Cells Only	Cells that are visible—not hidden. Use this option to avoid pasting hidden rows or columns along with visible rows and columns. Select the range, display the Go To Special dialog box, select this option, then copy the range.
Conditional Formats	Cells that have conditional formatting applied. ("Use Conditional Formatting," in Chapter 5, explains conditional formatting.) Under the Data Validation option, choose the All option button (the default) to select all cells. Select the Same option button to select only those that match the active cell.
Data Validation	Cells that contain data validation rules. Choose the All option button (the default) to select all cells. Select the Same option button to select only those that match the active cell.

TABLE 1-1   Go To Special Dialog Box Options

 *When multiple worksheets are selected, Excel displays* [Group] *in the title bar to remind you.*

Excel also offers two keyboard shortcuts for selecting worksheets:

- Press CTRL-SHIFT-PAGE DOWN to select the current and next worksheets. You can extend the selection further by pressing again to select the worksheet after the last selected worksheet.

- Press CTRL-SHIFT-PAGE UP to select the current and previous worksheets. You can extend the selection further by pressing again to select the worksheet before the first selected worksheet.

Get Help with Excel

To get help on using Excel, follow these steps:

1. Press F1 or click the Microsoft Office Excel Help icon at the right end of the Ribbon (the question mark icon). Excel displays the Excel Help window (see Figure 1-8).

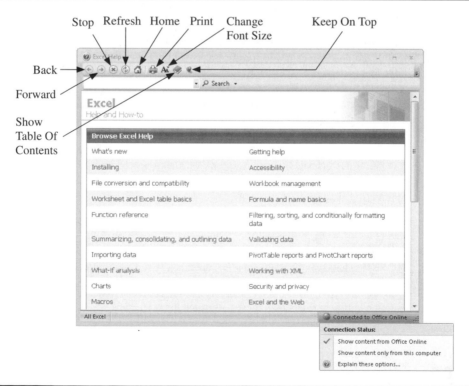

FIGURE 1-8 Use the Excel Help window to browse help topics or search for help.

You can switch between using Office Online help content and using only the help on your computer by using the drop-down list at the lower-right corner of the window.

2. To see what topics are available, click the links in the Browse Excel Help list.

3. To search for help, click in the Search box, type one or more keywords, and then click the Search button. You can confine the search to online content or offline content topics or to a particular help category either offline or online, by clicking the drop-down button on the Search button, and then choosing an item on the menu (shown here). Click a search result to display the related topic.

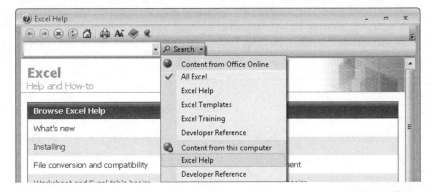

4. To control whether the Help window appears on top of other windows (such as the Excel window), click the Keep On Top button.

5. When you've finished using help, click the Close button (the × button) to close the Excel Help window.

Chapter 2

Configure Excel to Suit Your Working Needs

How to...

- Split a window to see different parts of it
- Open extra windows to view different parts of the same worksheet
- Hide and redisplay windows
- Zoom the display
- Keep key rows and columns on screen
- Set the most important options to make Excel suit your work style
- Load and unload add-ins
- Configure AutoCorrect to save time and effort

If you use Excel frequently, spend a little time configuring Excel to suit your working needs as closely as possible.

In an ideal world, you might dream of simply telling Excel to do your work for you. While this isn't possible yet, you *can* automate many routine tasks by creating macros in Visual Basic for Applications (VBA), the programming language built into Excel. Chapter 18 explains how to create macros with VBA.

More realistically, you can set many configurable options to specify how Excel's interface looks and behaves. By choosing settings that suit you, as discussed in this chapter, you can make the time you spend using Excel not only more comfortable, but also shorter and more productive.

In this chapter, you'll also learn how to display the appropriate sections of your worksheets so that you can see the information you need; how to load add-ins (extra components) to provide added functionality when you need it; and how to use the AutoCorrect feature to correct typos, expand abbreviations you define, and help enforce consistency in your worksheets.

Improve Your View with Splits, Extra Windows, Hiding, Zooming, and Freezing

You can greatly improve your view of data and your ability to work effectively with it by doing the following:

- Splitting the window to reveal two or four parts of it at the same time
- Opening extra windows to display other parts of the same workbook or worksheet
- Hiding windows you don't need (so that they don't get in the way)
- Zooming in and out to change your view of detail
- Freezing the display of rows and columns to keep relevant information on screen

This section shows you how to do all of these things.

Split the Excel Window to Show Separate Parts at Once

You can split a worksheet window into two or four panes so you can see two or four separate parts of the worksheet at once. Figure 2-1 shows an example of a window split into four panes to show different areas of the same worksheet.

The easiest way to apply a two-pane split is to drag the horizontal split box or the vertical split box to where you want the split to be. Then, if necessary, you can drag the other split box to create a four-pane split.

To split the window into four panes at once, position the active cell in the row above and the column to the left of which you want to split the window. Then choose View | Window | Split to split the window both ways—in other words, click the View tab on the Ribbon, go to the Window group (shown at the top of the next page), and then click the Split button.

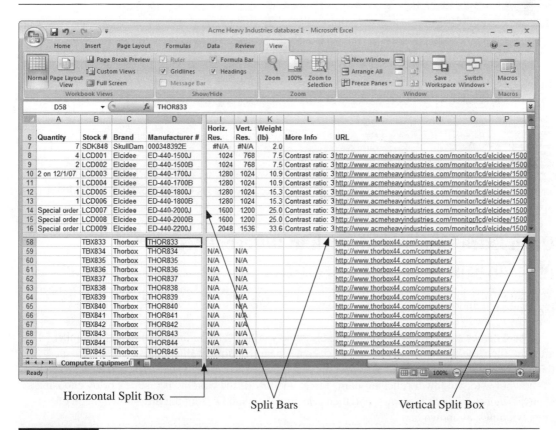

Horizontal Split Box ——   Split Bars   Vertical Split Box

| FIGURE 2-1 | Use Excel's window-splitting feature to display two or four separate parts of the same worksheet window at once. |

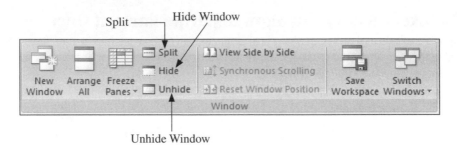

Split — Hide Window

Unhide Window

To adjust the horizontal or vertical split, drag the horizontal or vertical split bar. To adjust both split bars at once, drag where they cross. Excel shows shaded lines to indicate where the split will fall when you release the mouse button, as shown here.

ED-440-1800J	1280	1024	15.3	Contrast rat	3	http://www.acmeheavyindustries.com/m
ED-440-1800B	1280	1024	15.3	Contrast rat	3	http://www.acmeheavyindustries.com/m
ED-440-2000J	1600	1200	25.0	Contrast rat	3	http://www.acmeheavyindustries.com/m
ED-440-2000B	1600	1200	25.0	Contrast rat	3	http://www.acmeheavyindustries.com/m
ED-440-2200J	2048	1536	33.6	Contrast rat	3	http://www.acmeheavyindustries.com/m
THOR833						http://www.thorbox44.com/computers/
THOR834	N/A	N/A				http://www.thorbox44.com/computers/
THOR835	N/A	N/A				http://www.thorbox44.com/computers/
THOR836	N/A	N/A				http://www.thorbox44.com/computers/
THOR837	N/A	N/A				http://www.thorbox44.com/computers/
THOR838	N/A	N/A				http://www.thorbox44.com/computers/
THOR839	N/A	N/A				http://www.thorbox44.com/computers/
THOR840	N/A	N/A				http://www.thorbox44.com/computers/
THOR841	N/A	N/A				http://www.thorbox44.com/computers/

To remove a single split, double-click its split bar or drag it out of the worksheet window. To remove all splitting, double-click the split bars where they cross or choose, View | Window | Split.

Open Extra Windows to Work in Different Areas of a Worksheet

Another way of working more easily in two or more areas of a worksheet or workbook is to open two or more windows containing the same workbook. To open a new window, choose View | Window | New Window.

Excel names extra windows containing the same workbook by adding a colon and a number after the filename. For example, when you open a second window of Budget.xlsx, Excel renames the first window Budget.xlsx:1 and names the second window Budget.xlsx:2. You can easily switch from window to window by clicking in the target window (if the window is visible), or by choosing View | Window | Switch Windows, and then selecting the window from the drop-down menu of open windows, as shown here.

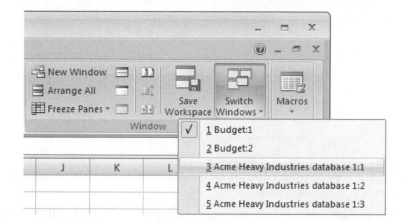

You can split each open window as needed, and you can hide and unhide windows as described later in this chapter.

When you open multiple windows on the same workbook, you can zoom each window independently of the other. (See "Zoom In and Out," later in this chapter for a discussion of zooming the display.) For example, you might zoom one window out to display an overview of a worksheet while you work in close-up in another window. By using two windows, you avoid having to zoom in and out in the same window.

Arrange Open Windows

You can arrange your workbook windows by using standard techniques to resize and position the windows:

- Click the Maximize Window button to maximize a window so that it occupies all the space in the Excel application window.
- Click the Restore Down button to restore it to its previous, nonmaximized size.
- Click the Minimize Window button to minimize a window.
- Drag the edges or corners of nonmaximized windows to resize them. Drag the windows by their title bar to position them where you want them to appear.

Arrange Windows Using the Arrange Windows Dialog Box

To arrange all nonminimized windows, follow these steps:

1. Choose View | Window | Arrange All. Excel displays the Arrange Windows dialog box, shown next.

2. Select the Tiled option button, Horizontal option button, Vertical option button, or Cascade option button as appropriate:

   ■ Tiling sizes each nonminimized window as evenly as possible to fill the space available in the Excel window. Tiling tends to be most useful for getting an overview of which workbook windows are open. You can then close any workbook windows you no longer need, or minimize (or hide) other workbook windows to get them out of the way before arranging the remaining windows horizontally or vertically.

   ■ The Horizontal and Vertical arrangements are good for comparing the contents of two or three windows. Horizontal is better for data laid out along rows; Vertical is better for data laid out down columns.

   ■ The Cascade arrangement is good for shuffling a stack of windows into an arrangement where each window is a reasonably large size but you can access any window instantly.

3. If you want the arrangement command to affect only the windows that belong to the active workbook (the one that has the focus), select the Windows Of Active Workbook check box.

4. Click the OK button. Excel closes the Arrange Windows dialog box and arranges the windows as you specified. If you don't like the effect, try another arrangement.

Arrange Minimized Windows Using the Arrange All Command

When all the open windows are minimized, you can choose View | Window | Arrange All to arrange the window icons neatly at the bottom of the Excel window.

Compare Two Windows Side by Side

You can use the Arrange Windows dialog box to position two windows alongside each other to compare their contents. But Excel also offers an option that goes one better and synchronizes the scrolling of the two windows so that you can compare their contents more easily.

To compare the contents of two windows, follow these steps:

1. Activate one of the windows whose contents you want to compare, e.g. by clicking in the window.

2. Choose View | Window | View Side By Side, shown next

View Side By Side ————   Synchronous Scrolling

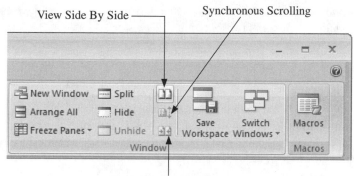

Reset Window Position

3. What happens next depends on how many windows you have open in Excel:

■   If you have only two windows open, Excel arranges them side by side. Skip the rest of this list.

■   If you have more than two windows open, Excel displays the Compare Side By Side dialog box:

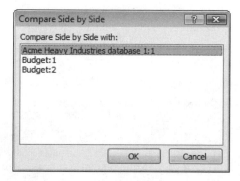

4. In the Compare Side By Side With list box, select the second window for the comparison.

5. Click the OK button. Excel closes the Compare Side By Side dialog box and arranges the windows to occupy the Excel application window.

You now have the two windows positioned so that you can see as much of their contents as fits within the windows. If you want to compare more data than fits within the windows, you can synchronize the scrolling of the two windows, so that when you scroll in one window, the other window scrolls along in the same direction and by the same amount.

To synchronize the scrolling, choose View | Window | Synchronous Scrolling. If you want to turn off synchronous scrolling, choose View | Window | Synchronous Scrolling again.

When you've finished comparing the windows, choose View | Window | View Side By Side to make Excel put the windows back the way they were arranged before.

 *The Synchronous Scrolling button is available only when you've used the Compare Side By Side command to position two windows side by side.*

Hide a Window

When you have many windows open, you may find that you don't need a particular window for a while. When this happens, click the window to make it active, and then hide it by choosing View | Window | Hide Window. This technique can help you both keep your Excel window uncluttered, and protect delete self data against inquisitive coworkers or passerby.

To redisplay a hidden window, follow these steps:

1. Choose View | Window | Unhide. Excel displays the Unhide dialog box:

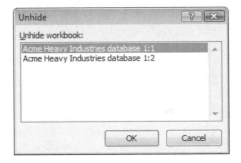

2. In the list box, select the window you want to redisplay.

3. Click the OK button. Excel closes the Unhide dialog box and reveals the specified window.

Zoom In and Out

To make your worksheets easier to read on screen, you can zoom in and out from 10 percent of normal size to 400 percent of normal size:

■ To zoom in or out by 10-percent increments, click the Zoom In (+) button or the Zoom Out (−) button on the Zoom slider at the right end of the status bar.

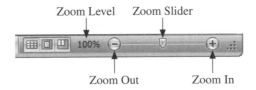

■ To zoom to a different percentage by hand, drag the Zoom slider on the status bar.

- To zoom to the largest size at which a particular range of cells fit in the window, select the range, and then choose View | Zoom | Zoom to Selection. This zoom is great for concentrating on a group of important cells.

- To zoom to a preset percentage or to a custom percentage, click the Zoom Percentage readout, or choose View | Zoom | Zoom. Excel displays the Zoom dialog box (shown here). Select the option button for the preset zoom percentage you want, or select the Custom option button, and then enter the exact percentage in the text box. Click the OK button. Excel closes the Zoom dialog box and zooms the window to the size you chose.

NOTE   *At tiny magnifications Excel hides the cell gridlines to improve visibility.*

Use Freezing to Keep Key Rows and Columns Visible

If you work on worksheets that contain more data than will fit on your monitor at a comfortable size, you'll often need to scroll up and down, or back and forth, to refer to labels and headings in the leftmost columns or topmost rows of the worksheet. Such frequent scrolling can be both frustrating and a waste of time.

To reduce scrolling, you can *freeze* specific rows and columns so that Excel keeps displaying them even though the other rows and columns scroll. For example, you can freeze column A and row 1 so that Excel keeps displaying them even when you navigate to the last cell in the worksheet.

To freeze just the top row in the window, choose View | Window | Freeze Panes | Freeze Top Row. To freeze just the leftmost column in the window, choose View | Window | Freeze Panes | Freeze First Column. These commands are new in Excel 2007 and make it easier to freeze just the top row or the leftmost column. (In earlier versions of Excel, you could freeze just the top row by selecting cell A2 and issuing the Freeze Panes command, or just the first column by selecting just cell B1 and issuing the Freeze Panes command.)

To freeze rows and columns, select the cell to the right of the column and below the row you want to freeze, and then choose View | Window | Freeze Panes | Freeze Panes. Excel displays a heavier line along the gridlines to show where the frozen section is. The frozen section then remains in place when you scroll the rest of the worksheet as usual. Figure 2-2 shows a worksheet with column A and the top six rows frozen. (The first five rows are scrolled off the top of the screen.)

To remove freezing, choose View | Window | Freeze Panes | Unfreeze Panes.

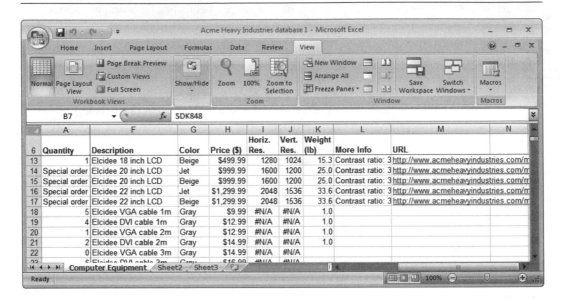

FIGURE 2-2   You can freeze the leftmost columns and topmost rows of a worksheet to keep them on screen as you scroll to the depths of the worksheet.

Set Options to Make Excel Easier to Use

Splits, extra windows, zooming, and freezing can make a huge difference in the way you use Excel. But to have Excel best suit the way you work, you must click the Office button, click Excel Options, and then configure various settings in the Excel Options dialog box. In this section, you'll learn about the options that affect the way Excel appears and behaves.

Excel offers dozens of options, some widely useful and others highly specialized. This section discusses the options most likely to make a difference to your work.

Some categories of options affect separate parts of Excel's functionality, rather than Excel's behavior as a whole. This book discusses these options in the section that covers their functionality, instead of presenting all the options here. Here are the details of where these options are discussed:

- "Troubleshoot Formulas," in Chapter 8, explains the Error Checking and Error Checking Rules options in the Formulas category.

- "Restrict Data and Protect Workbooks," in Chapter 14, discusses the options in the Trust Center category.

- Chapter 17 discusses how to customize Excel by using the options in the Customization category.

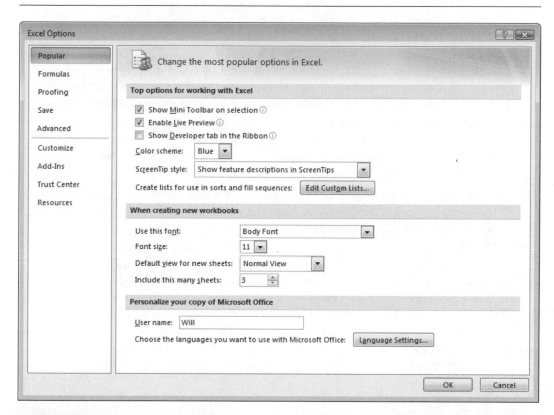

FIGURE 2-3   Start your customization by choosing options in the Popular category of the Excel Options dialog box.

Personalize Excel Using the Options in the Popular Category

The options in the Popular category of the Excel Options dialog box (see Figure 2-3) let you easily make sweeping changes to Excel's look and feel.

Top Options For Working with Excel

The Top Options For Working With Excel area offers the following options:

- **Show Mini Toolbar On Selection**   Select this check box if you want Excel to pop up the Mini Toolbar when you select text within a cell. The Mini Toolbar (shown here) contains widely used formatting commands, and having it appear automatically is normally useful. If you clear this check box, you can force the Mini Toolbar to appear by right-clicking the selection (which also displays the context menu).

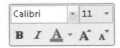

- **Enable Live Preview**   Select this check box if you want Excel to apply to your worksheets a preview of the formatting you choose so that you can see how it looks. For example, if you highlight a theme in the Themes panel, Excel shows you how it looks.

- **Show Developer Tab In The Ribbon**   Select this check box if you want Excel to display the Developer tab in the Ribbon. The Developer tab gives you access to VBA and XML controls, so you'll want to display it if you're creating macros, programming Excel, or creating XML-based workbooks.

- **Color Scheme**   In this drop-down list, select the color scheme you want to apply to the Excel window. Word, PowerPoint, and Excel share this setting, so if you change it in Excel, Word and PowerPoint change too.

- **ScreenTip Style**   In this drop-down list, choose Show Feature Descriptions In ScreenTips if you want to see the full-size ScreenTips that contain detailed explanations of options, choose Don't Show Feature Descriptions in ScreenTips if you want to see regular ScreenTips showing the name of the command or option, or choose Don't Show ScreenTips if you want to suppress all ScreenTips. Figure 2-4 shows a ScreenTip with the feature description on the left and a regular ScreenTip on the right.

- **Create Lists For Use In Sorts And Fill Sequences**   Chapter 3 shows you how to create custom lists that enable you to insert regular series of data swiftly and accurately in your worksheets.

When Creating New Workbooks

The When Creating New Workbooks area contains the following options:

- **Use This Font**   In this drop-down list, select the font you want to use as the standard font in all your workbooks. As in previous versions of Excel, you can choose a font by name, but in Excel 2007 you can choose the Body Font item to use the font specified in the theme used for the workbook. If you change theme, all the text formatted with the Body Font font takes on the new font and font color specified in the new theme. Each theme also includes a Headings Font item that's available to you in the Use This Font drop-down list, but you won't normally want to use the heading font as the standard font for your workbooks.

NOTE   *A theme is an overarching suite of formatting that applies to an entire workbook, including fonts, colors, and graphical effects. The advantage of using themes is that, by changing from one theme to another, you can completely change the look and feel of a workbook in moments.*

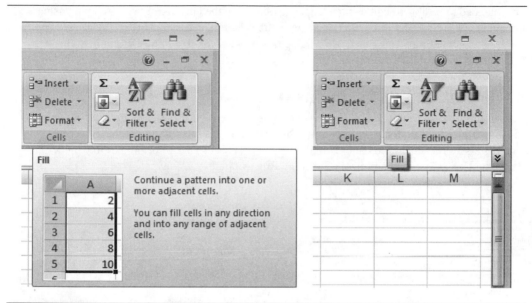

FIGURE 2-4 ScreenTips with feature descriptions (left) provide more detail about a command or option than regular ScreenTips (right), but you may find you don't need the extra information after you've been using Excel for a while.

- **Font Size**   In this drop-down list, select the point size to use as standard. Font sizes of 10, 11, or 12 points usually work well, depending on how much information you need to pack into a worksheet, and how easy to read you want it to be.

- **Default View For New Sheets**   In this drop-down list, select Normal View, Page Break Preview, or Page Layout View as the view you want Excel to apply each time you add a new worksheet or create a new workbook. Normal View is usually the best choice, but you may sometimes want to choose Page Layout View instead.

- **Include This Many Sheets**   Set the number of worksheets you want each new workbook to contain. The default number is 3. If you frequently have to add or delete worksheets, adjust the number accordingly. The limits are 1 and 255 sheets. You can add further worksheets to a workbook as needed.

Personalize Your Copy Of Microsoft Office

In the Personalize Your Copy Of Microsoft Office area, make sure your name appears as you want it in the User Name text box. If you set up Excel, you probably entered this information either during installation or the first time you ran Excel. But if someone else installed Excel, or if Excel came preinstalled on your computer, Excel may think you're called Authorized User.

If you need to be able to edit using a language other than the language Excel is already using (for example, U.S. English), click the Language Settings button, and then work in the Microsoft Office Language Settings dialog box. This dialog box enables you to add further editing languages and set your primary editing language.

Set Calculation and Formulas Options

The Formulas category in the Excel Options dialog box (see Figure 2-5) contains options for controlling how Excel performs calculations, displays and uses formulas, and checks errors. This section discusses the calculation and formulas options. "Troubleshoot Formulas," in Chapter 8, explains the Error Checking and Error Checking Rules options.

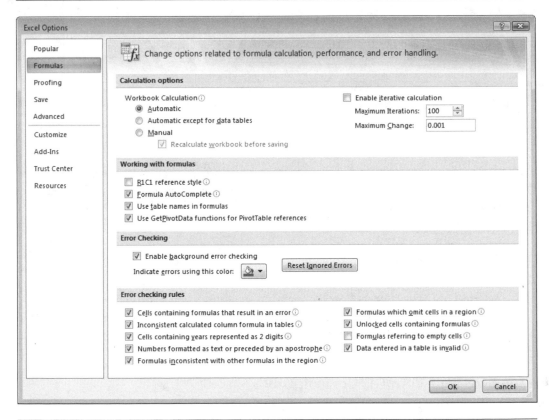

FIGURE 2-5   Unless you have special needs, most of the default settings in the Formulas category in the Options dialog box will probably do fine.

Calculation Options

The three option buttons in the Workbook Calculation area control how Excel calculates all worksheets. The default setting is the Automatic option button, which causes Excel to automatically recalculate all cells in a workbook when the value in any cell changes. So, by default, when you enter a new value in a cell, Excel automatically recalculates all the cells in the workbook. Normally, most of the cells won't be affected by any change you make, so the recalculation process is so quick as to be unnoticeable. This makes automatic recalculation the best choice for most users, because it ensures that all values in a workbook remain up-to-date no matter how many changes you make.

The exception is if you're using a workbook complex enough for recalculation to bog down your computer. For example, suppose you need to change a series of values in a physics calculation, and each value is involved in a set of complex calculations. In this case, automatic recalculation may take several seconds (or much longer) each time you enter or change the value in a cell, which will make for painfully slow progress. In this case, you would do better to select the Manual option button so that you can enter all the values without having to wait for each recalculation to finish before you could proceed.

If you select the Manual option button, you can select or clear the Recalculate Workbook Before Saving check box to control whether Excel recalculates formulas before saving the workbook. Recalculating before the save is the default and is usually a good idea, because it helps avoid someone subsequently opening the workbook and not realizing that some formula results aren't up to date.

The third option button, Automatic Except For Data Tables, performs automatic recalculation of all formulas except those in data tables. Depending on how your data is laid out, this option may give you the best of both worlds—you can enter data in data tables without recalculation slowing down the process, but Excel will recalculate all other formulas at each change.

If you choose the Automatic Except For Data Tables option button or the Manual option button, you can force recalculation of the entire workbook at any time by choosing Formulas | Calculation | Calculate Now, or by pressing F9. You can force recalculation of the worksheet (rather than the workbook) by choosing Formulas | Calculation | Calculate Sheet, or by pressing SHIFT-F9. The keyboard shortcuts are worth memorizing because you can issue them no matter which tab of the Ribbon is displayed—or if you've minimized the Ribbon to give yourself more space.

The Enable Iterative Calculation check box is a setting you won't need to change unless you must use circular references in your formulas. (A circular reference includes a calculation that refers to its own value.) Without iteration, circular references cause errors. If you need to use iteration, select the Enable Iterative Calculation check box, adjust the maximum permitted number of iterations in the Maximum Iterations text box, or adjust the maximum change (per iteration) in the Maximum Change text box.

Working With Formulas Options

The Working With Formulas area contains the following options:

- ■ **R1C1 Reference Style**   Select this check box if you want Excel to refer to cells using A1 reference style (column A, row 1) or R1C1 reference style (Row 1, Column 1). Almost everybody uses A1 reference style, which is the default, but you may occasionally need to use R1C1 reference style.

■ **Formula AutoComplete**   Select this check box if you want Excel to automatically complete the names of functions as you start typing them. This feature can help you enter complex formulas more quickly and accurately, so you'll probably want to turn it on.

■ **Use Table Names In Formulas**   Select this check box if you want to be able to use table names instead of ranges in formulas. Table names make referring to a table much easier, so you'll probably want to select this check box.

■ **Use GetPivotData Functions For PivotTable References**   Select this check box if you want to use the GetPivotData functions for references in PivotTables. Chapter 11 explains how to use PivotTables and PivotCharts.

Set Spelling Options

The Proofing category in the Excel Options dialog box (see Figure 2-6) lets you control how Excel corrects spelling. The Proofing category also contains AutoCorrect options, which are discussed in "Configure AutoCorrect to Save Time and Effort," later in this chapter.

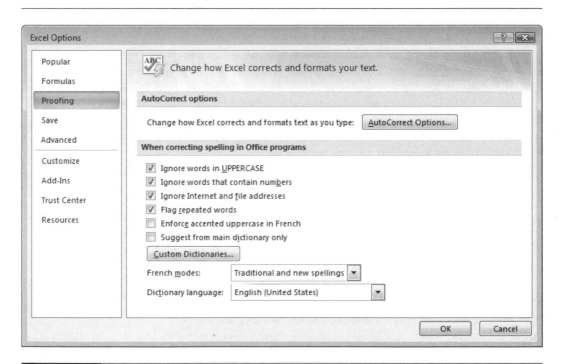

FIGURE 2-6   Choose spelling options in the Proofing category of the Excel Options dialog box.

The When Correcting Spelling In Office Programs area includes the following options:

- **Ignore Words In UPPERCASE**   Select this check box if you want the spelling checker to skip words in all capitals. Such skipping is useful when your workbooks contain uppercase words with product names or other nonstandard words.

- **Ignore Words That Contain Numbers**   Select this check box if you want the spelling checker to skip words that include numbers, such as Income08 or Site42. Turning on this option is usually helpful.

- **Ignore Internet And File Addresses**   Select this check box if you want the spelling checker to skip Internet addresses (for example, http://www.mcgraw-hill.com) and file paths. Turning on this option is usually helpful.

- **Flag Repeated Words**   Select this check box if you want the spelling checker to query the second instance of a word that's repeated. Turning on this option is usually helpful for catching unintended repetition in text-heavy cells.

- **Enforce Accented Uppercase In French**   Select this check box if you want Excel to display accents on uppercase letters in French words rather than hiding them.

- **Suggest From Main Dictionary Only**   Select this check box if you want the spelling checker to use only the main (built-in) dictionary rather than using your custom dictionaries as well (as it normally does). Normally, you'll want to clear this check box so that the spelling checker uses your custom dictionaries, but you may sometimes want to exclude them.

The Custom Dictionaries button lets you open the Custom Dictionaries dialog box, which you use to create, edit, and delete custom dictionaries. Chapter 6 shows you how to work with custom dictionaries.

Choose Save Options

The Save category in the Options dialog box (see Figure 2-7) are crucial for keeping valuable data as safe as possible.

Save Workbooks Options

The Save Workbooks area contains the following options:

- **Save Files In This Format**   In this drop-down list, choose the format you want to use for workbooks you save. Excel then uses this format as the standard format in the Save As dialog box; you can choose a different format for a workbook if you need one. Normally, you should choose Excel Workbook, the Excel 2007 format, which uses the .xlsx file extension. If you need to share your workbooks with people using earlier versions of Excel that cannot read Excel 2007 workbook files, choose Excel 97-2003 Workbook instead.

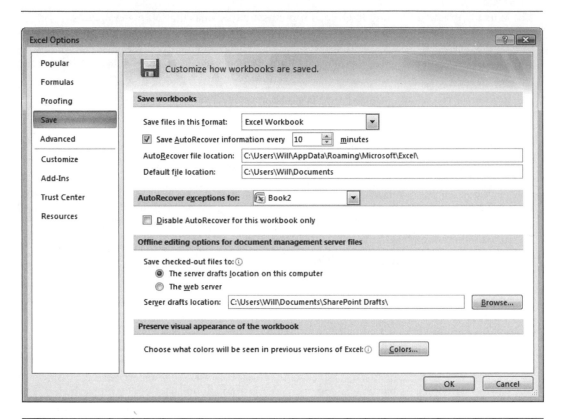

FIGURE 2-7 The Save category in the Options dialog box contains options for keeping your work safe from mishaps.

- **Save AutoRecover Information Every *NN* Minutes** Select this check box if you want the AutoRecover feature to automatically save a copy of your open workbooks in the background as you're working, so that you can recover from a disaster such as Excel crashing or your computer losing power. Usually, it's a good idea to select this check box. Set the value in the text box to a value that suits you. The default setting is 10 minutes, but you may want to set a shorter interval if you work rapidly, or if your computer has been unstable. You can set any interval from 1 minutes to 120 minutes.

NOTE
You may want to turn off AutoRecover if you prefer to save your documents manually every time you make an important change, or if you find that AutoRecover's automatic saves interfere with your work or your concentration. (The status bar displays Saving AutoRecover Info *and a progress readout during each AutoRecover save.)*

- **AutoRecover File Location**   In this text box, set the folder in which AutoRecover saves its files. The default location is the *%userprofile%*\Application Data\Microsoft\ Excel folder, where *%userprofile%* is the Windows environment variable that returns the path to your user profile folder. In a network environment, an administrator may have redirected the AutoRecover save location to a network drive so that AutoRecover files can be backed up centrally along with other files.

> **TIP**   *Entering a folder path correctly in the AutoRecover Save Location text box and the Default File Location text box is harder than it should be, because Excel doesn't let you browse to the folder. An easy way to enter the folder path correctly is to open a Windows Explorer window to the folder, copy the path from the address bar, and then paste it into the text box.*

- **Default File Location**   In this text box, set the folder that dialog boxes such as Open and Save As use initially. Excel normally uses the Documents folder (on Windows Vista) or the My Documents folder (on Windows XP). If you want Excel to display a different location, type it or paste it into this text box.

AutoRecover Exceptions For Option

The AutoRecover Exceptions For area lets you disable AutoRecover for a particular workbook (which you select in the AutoRecover Exceptions For drop-down list) while still using AutoRecover for all other workbooks. You may want to disable AutoRecover for a workbook so large that AutoRecover saves take a disruptive length of time, or for a workbook you don't care so much about.

Advanced Options

The Advanced category in the Options dialog box (see Figure 2-8) contains a wide variety of options for configuring Excel. This section discusses the options that are widely useful and that you will probably benefit from understanding, even if you choose to stay with Excel's default settings.

Editing Options

The Editing Options area includes the following options:

- **After Pressing Enter, Move Selection**   In the Direction drop-down list, choose the direction in which you want Excel to move the active cell after you press ENTER to finish editing in a cell. The default is to move down to the next cell. You might prefer to move right, so that you can work across a range of cells. If you want Excel to leave the same cell selected, clear the After Pressing Enter, Move Selection check box.

- **Automatically Insert A Decimal Point**   If you type sets of figures that all require a fixed number of decimal places, you can save keystrokes by selecting this check box and specifying the number of decimal places in the Places box. With this check box selected and 2 chosen in the Places box, when you type **4825** and move the active cell, Excel enters *48.25* (two decimal places).

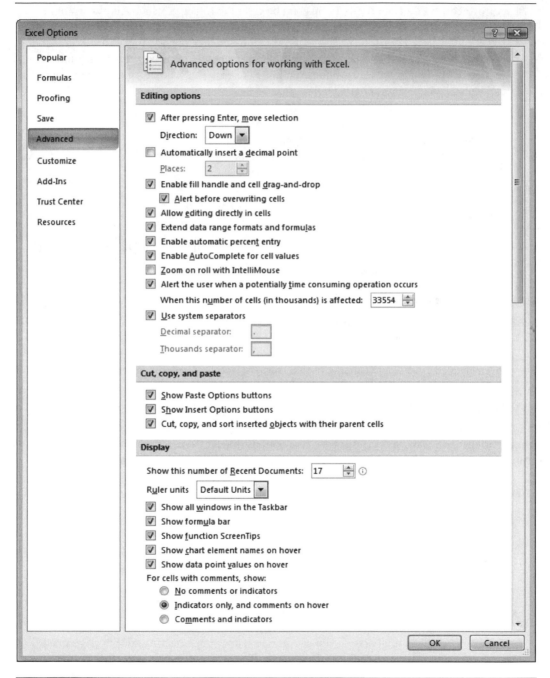

FIGURE 2-8 Many of the settings in the Advanced category in the Options dialog box are important to understand, even if you choose not to change the default settings. Scroll down to see the settings farther down the list.

■ **Enable Fill Handle And Cell Drag-And-Drop**   Select this check box if you want to use the AutoFill feature (see the section "Use AutoFill to Enter Data Series Quickly" in Chapter 3) and use drag and drop to copy or move the contents of cells. These features are usually helpful. If you leave them turned on, you can select or clear the Alert Before Overwriting Cells check box to control whether or not Excel warns you before overwriting cells that contain data when you perform a drag-and-drop operation.

■ **Allow Editing Directly In Cells**   Select this check box if you want to be able to double-click a cell to start editing it. This behavior is usually helpful.

■ **Extend Data Range Formats And Formulas**   Select this check box if you want Excel to apply repeated formats and formulas to new rows you add to the end of a list. This feature usually saves time and effort.

■ **Enable Automatic Percent Entry**   Select this check box if you want Excel to multiply percentage entries by 100 before displaying them. Most people find this option helpful—it enables you to enter percentages without thinking about them. When this option is turned off, typing **1** in a percentage-formatted cell displays 100%, typing **2** displays 200%, and so on; to enter 1%, you must type **.01**.

■ **Enable AutoComplete For Cell Values**   Select this check box if you want to use the AutoComplete feature. When you're typing text in a cell, AutoComplete suggests a matching item from another cell in the column once you've typed enough letters to identify it. For example, if you enter **Madrid** in cell A1, enter **Malaga** in cell A2, and type **mad** in cell A3, AutoComplete suggests *Madrid* to complete that cell. AutoComplete can greatly speed up entering repetitive information in columns. But if you find AutoComplete distracting, clear this check box.

■ **Zoom On Roll With IntelliMouse**   If you have an IntelliMouse or another mouse that has a wheel, you can select this check box and then use the mouse's roller to scroll in and out.

■ **Alert The User When A Potentially Time Consuming Operation Occurs**   Select this check box if you want Excel to warn you when you've started an operation that affects the number of cells specified in the When This Number Of Cells (In Thousands) Are Affected box (or more). The warning lets you choose not to complete the operation right now—for example, you might prefer to delay it till lunchtime.

■ **Use System Separators**   Select this check box (it should be selected by default) to use the decimal separator and the thousands separator set in your Windows configuration. For example, in U.S. English, Windows uses a period as the decimal separator and a comma as the thousands separator. If you need to use different separators, clear this check box, and then enter the separators in the Decimal Separator text box and the Thousands Separator text box.

Cut, Copy, And Paste Options

The Cut, Copy, And Paste area contains three important options:

- **Show Paste Options Buttons**   Select this check box if you want Excel to display the Paste Options button when you paste data. Clicking the Paste Options button displays a menu of options that allow you to change the format or content of data you've pasted if you find that the paste operation doesn't give the result you wanted. Having the button displayed is usually useful.

- **Show Insert Options Buttons**   Select this check box if you want Excel to display the Insert Options button when you insert cells (for example, by using a Home | Cells | Insert | Insert Cells command). The Insert Options button lets you change the way in which inserting the cells has affected the existing rows and columns in the worksheet. This feature is normally helpful.

- **Cut, Copy, And Sort Inserted Objects With Their Parent Cells**   Select this check box if you want Excel to include inserted objects (such as graphics) with the cells to which they are attached (their *parent* cells) when you cut, copy, or sort. This behavior is usually helpful.

Display Options

The Display area in the Advanced category of the Excel Options dialog box contains the following options:

- **Number Of Documents In The Recent Documents List**   Set the number of recent documents you want the Office button menu to display. Excel starts you off with 9 documents, but you can set any number from 0 to 50. Around 25 file names fit comfortably on the Office button menu and are enough for most purposes. Choose 0 documents if you want to prevent the Office button menu from letting your colleagues know which documents you've been working on.

- **Ruler Units**   In this drop-down list, choose Default Units if you want Excel to use the measurement units you're using in Windows—for example, inches. To use a different measurement, choose Inches, Centimeters, or Millimeters.

- **Show All Windows In The Taskbar**   Select this check box if you want Windows to display a separate taskbar button for each open window in Excel. Clear this check box if you want Windows to display a single taskbar button for Excel. Having separate taskbar buttons for each open workbook can enable you to switch from one workbook to another more easily, but some people find that the extra clutter on the taskbar outweighs this convenience.

- **Show Formula Bar**   Select this check box to display the Formula bar. The Formula bar is almost essential for working with formulas, so you'll normally want to display it.

■ **Show Function ScreenTips**   Select this check box to make Excel display ScreenTips showing the syntax of functions you type. Having the ScreenTips is usually helpful, especially when you're using functions with which you're not familiar.

■ **Show Chart Element Names On Hover**   Select this check box to make Excel display the names of chart elements when you hover the mouse pointer over them. (*Hover* means to hold the mouse pointer over an item for long enough for Windows to notice that it has stopped moving.) Even when you know what all the chart elements are called, the ScreenTips are often helpful, because in a complex chart they allow you to make sure that you're about to click the object you want, rather than another object that overlaps with it.

■ **Show Data Point Values On Hover**   Select this check box to make Excel display the values of data points in a chart when you hover the mouse pointer over them. This behavior is usually helpful.

■ **For Cells With Comments, Show**   Tell Excel what to display in an active cell that has a comment attached to it. Select the No Comments Or Indicators option button to hide the comments and indicators. Select the Indicators Only, And Comments On Hover option button to display a green indicator triangle in each commented cell and have Excel display a pop-up window showing the text of the comment when you hover the mouse pointer over the cell; this behavior is useful for worksheets that contain many comments. Select the Comments And Indicators option button if you want to display both the indicators and the floating comment windows all the time; this setting is useful when you need to ensure that the user sees the comments, but it's effective only when the worksheet contains relatively few comments.

Display Options For This Workbook

In the Display Options For This Workbook drop-down list (Figure 2-9 shows part of the Advanced category in the Excel Options dialog box), select the workbook you want to affect. Excel selects the active workbook in the drop-down list, so you may not need to change it. You can then select the following options for this workbook:

■ **Show Horizontal Scroll Bar**   Select this check box to make Excel display the horizontal scroll bar. Unless your worksheets are very small, you'll need both the horizontal scroll bar and the vertical scroll bar.

■ **Show Vertical Scroll Bar**   Select this check box to make Excel display the vertical scroll bar.

■ **Show Sheet Tabs**   Select this check box to make Excel display the worksheet tabs, which you use for navigating from one worksheet to another. You'll almost always want to display the tabs.

■ **Group Dates In The AutoFilter Menu**   Select this check box if you want Excel to automatically group dates by year and by month when you use the AutoFilter feature (discussed in the section "Filter a Table to Find Records That Match Criteria" in Chapter 9). Date grouping is usually helpful.

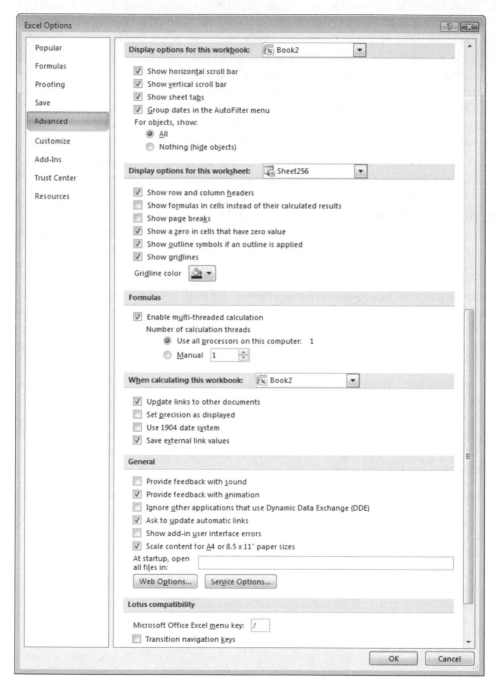

FIGURE 2-9 The Advanced category includes settings that are specific to a particular workbook and even to individual worksheets.

■ **For Objects, Show** In this area, select the All option button to make Excel display all objects, such as charts and graphics. Select the Nothing (Hide Objects) option button if you need temporarily to suppress graphical objects so that you can work with the data in the worksheet, or if a worksheet contains so many graphics that it scrolls slowly.

Display Options For This Worksheet

In the Display Options For This Worksheet drop-down list, select the worksheet you want to affect. Excel selects the active worksheet in the workbook chosen in the Display Options For This Workbook drop-down list. You can then choose the following options for the worksheet:

■ **Show Row And Column Headers** Select this check box to make Excel display the row and column headers, as it normally does. You may sometimes want to turn off the display of headers to make more space available on screen, or to hide the details of a collapsed outline or hidden cells or columns, but usually the headers help you keep track of which cell is active.

■ **Show Formulas In Cells Instead Of Their Calculated Results** Select this check box only when you want to see the actual formulas rather than the formula results in cells. Showing the formulas is useful when you're constructing or editing a worksheet, but normally you'll want to show the results.

■ **Show Page Breaks** Select this check box if you want Excel to display page breaks on worksheets. Seeing page breaks can be useful for laying out data but distracting for data entry.

■ **Show A Zero In Cells That Have Zero Value** Select this check box if you want Excel to display zeroes in cells that contain zero values. Clear this check box if you want Excel to display nothing in cells that contain zero values. Suppressing zero values can help you focus on nonzero values in worksheets.

■ **Show Outline Symbols If An Outline Is Applied** Select this check box to make Excel display outline symbols to indicate which outline sections are expanded and which are collapsed. Usually it's useful to see the outline symbols, but you may want to hide them when displaying outlined spreadsheets to an audience.

■ **Show Gridlines** Select this check box if you want Excel to display the gridlines for the worksheet, as it normally does. Seeing the gridlines is useful for most purposes, but you may want to turn off the display of gridlines when you're laying out a form.

■ **Gridline Color** If you choose to display gridlines, you can use this drop-down list to change their color from the default color (Automatic).

Formulas Options

The Formulas area in the Advanced category contains this option:

■ **Enable Multi-Threaded Calculation** Select this check box if you want Excel to be able to perform multi-threaded calculation, splitting complex calculations into separate *threads* (or components) and calculating them separately on your computer's separate processor cores or processors. Normally, you'll want to select this check box and select the Use All Processors On This Computer check box (even if your computer has only one processor with one core). If your computer has multiple processors or cores and you need to restrict Excel's usage of them, select the Manual option button, and then enter in the text box the number of processor or cores that Excel may use.

When Calculating This Workbook Options

In the When Calculating This Workbook drop-down list, select the workbook for which you want to choose options. Excel automatically selects the active workbook. You can then choose these options:

- **Update Links To Other Documents**   Select this check box if you want Excel to update links to other workbooks or other documents. Normally, you'll want Excel to do this, but you might want to clear this check box if you're working offline and don't have access to the linked documents.

- **Set Precision As Displayed**   Select this check box if you want Excel to change the numbers in the cells to match the precision with which they're displayed. For example, if you're using two decimal places in a worksheet, applying this feature would change the numbers in all the cells in the workbook to using two decimal places (including any rounding involved); $44.5593 would change to $44.56, and so on. This is a highly specialized feature that you'll seldom, if ever, need to use. (What you'll need much more often is to have Excel display only two decimal places for ease of reading but retain the real numbers unchanged "behind" the rounded number displayed.) If you do use Set Precision As Displayed, experiment first with a copy of your data, because the only way of undoing the change that Set Precision As Displayed makes is to revert to an unaffected copy of the data.

- **Use 1904 Date System**   Select this check box if you need to change Excel's serial date starting point from January 1, 1900, to January 2, 1904. Windows versions of Excel use 1900 as the starting date, while Mac versions of Excel use 1904. So when you import a workbook from Excel for the Mac, you'll usually need to select this check box to make serial dates display the correct values. If your Excel workbooks are Windows only, you don't need to worry about this option.

- **Save External Link Values**   Select this check box if you want Excel to store the value of external links in the workbook. Normally, storing the values is a good idea.

General Options

The General area in the Advanced category contains these options:

- **Provide Feedback With Sound**   Select this check box if you want Excel and the other Office applications to give you audio feedback when you take actions such as scrolling, using toolbars, or displaying dialog boxes. (Turning on sound feedback in one application turns it on for all of the Office applications.) To receive sound feedback, you must download the Office Sounds add-in from the Microsoft Office Download Center and install it. When you select this check box, Excel offers to open a browser window to the Microsoft Office Download Center.

■ **Provide Feedback With Animation**   Select this check box if you want Excel to use animated visual effects to accentuate actions you're performing. For example, when you insert a row (Insert | Row), Excel animates the process of sliding down the rows below it.

■ **Ignore Other Applications That Use Dynamic Data Exchange**   Select this check box if you want to make Excel ignore Dynamic Data Exchange (DDE) requests from other applications. DDE is an older technology for transferring data between applications and can pose a security risk.

■ **Ask To Update Automatic Links**   Select this check box if you want Excel to get your permission before it updates automatic links in workbooks. Having Excel prompt you before updating is usually helpful, especially if the links go to a document that may not be available.

■ **Show Add-In User Interface Errors**   Select this check box if you want Excel to display error messages for errors that occur in add-ins (discussed in the next section). Unless you're creating or debugging add-ins, it's usually more helpful to suppress the error messages.

■ **Scale Content For A4 or 8.5 × 11" Paper Sizes**   Select this check box if you want Excel to automatically scale (resize) content on 8.5 × 11" paper (the standard U.S. letter size) to fit A4 paper (an international standard paper size with slightly different dimensions), and vice versa. This option can save you plenty of printing problems.

■ **At Startup, Open All Files In**   If you need to open templates, workbooks, or add-ins automatically when you start Excel, enter the folder path in this text box. The easiest way to enter the path quickly and accurately is to copy it from the Address bar of a Windows Explorer window and paste it in.

Load and Unload Add-Ins

Excel includes several *add-ins,* optional components that you can load when you need the extra functionality that they provide. For example, the Euro Currency Tools add-in provides tools for working with the euro, which can be handy if you do business in Europe.

If you need an add-in frequently, you can always load it. But in general, it's not a good idea to load add-ins unless you need them, because they take up memory and may slow down your computer. So you should load add-ins when you need them, use them, and then unload them when you've finished.

To load or unload an add-in, follow these steps:

1. Click the Office button, and then choose Excel Options. Excel displays the Excel Options dialog box. In the left pane, click the Add-Ins category to display its contents.

2. In the Manage drop-down list toward the bottom of the dialog box, select Excel Add-Ins, and then click the Go button. Excel displays the Add-Ins dialog box (see Figure 2-10).

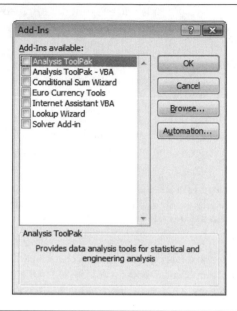

FIGURE 2-10 The Add-Ins dialog box lets you load and unload extra tools that add to Excel's functionality.

3. Select the check box for each add-in you want to load, and clear the check box for any loaded add-in you want to unload. To find an add-in that doesn't appear in the list, click the Browse button, use the resulting Browse button to select the add-in file, and then click the OK button.

4. Click the OK button. Excel closes the Add-Ins dialog box and loads or unloads the add-ins you specified.

Once you've loaded an add-in, you can use its features, which are usually implemented as extra groups or tabs on the Ribbon. The next illustration shows the Solutions group on the Formulas tab of the Ribbon, which includes the Conditional Sum Wizard, the Euro Conversion and the Euro Formatting tools, and the Lookup Wizard. Other add-ins appear on other tabs of the Ribbon. For example, if you load the Solver, you'll find it in the Analysis group on the Data tab.

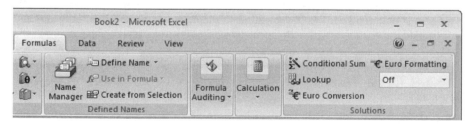

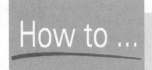 ## Add the Add-ins to Your Installation of Office

If your computer has a complete installation of Office, the add-ins will be installed; if it has a custom installation, they may be.

If you need to install the add-ins, follow these steps:

1. Choose Start | Control Panel. Windows opens a Control Panel window.

2. In Windows Vista, in Control Panel Home view, click the Uninstall A Program link under the Programs heading. In Windows XP, in Category view, click the Add Or Remove Programs link.

3. In the list of programs, select the Microsoft Office 2007 item, and then click the Change button.

4. Select the Add Or Remove Features option button, and then click the Continue button. Windows displays the Installation Options screen.

5. Expand the Excel item, and then expand the Add-ins item.

6. For each add-in you want to load, choose the Run From My Computer option. If you want to install all the add-ins, right-click the Add-Ins item, and then choose Run From My Computer from the shortcut menu.

7. Click the Continue button to update your Office installation.

Configure AutoCorrect to Save Time and Effort

AutoCorrect is an automatic correction feature that watches as you type and substitutes predefined replacement text when you type a group of characters that match one of its entries. AutoCorrect can not only save you the awkwardness of typos and some basic grammatical errors in your spreadsheets, but it can also make data entry faster and more consistent. It's well worth spending a few minutes understanding what AutoCorrect does and how it can help your work.

AutoCorrect is implemented in most of the Office applications, with text-only AutoCorrect entries stored in a central location so each application can access them. (Word can also use formatted AutoCorrect entries, which it doesn't share with the other applications.) The entries are stored in the MSO*nnnn*.acl file, where *nnnn* is the numeric designation (or *locale ID*, LCID) for the localization of Office you're using. On Windows Vista, Office stores the AutoCorrect file in the *%userprofile%*\AppData\Roaming\Microsoft\Office folder, while on Windows XP, Office stores the file in the *%userprofile%*\Application Data\Microsoft\Office folder. In both these paths, *%userprofile%* is the path to your user profile (for instance, C:\Users\Mike Smith on Windows Vista, or C:\Documents and Settings\Jane Petersen on Windows XP). For example, U.S. English AutoCorrect entries are stored in the MSO1033.acl file, because 1033 is the LCID for U.S. English.

 *If you use AutoCorrect extensively, back up your .ACL file. If you use multiple computers, you may want to copy the .ACL file from one computer to another so you don't need to re-create AutoCorrect entries manually.*

Configure AutoCorrect's Basic Settings

To configure AutoCorrect, open the AutoCorrect dialog box. Follow these steps:

1. Click the Office button, and then click Excel Options. Excel displays the Excel Options dialog box.

2. In the left pane, click the Proofing category to display its contents.

3. In the AutoCorrect Options area, click the AutoCorrect Options button. Excel displays the AutoCorrect dialog box with its AutoCorrect tab foremost (see Figure 2-11).

Choose settings to suit your needs:

■ **Show AutoCorrect Options Buttons** Select this check box if you want Excel to display a AutoCorrect Options button in worksheets next to each item that AutoCorrect has replaced. The AutoCorrect Options button gives you a visual indication of each AutoCorrect correction and enables you to undo a correction easily.

FIGURE 2-11 Configure AutoCorrect, and create and delete AutoCorrect entries, on the AutoCorrect tab of the AutoCorrect dialog box.

2

- **Correct TWo INitial CApitals**   Select this check box if you want AutoCorrect to lowercase the second of two initial capitals. AutoCorrect comes with some exceptions built in (such as "COs" and "JScript"), and you can add extra exceptions as necessary by clicking the Exceptions button and working on the INitial CAps tab of the AutoCorrect Exceptions dialog box.

- **Capitalize First Letter Of Sentences**   Select this check box if you want AutoCorrect to capitalize the first letter of everything it takes to be a sentence. Generally this feature works well, but sometimes you may disagree with what AutoCorrect considers to be a sentence. (This tends to be more of a problem with Word than with Excel.)

- **Capitalize Names Of Days**   Select this check box if you want AutoCorrect to capitalize the names of days. Usually this option is useful for speeding up data entry.

- **Correct Accidental Use Of cAPS LOCK Key**   Select this check box if you want AutoCorrect to try to detect when you've mistakenly switched on the Caps Lock key. AutoCorrect switches off the key and changes the case of the letters that should have been the opposite case. This option usually works well, but it may occasionally "fix" an oddly cased term that doesn't need fixing.

- **Replace Text As You Type**   Select this check box to turn on AutoCorrect's main feature—scanning for entries as you type and replacing them with their designated replacement text. You'll seldom want to clear this check box, unless you're using someone else's account on a computer, and you find AutoCorrect unexpectedly replacing text you type. By leaving this check box selected, and by creating as many AutoCorrect entries as is reasonable, you can make AutoCorrect shoulder part of the burden of entering text in your worksheets.

Create and Delete AutoCorrect Entries

AutoCorrect comes with many built-in entries that range from simple typos (for example, *abotu* instead of *about*) to basic grammatical mistakes (for example, *may of been* instead of *may have been*) and some symbols (for example, AutoCorrect corrects *(c)* to a copyright symbol, ©). You can add as many custom entries as you need, and you can replace or delete the built-in entries if you find them inconvenient.

Creating and deleting AutoCorrect entries is easy:

- To create an entry, enter the entry text in the Replace text box and the replacement text in the With text box. (You can paste copied text into either of these text boxes.) Either click the Add button to add the entry and keep the AutoCorrect dialog box open, or click the OK button to add the entry and close the AutoCorrect dialog box.

NOTE   *If an AutoCorrect entry with this name already exists, AutoCorrect prompts you to decide whether to overwrite it.*

How AutoCorrect Works

As you type, AutoCorrect examines each character. When you type a character that typically means you've finished typing a word, AutoCorrect compares the word (or, more precisely, the group of characters) against its list of entries. If the word matches an entry, AutoCorrect substitutes the replacement text for the word. If the word doesn't match an entry, AutoCorrect checks the word and its predecessor together to see if they match an entry. If so, AutoCorrect substitutes the replacement text. If not, AutoCorrect checks those two words with the word before them—and so on until it has checked all the complete words in the preceding 31 characters, at which point it gives up.

AutoCorrect entries can be up to 31 characters long and can contain spaces and punctuation. The replacement text for an entry can be up to 255 characters long—plenty to enable you to enter a short paragraph or two. (If you try to use more than 255 characters, AutoCorrect warns you that it'll need to shorten the replacement text.)

No entry's name should be a real word in any language you use; otherwise, AutoCorrect will replace that word each time you try to use it. The exception is if you *want* to prevent yourself from using a particular word. For example, if the word *purchase* sends your boss into conniptions, you can define AutoCorrect entries to change words based on *purchase* (such as *purchase, purchases, purchased, purchasing,* and so on) to their counterparts based on *buy*. AutoCorrect will then censor your language use gently and automatically.

AutoCorrect considers various characters to mean you've finished typing a word. As you'd guess, these characters include spaces, punctuation, tabs, and carriage returns. You might not guess that various symbols (such as % and #) trigger AutoCorrect checks, but they do.

- To delete an entry, select it in the list by scrolling or by typing its first few letters, and then click the Delete button.

- To change the name of an existing AutoCorrect entry, select it in the list, so that Excel enters its name in the Replace text box and its contents in the With text box. Type the new name, and then click Add to create a new entry with that name and contents. With the new entry created, delete the old entry.

Undo an AutoCorrect Correction

When AutoCorrect makes a correction that you don't want to keep, you can undo it by issuing an Undo command (for example, press CTRL-Z or click the Undo button on the Standard toolbar). But if you were typing fast at the time when AutoCorrect chose to kick in, you might need to undo a lot of typing (or other editing) before you can undo the AutoCorrect action.

To make corrections easier, Excel tracks corrections applied by AutoCorrect. When you hover your mouse pointer over an AutoCorrect correction, the application displays an AutoCorrect Options button that you can click to display a menu of AutoCorrect options. Your choices vary according to the context but include the option to undo this instance of the correction and to stop correcting this AutoCorrect entry (for the future).

Use AutoCorrect Most Effectively

AutoCorrect is wonderful for fixing typos as you type. But if you enter much text in your worksheets, define AutoCorrect entries for long words, complex terms, phrases, or sentences you enter frequently. By doing so, you can both accelerate your typing and avoid typos.

You can also use AutoCorrect for enforcing consistency. For example, if you work for the vice president for sales and marketing but tend to write the title as "Vice President of Sales and Marketing," create an AutoCorrect entry to change "Vice President of Sales and" to "Vice President for Sales and". AutoCorrect will then correct the error for you automatically when you make it. (Note that the phrase is too long to include "Marketing" in the AutoCorrect entry. But this has a hidden benefit—AutoCorrect will fire as you go on to type "Marketing." Otherwise, if the entry included "Marketing" and you typed the wrong phrase and no further, AutoCorrect wouldn't fire.)

To continue the previous example, you should create a shorter AutoCorrect entry (called something like "bossjob") that expands to your boss's correct title. The shorter entry will save you keystrokes and capitalization.

If you create many AutoCorrect entries, remembering entries that you use less frequently may be a problem. But there's nothing to stop you from creating multiple entries for the same replacement text.

Adding and Deleting AutoCorrect Exceptions

You can also define *AutoCorrect exceptions*—terms that you don't want AutoCorrect to automatically correct. Excel supports first-letter exceptions (for abbreviations such as *corp.* and for similar terms that end with punctuation) and initial-caps exceptions (for example, *IDs*).

To add and delete exceptions, click the Exceptions button on the AutoCorrect tab of the AutoCorrect dialog box, and then work in the AutoCorrect Exceptions dialog box:

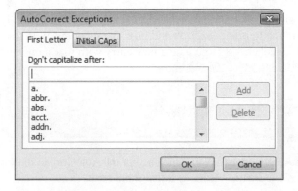

Choose AutoFormat As You Type Options

The AutoFormat As You Type page of the AutoCorrect dialog box (see Figure 2-12) contains three options for formatting that Excel can apply automatically as you type in a workbook:

- **Internet And Network Paths With Hyperlinks**   Select this check box to make Excel automatically change an Internet address (a URL—for example, http://www.mcgraw-hill .com) or a network path (for example, \\server\public\workbook2.xlsx) with a hyperlink. You can then CTRL-click the hyperlink to open the web page or the file. If you prefer not to have live hyperlinks in your workbooks, clear this check box.

- **Include New Rows And Columns In Table**   Select this check box if you want Excel to treat new rows and columns that you insert in a table as part of the table. This behavior is usually helpful.

- **Fill Formulas In Tables To Create Calculated Columns**   A calculated column is a method of automatically extending a formula so that it includes additional rows you add to a table. Calculated columns save time and effort, so you'll normally want to keep this check box selected.

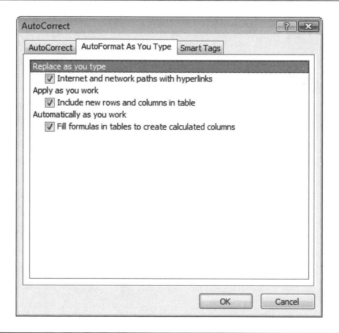

FIGURE 2-12   On the AutoFormat As You Type page of the AutoCorrect dialog box, choose which automatic-formatting features Excel should use.

FIGURE 2-13 On the Smart Tags page of the AutoCorrect dialog box, choose whether to label data with Smart Tags.

Choose Smart Tags Options

The Smart Tags page of the AutoCorrect dialog box (see Figure 2-13) lets you choose whether to use Smart Tags, which are pop-up buttons attached to certain types of information (you can choose which types). When you hover the mouse pointer over a Smart Tag, the Smart Tag's action button appears. You can then click the action button to display a menu of options for the item. For example, the Smart Tag for a person's name or telephone number contains an option that you can click to add the person or number to your Windows Contacts (on Windows Vista) or Windows Address Book (on Windows XP) directly from Excel, as shown here. A triangle in the lower-right corner of a cell indicates that a Smart Tag is available.

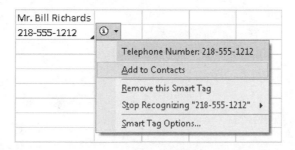

The Smart Tags page contains the following controls:

- **Label Data With Smart Tags**   This check box is the master control for Smart Tags. Select this check box if you want to use Smart Tags. Excel then enables the controls in the Recognizers list box.

- **Recognizers**   In this list box, select the check box for each type of Smart Tag you want Excel to recognize automatically. For example, you might select only the Telephone Number check box and the Person Name check box to have Excel recognize these two types of data and mark them with Smart Tags.

- **Check Workbook**   Click this button to make Excel search the workbook for data matching the recognizers you've chosen and apply a Smart Tag to each matching instance.

- **More Smart Tags**   Click this button to access more Smart Tags on the Microsoft website.

- **Show Smart Tags As**   In this drop-down list, choose how Excel should display Smart Tags: Indicator And Button, Button Only, or None (no indication).

- **Embed Smart Tags In This Workbook**   Select this check box if you want Excel to embed Smart Tags in the workbook, so that they remain available. If you want to remove Smart Tags from a workbook, clear this check box, save the workbook, and then close and reopen it.

Chapter 3

Create Spreadsheets and Enter Data

How to…

- ■ Create a workbook
- ■ Save a workbook
- ■ Create and save a template
- ■ Enter data in worksheets
- ■ Use AutoFill to enter data series quickly
- ■ Use Find and Replace
- ■ Recover your work if Excel crashes

Now that you know how to navigate Excel's interface, and you've chosen such customization options as necessary to make your work in Excel as smooth and comfortable as possible, you're ready to create workbooks of your own. This chapter shows you how to create and save both workbooks and the templates on which workbooks are based, how to enter data in worksheets manually and by using Excel's AutoFill feature, how to use Excel's Find and Replace features, and how to recover your work if Excel crashes.

Create a New Workbook

Each workbook is based on a *template*—a file that's used as the basis for the workbook. A template can contain anything from basic worksheets with minimal modifications from Excel's defaults, to a complete complex form with text, formatting, and even VBA macros, that requires the user to do nothing more than fill in a few pieces of information to complete the form. (For example, you might use such a template for an invoice, a business proposal, or a psychometric evaluation.)

When you need a new workbook, you have several options, which are discussed in the following sections:

- ■ You can create what Excel calls a "blank workbook"—a workbook with extremely basic settings. If you've just launched Excel by using the Start menu, Excel will have automatically created a blank workbook for you. A blank workbook is good when you need to set up an entire workbook from scratch, but often you can save time by using one of the other two options.

- ■ You can create a new workbook by cloning an existing workbook. This technique can save you huge amounts of time and repetitive work. In effect, you use the existing workbook as a kind of informal template for the new workbook.

- ■ You can create a new workbook based on a template. By using the right template, you can save a great deal of time and effort.

Create a New Blank Workbook

The easiest way to create a new blank workbook is to either press CTRL-N or follow these steps:

1. Click the Office button, and then click New on the menu. Excel displays the New Workbook dialog box (see Figure 3-1).

2. In the Templates panel on the left, make sure that the Blank And Recent item is selected. (Blank And Recent is normally selected when you open the New Workbook dialog box.)

3. In the Blank And Recent area, select the Blank Workbook item, and then click the Create button.

Create a New Workbook Based on an Existing Workbook

Once you've created and formatted a workbook to your (or your boss's) satisfaction, you can reuse it as the basis for other workbooks that use the same layout and formatting. Even if you need to make significant changes to the data in the new copy of the layout, you should be able to save considerable time and effort over creating the new workbook from scratch.

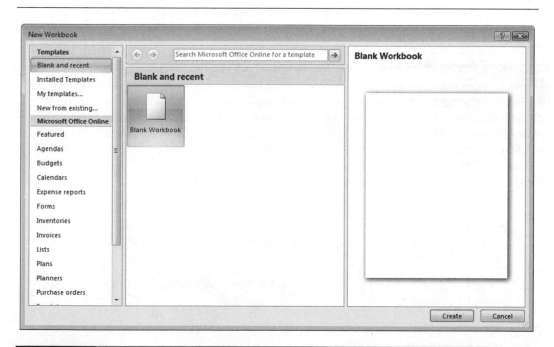

FIGURE 3-1   The New Workbook dialog box lets you create any kind of workbook, from a blank workbook to one that uses a template on the Microsoft Office Online site.

You can reuse an existing workbook in any of three ways:

- Use the New From Existing Workbook dialog box to create a new workbook based on an existing workbook, as described in this section. This is an informal but effective way of reusing material.

- Open the workbook as usual, and then use a Save As command to save a copy of the workbook under a different name for reuse. This method of reuse is even more informal but equally effective.

- Create a template from the workbook or, better still, create a template from scratch. See "Create and Save a Template," later in this chapter, for instructions.

To create a new workbook based on an existing workbook, follow these steps:

1. Click the Office button, and then click New. Excel displays the New Workbook dialog box.

2. In the Templates panel on the left, click the New From Existing item. Excel displays the New From Existing Workbook dialog box. This dialog box is a standard Windows Open dialog box with a different name.

3. Navigate to the folder that contains the workbook, and then select the workbook.

4. Click the Create New button. Excel closes the New From Existing Workbook dialog box and creates a new workbook based on the selected existing workbook.

Create a New Workbook Based on a Template

You can also create a new workbook based on a template—a template that you or your company has created, an template supplied with Excel, or a template that you download from the Microsoft Office Online website. See the next section for instructions on downloading templates from this site. See "Create and Save a Template," later in this chapter, for instructions on creating your own templates.

Create a New Workbook Based on a Template of Your Own

To create a new workbook based on a template stored in your user templates folder, follow these steps:

1. Click the Office button, and then click New. Excel displays the New Workbook dialog box.

2. In the Templates panel on the left, click the My Templates item. Excel displays the New dialog box (see Figure 3-2).

NOTE *If you divide your Excel templates into folders, the New dialog box displays a tab for each folder, as shown in Figure 3-2.*

3. If the templates are split among different pages in the New dialog box, click the appropriate tab to display its contents.

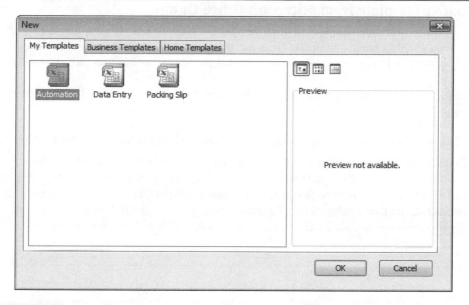

FIGURE 3-2   The New dialog box contains only your user templates, so until you create or download some templates, it will probably be empty.

4. Select the icon for the template. If necessary, use the Preview pane to check that you've selected the right template (some templates may not have previews available).

5. Click the OK button. Excel closes the Templates dialog box and creates a new document based on the template.

Create a New Workbook Based on an "Installed" Template

Excel comes with various templates that it installs in a subfolder of a Templates folder inside the Office folder within your Program Files folder. The folder is named with the locale ID (LCID) of the language you're using. For example, the LCID for U.S. English is 1033, so the templates are in the Program Files\Microsoft Office\Templates\1033 folder. Excel refers to these templates as "installed" templates.

To create a new workbook based on an installed template, follow these steps:

1. Click the Office button, and then click New. Excel displays the New Workbook dialog box.

2. In the Templates pane on the left, select the Installed Templates item.

3. In the Installed Templates list in the middle of the dialog box, select the template you want. Some of the templates have previews that appear in the right pane of the dialog box, allowing you to make sure that you've chosen the right template.

4. Click the Create button. Excel closes the New Workbook dialog box and creates a new workbook based on the template.

Download a Template from Microsoft Office Online

If you don't have a suitable template in your Templates folder or among your installed templates, you can download a template from the Microsoft Office Online site. This site has a wide variety of Excel templates, some of which are widely useful and professionally designed.

To create a new workbook based on a template from Microsoft Office Online, follow these steps:

1. Click the Office button, and then click New. Excel displays the New Workbook dialog box.

2. In the Templates pane on the left, go to the Microsoft Office Online section, and then choose the category of template you want: Agendas, Budgets, Calendars, Expense Reports, and so on. The New Workbook dialog box searches Office Online for that category of templates, and then displays a list of available templates. Figure 3-3 shows an example of the Invoices category, with one of the templates selected so that the preview appears.

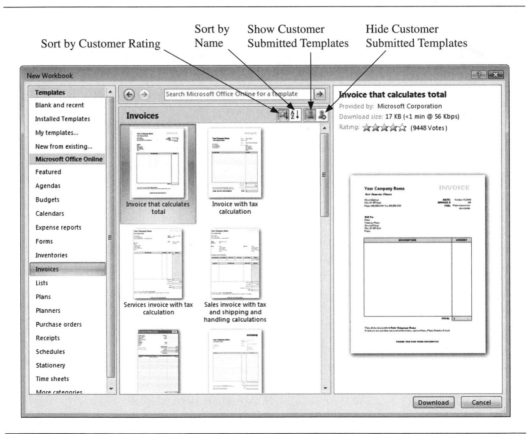

FIGURE 3-3   Use the preview of a Microsoft Office Online template to decide whether the template you've found will suit your needs.

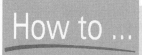

Divide Data Among Workbooks and Worksheets

Excel faces you with a choice of how to divide your data among workbooks and worksheets. Because each workbook can contain hundreds or even thousands of worksheets, you might be tempted to keep all of your data in a single workbook, allotting each subject to a different worksheet. That way, you need to open only one workbook to have access to all your data.

Even if your work involves a small enough quantity of data to fill only a handful of worksheets, keeping all of your data together is usually a mistake. Quite apart from increasing the risk of data loss or damage through a user error (for example, accidental deletion) or a hardware or software mishap, having all of your data together makes it hard to share some of the data with other people without sharing all of it. There are various ways around this—for example, you can copy or move a worksheet to a different workbook, or you can save a copy of the master workbook and delete all the sheets you don't want to share—but you'll be better off keeping separate data in separate workbooks in the first place.

In general, try to follow these rough guidelines:

- Divide data by subject and use a different workbook for each subject. For example, you might keep a workbook for your company's (or department's) sales, another workbook for staff details and salaries, another workbook for budgeting, and so on.

- Within each subject, divide the data into logical categories, and use a separate worksheet for each category. For example, in a staff workbook, you might keep staff address information on one worksheet, salary information on a second worksheet, and performance information on a third worksheet. (You might prefer to keep a separate worksheet for each employee, but doing so would make it much more difficult to sort employee details or compare employee performance.) Similarly, you might use separate worksheets for months, quarters, or years in a budget workbook.

If you're using Excel in your work for a company of any size, you'll probably find that the decisions for dividing data among workbooks and worksheets have already been made. If you get to make such decisions, be prepared to move worksheets to different workbooks when the need arises. See "Move and Copy Worksheets," in Chapter 4, for instructions. See Chapter 9 for a discussion of considerations for creating tables (long or complex lists) in Excel.

TIP *When viewing Microsoft Office Online templates, you can click the Sort by Customer Rating button to sort the templates by customer rating (for example, five stars) or the Sort by Name button to sort by name. If you want to see templates submitted by customers as well as templates developed by Microsoft and other companies, click the Show Customer Submitted Templates button so that it appears pushed in. To hide customer-submitted templates, click the Hide Customer Submitted Templates.*

3. Click a template to display its thumbnail or details. Use the View drop-down list to switch between viewing thumbnails and viewing details.

4. When you've selected the template you want, click the Download button. Excel downloads the template and creates a new workbook based on it. Excel saves the template in your user templates folder, so the next time you need it, you can find it in the New dialog box.

Save a Workbook

In theory, you can leave a workbook unsaved until you've finished working with it and are ready to close it. In practice, it's a good idea to save your work as soon as you've made changes that you wouldn't want to have to make again. You should save your work in case a problem occurs with Excel, Windows, or your computer (for example, a power outage or a hardware failure) that causes you to lose what you've been doing.

To begin with, you'll need to save the workbook for the first time, which involves giving the file a name and choosing which folder to save it in. After that, you can save changes to the workbook by issuing a Save command. At times, you may need to save a workbook under a different name (making a copy of it) or in a different format (for example, for sharing with someone who uses a different spreadsheet application). And for some workbooks, you may need to enter property information (attributes or metadata) to make the workbook more easily identifiable via searching. The following sections show you how to take these actions.

Save a Workbook for the First Time

To save a workbook for the first time, follow these steps:

1. Issue a Save command in any of the following ways to display the Save As dialog box. Figure 3-4 shows the Save As dialog box with choices made and key items labeled.

- ■ Click the Save button on the Quick Access toolbar.
- ■ Click the Office button, and then click Save.
- ■ Press CTRL-S or F12.

 When you're using Excel 2007 on Windows XP, the Save As dialog box is different: It doesn't have a small version and a large version, so all its controls are available all the time, and it doesn't contain the fields for tag information. Instead, you can enter tag information as discussed in the section "Enter Property Information for a Workbook," later in this chapter.

NOTE   *Excel normally displays the small version of the Save As dialog box first. To display the rest of the dialog box, click the Browse Folders button.*

Click the Recent Pages button to display a list of folders you've used recently

Click one of these arrows to display a list of the folders within the folder listed before the arrow

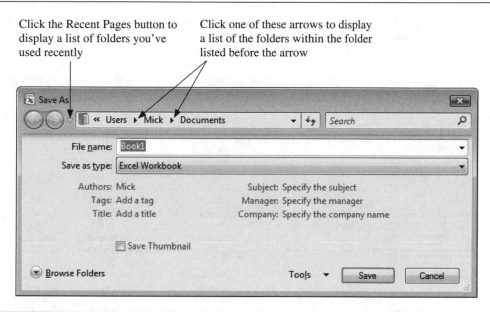

FIGURE 3-4   Use the Save As dialog box to set the file name, folder, format, and tag information for a workbook or template.

2. If you want to save the file in a folder other than the current folder, navigate to the folder you want to use:

■ On Windows Vista, use any of the arrow buttons in the Address bar at the top of the dialog box to navigate to a subfolder of the folder listed before the arrow button. Alternatively, click the Browse Folders button to display the folders area of the dialog box (see Figure 3-5), select the folder, and then click the Hide Folders button to hide the folders again.

■ On Windows XP, click a button in the Places Bar to navigate quickly to that place; display the Save In drop-down list and select the drive or folder; or double-click a folder displayed in the main area of the dialog box to open it.

3. Type the file name in the File Name text box:

■ The file name can be up to 255 characters in length including the folder path (the drive and all the folders leading to this folder).

■ In practice, most people find they can create usefully descriptive names by using 20 to 50 characters.

■ Very long file names can make Windows Explorer windows and common dialog boxes (such as the Open dialog box) hard to navigate, and listings such as the recently used files list on Excel's File menu have to truncate the names to display them.

The Favorite Links area lets you quickly access frequently used Windows folders

Click the Folders bar to display a folder tree that you can navigate like a Windows Explorer window

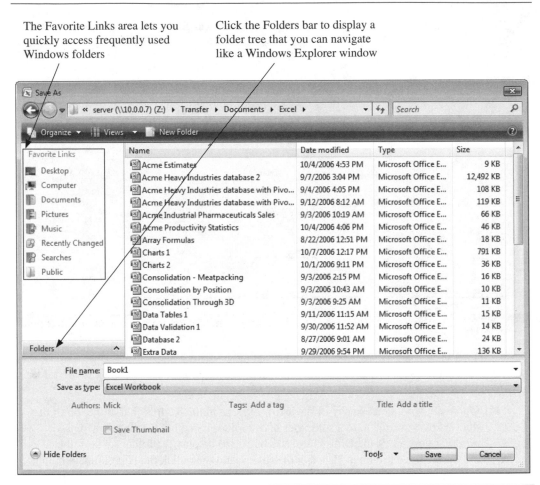

FIGURE 3-5 The full version of the Save As dialog box contains the folders area, which lets you choose the folder in which to save the workbook.

4. In the Save As Type drop-down list, choose the appropriate format:

   ■ Choose the Excel Workbook item for a normal workbook. This is the default format for Excel, so this item is normally selected already. (If you chose a different default format for workbooks, as discussed in the section "Preserve Backup Information For Your Workbook Options" in Chapter 2, Excel should have chosen that format for you.)

   ■ Choose the Excel Template item when creating a template.

   ■ Choose a different format when necessary. For example, if you need to share a workbook with someone who uses an older version of Excel, you may need to use the Excel 97-2003 format. Or if your company uses XML for data exchange, you may need to save workbooks in the XML Spreadsheet format. (Chapter 15 discusses XML.)

5. If you want to add information to the workbook so that you can search for it more easily, click in each field that you want to add, and then type a suitable value.

■ Excel automatically fills in the Authors field with your user name and the Company field with your company name (if you've set one), but you can add other authors or companies as necessary.

■ The names of the Title, Subject, and Manager fields suggest the types of information for which these fields are intended, but you can enter any information you want in these fields. For example, if you have no manager, you might choose to use the Manager field for the client's name.

■ Use the Tags field to enter any other information that doesn't fit into the other five categories. You can also add further information in other fields, as discussed in the section "Enter Property Information for a Workbook," later in this chapter.

6. If you want Excel to save a preview of the workbook in the file so that it appears in the Open dialog box in the future, select the Save Thumbnail check box.

7. Click the Save button. Excel closes the Save As dialog box and saves the workbook.

Save Changes to a Previously Saved Workbook

After saving a workbook as described in the previous section, you can save any unsaved changes to the workbook instantly by clicking the Save button on the Quick Access toolbar, pressing CTRL-S or SHIFT-F12, or clicking the Office button and then clicking Save.

Save a Workbook Under a Different Name

You can save a previously saved workbook under a different name by either clicking the Office button and then choosing Save As or pressing F12 to display the Save As dialog box again. Specify a new file name (or folder; or both), and then click the Save button.

This technique is useful for making a copy of a file you've been working on when you realize you don't want to overwrite the original file with the changes you've made—for example, when you start tweaking a planning budget and get carried away with the changes you make. This technique is also useful when you've opened a read-only file: In this case, you can't save changes to the existing file anyway, but you can save the file under a different name.

You can also use this technique as a quick way of making a copy of a file without leaving Excel. The more formal alternative is to use Windows Explorer to copy the file, rename the copy from its default name if necessary, and then double-click the copy to open it in Excel (if you need to work in the file).

These two techniques have almost the same result—a file with the same contents but a different name—but not quite. The difference is that creating a copy in Windows Explorer creates a file identical with the original file, whereas creating a copy by using a Save As command creates a new file with the same contents as the original file (assuming you haven't yet changed them) but with a different Modified date stamp. In most business or home contexts, the different date stamp is of little consequence, but in some sensitive situations, it may be better to create a copy that has the same date stamp as the original file.

Save a Workbook in a Different Format

By default, Excel saves files in its own Excel Workbook format.

Excel also lets you save workbooks in other formats, such as those used by earlier versions of Excel, for when you need to share data with people whose computers can't read Excel 2007 workbooks. You can even save the data from a workbook in universally readable formats, such as tab-delimited text or comma-separated values (CSV). You can override the default format either temporarily or permanently.

When you save a workbook in a non-Excel format, data and basic formatting should be saved without a problem, but complex formatting and advanced features may be stripped from the workbook during the conversion. So use a non-Excel format for workbooks only if you must; and even then, test the format with sample data first in case anything vital disappears from the workbook.

To save a workbook in a different format, follow these steps:

1. Open the workbook.

2. Click the Office button, and then click Save As. Excel displays the Save As dialog box.

3. Choose the format in the Save As Type drop-down list. Excel automatically changes the extension on the file to suit the format, so if you're using a Save As command to save a previously saved workbook in a different format, you won't need to change the file name.

4. Click the Save button.

 *If you usually or always need to save a file in another format than the Excel Workbook format, you can make Excel use that format as the default for new workbooks you save. To do so, click the Office button, and then click Excel Options. In the Excel Options dialog box, click the Save category, select the file type in the Save Files In This Format drop-down list, and then click the OK button.*

Enter Property Information for a Workbook

As you saw in the section "Save a Workbook for the First Time," earlier in this chapter, Excel running on Windows Vista encourages you to enter some fields of workbook metadata (data *about* the workbook rather than actual contents of the workbook) directly in the Save As dialog box. To make workbooks easier to identify via searches, and to help the Windows Indexing Service to store the appropriate key information about workbooks, you can enter property information by using the Properties bar and the Properties dialog box.

To open the Properties bar, click the Office button, click Prepare, and then click Properties on the Prepare submenu. Figure 3-6 shows the Properties bar, which contains the Author, Title, Subject, Keywords, Category, Status, and Comments fields.

For further properties, click the Document Properties drop-down list and then choose Advanced Properties. Excel displays the Properties dialog box. The Properties dialog box contains five tabs, which are discussed here.

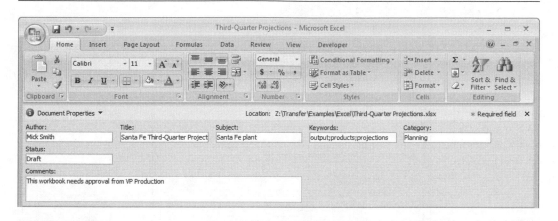

FIGURE 3-6   The Properties bar gives you quick access to the key properties for a workbook.

General Tab Properties

The General tab contains basic information about the file: its type (for example, Microsoft Excel Worksheet); the folder it's located in; its size; its MS-DOS name (in the 8.3 format—for example, ACMEPR~1.XLS); the dates it was created, last modified, and last accessed; and the status of its Read Only, Hidden, Archive, and System attributes. You can't manipulate any of this information directly on this tab.

Summary Tab Properties

The Summary tab (see Figure 3-7) contains Title, Subject, Author, Manager, Company, Category, Keywords, Comments, and Hyperlink Base fields. Excel automatically fills in the author information from the Author property of the template or, if that's blank, with your user name. Excel automatically fills in the Company field with the registered organization that's assigned to the copy of Windows you're using.

These fields are self-explanatory except for Hyperlink Base, which enables you to specify the base address for all of the hyperlinks in the workbook. For example, if you enter **http://www .acmeheavyindustries.com/** in the Hyperlink Base text box, you can then create a hyperlink to http://www.acmeheavyindustries/com/examples/example1.html by entering **examples/example1 .html** rather than the full address.

The Template readout shows the name of the template used for the workbook. This readout is blank if the workbook is a "new, blank" workbook.

Select the Save Thumbnails For All Excel Documents check box (on Windows Vista) or the Save Preview Picture check box (on Windows XP) if you want Excel to save a preview of the workbook in the file. If the workbook is visually distinctive, a preview can help you identify the workbook later. If all your workbooks look much the same, a preview won't be much help.

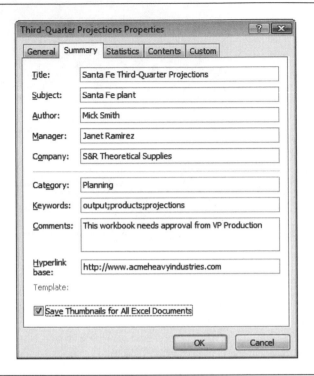

You can enter key information on the Summary tab of the Properties dialog box to make workbooks easier to identify without opening them.

Statistics Tab Properties and Content Tab Properties

The Statistics tab contains details on when the workbook was created, last saved, last modified, last accessed, and last printed, as well as on the person it was last saved by, the revision number, and the total time spent editing it.

The Contents tab provides a list of document contents, such as the worksheet names and the names of named ranges.

Custom Tab Properties

The Custom tab (see Figure 3-8) contains a variety of predefined properties that you can fill in. You can create custom properties by typing their names in the Name text box. You can also assign to a property the contents of the first cell in a named range in the workbook. This capability enables you to store the contents of specific cells automatically in the properties and thus have them indexed along with the other property information.

FIGURE 3-8   You can enter further identifying details for workbooks on the Custom tab of the Properties dialog box.

To add a property, follow these steps:

1. Select the property in the Name list, or type a new name to create a custom property.

2. In the Type drop-down list, select the appropriate type for the property: Text, Date, Number, or Yes or No. This choice isn't relevant if you're linking the property to a range in the workbook.

3. Enter the data for the property as appropriate:

  ■ For a Text, Date, or Number value, type it in the Value text box.

  ■ For a Yes or No choice, select the Yes option button or the No option button.

  ■ For information contained in a named range in a worksheet in the workbook, select the Link To Content check box. Excel displays a Source drop-down list that contains the named ranges in the workbook. Select the range from this list.

4. Click the Add button. Excel adds the property and data to the Properties list box. A property linked to a range displays a chain symbol beside it, as the Output property in Figure 3-8 does.

To delete a field, select it in the Properties list box, and then click the Delete button.

Save the Entire Workspace

Instead of just saving the workbooks you're using, you can save your entire *workspace*—the workbooks that are open and the way they're arranged, together with other settings that don't otherwise persist from one Excel session to another. Saving a workspace is great when you use multiple workbooks, multiple windows, or both in the course of your work. If you tend to have only a single workbook and window open at a time, you don't need to save your workspace.

To save your workspace, choose View | Window | Save Workspace, specify a file name and folder in the Save Workspace dialog box, and then click the Save button. Workspace files use the extension .xlw, and Excel suggests the default name resume.xlw for each workspace you save. If you use this default name, you automatically overwrite each previously saved workspace with the latest workspace you save. You may prefer to enter another name so that you can save multiple workspaces. Workspace files contain only the data about the workspace, not copies of the workbooks in it, so the files are very small and won't eat up your disk space.

After you close the Save Workspace dialog box, Excel prompts you to save any workbooks that contain unsaved changes.

The easiest way to open a workspace file is to click the Office button, and then choose the workspace file from the Recent Documents list. (If you often need to open the same workspaces, pin them to the Recent Documents list.)

You can also open a workspace file from the Open dialog box (press CTRL-O or click the Office button, and then click Open). The All Excel Files filter includes workspace files, but you can reduce the listing to only workspace files by choosing the Workspaces item in the drop-down list above the Open button.

 *If you save your workspace frequently, you may want Excel to open your last saved workspace automatically when you launch it. To do so, save the workspace file in a folder of its own, and enter the path to that folder in the At Startup, Open All Files In text box in the Advanced category of the Excel Options dialog box (click the Office button, and then click Excel Options). Don't save in this folder any files other than those you want opened for every Excel session.*

Create Your Own Templates

Excel ships with a small variety of built in templates, and, as you saw earlier in this chapter, you can download further templates from the Microsoft Office Online website. You can create as many of your own templates as you need, either starting from scratch or basing them on an existing workbook or template. If you work for a company, chances are that the company will provide you with templates that its developers and users have created to meet the company's business needs.

Understand What Templates Are and What They're For

A template file is the same as a workbook file, except that the template file uses the .xltx extension instead of the workbook's .xlsx extension. You can create a template simply by changing a workbook's extension from .xlsx to .xltx in Windows Explorer or another file-management program if you choose.

3

As you saw earlier in this chapter, you can base a new workbook on an existing workbook—so do you need templates at all? There's no absolute need to use templates, but keeping templates separate from workbooks tends to be cleaner and neater than basing new workbooks on existing workbooks and replacing or excising the parts that aren't relevant. By making your templates contain just the basic information for a workbook, you can avoid awkward errors such as forgetting to delete irrelevant information from a new workbook you've based on an existing workbook.

Understand Where Templates Are Stored

Excel keeps templates in two different folders:

- **Application Templates**   Application templates are ones that come with Excel. Excel stores these templates in the *%programfiles%*\Microsoft Office\Templates folder, where *%programfiles%* is the Windows environment variable that contains the path to your computer's Program Files folder.

- **User Templates**   User templates are templates you create or download or that your company provides for you. Excel stores user templates in the *%userprofile%*\Application Data\Microsoft\Templates folder on Windows Vista and in the *%userprofile%*\Application Data\Microsoft\Office folder on Windows XP, where *%userprofile%* is the Windows environment variable that contains the path to your user profile folder.

NOTE   *If you're using Excel on a corporate network, an administrator may have redirected the Templates folder to a different location—for example, a folder on a network drive—so that your templates can be backed up centrally.*

Create and Save a Template

To create a template, create a workbook in any of the ways covered earlier in this chapter: create a new blank workbook, create a workbook based on an existing workbook, or create a workbook based on a template. Set up the template so that it contains the data and formatting you want. Depending on the type of task it's intended to accomplish, a template might contain anything from a little cell formatting to a full layout that needs only a few cells to be filled in to become a complete workbook that you can save or print as required.

To save a template, follow these steps:

1. Click the Office button, and then choose Save As. Excel displays the Save As dialog box.

2. In the Save As Type drop-down list, select the Excel Template entry. Excel changes the folder to your Templates folder to help you save the template in the right place. (If you need to save the template in another folder, navigate to that folder now.)

NOTE   *If the template contains macros that you have created (see Chapter 18), choose the Excel Macro-Enabled Template item in the Save As Type drop-down list rather than the Excel Template item. Standard Excel templates cannot contain macros.*

3. Type the name for the template in the File Name text box.

4. If you want to save a preview picture of the template, select the Save Thumbnail check box. Having the preview picture enables the user to get a visual impression of the template from the preview pane in the New Workbook dialog box, which is usually helpful.

5. Click the Save button. Excel closes the Save As dialog box and saves the template.

After saving the template, close it (for example, click the Office button, and then click Close). Then create a new workbook based on the template to make sure that the template has the contents you expect and that it works as it should.

Enter Data in Worksheets

There are three main ways of entering data in worksheets: by typing data in manually, by using drag and drop to move or copy existing data, and by pasting in existing data that you've cut or copied. The following sections discuss these methods.

Enter Data Manually

You can enter data in a cell by selecting the cell, typing the entry, and then pressing ENTER or clicking the Enter button on the formula bar. Pressing ENTER moves the active cell to the next cell in the direction specified by the After Pressing Enter, Move Selection check box and Direction drop-down list in the Advanced category in the Excel Options dialog box. (The default direction is Down.) Alternatively, move to another cell by clicking in it, by using one of the arrow keys (↑, ↓, ←, or →), or by pressing TAB (to move right), SHIFT-TAB (to move left), or SHIFT-ENTER (to move the opposite way to that given by ENTER).

When entering data, you can work in either the cell itself or in the Formula bar. When you start editing in a cell, Excel places the insertion point in the cell, so if you want to work in the Formula bar instead, you need to click there. Entering data in the cell itself tends to be more straightforward, because you can see where the data will appear in the worksheet and whether it will fit in the cell. Entering data in the Formula bar is useful for long or complex entries for which a lack of space in the cell itself might prove distracting.

Excel also offers the following techniques for speeding up data entry:

- To enter the same data in each cell in a range, select the range, type the entry, and then press CTRL-ENTER.

- To enter data in multiple worksheets at once, CTRL-click the worksheet tabs to select the worksheets, and then enter the data. You can combine this technique with CTRL-ENTER to enter data in a range of cells on multiple worksheets at once.

NOTE   *"Use AutoFill to Enter Data Series Quickly," later in this chapter, explains how to use Excel's AutoFill feature to enter lists and series of data quickly in ranges of cells. Chapter 7 explains how to enter functions in cells, and Chapter 8 discusses how to enter formulas.*

To delete the existing contents of a cell or range, select that cell or range and press DELETE.

To replace the existing contents of a cell, simply create a new entry over the existing contents of the cell. To edit the existing contents of a cell, double-click the cell. Alternatively, move to the cell and press F2. You can then edit the text either in the cell itself (the default) or in the Formula bar (by clicking there).

Once you're editing the contents of a cell, the ← and → keys move the insertion point right and left one character at a time, so you can't use these keys (or ↑ or ↓) to enter the entry. Instead, you need to press ENTER, press TAB, click the Enter button on the Formula bar, or click in another cell.

To cancel the changes you've made in a cell, press ESC or click the Cancel button on the Formula bar.

Undo an Action

As in many Windows applications, you can undo actions in Excel. To undo an action, issue an Undo command in one of the following ways:

- Press CTRL-Z.

- Click the Undo button on the Quick Access toolbar to undo a single action. To undo multiple actions, click the drop-down button, and then choose the action up to which you want to perform the undo in the resulting list.

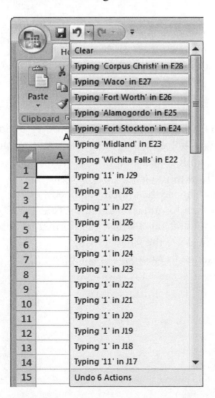

Redo an Undone Action

If you've undone one or more actions, you should be able to redo it or them by issuing a Redo command in either of the following ways:

- Press CTRL-Y.
- Click the Redo button on the Quick Access toolbar to redo a single action. To redo multiple actions, click the drop-down button, and then choose the action up to which you want to perform the redo in the resulting list.

Enter Data Using Drag and Drop

You can also enter data by using drag and drop as follows:

- Move the mouse pointer over one of the borders of the selection to produce the drag and drop pointer. (Don't click in the selection, because doing so will select the cell you click.)
- Drag and drop to move the selection. CTRL–drag and drop to copy the selection. If the destination cells contain data, Excel prompts you to decide whether to overwrite it, as shown here:

- Right-drag and drop to display a shortcut menu offering options such as Move Here, Copy Here, Copy Here As Values Only, Copy Here As Formats Only, Link Here, Create Hyperlink Here, Shift Down And Copy, Shift Right And Copy, Shift Down And Move, Shift Right And Move, and Cancel. Choose the option you need. Copying values (rather than formulas) is often useful, as is copying formatting. (You can also use the Format Painter to copy formatting. See the sidebar "Copy Formatting from One Range to Another" in Chapter 4 for details.)

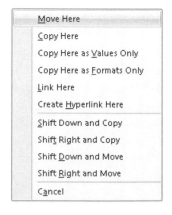

If drag-and-drop doesn't work, it may be turned off. To turn it back on, click the Office button, and then click Excel Options. In the Excel Options dialog box, click the Advanced category, select the Enable Fill Handle And Cell Drag-And-Drop check box in the Editing Options area, and then click the OK button.

Enter Data with Paste, Paste Options, and Paste Special

If you've used other Windows applications, you're probably familiar with the Windows Clipboard, the temporary storage area to which you can copy or cut a single item of data at a time so that you can paste it into another document or application. If you've used the Office applications, you're probably also familiar with the Office Clipboard, the Office-specific storage area to which you can copy or cut up to 24 separate items for pasting into Office programs.

Excel lets you cut, copy, and paste data from the Windows Clipboard or the Office Clipboard much as in the other Office applications, but with the following variations:

- When you copy an item, Excel displays a flashing border around it to indicate that the item is available for pasting. To paste a single time without using the Office Clipboard, select the destination and press ENTER; Excel removes the flashing border and clears the item from the Clipboard. To paste multiple times, issue a Paste command (for example, CTRL-V). Excel maintains the flashing border until you clear it by pressing ESC or starting to edit a cell.

- When you paste the contents of multiple cells, Excel uses the active cell as the top-left corner of the destination range. So you don't need to select the whole of the destination range, just its top-left cell.

- When you paste data, Excel displays a Paste Smart Tag below and to the right of the destination cells. Click this Smart Tag to display a menu of paste options, as shown next. For example, you can choose between maintaining the formatting of the source cell and matching the formatting of the destination cell, applying formatting only, or pasting a value rather than the formula that produces it. The available options depend on the type of data you've pasted.

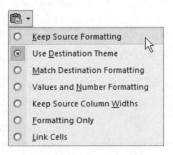

When the Smart Tag options don't give you the fine control you need, issue a Paste Special command from the Edit menu or the shortcut menu to display the Paste Special dialog box (see Figure 3-9).

The Paste section of the Paste Special dialog box offers these mutually exclusive options:

- **All**   Pastes everything copied: all values, formulas, formatting, and so on.
- **Formulas**   Pastes all data—formulas, constants, and so on—without formatting.
- **Values**   Pastes the values of formulas (rather than the formulas themselves) without formatting.
- **Formats**   Pastes all formatting without any data or formulas.
- **Comments**   Pastes all comments without other data.
- **Validation**   Pastes the data-validation criteria. (The section "Check Data Entry for Invalid Entries" in Chapter 14 explains data validation.)
- **All Using Source Theme**   Pastes everything copied except for the formatting that belongs to the theme in the source workbook. This option is useful for copying data and formatting from one workbook to another that uses a different theme.
- **All Except Borders**   Pastes all data and formatting except cell borders.
- **Column Widths**   Pastes the column widths without data and without other formatting.
- **Formulas And Number Formats**   Pastes formulas and number formatting only.
- **Values And Number Formats**   Pastes values and number formatting only.

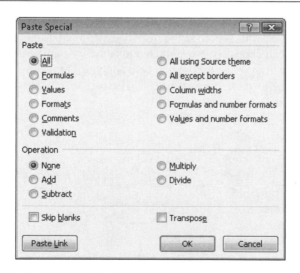

FIGURE 3-9   The Paste Special dialog box lets you choose exactly which formatting or data to paste in.

> **TIP**   *The Paste Special dialog box limits you to a single operation at a time, but you can use multiple Paste Special operations with the same data range to transfer multiple items.*

The Operation section of the Paste Special dialog box offers mutually exclusive options for adding, subtracting, multiplying, dividing, or performing no operation (the default). To use these options, follow these steps:

1. Copy to the Clipboard the cell or range that contains the number or numbers you want to add to or subtract from, or by which you want to multiply or divide, the other numbers.

2. Select the cell or range you want to affect.

3. Display the Paste Special dialog box, choose the appropriate Operation option, and click the OK button.

The final section of the Paste Special dialog box contains the following options, which you can use with the Paste options and Operation options:

- **Skip Blanks**   Prevents Excel from pasting blank cells.

- **Transpose**   Transposes rows to columns and columns to rows. This option can save you a huge amount of time when a colleague has laid out data across rather than down (or vice versa).

Link Data Across Worksheets or Across Workbooks

Most likely, your work in Excel involves many different worksheets or workbooks, some of which bear a relationship to one another. To avoid having to copy information manually from one worksheet or workbook to another each time it changes (let alone retype it), Excel lets you link data across worksheets or even across workbooks. For example, each departmental manager might maintain a separate workbook of productivity targets, with summaries from each of those workbooks linked to an executive-overview workbook used by the VPs.

To create a link, follow these steps:

1. Open the source workbook and the destination workbook. (If you're linking from one sheet of a workbook to another, open just that workbook).

2. In the source workbook, copy the relevant cell or range.

3. Display the destination sheet of the destination workbook, issue a Paste Special command to display the Paste Special dialog box, and then click the Paste Link button.

Excel updates links within the same workbook automatically and immediately when you change the data in the source. When you link from one workbook to another, here's what happens:

- If the source workbook is open and contains changes made since the destination workbook was last updated, Excel updates the links in the destination workbook when you open it.

- If the source workbook isn't open but contains changes made since the destination workbook was last updated, Excel's default behavior is to prompt you to update automatic links when you open the destination workbook. To make Excel update the links without prompting, clear the Ask To Update Automatic Links check box in the General area of the Advanced category in the Excel Options dialog box.

You can also force updating manually by choosing Data | Connections | Edit Links, and then working in the Edit Links dialog box. This dialog box also lets you check the status of a link, change a link's source, or break a link (for example, if the source isn't available now and never will be again). See "Edit, Update, and Break Links," in Chapter 16, for more information on working with links.

Use AutoFill to Enter Data Series Quickly

To enable you to fill in series of data quickly and easily in worksheets, Excel provides the AutoFill feature. You select one, two, or more cells that contain the basis for a series, and then drag the AutoFill handle—the black square that appears at the lower-right corner of the last cell selected—to show AutoFill the range of cells you want to fill with the series of data. AutoFill analyzes the starting cells, determines what the contents of the other cells should be, and enters the information automatically.

The best way to get the hang of AutoFill is to play around with it for a few minutes. Open a new, blank workbook, and then try the following examples to see how AutoFill works and what it does:

- Type **January** in cell A1, and then drag the AutoFill handle to cell D1, as shown here. As you drag, AutoFill displays a ScreenTip to show you the entry that the current cell will receive. When you release the mouse button, AutoFill enters the months February through April in the selected cells.

- Press CTRL-Z to undo the AutoFill operation, and then drag the AutoFill handle from cell A1 to cell M1 instead. AutoFill starts repeating the list after December, and enters January in cell M1.

- Type **0** in cell A2 and **5** in cell A3, select those cells, and then drag the AutoFill handle down column A. AutoFill continues the sequence by adding 5 to each number it enters in the successive cells.

NOTE   *AutoFill even works for multiple series of data at once, provided that each series is contained in a separate column or row. For example, if column A contains months and column B contains numbers, you can select both columns and drag the Autofill handle down to extend both series.*

3

■ Drag the AutoFill handle from cell A3 to the right. AutoFill repeats the data in cell A3 (the number 5), because there's no progression. You can use this behavior to extend a text label over a range of cells.

■ Hold down CTRL and drag the AutoFill handle from cell A3 to the right. Holding down CTRL forces AutoFill to increment the number entered in the single cell over the AutoFill range rather than copy the number.

■ Enter **Monday** in cell B2 and press CTRL-B to make it boldface. Then right-drag the AutoFill handle across to cell H2 and release the mouse button. AutoFill displays a context menu (as shown here) that includes options such as Copy Series, Fill Series, Fill Formatting Only, Fill Without Formatting, Fill Days, and Fill Weekdays. (For other content, the options Fill Months, Fill Years, Linear Trend, Growth Trend, and Series are available as appropriate.) Select the item you want. For example, select Fill Formatting Only to fill the series with the formatting from cell B2 but skip filling the cells with the content.

You can change the item that AutoFill has entered by clicking the AutoFill Options Smart Tag that appears below and to the right of the last cell in an AutoFill series and choosing another option from the resulting menu.

Create Custom AutoFill Lists

As well as being able to extrapolate AutoFill sequences from data in cells, Excel includes several custom lists for frequently used data: months, three-letter months (such as Jan and Feb), days of the week, and three-letter days of the week (such as Sun and Mon). You can supplement these by defining your own lists.

To create a custom list, follow these steps:

1. Click the Office button, and then click Excel Options. Excel displays the Excel Options dialog box.

2. If the Popular category isn't displayed, click it in the left panel.

3. Click the Edit Custom Lists button. Excel displays the Custom Lists dialog box (see Figure 3-10).

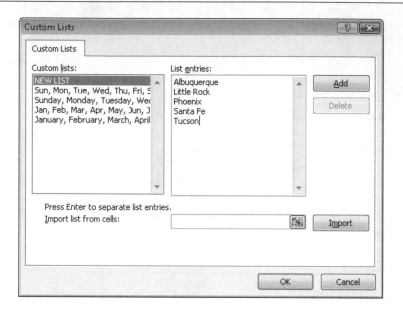

FIGURE 3-10 To speed up data entry, you can create custom AutoFill lists in the Custom Lists dialog box.

4. In the Custom Lists box, select the NEW LIST item.

5. Enter the list items in the List Entries text box, one to a line.

6. Click the Add button. Excel adds the list to the Custom Lists list box.

NOTE *You can import an existing list from a range of cells in a worksheet. Click the Collapse Dialog button at the right end of the Import List From Cells box to minimize the Custom Lists dialog box, select the range in the worksheet, and then click Import. (Alternatively, select the range of cells before displaying the Options dialog box.)*

7. When you've finished working with custom lists, click the OK button. Excel closes the Custom Lists dialog box and returns you to the Excel Options dialog box. Click the OK button to return to your workbook, where you can start using the custom lists you created.

To delete a custom list, select it in the Custom Lists box and click the Delete button.

Use Find and Replace

Excel includes Find and Replace functionality with plenty of power to make sweeping changes in your worksheets in moments.

To find items, choose Home | Editing | Find & Select | Find or press CTRL-F. Excel displays the Find tab of the Find And Replace dialog box. To replace items, choose Home | Editing | Find & Select | Replace or press CTRL-H; Excel displays the Replace tab of the Find And Replace dialog box. Figure 3-11 shows the two tabs of the Find And Replace dialog box expanded to show all their options.

To start with, Excel normally displays the reduced version of the Find And Replace dialog box. For a basic Find operation, enter the search text in the Find What text box, and then click Find Next to find the next occurrence or Find All to find all occurrences. For a basic Replace operation, enter the search text and replacement text, and then use the Find Next, Find All, Replace, and Replace All buttons as needed.

For more options, click the Options button to reveal the rest of the dialog box. These are the extra Find and Replace options:

- The Within drop-down list lets you specify whether to restrict the search or replace operation to the active worksheet (the default) or to the entire workbook.

- The Search drop-down list lets you choose whether to search by rows (the default) or by columns. Searching by columns can be quicker, but search performance is rarely an issue unless you're working with colossal worksheets.

TIP   *To reverse the search direction, hold down SHIFT and click Find Next.*

- The Look In drop-down list lets you specify whether to search formulas, values, or comments.

- The Match Case check box enables you to turn case-sensitive searching on and off. For example, you might need to find a term such as "New" without finding lowercase instances ("new").

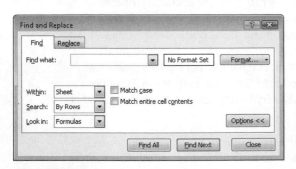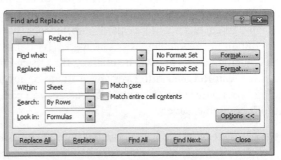

FIGURE 3-11   The full Find tab (left) and full Replace tab (right) of the Find And Replace dialog box.

- ■ The Match Entire Cell Contents check box enables you to restrict matches to only the entire contents of cells rather than partial contents. For example, you might need to find cells with the label "Tucson" without finding cells that included "Tucson" along with other text.

- ■ The Format button lets you search for or replace specific types of formatting that you either define using the Format Cells dialog box (choose Format | Format, as shown here) or specify by selecting a cell formatted that way (choose Format | Choose Format From Cell). You can replace text and formatting together or simply replace formatting on its own. This allows you to make sweeping changes to the formatting of your workbooks.

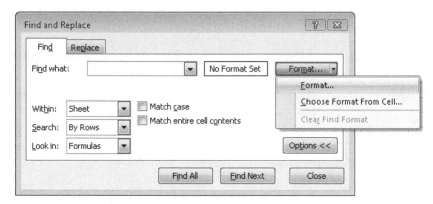

If you can't find an item that you're sure is in the worksheet, make sure that Find isn't set to use formatting. Click Format and choose Clear Find Format to clear Find formatting.

Recover Your Work If Excel Crashes

Creating spreadsheets on a computer rather than on paper can save you a huge amount of time, but it means your work is vulnerable to loss through user error, application crashes, operating system crashes, hardware failures, or power outages. To help you avoid losing data through mishaps, Excel has a feature called AutoRecover that automatically saves recovery copies of files that contain unsaved changes as you work. (By default, AutoRecover saves every 10 minutes. You can change this interval by clicking the Office button, choosing Excel Options, and using the Save AutoRecover Info Every *NN* Minutes controls in the Save category of the Excel Options dialog box.) After a crash or a power outage, you can then try to recover one of the versions that AutoRecover has saved.

Always save your work manually. AutoRecover may be able to save you from disaster, but you should never rely on it. If you're tempted to rely on AutoRecover, try thinking of it as akin to a fire sprinkler system—the sprinkler may save your home and its contents from disaster, but you'd probably rather not find out the hard way whether it actually works.

 **Minimize the Risk of Data Loss**

To minimize the risk of data loss, practice safe computing and use Excel and Office's recovery features. Here are some recommendations:

- Keep your computer hardware well maintained to reduce the risk of hardware failures.

- Use an uninterruptible power supply (UPS) to enable your desktop computer to ride out brownouts or brief blackouts and to enable you to save your work and shut down your computer if a longer power outage occurs. If you have a laptop computer, you shouldn't need a UPS, because your computer's battery can act as a backup. If your company's building has a backup power supply, you may not need a UPS for your computer.

- Keep Windows and your applications up-to-date by applying patches to eliminate known bugs and security vulnerabilities. Run Windows Update (choose Start | All Programs | Windows Update) periodically to check for patches to Windows and the applications you're using.

- Run an effective antivirus application. Update your antivirus application consistently and frequently.

- Back up your data to a removable disk or an Internet drive so that you can recover your data if your computer is destroyed, lost, or stolen. In a corporate environment, an administrator will probably back up your data centrally.

- Save your work frequently—perhaps even every time you've made a significant change.

- Configure AutoRecover options to save AutoRecover backups as often as necessary.

Use Windows Task Manager to Close a Hung Application

When a Windows application *hangs* (stops responding to the keyboard and mouse), Windows may notice and close the application for you. If Windows allows the application to continue running, you can use Windows Task Manager to shut down the application. Closing the application this way usually loses any unsaved changes in the files you had open in that application.

If Excel stops responding, follow these steps:

1. Make sure nothing easily fixable is wrong:

   ■ Check that you don't have a dialog box open for the application but hidden behind another window.

   ■ If you're running a VBA macro, wait for it to stop. Windows lists an application as Not Responding when it's under VBA's control but is otherwise fine.

   ■ Wait for a couple of minutes to see if the application starts responding again.

2. Right-click the notification area or open space in the Taskbar, and then choose Task Manager from the shortcut menu. Windows displays the Windows Task Manager window (see Figure 3-12).

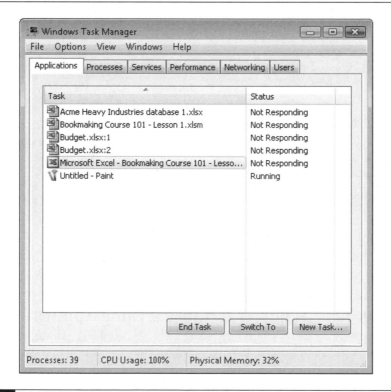

FIGURE 3-12   You may need to use Windows Task Manager to close Excel if it stops responding to the keyboard and mouse.

3. Select the Excel item that's not responding, and then click the End Task button. Windows displays a dialog box such as the one shown there, giving you the choice of restarting the program, closing the program, or waiting for the program to respond.

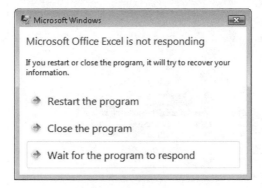

4. Click the Restart The Program button. Windows collects data about the problem, and then lets you choose whether to send information to Microsoft about it, as shown here.

5. Click the Send Information button or the Cancel button as you see fit. Generally, it's worth reporting an error once or twice to make sure that Microsoft is working on it, but beyond that, there's little point. Microsoft doesn't respond directly to error reports that users send in. You can click the View Details button to see the list of files that Windows will send to Microsoft if you choose to proceed.

6. Windows then restarts Excel for you. You may be able to recover your data, as described in the next section.

Recover a Workbook from an AutoRecover File

When Excel restarts after a crash or after being closed by Windows Task Manager, it displays the Document Recovery task pane (shown here) on the left of the application window.

The Document Recovery task pane lists any files the application has recovered, together with original versions of the documents:

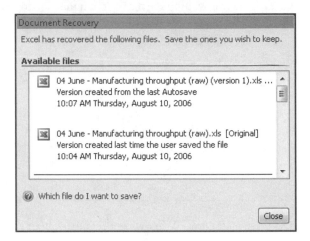

When you hover the mouse pointer over the entry for an available file in the Document Recovery task pane, the application displays a drop-down button on the right side of the entry. Click the button to display the menu, then choose Open, Save As, Delete (for AutoRecover versions only, not for original files), or Show Repairs. Once you've opened a document, the menu offers the choices View, Save As, Close, and Show Repairs. The Show Repairs item displays the Repairs dialog box with a report showing which errors (if any) were detected and repaired in the file.

After deciding which recovered file to keep, click the Office button, choose Save As to display the Save As dialog box, and then save the file under a different name than the original file. This way, you'll be able to go back to the original file if you subsequently discover that the recovered file has problems you didn't identify when viewing it.

Click the Close button to close the Document Recovery task pane. If the pane contains recovered files that you haven't opened, Excel displays the dialog box shown here to ask if you want to view the files the next time you start Excel or remove the files. Choose the Yes, I Want To View These Files Later option button or the No, Remove The Files, I Have Saved The Files I Need option button as needed, and then click the OK button.

Approach the recovery of documents with as calm a mind as possible. Don't fall sobbing with relief on a recovered document and save it over your old document before making sure it contains usable data without errors.

Chapter 4

Format Worksheets for Best Effect

How to...

- Add, delete, and manipulate worksheets
- Format cells and ranges
- Understand the number formats that Excel offers
- Apply visual formatting to cells and ranges
- Use conditional formatting to make remarkable values stand out
- Apply canned formatting instantly with AutoFormat
- Create and use styles to apply consistent formatting easily

As you saw in Chapter 3, Excel makes it easy to navigate in and enter data in worksheets. Excel also offers a wide variety of formatting options for presenting the data in worksheets as effectively as possible.

In this chapter, you'll learn how to manipulate worksheets in a workbook before moving on to discover how to format cells and ranges by using the many types of formatting that Excel supports.

Add, Delete, and Manipulate Worksheets

By default, each new Excel workbook you create contains three worksheets. In the following sections, you'll learn how to add, delete, hide, and redisplay worksheets; move and copy worksheets; rename worksheets; and change the formatting on default new worksheets that you create.

Add, Delete, Hide, and Redisplay Worksheets

When setting up a workbook, you'll often need to add further worksheets, either temporarily or permanently. For simple workbooks, you may need to delete worksheets. You may also need to hide worksheets from view so that your colleagues can't see them—but so that you can redisplay them when you need them.

Add a Worksheet

You can add a worksheet in either of these ways:

- **Add a worksheet after the last existing worksheet** Click the Insert Worksheet button that appears after the last worksheet tab, as shown here. If you need the new worksheet at a different position, you can drag it there.

■ **Add a worksheet before a particular worksheet**   Right-click the tab of the worksheet before which you want to insert the worksheet, and then choose Insert from the shortcut menu. Excel displays the Insert dialog box. Select the Worksheet item on the General tab, and then click the OK button. Alternatively, select the worksheet tab before which you want the new worksheet, and then choose Home | Cells | Insert | Sheet or press either SHIFT-F11 or ALT-SHIFT-F1.

 *You can change the default number of worksheets in a new workbook by adjusting the value in the Include This Many Sheets text box in the Popular category in the Excel Options dialog box (click the Office button, and then click Excel Options).*

Delete a Worksheet

To delete a worksheet, right-click its tab and choose Delete from the shortcut menu, or select the sheet, and then choose Home | Cells | Delete | Sheet. If the worksheet has no contents, Excel deletes it without comment. But if the worksheet contains data, Excel prompts you as shown here. Click the Delete button if you're sure you want to delete the worksheet.

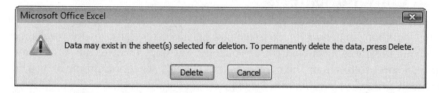

Hide and Redisplay a Worksheet

When you don't need to see a worksheet, or you need your colleagues not to see it, you can hide it from view. To do so, right-click the worksheet tab, and then choose Hide from the shortcut menu.

To display the worksheet again, right-click any worksheet tab, and then choose Unhide from the shortcut menu. Excel displays the Unhide dialog box (shown here). Select the worksheet, and then click the OK button.

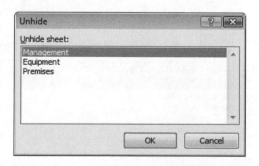

Recover from Deleting the Wrong Worksheet

If you delete the wrong worksheet, the only way to recover your work is to revert to the previously saved version of the workbook—if that version of the workbook contains the worksheet. (If you've just inserted the worksheet in the workbook, entered data on it, and then deleted it, you're stuck.)

To revert to the previously saved version of the workbook, close the workbook without saving changes to it, and then open the workbook again.

When you close the workbook like this, you'll also lose any other unsaved changes to the workbook, so this isn't an action to take lightly. But if the alternative is losing a worksheet that contained valuable information, losing other unsaved changes may be worthwhile.

Move and Copy Worksheets

In a workbook that contains few worksheets, the easiest way to move a worksheet to a new position in the workbook is to drag its tab to the new position. You can copy the worksheet instead of moving it by holding down CTRL as you drag. The copy receives the same name as the original worksheet followed by the number two in parentheses. For example, if you copy a worksheet named *Summary*, Excel names the copy *Summary (2)*.

In a workbook that contains many worksheets, it's easier to use the Move Or Copy dialog box to move or copy a worksheet. Follow these steps:

1. Select the worksheet or worksheets that you want to move or copy.

2. Right-click a selected worksheet tab, and then choose Move Or Copy from the shortcut menu. Alternatively, choose Home | Cells | Format | Move Or Copy Sheet. Excel displays the Move Or Copy dialog box, as shown here:

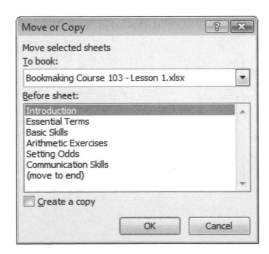

3. Select the destination in the Before Sheet list box.

4. To copy the worksheet rather than move it, select the Create A Copy check box.

5. Click the OK button to close the Move Or Copy dialog box. Excel moves or copies the worksheet.

The Move Or Copy dialog box also enables you to move or copy a worksheet to a different workbook. Open the workbook and follow the previous steps, but in the To Book drop-down list, select the destination workbook.

Rename a Worksheet

By default, Excel names worksheets Sheet1, Sheet2, and so on. You can rename worksheets with new names of up to 31 characters. Usually, it's best to keep worksheet names considerably shorter than the maximum length so that there's enough room for several tabs to appear at once on an average-resolution screen.

To rename a worksheet, follow these steps:

1. Double-click the worksheet's tab, or right-click the tab and then choose Rename from the shortcut menu. Excel selects the existing name.

2. Type the new name over or edit the existing name.

3. Press ENTER or click elsewhere.

TIP   *To make a worksheet tab easier to identify among its siblings, you can change its color. Right-click the tab, choose Tab Color, and then choose the color from the color panel.*

Format Cells and Ranges

As you've seen already in this book, the cell is the basis of the Excel worksheet. A cell can contain any one of various types of data—numbers (values that can be calculated), dates, times, formulas, text, and so on—and can be formatted in a variety of ways. You can adjust everything from the formats in which Excel displays different types of data, to alignment, to background color and gridlines.

The most basic type of formatting controls the way in which Excel displays the data the cell contains. For some types of entries, Excel displays the literal contents of the cell by default; for other types of entries, Excel displays the results of the cell's contents. For example, when you enter a formula in a cell, Excel normally displays the results of the formula rather than the formula itself. So to be sure of the contents of a cell, you need to make it the active cell or edit it. Excel displays the literal contents of the active cell in the Formula bar; and, when you edit a cell, Excel displays its literal contents in both the cell itself and in the Formula bar.

Even when Excel displays the contents of the cell, it may change the contents for display purposes. For example, when you enter a number that's too long to be displayed in a General-formatted cell, Excel converts it to scientific notation using six digits of precision. Similarly, Excel rounds display numbers when they won't fit in cells, but the underlying number remains unaffected.

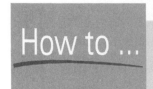

Change the Default Formatting on New Worksheets and Workbooks

You can change the default formatting of the workbook and worksheets that Excel uses for the New Blank Workbook command by creating a template named Book.xltx in the XLSTART folder. Here's where to find this folder, where *%userprofile%* is the Windows environment variable that returns the path to your user profile folder:

- **Windows Vista**   *%userprofile%*\AppData\Roaming\Microsoft\Excel\XLSTART
- **Windows XP**   *%userprofile%*\Application Data\Microsoft\Excel

Before you can navigate to the XLSTART folder, you'll need to display hidden files and folders (if you haven't already done so). To do so:

- On Windows Vista, choose Start | Computer to open a Computer window. Click the Organize button, choose Folder And Search Options, and then click the View tab in the Folder Options dialog box. In the Advanced Settings list box, select the Show Hidden Files And Folders option button, and then click the OK button.

- On Windows XP, choose Start | My Computer to open a My Computer window. Choose Tools | Folder Options, and then click the View tab in the Folder Options dialog box. Select the Show Hidden Files And Folders option button, and then click the OK button.

Then open a Windows Explorer window to the XLSTART folder (for example, press WINDOWS KEY + R, enter the path shown above in the Run dialog box, and then press ENTER) and take either of the following actions:

- If you have a workbook or template that contains the default formatting that you want to use for new worksheets and workbooks, copy it to the XLSTART folder. Press F2 and rename the copy Book.xltx. (If the file was a workbook, Windows displays a Rename dialog box that warns you about the change of file extension. Click the Yes button.) Open Book.xltx and delete any contents you don't want to have in the new default worksheets and workbooks. Save and close the file.

- If you don't have a workbook or template that contains the default formatting you want to use for new worksheets and workbooks, create a new one. In the XLSTART folder, right-click in the document area and choose New | Microsoft Office Excel Worksheet from the shortcut menu. Name the new workbook Book.xltx. Windows displays a Rename dialog box that warns you about the change of file extension. Click the Yes button. Open Book.xltx, set it up with the default formatting you want to use for new worksheets and workbooks, save it, and then close it.

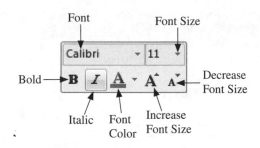

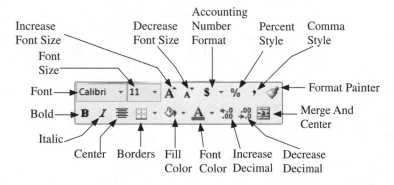

FIGURE 4-1   Excel automatically displays the smaller Mini Toolbar (top) when you select text. You can display the larger Mini Toolbar (bottom) by right-clicking a cell or a selection.

Apply Number Formatting

You can apply formatting to cells and ranges in three ways:

- The Mini Toolbar (see Figure 4-1) provides instant access to frequently used formatting. Excel displays the smaller version of the Mini Toolbar automatically when you select text within a cell. You can display the larger version by right-clicking a cell or a selection.

- The Home tab of the Ribbon contains many formatting options in the Font group, Alignment group, and Number group, as shown here.

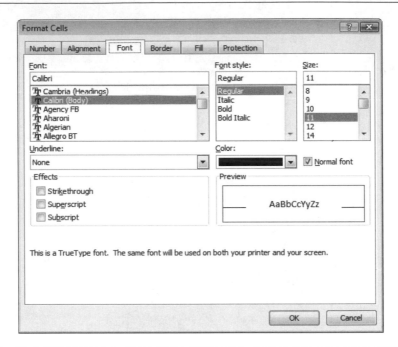

FIGURE 4-2 The Format Cells dialog box offers many options for formatting the active cell or selected ranges.

- The Format Cells dialog box (see Figure 4-2) includes the full range of cell formatting on its six tabs. You can display the Format Cells dialog box in any of these ways:

  - Press CTRL-1.

  - Right-click a cell or selection, and then choose Format Cells from the shortcut menu.

  - Click the Format Cells button in the lower-right corner of the Font group, the Alignment group, or the Number group on the Home tab of the Ribbon. The Format Cells button is the tiny button with the arrow pointing downward and to the right. Clicking the Format Cells button in the Font group displays the Font tab of the Format Cells dialog box; clicking the button in the Alignment group displays the Alignment tab; and clicking the button in the Number group displays the Number tab.

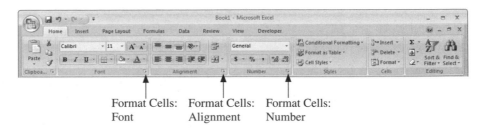

Format Cells: Format Cells: Format Cells:
Font   Alignment   Number

If you prefer to work with the Ribbon minimized, you can put formatting commands on the Quick Access toolbar. Chapter 17 explains how to customize Excel.

You'll learn about most of the options in the Format Cells dialog box later in this chapter. Other options, such as those for locking and protecting cells, you'll learn about later in this book.

You can also apply some font formatting via standard Office shortcuts (such as CTRL-B for boldface, CTRL-I for italic, and CTRL-U for single underline).

Understand Excel's Number Formats

To make Excel display the contents of a cell in the way you intend, apply the appropriate number format. You can apply number formats manually in several ways, but Excel also applies number formats automatically when you enter text that matches one of Excel's triggers for a number format. By knowing these triggers, you can both, use them to apply formatting and to avoid having Excel apply the number formats unexpectedly.

The Number group on the Home tab of the Ribbon (shown here with labels) contains buttons for the most widely used number formats and a drop-down list that lets you access the other number formats.

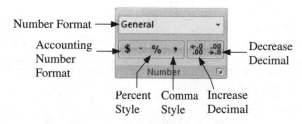

You can also apply number formats from the Number tab of the Format Cells dialog box (see Figure 4-3). The Number tab offers 12 categories of built-in formats. The following sections discuss these formats.

General Number Format

The General number is the default format for all cells on a new worksheet (unless you've customized it). General displays up to 11 digits per cell and doesn't use thousands separators.

You can apply General format by pressing CTRL-SHIFT-~ (tilde).

Number Format

The Number formats let you specify the number of decimal places to display (0 to 30, with a default of 2), whether to display a thousands separator (for example, a comma in U.S. English formats), and how to represent negative numbers.

You can make Excel apply the Number format with the thousands separator by including a comma to separate thousands or millions (for example, enter **1,000**, **1,000,000**, or **1,000000**— only one appropriately placed comma is necessary, although you can include more if you find it easier to enter the number that way).

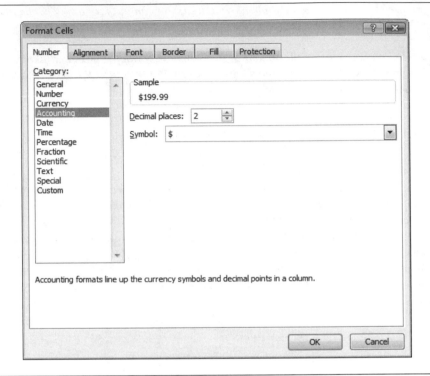

FIGURE 4-3   Use the options on the Number tab of the Format Cells dialog box to apply number formatting.

Currency Format

The Currency formats let you specify the number of decimal places to display (0 to 30, with a default of 2), which currency symbol to display (if any), and how to represent negative numbers.

You can make Excel apply Currency format by entering the appropriate currency symbol before the number. For example, enter **$4** to make Excel display dollar formatting. If you enter one or more decimal places, Excel applies Currency format with two decimal places. For example, if you enter **$4.1**, Excel displays *$4.10*.

Accounting Format

The Accounting formats let you specify the number of decimal places to display (0 to 30, with a default of 2) and which currency symbol to display (if any). The currency symbol appears flush left with the cell border, separated from the figures. The Accounting formats represent negative numbers with parentheses around them—there's no choice of format.

You can apply the Accounting format quickly by clicking the Currency Style button on the Formatting toolbar.

Date Format

The Date formats offer a variety of date formats based on the locale you choose. These options are easy to understand. What's more important to grasp is how Excel stores dates and times.

Excel treats dates and times as serial numbers representing the number of days that have elapsed since 1/1/1900, which is given the serial number 1. For example, the serial date 39416 represents November 30, 2007.

Excel for the Macintosh uses a different starting date—January 2, 1904—instead of January 1, 1900. If you use spreadsheets created in Excel for the Mac in Windows versions of Excel, you'll need to select the Use 1904 Date System check box in the When Calculating This Workbook section of the Advanced category in the Excel Options dialog box to get Excel to display the dates correctly.

4

For computers, serial dates (and times) are a snap to sort and manipulate: to find out how far apart two dates are, the computer need merely subtract one date from the other, without having to consider which months are shorter than others or whether a leap year is involved. For humans, serial dates are largely inscrutable, so Excel displays dates in your choice of format.

If you want, you can enter dates by formatting cells with the Date format and entering the appropriate serial number, but most people find it far easier to enter the date in one of the conventional Windows formats that Excel recognizes. Excel automatically converts to serial dates, and formats with a Date format any entry that contains a hyphen (-) or a forward slash (/) and matches one of the date and time formats Windows uses. For example, if you type **11/30/07**, Excel assumes you mean November 30, 2007.

If you don't specify the year, Excel assumes you mean the current year.

Time Format

The Time formats offer a variety of time formats based on 12-hour and 24-hour clocks. These options are easy to understand. Excel treats times as subdivisions of days, with 24 hours making up one day and one serial number. So, given that 39448 is the serial date for January 1, 2008, 39448.5 is noon on that day, 39448.25 is 6AM, 39448.75 is 6PM, and so on.

You can make Excel automatically format an entry with a time format by entering a number that contains a colon (for example, 12:00) or a number followed by a space and an uppercase or lowercase *a* or *p* (for example, **1 P** or **11 a**).

Percentage Format

The Percentage format displays the value in the cell with a percent sign and with your choice of number of decimal places (the default is two). For example, if you enter **71** in the cell, Excel displays *71.00%* by default.

You can make Excel automatically format an entry with the Percentage format by entering a percent sign after the number—for example, **9%**. If you enter no decimal places, Excel uses none. If you enter one or more decimal places, Excel uses two decimal places. You can change the number of decimal places displayed by formatting the cell manually.

Fraction Format

Excel stores fractions as their decimal equivalents—for example, it stores ¼ as 0.25. To display fractions (for example, ¼) and compound fractions (for example, 11¼) in Excel, use the Fraction formats. Excel offers fraction formats of one digit (for example, ¾), two digits (for example, 16/18), and three digits (for example, 303/512)—halves, quarters, eighths, sixteenths, tenths, and hundreds.

Before worrying about fractions being displayed as their decimal equivalents, however, you need to worry about entering many fractions in a way that Excel won't mistake for dates. For example, if you enter **1/4** in a General-formatted cell, Excel converts it to the date 4-Jan in the current year.

To enter a fraction in a General-formatted cell, type a zero, a space, and the fraction—for example, type **0 1/4** to enter ¼. To enter a compound fraction in a General-formatted cell, type the integer, a space, and the fraction—for example, type **11 1/4** to enter 11¼. Excel formats the cell with the appropriate Fraction format, so the fraction is displayed and stores the corresponding decimal value.

If you need to enter simple fractions consistently in your worksheets, format the relevant cells, columns, or rows with the Fraction format ahead of time.

Scientific Format

Scientific format displays numbers in an exponential form—for example, 567890123245 is displayed as 5.6789E+11, indicating where the decimal place needs to go. You can change the number of decimal places displayed to anywhere from 0 to 30; the default is 2.

You can make Excel apply Scientific format by entering a number that contains an *e* in any position but the ends (for example, **3e4** or **12345E17**).

Text Format

Text format is for values that you want to force Excel to treat as text so as to avoid having Excel automatically apply another format. For example, if you keep a spreadsheet of telephone numbers, you might have some numbers that start with 0. To prevent Excel from dropping what appears to be a leading zero and converting the cell to a number format, you could format the cell as Text. (You could also use the Special format for phone numbers, discussed in the next section.) Similarly, you might need to enter a value that Excel might take to be a date (for example, **1/2**), a time, a formula, or another format.

Excel left-aligns Text-formatted entries and omits them from range calculations—for example, SUM()—in which they would otherwise be included.

You can make Excel format a numeric entry with the Text format by entering a space before the number.

For safety, force the Text format by typing a space before a numeric entry or manually format the cell as Text before *entering data in it. If you apply the Text format to numbers you've already entered, Excel will continue to treat them as numbers rather than as text. You'll need to edit each cell (double-click it, or press F2, and then press ENTER to accept the existing entry) to correct this error.*

Special Format

The Special formats provide a locale-specific range of formatting choices. For example, the English (United States) locale offers the choices Zip Code, Zip Code + 4, Phone Number, and Social Security Number.

As you'll quickly realize, these formats are all rigidly defined; most are separated by hyphens into groups of specific lengths. (Phone numbers are less rigid than the other formats, but Excel handles longer numbers—for example, international numbers—as well as can be expected.)

Special formats enable you to quickly enter numbers of the given type and have Excel enter the hyphens automatically for you. For example, if you format a cell with the Social Security Number format and enter **623648267**, Excel automatically formats it as 623-64-8267.

Custom Format

The Custom format enables you to define your own custom formats for needs that none of the built-in formats covers.

As explained in the previous sections, Excel includes a variety of built-in formats that cover general, numeric, currency, percentage, exponential, date, time, and custom numeric formats. You can also design your own custom formats based on one of the built-in formats.

To define a custom format, follow these steps:

1. Click in a cell, type sample text for the format in the cell, and press ENTER. Then click the cell again to select it. (Excel then displays the sample text in the format you're creating, which helps you see the effects of your changes.)

2. Display the Number tab of the Format Cells dialog box. For example, click the Format Cells button in the lower-right corner of the Number group on the Home tab of the Ribbon.

3. In the Category box, select the Custom item.

4. In the Type list box, select the custom format on which you want to base your new custom format. Excel displays the details for the type in the Type text box.

5. If the details for the type extend beyond the Type text box, double-click in the Type text box to select all of its contents, issue a Copy command (for example, press CTRL-C), and then paste the copied text into a text editor, such as Notepad. (For a shorter type, you can work effectively in the Type text box. For a longer type, it's easier to have enough space to see the whole type at once.)

6. Enter the details for the four parts of the type, separating the parts from each other with a semicolon. (See the detailed explanation after this list.)

7. If you're working in a text editor, copy what you typed and paste it into the Type text box. Check the sample text to make sure it seems to be correct.

8. Click the OK button.

Each custom format consists of format codes that specify how Excel should display the information. Each custom format can contain four formats. The first format specifies how to display positive numbers, the second format specifies how to display negative numbers, the third format specifies how to display zero values, and the fourth format specifies how to display text. The four formats are separated by semicolons. You can leave a section blank by entering nothing between the relevant semicolons (or before the first semicolon, or after the last semicolon).

Table 4-1 explains the codes you can use for defining custom formats.

Code	Meaning	Example
[*color name*]	Display the specified color.	Enter the appropriate color in brackets as the first item in the section: [Black], [Red], [Blue], [Green], [White], [Cyan], [Magenta], or [Yellow]. For example, **#,##0_);[Magenta](#,##0)** displays negative numbers in magenta.
Number Format Codes		
#	Display a significant digit.	##.# displays two significant digits before the decimal point and one significant digit after it. (A *significant digit* is a nonzero figure.)
0	Display a zero if there would otherwise be no digit in this place.	00000 displays a five-digit number, packing it with leading zeros if necessary. For example, if you enter **4**, Excel displays *00004*.
%	Display a percentage.	#% displays the number multiplied by 100 and with a percent sign. For example, **2** appears as *200%*.
?	Display as a fraction.	# ????/???? displays a number and four-digit fractions—for example, 4 1234/4321.
.	Display a decimal point.	##.## displays two significant digits on either side of the decimal point.
,	Two meanings: display the thousands separator *or* scale the number down by 1,000.	Thousands separator example: $#,### displays the dollar sign, four significant digits, and the thousands separator.
		Scale by 1,000 example: €#.##,,, " billion" displays the euro symbol, one significant digit before the decimal point and two after, the number scaled down by a billion, and the word *billion* (after a space). For example, if you enter **9876543210**, Excel displays *€9.88 billion*.
Date and Time Format Codes		
d	Display the day in numeric format.	d-mmm-yyyy displays 1/1/08 as *1-Jan-2008*.
dd	Display the day in numeric format with a leading zero.	dd/mmm/yy displays 1/1/08 as *01/Jan/08*. Use leading zeros to align dates.
ddd	Display the day as a three-letter abbreviation.	ddd dd/mm/yyyy displays 1/1/08 as *Tue 01/01/2008*.

TABLE 4-1 Codes for Creating Custom Formats

Code	Meaning	Example
dddd	Display the day in full.	dddd, dd/mm/yyyy displays 1/1/08 as *Tuesday, 01/01/2008*.
m	Display the month in numeric format.	d/m/yy displays 1/1/08 as *1/1/08*.
mm	Display the month in numeric format with a leading zero.	dd/mm/yy displays 1/1/08 as *01/01/08*.
mmm	Display the month as a three-letter abbreviation.	dd-mmm-yy displays 1/1/08 as *01-Jan-2008*.
mmmm	Display the month in full.	d mmmm, yyyy displays 1/1/08 as *1 January, 2008*.
mmmmm	Display the month as a one-letter abbreviation.	January, June, and July appear as *J;* April and August appear as *A;* and so on. This code is seldom useful because it tends to be visually confusing.
yy	Display the year as a two-digit number.	d/m/yy displays 1/1/08 as *1/1/08*.
yyyy	Display the year in full.	d-mmm-yyyy displays 1/1/08 as *1-Jan-2008*.
h	Display the hour.	h:m displays 1:01 as *1:1*.
hh	Display the hour with a leading zero.	hh:mm displays 1:01 as *01:01*.
m	Display the minute.	h:m displays 1:01 as *1:1*.
mm	Display the minute with a leading zero.	hh:mm displays 1:01 as *01:01*. To distinguish mm from the months code, you must enter it immediately after hh or immediately before ss.
s	Display the second.	h:m:s displays 1:01:01 as *1:1:1*.
ss	Display the second with a leading zero.	hh:mm:ss displays 1:01:01 as *1:01:01*.
.0, .00, .000	Display tenths, hundredths, or thousandths of seconds.	h:mm:ss.00 displays 1:01:01.11 as *1:01:01.11*. Use further zeros for greater precision.
A/P	Display A for A.M. and P for P.M.	h:mm A/P displays 1:01 as *1:01 A*. You can use uppercase A/P or lowercase a/p to specify which case to display.
AM/PM	Display AM for A.M. and PM for P.M.	h:mm am/pm displays 13:01 as *1:01 PM*. Excel uses uppercase regardless of which case you use.
[]	Display the elapsed time in the specified unit.	[h]:mm:ss displays the elapsed time in hours, minutes, and seconds—for example, *33:22:01*.

Text Format Codes

_	Display a space as wide as the specified character.	_) makes Excel enter a space the width of a closing parenthesis—for example, to align positive numbers with negative numbers surrounded by parentheses.

TABLE 4-1   Codes for Creating Custom Formats (*continued*)

Code	Meaning	Example
*	Repeat the specified character to fill the cell.	*A makes Excel fill the cell with A characters. Sometimes useful for drawing attention to particular values—for example, zero values.
\	Display the following character.	[Blue]$#,###.00 *;[Red]$#,###.00 \D displays positive numbers in blue and followed by an asterisk, and negative numbers in red and followed by a *D*.
"string"	Display the string of text.	$#,##0.00" Advance" displays the word *Advance* after the entry. Note the leading space between the " and the word.
@	Concatenate the specified string with the user's text input.	"Username: "@ enters **Username:** and a space before the user's text input. This works only in the fourth section (the text section) of a custom format.
N/A	Display the specified character.	$ - + = / ( ) { } : ! ^ & ' ' ~ < > [SPACE]

TABLE 4-1   Codes for Creating Custom Formats (*continued*)

Apply Visual Formatting

After telling Excel how to represent the data you enter in worksheet cells, you'll probably want to apply formatting to the worksheets to make them more readable. Excel offers a wide range of formatting options, most of which are easy to understand and applicable to a cell or range.

This section outlines the main types of formatting that Excel offers for individual cells. You can apply some of these formatting options from the Mini Toolbar, more of them from the Home tab of the Ribbon, and all of them from the Format Cells dialog box. But what you should do first is apply a theme to your workbook.

Apply a Theme

A *theme* is a suite of formatting that you apply to an entire workbook rather than to individual worksheets, ranges, or cells. By changing the theme, you can change the overall "look and feel" of the workbook in moments. A theme includes:

■ **Twelve colors**   Each theme has four colors for text and backgrounds, six accent colors for items such as charts and graphs, and one color each for hyperlinks and followed hyperlinks. Microsoft's designers set up the text and background colors so that light colors are legible against the dark colors and dark colors are legible against the light colors. Similarly, the designers chose accent colors that are always visible against the background colors. The net result is that you have a choice of colors for text and backgrounds that should always work in combination, even though you will need to experiment with different combinations of colors to produce a result that appeals to you.

■ **Two fonts** Each theme has a Heading font (used for headings) and a Body font (used for body text).

■ **Graphical effects** Each theme has colored and shaded graphical effects for items such as AutoShapes (easy-to-use shapes that you can use in worksheets).

To apply a theme to the active workbook, follow these steps:

1. Click the Page Layout tab of the Ribbon to display its contents.

2. In the Themes group, click the Themes button to display the Themes panel (shown on the left in Figure 4-4), and then hover the mouse pointer over a theme to preview its effect on the worksheet or worksheets that are visible. When you find the theme you want, click the name to apply it.

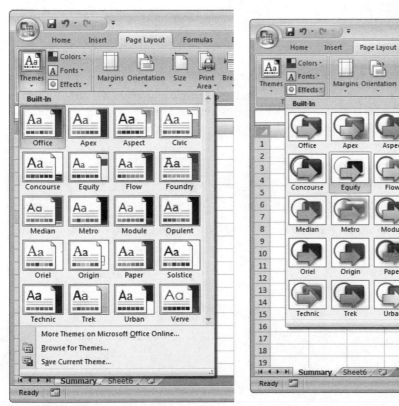

FIGURE 4-4   The Themes panel (left) lets you preview a theme before you apply it. You can also apply colors, fonts, or graphical effects (shown here on the right) as needed.

3. If you want to change the colors used in the theme, go to the Themes group, click the Colors button, and then choose a set of colors from the Colors panel. You can also create a custom set of colors by clicking the Create New Theme Colors button at the bottom of the Colors panel, and then working in the Create New Theme Colors dialog box.

4. If you want to change the fonts used, in the Themes group, click the Fonts button, and then choose a pair of fonts from the Fonts panel. Some of the pairs use two different fonts, while others use different sizes of the same font. You can also create a custom set of fonts by clicking the Create New Themes Fonts button at the bottom of the Fonts panel, and then working in the Create New Theme Fonts dialog box.

5. If you want to change the graphical effects used, in the Themes group, click the Effects button, and then choose a set of effects from the Effects panel (shown on the right in Figure 4-4).

Font Formatting

The controls on the Font group in the Home tab of the Ribbon and on the Mini Toolbars let you quickly change fonts, font size, font style (regular, bold, italic, or bold italic), underline, and color. You can also work on the Font tab of the Format Cells dialog box (shown on the left in Figure 4-5).

Alignment, Text-Control, and Orientation Formatting

Alignment formatting lets you change cells' horizontal and vertical alignment. Options include horizontal centering across the selection (which can be useful for centering a heading over several columns), vertical centering in a cell whose height you've increased, and indentation.

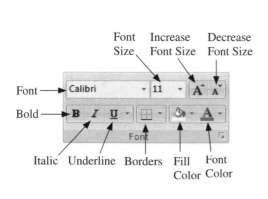

FIGURE 4-5 Use the Font group in the Home tab of the Ribbon (left) or the Font tab of the Format Cells dialog box (right) to apply font formatting.

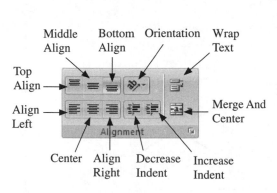 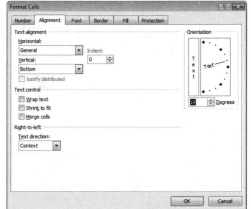

FIGURE 4-6	Use the controls in the Alignment group on the Home tab of the Ribbon to quickly apply alignment without displaying the Format Cells dialog box—or simply use the Alignment tab (right).

The Mini Toolbar includes a Center button for quickly centering the contents of a cell, but the options you'll need most of the time are in the Alignment group on the Home tab of the Ribbon (see Figure 4-6). You can also use the controls on the Alignment tab of the Format Cells dialog box (shown on the right in Figure 4-6).

Orientation formatting lets you change the orientation of the text—for example, you may need to set text at a slant for special emphasis, or create a vertical heading to save space. The Text Direction drop-down list on the Alignment tab of the Format Cells dialog box lets you set the direction of the text: Left-to-Right, Right-to-Left, or Context (Excel decides based on the context).

Text-control formatting lets you choose whether to wrap text in the cell, shrink it to fit the cell, or merge multiple cells into one cell. Wrapping text can greatly improve long entries, and you can break lines manually by pressing ALT-ENTER.

 Be careful with the Shrink To Fit option—when it resizes the display of some cells to make their contents fit the column but leaves other cells at full size, it can produce the effect of formatting errors. For more control, resize your columns or fonts manually.

Border Formatting

The Borders button on the Mini Toolbar (shown on the left in Figure 4-7) and the Font panel of the Home tab let you quickly apply standard borders. For example, you might put a bottom double border on the last cell in a column before the cell containing a total.

For more border options and a greater choice of border weights and colors, work on the Border tab of the Format Cells dialog box (shown on the right in Figure 4-7). Select the style and color, then click the preview pane to apply a line. Click an applied line to remove it.

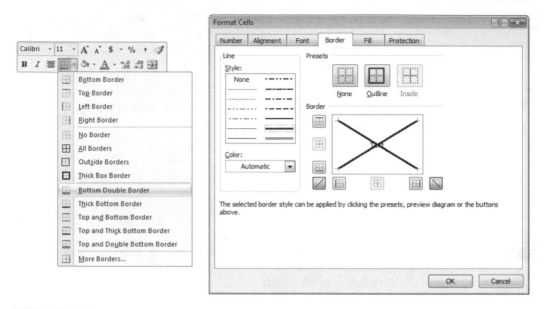

FIGURE 4-7
You can apply borders from the Borders button on the Mini Toolbar (left) or the Border tab of the Format Cells dialog box (right).

How to ... Copy Formatting from One Range to Another

To copy formatting from one cell or a range of cells to another cell or range of cells, use the Format Painter feature. Follow these steps:

1. Select the cell or range that has the formatting you want to copy.

2. Click the Format Painter button (the button with the paintbrush icon) on the Mini Toolbar or the Clipboard group on the Home tab of the Ribbon. Excel changes the mouse pointer to a brush and displays a flashing outline around the cell or range that contains the copied formatting.

3. Click the cell, or drag over the range, to which you want to apply the formatting. Excel applies the formatting.

After applying the formatting, Excel restores the normal mouse pointer. If you need to apply the formatting to multiple cells or ranges, double-click the Format Painter button to lock the feature on. Apply the formatting to all the cells or ranges, and then press ESC or click the Format Painter button again to unlock the feature.

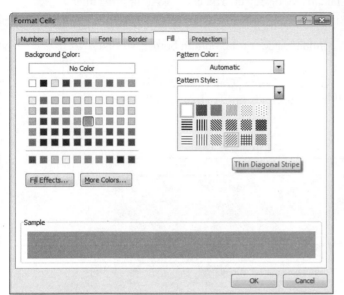

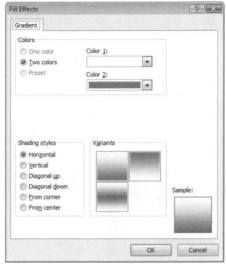

FIGURE 4-8   Fill effects from the Fill tab of the Format Cells dialog box (left) and the Fill Effects dialog box (right) can greatly change the look of a worksheet.

Fill Formatting

Fill formatting lets you apply solid shades of color or colored patterns to add emphasis or create a design. These options appear on the Fill tab of the Format Cells dialog box (shown on the left in Figure 4-8). You can click the Fill Effects button and use the Fill Effects dialog box (shown on the right in Figure 4-8) to control the color gradient and the shading style.

Protection Formatting

Protection formatting enables you to lock or hide particular cells. Locking and hiding takes effect only when you protect the worksheet. The section "Protect Cells, a Worksheet, or a Workbook," in Chapter 14, explains how to protect your work.

Format Rows and Columns

In most worksheets you create, you'll need to change some columns from their standard widths to widths better suited to the data entered in their cells. Similarly, you may need to change row height—for example, to accommodate objects or taller text you enter for headings.

The fastest and most effective way to change the width of a column or the height of a row is by using Excel's AutoFit feature. AutoFit resizes a column to just wider than its widest entry and resizes a row to just high enough for its tallest character or object. You can use AutoFit in either of these ways:

- Double-click the right border bar of a column header or the bottom border bar of a row header.
- Select the column (or its widest cell) and choose Home | Cells | Format | AutoFit Column Width (see Figure 4-9), or select a cell in the row and choose Home | Cells | Format | AutoFit Row Height).

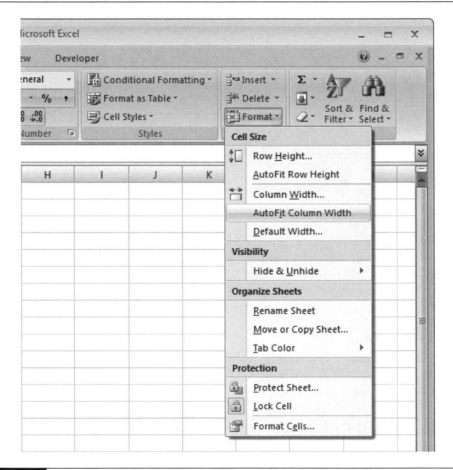

FIGURE4-9 The Format drop-down menu in the Cells group on the Home tab of the Ribbon contains AutoFit commands for automatically adjusting row height and column width.

You can also change column width and row height manually by dragging the appropriate column border bar or row border bar. Excel displays a ScreenTip showing the size to which you've currently dragged. The column-width ScreenTip shows the number of characters and the number of pixels; the row-height ScreenTip shows the number of points and the number of pixels.

To set an exact column width, choose Home | Cells | Format | Column Width, and then enter the width in characters in the Column Width dialog box. You can use any value from 0 to 255 characters. Similarly, you can change row height by choosing Home | Cells | Format | Row Height, and then entering the row height in points in the Row Height dialog box. You can set row height to any value between 0 and 409 points.

> **NOTE** *You can change the standard column width for the active worksheet by choosing Home Cells | Format | Default Width, typing the width you want, and clicking the OK button. Excel doesn't apply this new standard width to any columns you've already adjusted.*

> **TIP** *Use the Column Widths option button in the Paste Special dialog box to copy column widths to another worksheet without including their data. This trick is helpful when you need to set up several worksheets with the same column widths.*

You can hide selected rows and columns by choosing Home | Cells | Format | Hide & Unhide | Hide Rows or Home | Cells | Format | Hide & Unhide | Hide Columns. Alternatively, select the rows or columns, right-click a column heading or row heading, and then choose Hide from the shortcut menu. Hidden rows and columns can be a great way of hiding the workings of your spreadsheets from inquisitive eyes, but you have to be aware of them when you copy data and paste it, because Excel includes them in the Paste operation. This can produce some unpleasant surprises, particularly when you're working under pressure of time.

To redisplay hidden rows or columns, select the row headings or column headings around the hidden rows or columns, or select the whole worksheet to redisplay all hidden rows and columns. Then either right-click the row headings or column heading and choose Unhide from the shortcut menu, or choose Home | Cells | Format | Hide & Unhide | Unhide Rows or Home | Cells | Format | Hide & Unhide | Unhide Columns.

Use Conditional Formatting

The formatting you've used so far is constant formatting—once you've applied it to a cell, range, column, or row, there it stays until you change it. But Excel also lets you use *conditional formatting,* formatting that Excel uses only when specified conditions are met. You can use conditional formatting to draw attention to missing data, highlight values that are so atypical as to merit checking, or simply to pick out the top 10 or bottom 10 scores in a list.

> **NOTE** *Conditional formatting is especially useful in tables (discussed in Chapter 9) and PivotTables (discussed in Chapter 11).*

Conditional formatting is similar to the effect produced by some predefined number formats—for example, those that display negative numbers in a different color—but more subtle, in that you can set careful triggers for applying the formatting.

To apply conditional formatting, follow these steps:

1. Choose the item you want to affect:

   - ■ To affect a range of cells, select that range.

   - ■ To affect an entire worksheet, make that worksheet active.

   - ■ To affect an entire table (discussed in Chapter 9), click anywhere in the table.

   - ■ To affect an entire PivotTable, make the PivotTable's worksheet active.

2. Choose Home | Styles | Conditional Formatting to display the Conditional Formatting panel, choose the category you want, and then select the item you want. Excel displays the dialog box for that type of condition. For example, if you choose Home | Styles | Conditional Formatting | Top/Bottom Rules | Top 10 Items (as shown in Figure 4-10), Excel displays the Top 10 dialog box shown here.

3. Use the controls in the dialog box to specify the condition and how to format the cells that meet it. For example, in the Top N dialog box, choose the percentages you want (say, the Top 10 percent) and the type of formatting you want to apply.

4. Click the OK button. Excel closes the dialog box and applies the conditional formatting.

 *You can apply multiple conditions to the same cells. Excel evaluates the conditions in order and stops evaluating them after it finds one that's true. So to make your conditional formatting effective, you must arrange your conditions in the correct order. See "Manage Conditional Formatting Rules," later in this chapter, for a discussion of how to rearrange your rules.*

Create a New Formatting Rule

Excel comes with an impressive variety of conditional formatting rules, but sometimes you'll need to create a rule of your own. To create a rule, follow these general steps:

1. Select the cells you want to affect.

2. Choose Home | Styles | Conditional Formatting | New Rule. Excel displays the New Formatting Rule dialog box (see Figure 4-11).

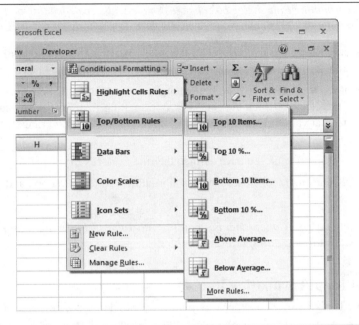

FIGURE 4-10   The Conditional Formatting panel breaks down conditional formatting into categories of easy-to-apply rules.

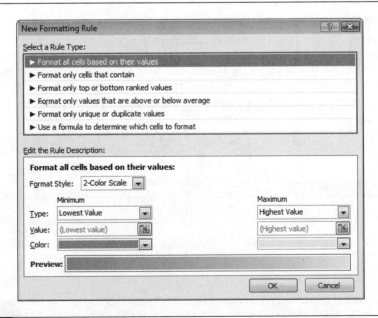

FIGURE 4-11   Use the New Formatting Rule dialog box to create a new conditional formatting rule.

The New Formatting Rule dialog box changes shape and size depending on the rule you're editing, so it may look different from the dialog box shown here.

3. In the Select A Rule Type list box, select the item you want to edit. Excel displays the controls available for this item in the Edit The Rule Description box.

4. Use the controls to change the rule. For example, you can change the colors, types, or values of the cells you want the conditional formatting to affect; or you can choose whether to format values that are above the average for the selected range or below the average for it.

5. Repeat steps 2 and 3 until you have defined the rule as necessary.

6. Click the OK button. Excel closes the New Formatting Rule dialog box and applies the rule to the cells.

See the section "Use Conditional Formatting with Tables" in Chapter 9 for examples of using conditional formatting rules with tables.

Manage Conditional Formatting Rules

When you've applied only a single conditional formatting rule to a range of cells, a worksheet, a table, or a PivotTable, you'll probably find it easy to remember what type of rule it is and what its criteria are. But when you apply multiple rules to the same cells, conditional formatting can get confusing. Or you may need to find out which conditional formatting rules someone else has applied.

To see which conditional formatting rules are applied to cells, follow these steps:

1. Select the cells you want to affect.

2. Choose Home | Styles | Conditional Formatting | Manage Rules. Excel displays the Conditional Formatting Rules Manager dialog box (see Figure 4-12).

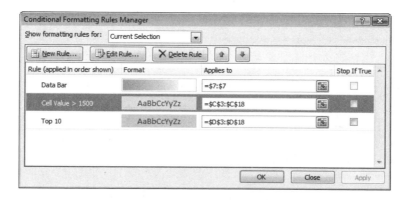

FIGURE 4-12 Use the Conditional Formatting Rules Manager dialog box to see which rules apply to particular cells and to change the order in which Excel applies the rules.

3. Make sure the Show Formatting Rules For drop-down list shows the item you want to affect. If not, choose the right item.

4. In the main list box, examine the rules, and change them as needed:

- To change the order of the rules, select a rule, and then use the Up button or Down button to move it to a different place in the list.

- To delete a rule, select it, and then click the Delete Rule button.

- To edit a rule, select it, click the Edit Rule button, and then work in the Edit Formatting Rule dialog box. This dialog box has the same controls as the New Formatting Rule dialog box.

- To create a new rule, click the New Rule button, and then work in the New Formatting Rule dialog box. After you've created the rule, move it to the right position in the list.

- To change the range to which a rule applies, click the Collapse Dialog button next to the rule's Applies To box, select the correct range, and then click the Collapse Dialog button again. For example, you might have accidentally applied one rule to a cell rather than to the entire range you intended.

- If you want Excel to stop evaluating rules when it finds one to be true, select the Stop If True check box next to the rule.

5. Click the OK button. Excel closes the Conditional Formatting Rules Manager dialog box and applies the modified rules.

Clear the Conditional Formatting Rules from a Range or a Worksheet

To clear the conditional formatting rules from a range of cells or from an entire worksheet, follow these steps:

1. Choose the item you want to affect. For example, select the range of cells, or activate the worksheet.

2. Choose Home | Styles | Conditional Formatting | Clear Rules, and then choose Clear Rules From Selected Cells, Clear Rules From Entire Sheet, Clear Rules From This Table, or Clear Rules From This PivotTable from the submenu, as appropriate.

Use Table Formatting to Apply Canned Formatting Quickly

Excel also offers preset formatting options for tables. These options, which you find in the Format As Table drop-down panel in the Styles group on the Home tab of the Ribbon, allow you to apply formatting quickly and consistently to tables. Chapter 9 shows you how to use table formatting.

Use Styles

Like Word's documents and templates, Excel's workbooks and templates include many built-in styles that you can use to apply predefined sets of formatting quickly and easily. You can modify the built-in styles, create styles to meet your own formatting needs, and copy styles from one workbook or template to another workbook or template as needed.

Each default new workbook contains several dozen styles broken up into the following categories, which you can see on the Cell Styles panel in Figure 4-13.

- **Good, Bad And Neutral** This category includes Normal, Bad, Good, and Neutral styles. Excel uses Normal style for each cell by default until you apply another style. Bad, Good, and Neutral styles are used for conditional formatting.

- **Data And Model** This category includes Calculation, Check Cell, Followed Hyperlink, Hyperlink, Input, Linked Cell, Note, Output, and Warning Text Styles. Excel uses the Hyperlink style to mark hyperlinks that you haven't yet clicked and the Followed Hyperlink style to mark hyperlinks that you have clicked. (Hyperlink appears only when the active workbook contains one or more hyperlinks; Followed Hyperlink appears only when the active workbook contains one or more hyperlinks you've clicked.) The other styles are for special purposes; you'll meet them later in this book.

- **Titles And Headings** This category includes Heading 1, Heading 2, Heading 3, and Heading 4 styles (for different levels of headings), a Sheet style (for worksheet headings), and a Total style (for totals).

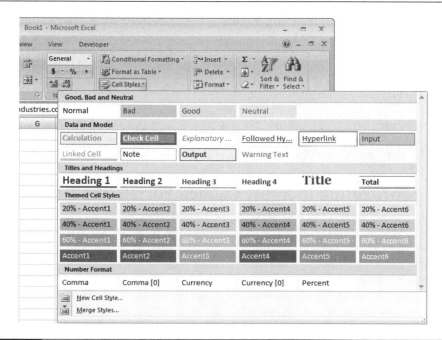

FIGURE 4-13 The Cell Styles pane divides the styles into categories.

- ■ **Themed Cell Styles**   This category includes three Emphasis styles (for making particular cells stand out) and six different Accent colors for applying themed shading. The Accent colors are numbered 1 through 6. Each Accent color has four different degrees of shading; for example, Accent 1 has Accent1 (which has 100 percent shading), 20%-Accent1, 40%-Accent 1, and 60%-Accent 1.

- ■ **Number Format**   This category contains these five number formats, which you can apply from the Number group as discussed earlier in this chapter:

Style	Example Using 1000	Explanation
Comma	1,000.00	Uses a thousands separator and two decimal places.
Comma [0]	1,000	Uses a thousands separator and no decimal places.
Currency	$1,000.00	Uses a currency symbol, a thousands separator, and two decimal places.
Currency [0]	$1,000	Uses a currency symbol, a thousands separator, and no decimal places.
Percent	100000%	Uses a percent symbol and multiplies the number by 100.

Apply a Style

Excel applies Normal style to all cells in the default workbook format. You can apply the Comma style, the Percent style, and the Currency style from the corresponding buttons on the Formatting toolbar. Excel applies the Hyperlink style automatically to any cell in which you enter a recognizable URL or path, and changes the style to Followed Hyperlink when you click the hyperlink.

Turning off Excel's automatic creation of hyperlinks can be done in two ways, click the Smart Tag on a hyperlink, and then choose Stop Automatically Creating Hyperlinks from the menu. Alternatively, click the Office button, and then click Excel Options. In the Excel Options dialog box, click the Proofing category, and then click the AutoCorrect Options button. On the AutoFormat As You Type tab of the AutoCorrect dialog box, clear the Internet And Network Paths With Hyperlinks check box. Click the OK button to close each dialog box.To apply other styles, use the Cell Styles panel.

Create Your Own Styles

You can create your own styles either from scratch (as discussed here) or by modifying an existing style (as discussed next).

To create a style from scratch, follow these steps:

1. Apply the formatting for the style to a cell. If you like, you can use a style as the basis for your formatting, and then adjust that formatting rather than creating the entire style from scratch.

2. Select that cell.

3. Click the Cell Styles button to display the Styles panel, and then choose New Cell Style. Excel displays the Style dialog box (see Figure 4-14).

4. In the Style Name text box, type the name for the new style.

5. Clear any check boxes for formatting you don't want to include in the style.

6. If you need to change the formatting for the style, click the Format button, and then work in the Format Cells dialog box. Click the OK button to return to the Style dialog box.

7. Click the OK button to close the Style dialog box. Excel creates the style and adds it to the Custom list at the top of the Styles panel.

Modify a Style

To modify an existing style to better suit your needs, follow these steps:

1. Click the Cell Styles button to display the Styles panel, right-click the style, and then choose Modify from the shortcut menu. Excel displays the Style dialog box.

FIGURE 4-14   Use the Style dialog box to specify which formatting goes into your new style. If you haven't set the style up fully before opening the Style dialog box, click the Format button, and then use the Format Cells dialog box to adjust the style's formatting.

> **TIP**   *Instead of modifying a style itself, you may want to duplicate the style, and then modify the duplicate. To duplicate a style, click the Cell Styles button to display the Styles panel, right-click the style, and then choose Duplicate from the shortcut menu. Excel creates a duplicate of the style, gives it the original style's name followed by 2, and then opens the Style dialog box so that you can modify the style.*

2. In the Style Includes area, select the check box for each formatting type that you want to include: Number, Alignment, Font, Border, Fill, or Protection.

3. To change the style's formatting, click the Format button, work in the Format Cells dialog box, and then click the OK button to return to the Style dialog box.

4. Click the OK button. Excel closes the Style dialog box and implements your changes to the style.

> **TIP**   *If you work with styles frequently, you may want to place the style gallery on the Quick Access Toolbar so that you can reach the styles when a different tab of the Ribbon than the Home tab is displayed, or when you've minimized the Ribbon. To put the style gallery on the Quick Access Toolbar, click the Cell Styles button to display the panel, right-click any style, and then choose Add Gallery To Quick Access Toolbar from the shortcut menu.*

Delete a Style

If you no longer need a style, you can delete it. To do so, click the Cell Styles button to display the panel, right-click the style, and then choose Delete from the shortcut menu. Excel deletes the style and reapplies the Normal style to any cells in the workbook that were formatted with the style.

> **NOTE**   *You can delete any style except the Normal style, which Excel protects.*

Merge Styles from Another Workbook

If you create your own styles in a workbook or template, you may want to use them in another workbook or template. You can copy styles from one workbook (or template) to another by performing what Excel calls a *merge styles* operation.

To merge styles from one workbook to another, follow these steps:

1. Open the source workbook (or template) and the destination workbook (or template).

2. Activate the destination workbook (or template). For example, click in it.

3. Choose Home | Styles | Cell Styles | Merge Styles. Excel displays the Merge Styles dialog box, shown next.

4. Select the source workbook (or template), and then click the OK button. Excel closes the Merge Styles dialog box and merges the styles into the destination workbook or template.

Chapter 5

Add Graphics and Drawings to Worksheets

How to...

- Understand how Excel handles graphical objects
- Insert clip art in worksheets
- Work with shapes, AutoShapes, and WordArt
- Add graphics to worksheets
- Add diagrams to worksheets

To give worksheets more visual impact, or simply to make them more comprehensible, you'll often need to add pictures, shapes, diagrams, or other graphical objects. In this chapter, you'll learn about the wide variety of features that Excel offers for adding graphical objects—everything from a modest shape or textual note to a highly professional organization chart—to worksheets.

Understand How Excel Handles Graphical Objects

Although Excel worksheets appear to be flat, Excel actually treats them as consisting of several different layers. The primary layers are the text layer (which contains the cells of the worksheet) and the drawing layer. When you open a workbook, you work in the text layer until you specifically go to work with an object that resides in a different layer—for example, a graphical object in the drawing layer.

The layers are transparent unless they contain an object, so when you look at a worksheet, you see the contents of all the layers together, making up the entire appearance of the worksheet. You can change the order in which the layers appear, so you can change the way that objects appear to be superimposed on each other. For example, you can position a graphic so that it appears behind the cells of a worksheet, inline with the cells, or in front of the cells, blocking the view to them.

The drawing layer consists of as many sublayers as you need. You can create multiple objects in the drawing layer, either keeping them separate from each other, or arranging them into groups that you can keep together and manipulate with a single command. You can arrange objects in the drawing layer so that they overlap each other, and you can alter the order in which they appear by moving the objects forward (up the stack of sublayers toward the top), or backward (down the stack of sublayers toward the bottom).

When you start working with an object in the drawing layer, the Ribbon automatically displays a set of extra tabs containing tools for working with that type of object. For example, when you insert or select a SmartArt item, the Ribbon displays the SmartArt Tools tab set, which includes a Design tab and a Format tab (see Figure 5-1). When you insert or select a picture, the Ribbon displays the Picture Tools set, which has just a Format tab. When you insert a chart, the Ribbon displays the Chart Tools set, which has a Design tab, a Layout tab, and a Format tab. The controls on the Format tab change to suit the type of graphical object you're working with.

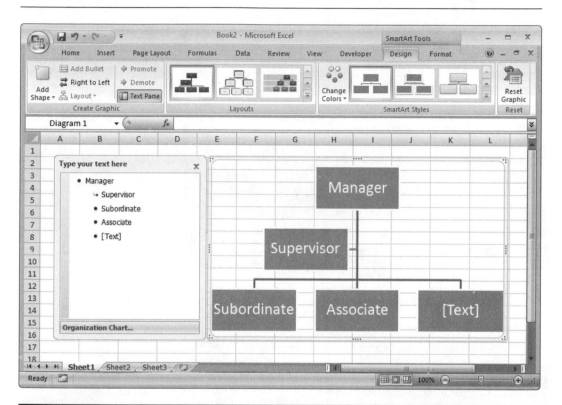

FIGURE 5-1   The Ribbon automatically displays extra tabs when you start working with a graphical object.

Insert Clip Art, Photographs, Movies, and Sounds in Worksheets

Clip art is generally understood to mean pictures, but Office's Clip Art feature lets you easily access and insert a wide selection of graphics, photographs, movie clips, and sounds that you can use freely in your documents, and insert them easily. When using these items, exercise discretion and restraint—a unique picture may still be worth the thousand words of the cliché, but a tired clip-art graphic may detract from a workbook rather than enhance it.

To insert one of Office's included "clip art" items, follow these steps:

1. Select the cell at whose upper-left corner you want to position the upper-left corner of the item. You can move the item later as needed.

2. Choose Insert | Illustrations | Clip Art. Excel displays the Clip Art task pane. Figure 5-2 shows the Clip Art task pane after a successful search.

FIGURE 5-2   The Clip Art task pane makes it easy to find clip art, photos, movies, and sounds to insert in your worksheets.

3. Use the Search For box, the Search In drop-down list, and the Results Should Be drop-down list to specify which types of files you're looking for:

    ■ In the Search For box, specify one or more keywords.

    ■ In the Search In drop-down list, choose which collections to search (or choose Everywhere).

    ■ In the Results Should Be drop-down list, choose the media types you're interested in: All Media File Types, Clip Art, Photographs, Movies, or Sounds.

4. Click the Go button. Excel searches for matching media types and displays them in the pane.

NOTE   *The first time you search, a Microsoft Clip Organizer dialog box prompts you to decide whether to include extra clip art images and photos from Microsoft Office Online in your searches. If you have a fast Internet connection, searching Microsoft Office Online is usually a good idea, as you'll find a wider range of images.*

Once you find a clip that matches your needs, you can insert it in your worksheet by clicking its thumbnail. You can also move the mouse pointer over the thumbnail, click the drop-down button that appears, and choose one of the following actions from the menu (shown here):

5

- ■ **Insert**   Inserts the clip, just as if you had clicked the thumbnail.
- ■ **Copy**   Copies the clip so you can paste it elsewhere.
- ■ **Delete From Clip Organizer**   Deletes the clip from all collections in the Clip Organizer. Office makes you confirm the deletion in case you misclicked. This option is available only for clips you add, not for clips that come with Office.
- ■ **Copy To Collection**   Displays the Copy To Collection dialog box so you can add a copy of the clip to another collection—for example, your Favorites. This option is useful for making a collection of clips you use often. This option is available only for clips stored on local drives.
- ■ **Make Available Offline**   Displays the Copy To Collection dialog box so you can download this clip from its online source to one of your collections. This option is available only for online clips.
- ■ **Move To Collection**   Displays the Move To Collection dialog box so you can move the clip to another collection. This option is useful for relocating clips in your collections. You can move only clips you add to the collection, not the clips included with Office.
- ■ **Edit Keywords**   Displays the Keywords dialog box (see Figure 5-3), in which you can add, modify, or delete the keywords associated with the clip. You can't change the keywords for the clips included with Office, only those for clips you add.
- ■ **Find Similar Style**   Searches for clips that have a similar style to the clip from which you issue this command. This option is useful when you need multiple clips in the same

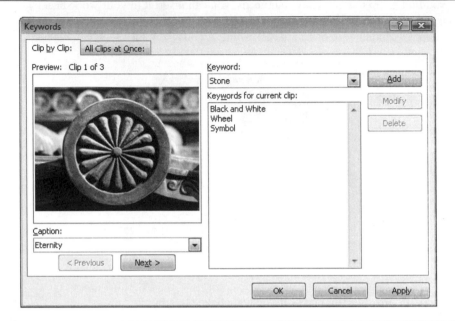

FIGURE 5-3 You can associate keywords with clips you add to the collection, which helps you search for them in the future.

style to convey a certain impression in a document. The clips returned by a style search can span an interesting range of subjects and keywords.

■ **Preview/Properties** Displays the Preview/Properties dialog box (see Figure 5-4), in which you can view the image and its details. The Paths section of this dialog box shows the full path for the image's file and the catalog that contains the image.

To organize your clips, click the Organize Clips link at the foot of the Clip Art task pane. Excel opens the Microsoft Clip Organizer applet (see Figure 5-5). In the figure, the Animals collection is selected in the Collection List task pane. This is why the word *Animals* appears in the title bar.

These are the key commands for working with Microsoft Clip Organizer:

■ To navigate your collections, click the Collection List button, and then work in the Collection List task pane.

■ To search for clips, click the Search button, and then use the Search task pane.

■ To add clips, choose File | Add Clips To Organizer, and then choose Automatically, On My Own, or From Scanner Or Camera from the submenu.

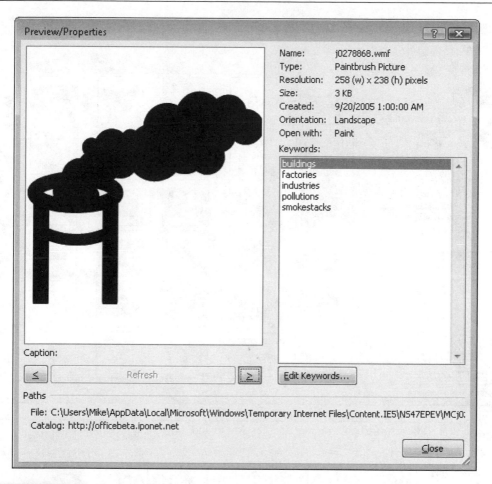

Preview/Properties

Name: j0278868.wmf
Type: Paintbrush Picture
Resolution: 258 (w) x 238 (h) pixels
Size: 3 KB
Created: 9/20/2005 1:00:00 AM
Orientation: Landscape
Open with: Paint
Keywords:

buildings
factories
industries
pollutions
smokestacks

Caption:

< | Refresh | >   Edit Keywords...

Paths

File: C:\Users\Mike\AppData\Local\Microsoft\Windows\Temporary Internet Files\Content.IE5\NS47EPEV\MCj0:
Catalog: http://officebeta.iponet.net

Close

FIGURE 5-4   Use the Preview/Properties dialog box to check an image's details.

- To edit the keywords for a selected clip, choose Edit | Keywords. Alternatively, click the clip's button, and then choose Edit Keywords from the drop-down menu.

- To compact your clips collection so that it takes up as little space as possible, choose Tools | Compact.

NOTE   *After inserting a picture, you can use the controls on the Picture Tools | Format tab to configure the picture. You'll learn how to use these controls later in this chapter.*

FIGURE 5-5 Microsoft Clip Organizer enables you to add, browse, collate, and search clips.

Work with Shapes, AutoShapes, and WordArt

Excel provides two types of tools for creating drawing objects:

- *Shapes* range from basic shapes (such as squares and circles) to more complex shapes with some built-in intelligence.
- *WordArt* items are pictures made by applying effects to text.

In the following sections, you'll learn how to work with these objects.

Add Shapes

To add a shape to a workbook, follow these steps:

1. Choose Insert | Illustrations | Shapes to display the Shapes panel (see Figure 5-6).
2. Click the shape you want. Excel changes the mouse pointer to a crosshair.

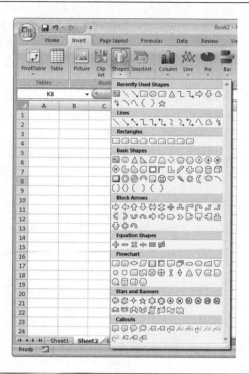

FIGURE 5-6 The Shapes panel provides a wide variety of shapes, from lines and basic shapes to flowchart shapes and callouts.

3. Click in the worksheet to position one corner of the shape. It doesn't matter which corner you position, so position whichever corner is most convenient.

4. Drag to the size you want the shape to be. When you release the mouse button, the application restores the mouse pointer.

You can also center the shape, constrain it, or create multiple shapes of the same type:

- To create the shape centered on the point where you click and start dragging, instead of having one corner of the shape (or the rectangular frame that surrounds a nonrectangular shape) appear there, hold down CTRL as you click and drag.

- To constrain a rectangle to a square, or to constrain an ellipse to a circle, hold down SHIFT as you click and drag.

- Hold down CTRL-SHIFT to apply both the centering and the constraint.

- To create multiple shapes of the same type (for example, several rectangles), right-click the tool, and then choose Lock Drawing Mode from the shortcut menu. Then, when you release the mouse button after creating a shape, the tool remains active, so that you can create another shape of the same type. Press ESC to toggle the tool off when you've finished creating all the shapes of that type. (Alternatively, click another tool to start using that tool.)

Add WordArt Objects to Worksheets

Another element you can add to worksheets is a WordArt object. WordArt is an Office applet for creating text-based designs, such as logos or decorations.

 *Like all means of making text more difficult to read, WordArt is best used only when necessary and, even then, only in moderation.*

To insert a WordArt object in a drawing, follow these steps:

1. Choose Insert | Text | WordArt. Excel displays the WordArt panel, as shown here.

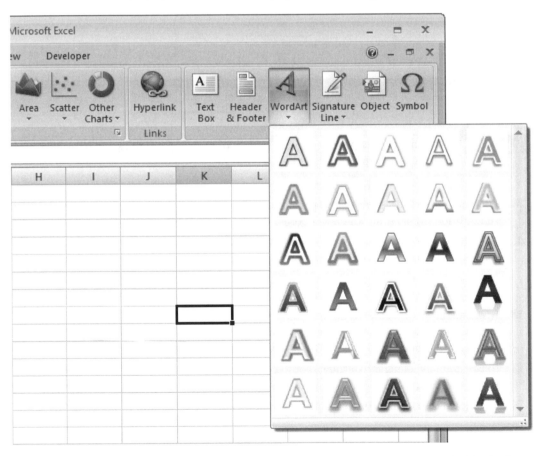

2. Click the style of WordArt item you want. Excel displays a WordArt placeholder in the middle of the window, as shown here:

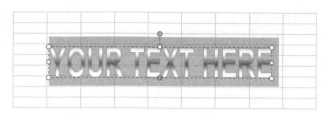

3. Type the text you want the WordArt to have. The WordArt shape takes on the text, as shown here:

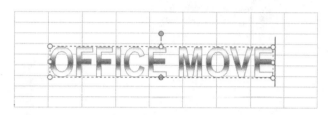

4. If necessary, change the WordArt's size:

- ■ To resize the WordArt item proportionally, drag one of the corner handles.
- ■ To resize the WordArt item only horizontally or vertically, drag one of the handles in the middle of the sides or the top or bottom.

5. If you want to slant the text, drag the pink slant handle to the left or right, and stop when you get the effect you want.

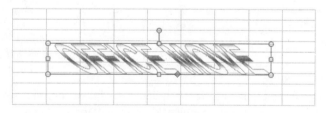

6. If you want to rotate the text, move the mouse pointer over the green rotation handle attached to the WordArt object, and then drag left to rotate it counterclockwise or right to rotate it clockwise, as shown here.

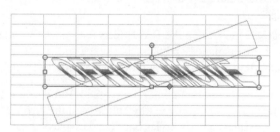

7. To format some of the text in the WordArt object with a different style, select that text by dragging through it. Then click the Quick Style button on the Format tab of the Drawing Tools section of the Ribbon, and choose the style in the Applies To Selected Text area of the Quick Styles panel, as shown here:

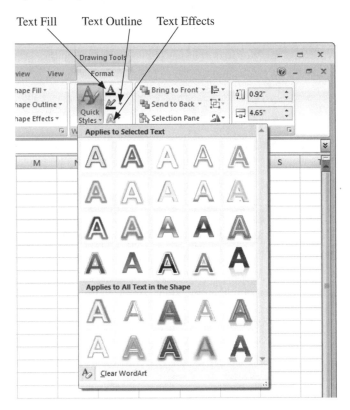

8. To apply a fill to the text, click the Text Fill button, and then choose a color from the Text Fill panel. You can also choose a picture, a gradient, or a texture.

9. To apply an outline to the text, click the Text Outline button, and then choose the color from the Text Outline panel. The Weight submenu lets you choose the weight (or thickness) of the outline, and the Dashes submenu lets you choose the style (for example, solid, dotted, or dashed).

10. To apply an effect to the text, click the Text Effects button, choose the category of text effect from the Text Effects panel, and then choose the specific type from the subpanel. Figure 5-7 shows the Text Effects panel with the Transform subpanel displayed.

By now, your WordArt item should be looking pretty good. But if you want to adjust it further, click the Format Text Effects button, the tiny button with the arrow pointing downward and to the right that appears in the WordArt Styles bar. Excel displays the Format Text Effects dialog box (see Figure 5-8). Choose settings, watching the preview that Excel automatically applies to the WordArt, and then click the Close button.

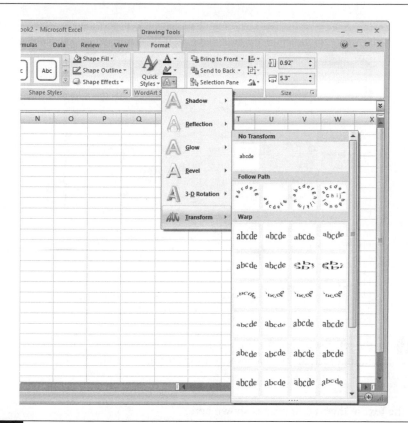

FIGURE 5-7   The Transform subpanel on the Text Effects panel lets you apply a particular shape to the WordArt object.

Add Text to a Shape

You can add text inside just about any shape that has enough space available—that is, most shapes apart from those in the Lines category and a few of the others. To add text, follow these steps:

1.   Right-click the shape, and then choose Edit Text from the shortcut menu. Excel displays an insertion point in the shape.

NOTE   *If the Edit Text command doesn't appear on the shortcut menu, you can't add text to the shape. Instead, place a text box or one of the shapes from the Callouts category next to the line. Then format the line color for the text box or Callout with the No Line option, and set the Fill color to No Fill (as discussed later in this chapter).*

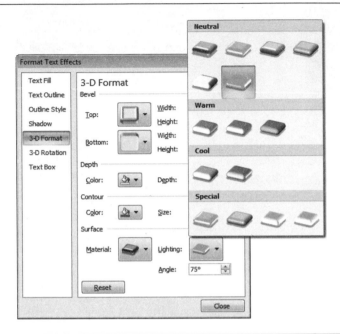

In the left list box of the Format Text Effects dialog box, click the category you
want to affect, and then choose settings using the controls that Excel displays.

2. Type the text in the AutoShape, as shown here.

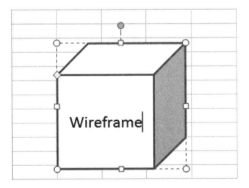

3. If you want to change the formatting, select the text, and then apply formatting as
discussed in Chapter 4.

4. Click elsewhere to select another object, or right-click the shape again, and then choose
Exit Edit Text from the shortcut menu.

Format a Drawing Object

You can format a selected drawing object by using the controls on the Format tab of the Drawing Tools section of the Ribbon, or by using the Format dialog box for the shape. The capabilities of the two overlap, but generally speaking the Format tab is better for making sweeping changes to a shape's look, while the Format dialog box is better for finer adjustments. To display the Format dialog box, right-click the drawing object and issue the Format command from the shortcut menu. The name of the command and the dialog box depend on the object you're formatting—for example, Format Picture for a picture, or Format Shape for a shape.

Apply a Style and Graphical Effects to a Drawing Object

5

The best way to start formatting a drawing object is to give it a suitable style and then adjust the fill, outline, and effects as necessary. Follow these steps:

1. Select the drawing object. Excel displays the Drawing Tools section of the Ribbon and selects the Format tab. (If Excel doesn't select the Format tab, click it.)

2. Click the Shape Styles drop-down button, and then choose the style either from the Shape Styles panel or from the Other Theme Fills panel (see Figure 5-9).

3. To change the fill of the shape, click the Shape Fill button in the Shape Styles group, and then choose a fill from the Shape Fill panel (see Figure 5-10).

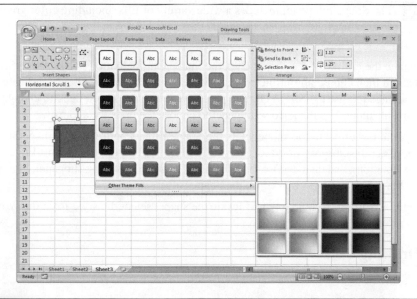

FIGURE 5-9   Begin formatting a drawing object by applying a style to give it an overall look.

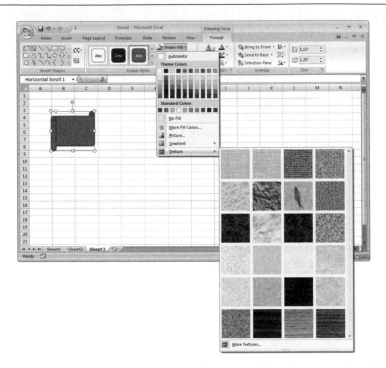

FIGURE 5-10 The Shape Fill panel includes a wide variety of fills, including color gradients and textures.

4. To change the outline of the shape, click the Shape Outline button in the Shape Styles group, and then choose an outline color, weight, or style from the Shape Outline panel. You may need to use the Shape Outline panel twice or more if you need to change more than one attribute. Use the Arrow subpanel to choose the ends for an arrow.

5. To apply a new effect to the shape, click the Shape Effects button in the Shape Styles group, select the category of effect (Preset, Shadow, Reflection, Glow, Soft Edges, Bevel, or 3-D Rotation), and then choose the effect itself from the resulting subpanel. Figure 5-11 shows the 3-D Rotation subpanel on the Shape Effects panel.

6. To apply a WordArt style to any text inside the shape, select the style from the WordArt Styles group.

Resize a Drawing Object

You can resize a drawing object in the following ways:

■ Drag a sizing handle on the object with the mouse.

■ Select the object, and then use the Height control and Width control in the Size group on the Format tab.

FIGURE 5-11   The Shape Effects panel gives you a wide choice of effects, including 3-D Rotation effects.

■   Click the Size And Properties button (the tiny button with the arrow pointing down and to the right) in the Size group on the Format tab, and then work on the Size tab in the Size And Properties dialog box (see Figure 5-12). The key setting here is the Lock Aspect Ratio check box. If this check box is selected, Excel maintains the object's aspect ratio, so if you change the height, the width changes correspondingly.

NOTE   *The Crop From controls and Reset button on the Size And Properties dialog box work only for objects such as pictures.*

Choose Whether an Object Moves with Text and Whether It Prints

When you position an object in a worksheet, Excel positions it relative to cells. If you then move or resize cells, Excel moves or resizes the object to match. Normally, this behavior is helpful, but you may sometimes want to prevent Excel from resizing an object or from moving it at all.

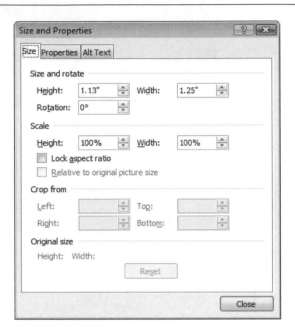

FIGURE 5-12   Use the options on the Size tab of the Size And Properties dialog box to resize or rotate an object.

To do so, click the Size And Properties button in the Size group on the Format tab, and then click the Properties tab in the Size And Properties dialog box (see Figure 5-13). You can then choose the following options:

- **Object Positioning area**   Select the Move And Size With Cells option button, the Move But Don't Size With Cells option button, or the Don't Move Or Size With Cells option button, as needed.

- **Print Object**   Select this check box if you want the object to print along with the worksheet. Clear the check box if you want to suppress the object in printouts. For example, you might want to use shapes to include instructions for completing a worksheet, but not have the shapes appear on printouts.

- **Locked**   Select this check box to lock the object in place. To make the locking take effect, you then need to protect the workbook, as described in the section "Restrict Data and Protect Workbooks," in Chapter 14.

- **Lock Text**   Select this check box to lock the text contained in the object. Again, you need to protect the workbook to make the locking take effect.

Specify Alternative Web Text for an Object

On the Alt Text tab of the Size And Properties dialog box for an object, you can specify alternative text to be displayed while a web browser is loading the picture, when the picture isn't available,

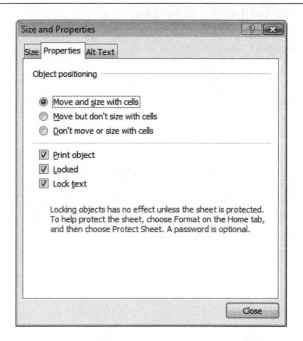

FIGURE 5-13   The Properties tab of the Size And Properties dialog box

or when the user has chosen not to display pictures. For example, you might supply a text description of the picture so that the user knows what they're missing.

Position Drawing Objects

You can position drawing objects in various ways. You can drag objects roughly into position, nudge them precisely into position, use the Size And Properties dialog box to position them by specifying measurements, align one object according to another, and create groups of objects that you can format and move together. You can also choose whether objects snap to the grid or not.

Drag and Nudge Objects

To position an object roughly where you want it, drag the object. To constrain the movement to either horizontal or vertical, SHIFT-drag the object.

To move an object a shorter distance, *nudge* it. Select the object and press the appropriate arrow key ($\uparrow$, $\downarrow$, $\leftarrow$, or $\rightarrow$) to move the object one square up, down, left, or right on the underlying grid that Excel uses for positioning objects.

Snap an Object to the Grid or to a Shape

For positioning objects on a worksheet, Excel lets you choose the following settings on its Picture Tools | Format | Arrange | Align menu:

- **Snap To Grid**   Controls whether an object *snaps* (jumps) to Excel's underlying drawing grid or not when you move it close to a gridline. Having this setting turned on is usually helpful.

- **Snap To Shape**   Controls whether an object snaps to another shape when you move it close to that shape.

- **View Gridlines**   Controls whether Excel displays the cell gridlines in the worksheet. You may want to turn off the display of gridlines temporarily when positioning many objects, but gridlines are usually helpful when you're working with data.

Align an Object Relative to Another Object

Instead of positioning an object by a gridline or a shape, you can align an object relative to another object. To do so, follow these steps:

1. Select the object according to which you want to align the other object or objects.

2. Hold down SHIFT, and then click to select the other objects.

3. Choose Picture Tools | Format | Arrange | Align, and then choose the appropriate command from the menu. Most of the options are self-explanatory, but the following options merit explanation:

   - The Align Center option applies horizontal centering, while the Align Middle option applies vertical centering.

   - The Distribute Horizontally option and the Distribute Vertically option place the objects evenly across the area. These commands are available only when you have three or more objects selected.

Group and Ungroup Objects

When you've selected multiple objects by SHIFT-clicking or CTRL-clicking, you can treat them as an informal group—for example, you can drag an object to move all the objects, or apply shared formatting to all the objects at once.

To apply formal grouping so that you can quickly work with these objects as a unit in the future, choose Picture Tools | Format | Arrange | Group command, or right-click one of the objects and choose Group | Group from the context menu. Excel puts a single box around the objects instead of a separate box around each object.

To ungroup grouped objects, choose Picture Tools | Format | Arrange | Ungroup. To regroup objects, choose Picture Tools | Format | Arrange | Regroup.

Layer Drawing Objects

To adjust the layer order in which drawing objects appear, follow these steps:

1. Click the object you want to affect, and then click the Format tab of the Drawing Tools section or Picture Tools section of the Ribbon.

2. In the Arrange group, choose the action you want:

   ■ To bring the object all the way to the topmost layer, click the Bring To Front button.

   ■ To bring the object up the stack by one layer, click the Bring To Front drop-down list, and then choose Bring Forward.

   ■ To send the object all the way to the lowest layer, click the Send To Back button.

   ■ To place the object one layer farther down the stack, click the Send To Back drop-down list, and then choose Send Backward.

NOTE *You can also right-click an object and then issue the Bring To Front, Bring Forward, Send To Back, and Send Backward commands from the context menu.*

When you've layered objects on top of each other, you may find it hard to select objects that are partly or wholly overlaid by other objects. If so, click the Selection Pane button in the Arrange group, and then click the object in the Selection And Visibility pane (see Figure 5-14). You can use the Reorder buttons in the Selection And Visibility pane to move an object up and down the stack of objects, or clear the box next to the object to hide it temporarily. To hide all objects so that you can see the worksheet, click the Hide All button; to get them back, click the Show All button.

FIGURE 5-14   The Selection And Visibility pane lets you click an object's name in the Shapes On This Sheet list box to select the object.

Use Text Boxes to Position Text Wherever You Need It

As you saw earlier in this book, you can wrap text to fit more text in a cell—but increasing the depth of the cell increases the depth of the whole row, which can cause problems with layout. If you need to position text precisely, a text box gives you much greater flexibility. You can use text boxes to create anything from labels for chart elements to explanatory paragraphs of text.

To create a text box, follow these steps:

1. Choose Insert | Text | Text Box. Excel changes the mouse pointer to a downward-pointing arrow.

2. Click in the worksheet where you want to place one corner of the text box, and then drag diagonally to create a text box of the size you want. Excel displays the text box as a blank area surrounded by a dotted border and sizing handles, with a green rotation handle above it, as shown here.

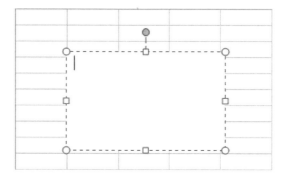

3. Type the text for the text box, creating paragraphs if needed by pressing ENTER. You can also paste text in from another worksheet or another program.

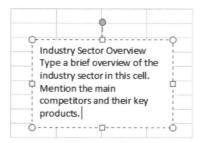

4. Format the text as you want it. Select one or more characters, and then use the controls on the Font group on the Home tab of the Ribbon, or right-click, choose Font from the shortcut menu, and then work in the Font dialog box (see Figure 5-15). Most of the options in this dialog box are easy to grasp. The Offset box works with the Superscript

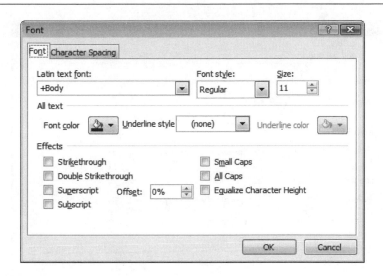

FIGURE 5-15   The Font dialog box

check box for raised characters and the Subscript check box for lowered characters. The Equalize Character Height check box makes all characters in the text the same height, which can look dramatic but renders them hard to read.

5. To apply paragraph formatting, right-click the paragraph you want to affect, choose Paragraph from the shortcut menu, and then work in the Paragraph dialog box (see Figure 5-16). You can add extra space before and after a paragraph, or click the Tabs button to set custom tab stops for a text box.

6. Use the options in the Shape Styles group on the Format tab to choose a style, fill, outline, and any effects for the text box. Effects can be amusing, but they seldom make the text more readable.

7. To format internal margins or alignment on the text box, right-click the text box, choose Format Shape from the context menu, and then work in the Text Box category in the Format Shape dialog box (see Figure 5-17). The Text Box category lets you choose vertical alignment and text direction, make the text box resize itself to fit its contents, or set internal margins. For example, you might select the Resize Shape To Fit Text check box to make Excel automatically enlarge the text box as you add more text to it. You can even set up columns within the text box by clicking the Columns button, and then working in the Columns dialog box.

NOTE   *Unlike in Word, you can't make text flow automatically from one text box to another in Excel.*

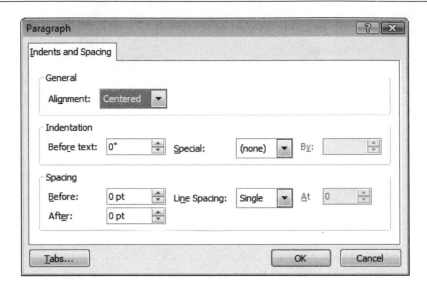

FIGURE 5-16 The Paragraph dialog box lets you set alignment, indentation, and line spacing.

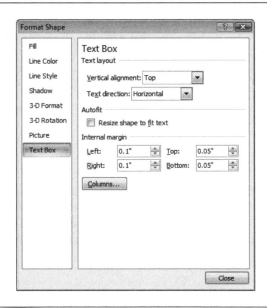

FIGURE 5-17 The Text Box category in the Format Shape dialog box

Add Pictures to Worksheets

To enhance your workbooks, you'll often need to insert a picture, such as a custom illustration, photograph, or screen capture, and then adjust it—for example, by changing its contrast or cropping it.

Insert a Picture

To insert a picture, follow these steps:

1. Select the cell where you want the upper-left corner of the picture to appear. (The picture isn't placed *in* this cell but is aligned with its borders.)
2. Choose Insert | Illustrations | Picture. Excel displays the Insert Picture dialog box, which is a common Open dialog box.
3. Navigate to the picture you want to add, and then select it.
4. Click the Insert button. Excel closes the Insert Picture dialog box and inserts the picture.

Crop a Picture

If you don't want to show the whole of a picture, you can *crop* it, cutting off the parts you don't want to keep. To crop a picture, follow these steps:

1. Click the picture to select it.
2. Click the Format tab on the Picture Tools section of the Ribbon, and then click the Crop button in the Size area. Excel displays crop handles at each corner and at the midpoint of each side.
3. Drag a crop handle to crop the picture:
    - SHIFT-drag a corner crop handle to crop proportionally.
    - CTRL-drag a crop handle to crop from both sides simultaneously.
    - CTRL-SHIFT-drag to crop proportionally and from both sides.

For more precise cropping, choose Format | Size | Size And Properties, and then use the Crop From controls on the Size tab of the Size And Properties dialog box.

Format a Picture

The Format tab of the Picture Tools section of the Ribbon lets you quickly and easily make sweeping changes to a picture.

Change a Picture's Brightness, Contrast, or Color

Start by making any needed changes to the picture's brightness, contrast, and colors by using the Brightness panel, the Contrast panel, and the Recolor panel in the Picture Tools group. These tools are easy to use but can make a dramatic difference to how a picture looks.

If you produce an effect you don't like, click the Reset Picture button in the Picture Tools group to restore the picture to its former state. If you decide that a different picture would look better, click the Change Picture button, and then choose the new picture.

When you use the Change Picture button to replace one picture with another, Excel retains the picture's position, size, and formatting. By contrast, if you delete the picture and insert another picture, you have to start again from scratch. (Sometimes starting again from scratch may be the better option, but it's good to have the choice of continuing with your current settings.)

Compress the Pictures in a Workbook

If you use large pictures in a workbook, its file size increases rapidly. You can reduce this problem by telling Excel to compress the pictures. Follow these steps:

1. If you want to compress only some pictures, select them. Otherwise, click one picture so that Excel makes the Picture Tools section of the Ribbon available.

2. Click the Compress Pictures button in the Adjust group on the Format tab. Excel displays the Compress Pictures dialog box, shown here:

3. If you want to compress only the picture or pictures you chose in step 1, select the Apply To Selected Pictures Only check box. To compress all the pictures, leave this check box cleared.

4. Click the Options button. Excel displays the Compression Settings dialog box, shown here:

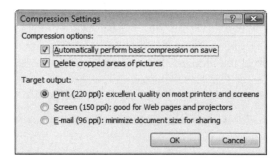

5. In the Compression Options area, select the Automatically Perform Basic Compression On Save check box if you want Excel to use its normal compression whenever you

save the workbook. (This compression retains high quality but minimizes bloat.) Select the Delete Cropped Areas Of Pictures check box if you want Excel to get rid of any parts you crop off pictures. If you clear this check box, Excel merely hides the "cropped" parts. This hiding is good if you want to be able to restore the cropped parts, but it's bad for file size, and it may also have security implications (for example, a customer may be able to restore a part of a graphic that you had intended to crop off a worksheet).

6. In the Target Output area, select the Print (220 ppi) option button, the Screen (150 ppi) option button, or the E-mail (96 ppi) option button to tell Excel what picture quality you need (*ppi* is pixels per inch). If you're not sure, use the Print setting—you can always reduce it later, but you can't restore information if you choose a lower setting.

7. Click the OK button. Excel closes the Compression Settings dialog box and displays the Compress Pictures dialog box.

8. Click the OK button. Excel compresses the pictures in the workbook.

Add SmartArt to Worksheets

Individual shapes and pictures can make a huge difference to your worksheets, but you'll often need to create more complex diagrams. You can combine shapes as needed to create diagrams, but first you should try Excel's SmartArt feature, which makes inserting various types of diagram in your worksheets a snap.

This section uses an organization chart as an example, as this is one of the most widely used forms of diagrams. The other SmartArt items work in similar ways.

 SmartArt is a huge improvement on the Diagram applet and Organization Chart applet in Excel 2003 and earlier versions.

Insert a SmartArt Graphic

To insert a SmartArt graphic, follow these steps:

1. Click the cell in which you want to place the upper-left corner of the SmartArt graphic. You can move the SmartArt graphic later if needed.

2. Choose Insert | Illustrations | SmartArt. Excel displays the Choose A SmartArt Graphic dialog box (see Figure 5-18). This dialog box breaks the diagrams up into List, Process, Cycle, Hierarchy, Relationship, Matrix, and Pyramid categories. The Hierarchy category offers various designs of organization charts.

3. In the left panel, select the category of SmartArt you want. For example, if you want to create an organization chart, select the Hierarchy category. Excel displays the available diagrams in the main box.

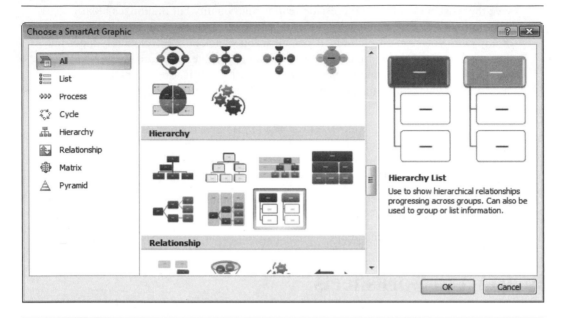

FIGURE 5-18   The Choose A SmartArt Graphic dialog box

4. Click the diagram you want, and then use the sample picture and description to verify that it's suitable.

5. Click the OK button. Excel closes the Choose A SmartArt Graphic dialog box, inserts the diagram in the worksheet, and displays the SmartArt Tools section of the Ribbon (see Figure 5-19), which contains a design tab and a Format tab. The Text pane contains paragraphs that map to the shapes in the SmartArt and lets you work on the text separately from the layout.

6. Enter text by clicking a paragraph in the Text pane and then typing the text.

7. To add a shape to the diagram, click the paragraph or shape to which the new item will be related, click the Add Shape button in the Create Graphic group, and then choose a command from the menu. For example, the Hierarchy diagrams offer the Add Shape After, Add Shape Before, Add Shape Above, Add Shape Below, and Add Assistant commands (see Figure 5-20).

8. If you need to change the layout of the diagram, select the new layout in the Layouts panel. SmartArt lets you change from one kind of a diagram to another without losing the data you've entered, although you may need to rearrange the data to suit the new layout you've chosen.

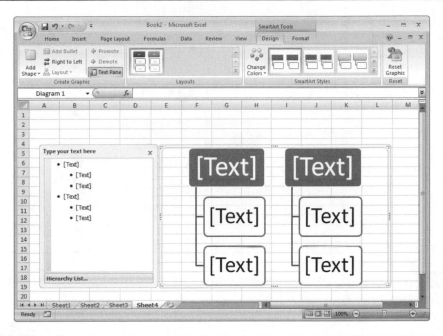

FIGURE 5-19   When you've selected a SmartArt item, the Ribbon displays the SmartArt Tools section.

Format a SmartArt Diagram

Once you've entered the text for your SmartArt diagram, you can format it so that it looks attractive and polished. Follow these steps:

1. Click the Format tab on the SmartArt Tools section of the Ribbon to display the formatting tools, shown here:

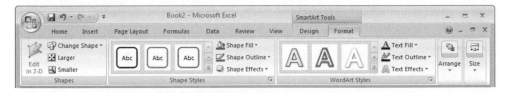

2. To change the shape used for an individual shape in the diagram, click the shape, click the Change Shape button in the Shapes group, and then choose the shape from the Change Shape panel.

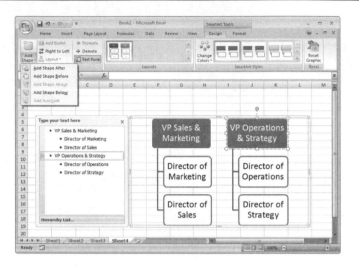

FIGURE 5-20   In a hierarchy, you can use the Promote button and Demote button to promote
and demote the selected item.

3. To change the size of an individual shape, click the shape, and then click the Larger
button or the Smaller button in the Shapes group.

4. Click the Shape Styles drop-down button, and then choose a graphical style for the
SmartArt from the Shape Styles panel.

5. If necessary, use the Shape Fill panel, the Shape Outline panel, or the Shape Effects
panel to adjust the shape style you chose.

6. If you want to apply a WordArt style to the text in the SmartArt shapes, use the controls
in the WordArt Styles group. Make sure the result is readable.

7. To change the size of your SmartArt diagram, either drag a sizing handle, or use the
Height and Width controls in the Size group.

Chapter 6

Check, Lay Out, and Print Worksheets

How to...

- Check the spelling in worksheets
- Set the print area to specify which parts of a worksheet to print
- Specify the paper size and orientation
- Scale a printout to fit the paper
- Use Print Preview to see how the printout will look
- Add useful headers and footers
- Set and adjust page breaks
- Check and change margins
- Include extra items in the printout
- Repeat row titles or column titles on subsequent pages
- Print a worksheet instantly with default settings
- Print a worksheet by using the Print dialog box

Once you develop a worksheet, you may need to print it out to share with other people. Before you print, check that the worksheet doesn't contain any spelling mistakes that will return to haunt you, and that Excel knows which area of the worksheet you want to print. You should also add headers and footers to identify the printout amidst the morass of papers that your colleagues probably collect, and make sure that the worksheet is laid out correctly on suitably sized paper.

Beyond these basics, you may sometimes want to include extra items in the printout, or repeat row titles or column titles across multiple pages of a worksheet. In this chapter, you'll learn how to do all this and more.

Check the Spelling in Worksheets

Spelling is a great task for computerization, because any given word is spelled either correctly or incorrectly; there are no gray areas. Excel shares the powerful spell checker that is included with Office, which enables you to identify and correct any misspelled words in worksheets.

While the spell checker can root out every misspelled word, be aware that it doesn't catch words that are spelled correctly but used incorrectly. For example, if you've written "You're Debts" instead of "Your Debts," the spell checker can't help you, although AutoCorrect automatically fixes some incorrect usages (such as replacing the incorrect "their are" with the correct "there are"). To catch usage errors such as these, read through your work carefully or (better) ask someone else to read through it for you.

Run a Spell Check

To start a spell check, choose Review | Proofing | Spelling or press F7.

The spell checker searches for spelling errors and displays the Spelling dialog box (see Figure 6-1) if it finds an error. In this dialog box, you can choose whether to ignore one or all instances of the disputed word, add it to the dictionary, change this or all instances to one of the suggested words, or create an AutoCorrect entry to automatically correct the word to one of the suggested words.

Usually it's best to start a spell check from the beginning of the worksheet. To do so, click the first cell in the worksheet. If you start a spell check from elsewhere in a worksheet, when the spell checker reaches the end of the worksheet, it asks you whether you want to continue at the beginning. Alternatively, you can check the spelling of a particular range by selecting the range before starting a spell check.

Excel displays a message box when the spell check is complete. If the spell checker found no errors in the worksheet, you'll see this message almost immediately.

NOTE   *Excel's default settings for the spell checker work for many people, but you may want to customize them to better suit your needs. To configure spelling options, click the Office button, choose Excel Options, and then click the Proofing category in the Excel Options dialog box. See "Set Spelling Options" in Chapter 2 for a discussion of these options.*

6

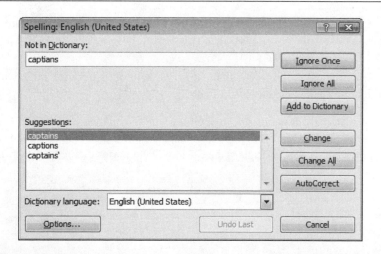

FIGURE 6-1   The Spelling dialog box offers suggestions for correcting apparent spelling errors in worksheets.

How to ... Use Custom Dictionaries

The spell checker uses a shared dictionary that's installed by default in the \Program Files\Common Files\Microsoft Shared\Proof folder. The actual dictionary file varies based on which language you're using. This dictionary contains a wide range of words for that language, but you may need to supplement the dictionary with special words and technical terms that you use in your work. To do so, you can use one or more custom dictionaries.

A custom dictionary is a text file that contains a list of words that the spell checker shouldn't query—words that you've told the spell checker are okay. Office starts you off with a custom dictionary named Custom.dic, which it stores in the *%userprofile%*\AppData\ Roaming\Microsoft\Proof folder on Windows Vista or the %userprofile%\Application Data\Microsoft\Proof folder on Windows XP. Office's default setting is to add words to this dictionary when you issue an Add command from the spell checker.

If you add all of the extra words to this one dictionary, you at least know where they are. So if, for example, you mistakenly add a real spelling error to the custom dictionary, you know which dictionary to remove it from. But you may find it better to maintain a separate custom dictionary for each separate topic area—for example, one custom dictionary for part names and another custom dictionary for customer names. The two main advantages to separating terms into different dictionaries are that you can:

- Load and unload the dictionaries as necessary. That way, you can make sure that—to continue the example—your parts database doesn't have misspellings that are permitted only in your customer lists.

- Share an individual dictionary with other people without burdening them with extra words that the spell checker doesn't like.

To work with custom dictionaries, click the Office button, and then choose Excel Options. In the left panel of the Excel Options dialog box, click the Proofing category, and then click the Custom Dictionaries button. Excel displays the Custom Dictionaries dialog box, shown here:

From this dialog box, you can perform several tasks as needed:

- ■ To specify which dictionaries to use, select or clear the appropriate check boxes.

- ■ To edit a dictionary, select it, click the Edit Word List button, and work in the resulting dialog box. You may want to edit a dictionary to remove incorrect words that you accidentally added, or to add a large number of words you know the spell checker will disagree with. (For smaller numbers of words, it's usually quicker to add them individually when the spell checker disagrees with them during a spell check.)

- ■ To make a different dictionary the default, select the dictionary, and then click the Change Default button.

- ■ To create a new dictionary, click the New button, specify the name and location in the Create Custom Dictionary dialog box, and then click the OK button.

- ■ To add an existing dictionary, click the Add button, navigate to and select the dictionary file, and then click the OK button.

- ■ To remove a dictionary from the list (but not from your computer), select it, and then click the Remove button.

- ■ To browse for another type of file than a .DIC dictionary file, click the Browse button, select the file in the File Open dialog box, and then click the Open button.

When you've finished working in the Custom Dictionaries dialog box, click the OK button. Excel closes the Custom Dictionaries dialog box and returns you to the Excel Options dialog box. Click the OK button.

Set the Print Area

To tell Excel which cells of a worksheet to print, set the *print area*. You can do this by using the Print Area | Set Print Area command in the Page Setup group of the Page Layout tab (shown here), or by using the Page Setup dialog box.

If you don't set the print area manually, Excel assumes that you want to print all the cells that contain data or objects. As long as you've created a spreadsheet in a single area of the worksheet, this assumption works well. But if you've used some distant cells for notes or scratch calculations, Excel will happily waste wads of paper printing all of the intervening blank cells. So in most cases, you should set the print area manually to make sure that Excel prints only what you want printed.

The print area doesn't have to be one range of contiguous cells—you can select multiple ranges by CTRL-clicking. When you issue the Set Print Area command, Excel creates a print area around each range of cells. Excel then prints each range of cells on a separate page.

Set the Print Area Using the Set Print Area Command

To set the print area using the Set Print Area command, follow these steps:

1. Select the range of cells that you want to print.

2. Choose Page Layout | Page Setup | Print Area | Set Print Area. Excel places a dotted line around the cells.

Set the Print Area from the Page Setup Dialog Box

To set the print area from the Page Setup dialog box, follow these steps:

1. Choose Page Layout | Page Setup | Page Setup (click the small arrow at the right end of the bar that says Page Setup). Excel displays the Page Setup dialog box.

2. Click the Sheet tab to display its contents (see Figure 6-2).

3. Click the Collapse Dialog button in the Print Area box. Excel collapses the dialog box to its title bar.

4. Click and drag in the worksheet to select the area you want to print.

5. Click the Collapse Dialog button. Excel restores the Page Setup dialog box.

6. Click the OK button. Excel closes the Page Setup dialog box.

Using the Sheet tab to set the print area is normally most useful when you're adjusting other settings in the Page Setup dialog box.

How Excel Handles the Print Area

Here are the details of how Excel handles the print area:

■ Excel saves the print area set for each worksheet, so you don't need to set the print area again until you need to print a different area of a worksheet.

■ If you add or delete rows or columns within the print area, Excel adjusts the boundaries of the print area to compensate.

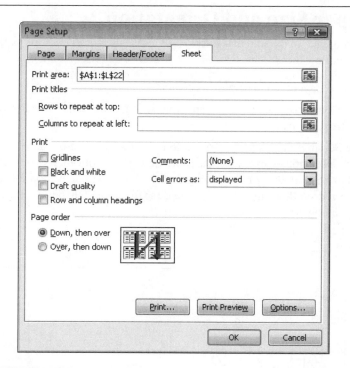

FIGURE 6-2   You can set the print area on the Sheet tab of the Page Setup dialog box.

- If you add cells to the print area and use the Shift Cells Right option or the Shift Cells Down option rather than the Entire Row option or the Entire Column option, Excel doesn't adjust the boundaries of the print area. Data that was previously in the print area can move out of the print area.

- If you delete cells (rather than entire rows or columns) within the print area, Excel doesn't adjust the boundaries of the print area. Data that was previously outside the print area may move inside the print area.

In short, if you've added cells to or deleted cells from the active area of a worksheet, it's a good idea to check that the print area is correct before you print.

Change or Clear the Existing Print Area

To change the print area, set the print area again. To clear the print area and return to the default print settings, choose Page Layout | Page Setup | Print Area | Clear Print Area.

Specify the Paper Size and Orientation

After setting the print area, make sure that Excel is set to use the correct size of paper and the correct orientation. Follow these steps:

1. Click the Page Layout tab to display its contents.

2. In the Page Setup group, click the Orientation button, and then choose Portrait or Landscape from the panel.

3. In the Page Setup group, click the Size button, and then choose the paper size from the panel. To choose another size, click the More item at the bottom. Excel displays the Page tab of the Page Setup dialog box (see Figure 6-3), where you can choose the paper size in the Paper Size drop-down list. When you're done, click the OK button. Excel closes the Page Setup dialog box.

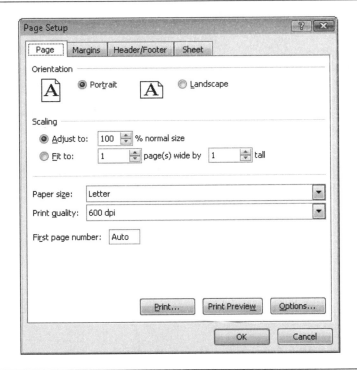

FIGURE 6-3 The Page tab of the Page Setup dialog box lets you choose paper orientation and size, and specify scaling, if necessary, to better fit the paper.

Scale the Printout to Fit the Paper

Often, to get the print area to appear on one or more sheets of paper, you need to scale the printout to the right size. Usually you'll need to scale down the printout, but sometimes you may need to scale it up. To scale the printout, choose Page Layout | Page Setup | Page Setup to display the Page Setup dialog box, and then use the options in the Scaling section of the Page tab.

The Scaling section of the Page tab offers two scaling options:

- **Adjust To *NN*% Normal Size**   Use this option button and text box to specify an exact percentage. This option tends to be less useful than the Fit To *NN* Page(s) Wide By *NN* Tall option unless you happen to know the scaling percentage that a given print area needs for printing. You can set any size from 10 percent to 400 percent, instead of the default 100 percent.

- **Fit To *NN* Page(s) Wide By *NN* Tall**   Use this option button and text boxes to resize a print area to fit on a specific number of pages—for example, 2 pages wide by 1 page tall. This option can save you time and paper, but always use Print Preview to check that the results will look acceptable before you commit them to paper. Excel will happily scale down worksheets so small that you need a magnifying glass to read the text.

When you've finished scaling the printout, click the OK button. Excel closes the Page Setup dialog box.

Use Print Preview to See How the Printout Will Look

Use Print Preview (see Figure 6-4) to make sure that the worksheet will fit on the paper and look as you want it to. You can display the active worksheet in Print Preview in any of these ways:

- Click the Office button, click the arrow next to Print, and then choose Print Preview.
- Click the Print Preview button on any tab of the Page Setup dialog box.
- Click the Preview button in the Print dialog box.

From Print Preview, you can:

- Click the Next Page button or the Previous Page button to navigate to the printout's next page or previous page. (These buttons are unavailable if there is no next page or previous page.)
- Click the Zoom button to toggle zooming between being zoomed in and zoomed out.
- Click the Print button to display the Print dialog box.
- Click the Page Setup button to display the Page Setup dialog box.
- Select the Show Margins check box to toggle the display of the margin guidelines. (See "Check and Change Margins," later in this chapter.)
- Click the Close Print Preview button to exit Print Preview.

6

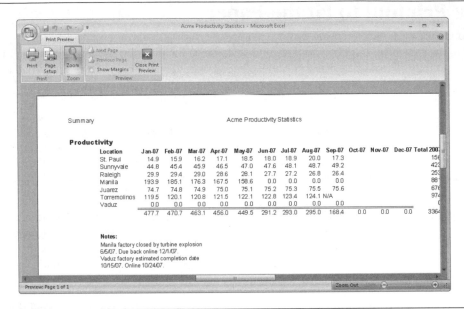

FIGURE 6-4   Use Print Preview to check the print layout before printing a worksheet.

Add Effective Headers and Footers to Worksheets

Excel provides easy-to-use features for adding headers and footers to worksheets to help you keep your printouts in good order. Each worksheet in a workbook has its own header and footer, so you can give each worksheet exactly the right header, footer, or both.

To create headers and footers, follow these steps:

1. Select the worksheet that you want to affect.

2. Choose Insert | Text | Header And Footer. Excel adds the Header & Footer Tools section to the Ribbon and displays the Design tab and the header section of the worksheet, as shown here. The header and footer sections are each divided into left, center, and right sections. Each section can contain separate information.

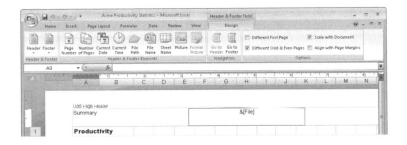

3. To create a standard header or footer based on information such as the page number, sheet name, workbook name, author name, date, or a combination of these, click the Header button or Footer button in the Header & Footer group, and then choose the header or footer from the panel.

4. To switch between the header area and the footer area, click the Go To Footer button or the Go To Header button in the Navigation group. If you can see both the header area and the footer area, you can simply click in them.

5. To create a custom header or footer, click in the section to which you want to add text or an element. You can type text wherever you need it, or click the element's button in the Header & Footer Elements group. For example, you might click in the left section, and then click the Current Date button. Excel enters a code representing the element—for example, **&[Date]** for the date, or **&[Tab]** for the worksheet's name.

6. To format text or an element, select it, click the Home tab, and then use the controls in the Font group.

7. To add a picture to a header or footer, click in the appropriate section. Click the Picture button in the Header & Footer Elements group, select the picture in the Insert Picture dialog box, and then click the Insert button. Click the Format Picture button, and then use the Format Picture dialog box to set the picture's size, rotation, and any cropping.

8. To set options for the header and footer, select or clear the check boxes in the Options group:

- **Different First Page**   Select this check box if you want the first page of your printout to have a different header or footer. This setting is useful when you need to put more information on the first page of a printout, to suppress the header or footer on the first page, or to have the second-page and later headers or footers say "continued" or something similar. When you select this check box, Excel displays *First Page Header* and *First Page Footer* on the first page for clarity. After setting up the first page header and footer, go to the second page, and then set up the header and footer for the rest of the pages.

- **Different Odd & Even Pages**   Select this check box if you need to have different headers and footers on odd and even pages. Excel displays *Odd Page Header*, *Odd Page Footer*, *Even Page Header*, and *Even Page Footer* on the header and footer sections so that you can see which header or footer you're working on.

- **Scale With Document**   Select this check box if you want Excel to apply any scaling (resizing) to the header and footer, as well as to the document (for example, when shrinking the print area to fit on a certain number of pages). Scaling is usually a good idea, but you may sometimes need to print headers and footers at their real size even when you scale the document.

- **Align With Page Margins**   Select this check box if you want Excel to align the header and footer with the left and right margin of the page.

9. When you've finished working in the header or footer, click any cell in the worksheet. Excel removes the Header & Footer Tools section from the Ribbon.

6

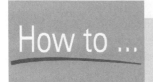 **Create Headers and Footers the Old Way**

If you've used Excel 2003 or an earlier version, you're probably used to creating headers and footers by using the Header/Footer tab of the Page Setup dialog box and the Header dialog box and Footer dialog box to which it gives you access. Good news: You can still create headers and footers this way if you prefer. Choose Page Layout | Page Setup | Page Setup, and then click the Header/Footer tab, and you can work just as before.

 *If you regularly need to add headers and footers to worksheets, add the headers and footers to the templates on which the worksheets are based so that you don't have to create them manually for each new workbook.*

Set and Adjust Page Breaks

For a print area that'll print on multiple pages, Excel automatically positions page breaks between the cells that will fall on different pages. You can adjust these page breaks manually as needed. Typically, you'll want to start by setting page breaks where they'll produce a logical division in your spreadsheets—or at least prevent crucial information that belongs together from being broken across two pages. After setting manual page breaks, you can reposition any of the automatic page breaks that fall in awkward places. (Setting the manual page breaks is likely to affect the automatic page breaks.)

Switch to Page Break Preview

To see where page breaks currently fall, click the Page Break Preview button on the status bar, shown here, or choose View | Workbook Views | Page Break Preview. Excel displays the worksheet in Page Break Preview (see Figure 6-5), with the pages divided and numbered.

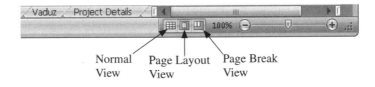

Reposition an Automatic Page Break

To reposition an automatic page break, move the mouse pointer over it so that the mouse pointer changes to a two-headed arrow, and then drag the page break to where you want it.

When you move an automatic page break, Excel changes it to a manual page break.

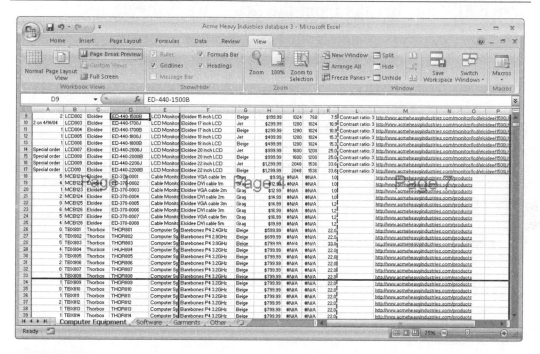

FIGURE 6-5 In Page Break Preview, dashed blue lines indicate automatic page breaks and solid blue lines indicate manual page breaks.

Set a Manual Page Break

To set a manual page break, follow these steps:

1. Select the cell above and to the left of which you want to insert the new page break.

2. Choose Page Layout | Page Setup | Breaks | Insert Page Break. Alternatively, right-click the cell, and then choose Insert Page Break from the context menu.

Remove a Manual Page Break

To remove a manual page break, follow these steps:

1. Select the cell below and to the right of the page break.

2. Choose Page Layout | Page Setup | Breaks | Remove Page Break. Alternatively, right-click the cell, and then choose Remove Page Break from the shortcut menu.

Remove All Page Breaks from the Active Worksheet

To remove all page breaks from the active worksheet, choose Page Layout | Page Setup | Breaks | Reset All Page Breaks.

When you've finished working in Page Break Preview, click the Normal View button on the status bar or choose View | Workbook Views | Normal to return to Normal view.

Check and Change Margins

To make printouts fit the page, set suitable margins. You can set anything from the tiny margins that laser printers need (laser printers can't print right up to the edge of the paper) to margins generous enough for scribbling paragraphs of complex notes. Excel starts you off with default margins for predefined paper sizes, but often you'll need to change them.

To set margins, choose Page Layout | Page Setup | Margins, and then choose Normal, Wide, or Narrow from the Margins panel (shown here).

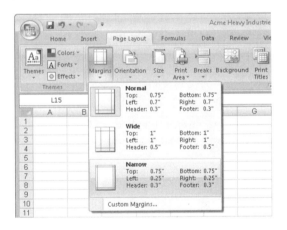

If none of these preset margin types suits you, click Custom Margins. Excel displays the Margins tab of the Page Setup dialog box (see Figure 6-6). On this tab, you can:

- Use the Top box, Bottom box, Left box, and Right box to set the top, bottom, left, and right margins.

- Use the Header box to specify the distance between the header and the top of the page, and the Footer box to specify the distance between the footer and the bottom of the page.

- Select the Horizontally check box if you want to center the printout on the page horizontally. Select the Vertically check box if you want to center the printout on the page vertically.

TIP *You can also use the Margins tab to center the printout horizontally or vertically on the page.*

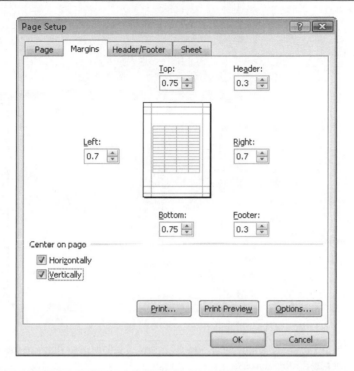

6

FIGURE 6-6   Use the Margins tab of the Page Setup dialog box to set custom margins for a printout.

After setting margin distances on the Margins tab, click the Print Preview button to display the worksheet in Print Preview. Then select the Margins check box in the Preview group to make Excel display guidelines where the margins and the header and footer areas fall (see Figure 6-7). You can change the margins and the header and footer areas by dragging these guidelines—for example, if you notice that a deep header or footer is crashing into the worksheet. You can also drag the markers along the top border of the page to change column widths—for example, if you notice that a cell is too wide for its column.

After checking the margins, click the Close Print Preview button (or press ESC) to exit Print Preview.

Choose Which Items to Include in the Printout

Excel's default settings are to print the contents of cells in the print area that you specify but not print items such as gridlines, row headings and column headings, or comments attached to cells in the print area.

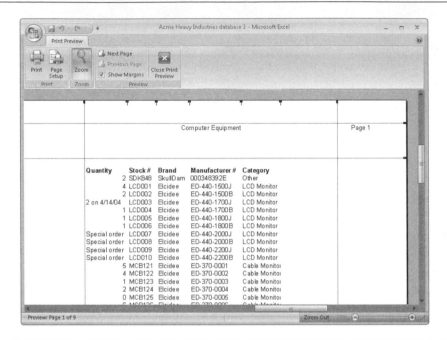

FIGURE 6-7 In Print Preview, select the Show Margins check box to display the margins and header and footer areas.

If you want to print gridlines or headings, select the appropriate Print check box in the Sheet Options group on the Page Layout tab (shown here):

To reach the full set of options, choose Page Layout | Page Setup | Print Titles. (You can also click the tiny Page Setup: Sheet button at the right end of the Sheet Options bar, but the Print Titles button is easier.) Excel displays the Sheet tab of the Page Setup dialog box (shown in Figure 6-2, earlier in this chapter).

The Sheet tab enables you to:

- Print gridlines and row and column headings.
- Print colors as black and white (for a monochrome printer).

- Use draft quality for faster printing and lower ink use.

- Include comments. If you do, choose whether to print them at the end of the worksheet or in the positions in which they appear on the worksheet.

- Specify how to deal with cells that contain errors: display them, print blank cells, print two dashes (**--**), or print **#N/A** to indicate that they're not applicable.

- Change the page order from Down, Then Over (the default) to Over, Then Down to specify how Excel paginates and numbers multipage printouts.

Repeat Row Titles or Column Titles on Subsequent Pages

6

If the printout of a worksheet continues to a second or subsequent page, it's usually a good idea to repeat the row titles or column titles (or both) on each page after the first to make them easy to read. Otherwise, you'll see your readers carefully folding the second sheet over at the end of the white space and lining up the crease with the columns on the first sheet so that they can see what's what.

To repeat row titles or column titles, follow these steps:

1. Choose Page Layout | Page Setup | Print Titles. Excel displays the Sheet tab of the Page Setup dialog box.

2. Click the Collapse Dialog button in the Rows to Repeat at Top box, select the rows you want to repeat, and then click the Collapse Dialog button to restore the dialog box.

3. Click the Collapse Dialog button in the Columns to Repeat at Left box, select the columns you want to repeat, and then click the Collapse Dialog button to restore the dialog box.

4. Click the OK button. Excel closes the Page Setup dialog box.

Print Worksheets

When a worksheet is ready to print, you can print it with any necessary options by using the Print dialog box. If you often need to print the same print area, you can put the Quick Print button on the Quick Access Toolbar, and then click that button to print instantly.

Control Printing Using the Print Dialog Box

For normal printing, when you need to control what you print and how you print it, click the Office button, and then click Print. Excel displays the Print dialog box (see Figure 6-8).

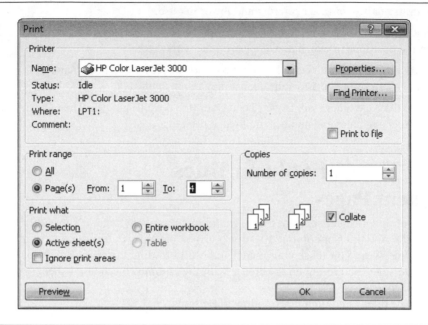

FIGURE 6-8 Use the Print dialog box to choose what to print, which printer to use, and whether to print multiple copies.

Choose Options in the Print Dialog Box

In the Print dialog box, you can:

- Choose the printer in the Name drop-down list.

If your computer is running Windows Vista Business Edition or Windows XP Professional and is part of a Windows Server network, you can click the Find Printer button and use the Find Printers dialog box to locate available printers. You can't use the Find Printer button on home networks.

- Specify which pages to print in the Print Range group box. The default is to print all pages in the print area. To print only some pages, enter the starting number in the From box and the ending number in the To box. When you enter the first of these values, Excel selects the Page(s) option button automatically.

- Choose what to print in the Print What group box. The default is to print the active worksheet. You can also choose to print the current selection, the entire workbook, or the current table (if one is selected). Select the Ignore Print Areas check box if the item you want to print (for example, a selection) isn't set as the print area.

■ Set the number of copies to print in the Number Of Copies box. The default is one copy. If you print multiple copies, select the Collate check box to print the full set of each copy at once (followed by the next copy), or clear the Collate check box to print all of the copies of each page together (followed by all of the copies of the next page).

■ To print to a file instead of printing to paper (or to a fax printer), select the Print To File check box. When you click the OK button in the Print dialog box, Excel displays the Print To File dialog box. Type or paste the path and file name for the print file in the Output File Name text box, and then click the OK button. Excel then creates a print file that you can send or take to another computer (for example, to a specialist print shop for high-quality printouts) for printing.

Choose Further Options in the Printer Properties Dialog Box

You can choose further options by clicking the Properties button in the Print dialog box and working in the Properties dialog box for the printer. The contents of the Properties dialog box varies greatly depending on the printer, but you'll often find options such as these:

■ Printing in back-to-front order instead of the default front-to-back order. (Back-to-front order is sometimes useful for photocopying tasks.)

■ Printing multiple pages on the same sheet of paper.

■ Using different paper trays. For example, you might need to print invoices on letterhead loaded into a separate paper tray than plain paper.

■ Using different print quality—for example, 300 dpi (dots per inch) instead of 600 dpi.

After choosing options, click the OK button. Excel closes the Properties dialog box.

 You can also display the Properties dialog box for the printer by clicking the Options button on any of the tabs in the Page Setup dialog box.

Print Your Work

After choosing the appropriate options, click the OK button in the Print dialog box to print your work.

Put the Quick Print Button on the Quick Access Toolbar for Instant Printing

If you often need to print the same print area, going through the Print dialog box is a waste of time. Instead, you can put the Quick Print button on the Quick Access Toolbar for one-click printing. To do so, click the Customize Quick Access Toolbar button (the drop-down button at the right end of the Quick Access Toolbar), and then choose Quick Print from the drop-down menu, selecting the check box next to the Quick Print item.

Once you've chosen a print area and suitable print settings for the worksheet, you can then print instantly by clicking the Quick Print button on the Quick Access toolbar. Excel prints the active worksheet with the existing print settings without displaying the Print dialog box.

You can also print by clicking the Quick Print button without explicitly setting a print area or other settings. Excel prints the worksheet up to the last cell that contains data, using automatic page breaks and the default paper size. For a small worksheet that occupies less than one sheet of paper, printing this way can give tolerable results. But in most cases, you'll do better to set up the printouts manually, as described earlier in this chapter.

Part II

Calculate, Manipulate, and Analyze Data

Chapter 7

Perform Calculations with Functions

How to...

- Understand what functions are and what their components are
- Enter functions in worksheets
- Nest one function inside another function
- Edit a function in a worksheet
- Monitor calculations with the Watch window
- See examples of functions in action

To manipulate data and perform calculations with Excel, you use formulas and functions. A *formula* is a set of instructions for performing a calculation, while a *function* is a predefined formula for a standard calculation.

In this chapter, you'll start using Excel's built-in functions in worksheets. You'll learn what functions are and how you enter them in worksheets. You'll also learn about the various categories of functions that Excel provides, with examples of some of the most useful functions in each category.

In the next chapter, you'll learn how to create your own formulas to perform calculations that require more flexibility than the built-in functions provide.

Understand Functions

Excel includes a large number of *functions*—built-in, predefined formulas for standard calculations. Excel's functions range from the everyday to the highly specialized. For example, the SUM() function adds two or more values together and displays the result, whereas the MINVERSE() function produces the inverse matrix for a specific matrix. SUM() is very widely used, but MINVERSE() much less so.

Understand the Components of a Function

Each function has a name entered in capitals and followed by a pair of parentheses—for example, SUM(), MAX(), or DATEVALUE(). Almost all functions have one or more *arguments,* which specify the elements and types of information you give them in order to get a valid result. Some functions, such as =NOW(), =TODAY(), and =NA(), require no arguments at all, but these functions are very much the exceptions that prove the rule.

The rules that govern the types of information a function needs are called its *syntax.* Excel shows required arguments in boldface, optional arguments in regular font, and an ellipsis to indicate where you can use further arguments of the same type.

For example, the syntax for the =SUM() function is

```
SUM(number1,number2,...)
```

Here, number1 is a required argument that specifies the first number to include in the sum: you can't have a SUM without a number (although the number can be zero or negative). By contrast, number2 is an optional argument that specifies the second number, if there is one. The ellipsis indicates that you can use further arguments—number3, number4, and so on—as necessary to tell the function to include further numbers in the calculation.

Enter Functions in Worksheets

You can enter a function in the active cell in three ways:

- Type the function directly into the cell.

- Choose a function from one of the drop-down panels in the Function Library group on the Formulas tab of the Ribbon, and then use the Function Arguments dialog box to specify any arguments the function needs.

- Click the Insert Function button in the Function Library group, and then use the Insert Function dialog box.

The following sections discuss these ways of entering a function and explain when to use each method.

Type a Function Directly into a Cell

The most straightforward way to enter a function is to type it and its arguments directly into the cell. Use this way when you're familiar with the function you're entering and need minimal assistance.

When you've typed enough to identify the function you're entering, Excel displays a ScreenTip that shows the syntax for the function and tracks your progress in entering the argument. The ScreenTip includes links that you can click to select an argument you've previously entered, or to return to the argument you're currently entering.

Here's an example of entering the SUM() function by typing it directly into the active cell. To try it out, follow these steps:

1. Click the Office Button, and then click New, to create a new blank workbook.

2. Click in cell A1, type **34**, and then press Enter.

3. Click in cell A2 if it's not selected already. (Usually, Excel selects the next cell when you press Enter after typing a value in a cell.) Type **66**, and then press Enter.

4. Select cell A3 if it isn't already selected.

5. Type **=s**. Excel displays a list of the functions starting with the letter S and displays a ScreenTip explaining the highlighted function, as shown here:

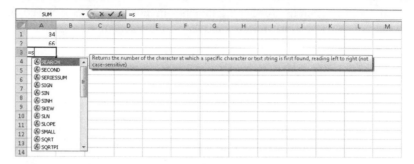

6. Type **um(**. As soon as you type the opening parenthesis, Excel recognizes the function name and displays the ScreenTip, as shown here, to remind you of the syntax required. The boldface (on the number1 argument here) shows you the information that you need to enter next:

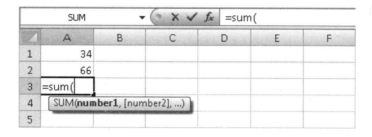

 *You don't have to enter function names in capitals—Excel automatically changes the names to capitals for you.*

7. Type **a1** after the opening parenthesis. Excel recognizes the cell reference and applies a blue outline to the cell to help make sure you've entered the correct cell:

8. Type **,** (a comma) after a1. Excel removes boldface from the number1 argument (which you've entered) and applies it to the number2 argument, which you need to enter next:

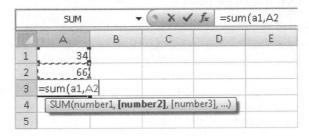

9. Click cell A2 to enter its address as the second argument in the function, as shown here. Excel applies a flashing outline to the cell and enters its address in green:

10. Type the closing parenthesis for the function, and then click the Enter button (the button with the check mark) in the Formula bar. Excel enters the function in the cell and displays its result. The next illustration shows the function result displayed in the active cell and the function itself displayed in the Formula bar:

Use the Function Library Drop-Down Panels

The next way to enter a function is to use one of the drop-down panels in the Function Library group on the Formulas tab of the Ribbon (shown here).

Use this way of entering functions when you need to:

■ **Insert a common function** The AutoSum drop-down panel contains the Sum, Average, Count Numbers, Max, and Min functions. The More Functions entry displays the Insert Function dialog box.

■ **Insert a function you've used recently** The Recently Used drop-down panel contains the last 10 functions you used.

■ **Pick a function by category** Sometimes, you'll know the category of function you need but not the exact function. When this happens, choose the category, and then choose the function from the panel. For example, click the Date & Time button, and then choose a date or time function from the panel.

At the bottom of each panel is an Insert Function entry that displays the Insert Function dialog box (discussed in the "Use the Insert Function Dialog Box" section, next).

To enter one of the functions from the AutoSum panel, follow these steps:

1. Select the cell in which you want to enter the function. Often, the cell will be immediately beneath the column of figures, or immediately to the right of the row of figures, on which you want to use the function.

2. Click the AutoSum button if you want to enter the SUM() function, or click the drop-down button, and then select another function from the panel, as shown here:

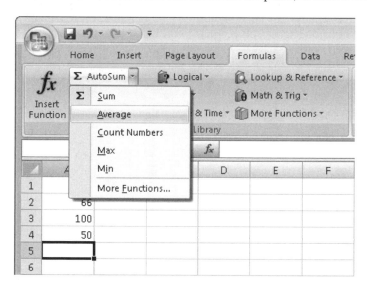

3. Excel enters the function in the active cell. If Excel detects numeric entries in the cells above or to the left of the active cell, it selects the cells as a suggestion for what you may want to enter in the function, as shown here:

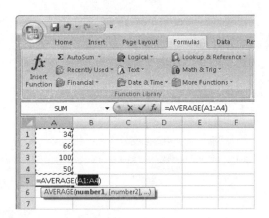

4. Edit the selection (or create a new selection) as necessary:

- If Excel has selected almost the correct range for the function, drag one of the borders of the automatic selection to select the correct range.

- If Excel has selected completely the wrong range for the function, or hasn't identified any suitable range to select, click and drag to select the correct range.

- Instead of clicking and dragging to select the range, you can type the start cell address and end cell address within the function.

5. Press ENTER to enter the function in the cell.

To enter a function from one of the other drop-down panels in the Function Library group, follow these steps:

1. Select the cell in which you want to enter the function.

2. Click the Recently Used button or the category button. Excel displays the panel of functions. Here is the Logical panel:

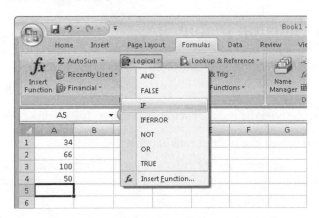

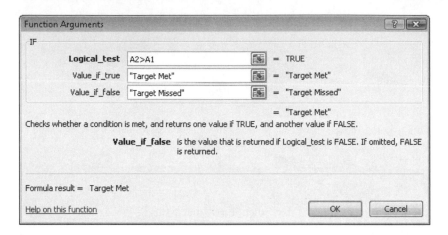

The Function Arguments dialog box shows you which arguments the function you selected requires.

3. Click the function you want. Excel enters the function in the cell and displays the Function Arguments dialog box, which shows the arguments required by the function. Figure 7-1 shows the arguments required by the IF function with values entered. If you enter a function that requires no arguments, the Function Arguments dialog box tells you so.

4. Enter each required argument and as many optional arguments as necessary in the Function Arguments dialog box. For many arguments, you can click a Collapse Dialog button, select the right cell in the worksheet, and then click the Collapse Dialog button again.

5. When you've entered all the arguments, click the OK button. Excel closes the Function Arguments dialog box and enters the function in the cell.

Use the Insert Function Dialog Box

The third way of entering a function is by using the Insert Function dialog box, which walks you through the process of choosing a function and specifying its arguments correctly. Use this dialog box when you need to browse for a function, or if you simply want to use a single way to enter all functions.

To enter a function by using the Insert Function dialog box, follow these steps:

1. Select the cell in which you want to enter the function.

2. Click the Insert Function button (the *fx* button) on the Formula bar, or choose Formulas | Function Library | Insert Function. Excel displays the Insert Function dialog box (see Figure 7-2).

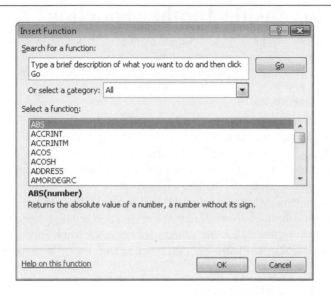

FIGURE 7-2   The Insert Function dialog box walks you through the process of choosing a function and entering the arguments it needs.

3. Select the function you want to enter in any of these ways:

■ If the Select A Function box already contains the function, click the function.

■ Select the function's category in the Or Select a Category drop-down list; then click the function in the Select A Function box.

■ Type keywords describing the function in the Search For A Function text box, and then click the Go button. Excel displays matching functions in the Select A Function box under the Recommended category. Click the function you want.

4. Check that the description of the function below the Select A Function box matches your expectations. (If necessary, click the Help On This Function link to display Excel's help entry on the function.)

5. Click the OK button. Excel displays the Function Arguments dialog box.

6. Enter the data in each argument box in turn, either by typing in the data or by clicking the Collapse Dialog button for the argument, using the mouse to select the appropriate cell or range references, and then clicking the Collapse Dialog button again. As you work, Excel displays information on the current argument and, as soon as appropriate, the result of the formula. Again, you can click the Help On This Function link to access help information.

7. Click the OK button. Excel closes the Function Arguments dialog box and enters the function in the cell.

Nest One Function Inside Another Function

To achieve the calculations you need, you'll often use multiple functions in sequence. You can do this by entering a function in one cell, and then using another function in another cell to work on the result of that function. But you can also achieve the same effect in a single cell by nesting one function within another. Excel supports nesting up to 64 functions, so you can create highly involved calculations.

To nest one function within another, follow the procedure described in the "Use the Insert Function Dialog Box" section, earlier in this chapter, up to step 5. You'll have noticed that when the Insert Function dialog box or the Function Arguments dialog box appears, Excel replaces the Name box to the left of the Formula bar with a box (called the Function box) that contains the name of the last function you used.

In the Function Arguments dialog box, select the argument box in which you want to enter the nested function. Then click the drop-down list next to the Function box and choose either one of the listed functions (the list shows the last ten you've used), or select the More Functions entry to display the Insert Function dialog box again. Then select the function and specify its arguments as usual.

Edit a Function in a Worksheet

To edit a function you've entered, select the cell that contains the formula, and then click the Insert Function button on the Formula bar or choose Formulas | Function Library | Insert Function. Excel displays the Function Arguments dialog box again. Edit the function by using the same techniques as for creating the function in the first place.

Monitor Calculations with the Watch Window

Excel's Watch window (see Figure 7-3) is a tool for monitoring the value of specific cells in one or more workbooks as you work. The cells can be on any of the worksheets in the workbooks or on a worksheet in a linked workbook. You may find the Watch window useful for working with either functions or formulas, especially when you're constructing complex worksheets or troubleshooting problems: instead of having to move to different points in your workbook to check values as they change, you can put them all in one place.

To use the Watch window, follow these steps:

1. Choose Formulas | Formula Auditing | Watch Window. Excel opens the Watch window.

2. Add watch cells to the Watch window:

   ■ Click the Add Watch button. Excel displays the Add Watch dialog box, as shown here:

FIGURE 7-3   Use the Watch window to monitor the values of particular cells during calculations.

- ■ Type the address or name of the cell, or click the Collapse Dialog button, select the cell, and then click the Collapse Dialog button again.

- ■ Click the Add button. Excel adds the watch item to the Watch window.

3. If necessary, delete a watch cell: click the cell in the Watch window, and then click the Delete Watch button.

4. To sort the cells by a column, click that column heading.

5. To go to a watch cell, double-click it in the Watch window.

6. To close the Watch window, click its Close button (the × button) or choose Formulas | Formula Auditing | Watch Window again.

Examples of Functions in Action

Excel offers 11 categories of built-in functions: Cube, Database, Date & Time, Engineering, Financial, Logical, Information, Lookup & Reference, Math & Trig, Statistical, and Text. The following sections introduce each category, discuss those functions you're most likely to find useful, and provide brief examples of most types of functions. Some categories contain too many functions to list all of them here. To access one of the main categories of functions, click the category button in the Function Library group: Financial, Logical, Text, Date & Time, Lookup & Reference, or Math & Trig. To access one of the less-used categories of functions, click the More Functions button, and then choose Statistical, Engineering, Cube, or Information in the panel (shown here).

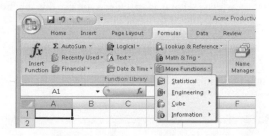

Alternatively, click the Insert Function button in the Formula bar or choose Formulas | Function Library | Insert Function. Excel displays the Insert Function dialog box. Select the category in the Or Select A Category drop-down list.

Cube Functions

Excel's seven cube functions let you bring data from an Online Analytical Processing (OLAP) cube drawn from SQL Server Analysis Services into a worksheet. Briefly, an *OLAP cube* is an array of data drawn from a relational database. The purpose of an OLAP cube is to allow faster analysis of the data than the database itself would permit.

To use the cube functions, you must have access to an OLAP cube connected via SQL Server Analysis Services to a database, which you'll normally have only in a corporate setting. Table 7-1 lists the cube functions and what they return.

Database Functions

Excel's 12 database functions are for identifying which values in an Excel database or table match certain criteria. For example:

- DCOUNT returns the number of records that match the criteria.
- DSUM adds the numbers in the specified column of the records that match the criteria.
- DSTDEVP returns the standard deviation based on the entire population of entries that match the criteria.

Chapter 9 discusses how to create databases and tables in Excel.

Function	What It Returns
CUBEKPIMEMBER	A key performance indicator (KPI) from the specified connection in the OLAP cube
CUBEMEMBER	The specified member or *tuple* (an intersection of two dimensions) from the OLAP cube
CUBEMEMBERPROPERTY	The value of the specified member property from the cube
CUBERANKEDMEMBER	The cube member at the rank specified—for example, the fifth item in the cube
CUBESET	The set of data specified (you use this function to define a calculated set of data on the server)
CUBESETCOUNT	The number of items in the specified set
CUBEVALUE	The aggregate value of the cube, using the filters specified

TABLE 7-1 Excel's Cube Functions

Date and Time Functions

Excel's date and time functions, explained in Table 7-2, are widely useful in worksheets for a variety of operations.

Function	What It Returns
DATE	Serial number of the specified date
TIME	Serial number of the specified time
DATEVALUE	Serial number of the specified text-formatted date
TIMEVALUE	Serial number of the specified text-formatted time
DAY	Day of the month for the specified serial date, as a serial number between 1 and 31
MONTH	Month of the year for the specified serial date, as a serial number between 1 and 12
YEAR	Year for the specified serial date (for example, 2007)
YEARFRAC	Year fraction giving the number of whole days between the specified starting date and the specified ending date
DAYS360	Number of days between the two specified dates, based on a 360-day year (used for some accounting purposes)
HOUR	Hour for the specified serial time, as a serial number between 0 and 23
MINUTE	Minute for the specified serial time, as a serial number between 0 and 59
SECOND	Second for the specified serial time, as a serial number between 0 and 59
TODAY	Current date, formatted as a date
NOW	Current date and time, formatted as a date and time
WEEKNUM	Number of the specified week in the year
WEEKDAY	Weekday for the specified day, as a serial number between 1 (Sunday) and 7 (Saturday)
WORKDAY	Serial number of the date the specified number of workdays before or after the specified date
NETWORKDAYS	Number of whole workdays between the two specified dates ("net workdays" rather than "network days")
EDATE	Serial number of the date the specified number of months before or after the specified start date
EOMONTH	Serial number of the last day of the month the specified number of months before or after the specified date

TABLE 7-2   Excel's Date and Time Functions

Here are three examples of using the date and time functions:

- **=TODAY()** enters the current date in a cell, and **=NOW()** enters the current date and time, in an automatically updating form.
- **=DATEVALUE("2007-4-1")** converts the text string "2007-4-1" to its corresponding serial date.
- **=HOUR("11:45 PM")** returns *23*, the hour derived from 11:45 P.M.

Engineering Functions

Excel contains about 40 engineering functions, of which some are highly specialized (such as the Bessel functions) and others more widely used (such as the functions that convert numbers among binary, octal, decimal, and hexadecimal systems). Table 7-3 explains the engineering functions.

Function	What It Returns
BESSELI	Modified Bessel function In(x), contour integral.
BESSELJ	Bessel function Jn(x), also called cylindrical harmonics.
BESSELK	Modified Bessel function Kn(x), also called Basset function or Macdonald function.
BESSELY	Bessel function Yn(x), also called Neumann functions or Weber functions.
BIN2DEC	Decimal (base 10) equivalent of the specified binary (base 2) number.
BIN2HEX	Hexadecimal (base 16) equivalent of the specified binary (base 2) number.
BIN2OCT	Octal (base 8) equivalent of the specified binary (base 2) number.
COMPLEX	Complex number produced by real and imaginary coefficients.
CONVERT	Equivalent value in the specified destination measuring system of the value in the specified source measuring system. For example, you can convert yards to meters, joules to thermodynamic calories, or Celsius to Fahrenheit.
DEC2BIN	Binary (base 2) equivalent of the specified decimal (base 10) number.
DEC2HEX	Hexadecimal (base 16) equivalent of the specified decimal (base 10) number.
DEC2OCT	Octal (base 8) equivalent of the specified decimal (base 10) number.
DELTA	1 if the two numbers are equal, 0 if they are not.
ERF	Error function between the specified lower limit and specified upper limit.
ERFC	Complementary error function.
GESTEP	1 if the specified number is greater than the specified threshold, 0 if it is not.

TABLE 7-3   Excel's Engineering Functions (*continued*)

Function	What It Returns
HEX2BIN	Binary (base 2) equivalent of the specified hexadecimal (base 16) number.
HEX2DEC	Decimal (base 10) equivalent of the specified hexadecimal (base 16) number.
HEX2OCT	Octal (base 8) equivalent of the specified hexadecimal (base 16) number.
IMABS	Modulus (absolute value) of a complex number.
IMAGINARY	Imaginary coefficient of a complex number.
IMARGUMENT	Angle expressed in radians for the specified complex number.
IMCONJUGATE	Complex conjugate of the specified complex number.
IMCOS	Cosine of the specified complex number.
IMDIV	Quotient of the specified two complex numbers.
IMEXP	Exponential of the specified complex number.
IMLN	Natural logarithm of the specified complex number.
IMLOG10	Base-10 logarithm of the specified complex number.
IMLOG2	Base-2 logarithm of the specified complex number.
IMPOWER	Specified complex number raised to the specified power.
IMPRODUCT	Product of the specified complex numbers.
IMREAL	Real coefficient of the specified complex number.
IMSIN	Sine of the specified complex number.
IMSQRT	Square root of the specified complex number.
IMSUB	Difference between the two specified complex numbers.
IMSUM	Sum of the specified complex numbers.
OCT2BIN	Binary (base 2) equivalent of the specified octal (base 8) number.
OCT2DEC	Decimal (base 10) equivalent of the specified octal (base 8) number.
OCT2HEX	Hexadecimal (base 16) equivalent of the specified octal (base 8) number.

TABLE 7-3   Excel's Engineering Functions (*continued*)

Here are three examples of using the engineering functions:

■ **=CONVERT(454,"g","lbm")** converts 454 grams to pounds.

■ **=DEC2HEX(1000)** converts the decimal (base 10) value 1000 to its hexadecimal (base 16) equivalent.

■ **=IMSQRT(B12)** returns the square root of the complex number contained in cell B12.

Financial Functions

Excel includes several dozen financial functions, explained in Table 7-4, that cover the range from common calculations to highly specialized uses.

Function	What It Returns
ACCRINT	Interest accrued on a security that pays interest periodically
ACCRINTM	Interest accrued on a security that pays interest on maturity
AMORDEGRC	An asset's prorated linear depreciation for each accounting period (French accounting system)
AMORLINC	An asset's prorated linear depreciation for each accounting period (French accounting system)
COUPDAYBS	Number of days from the coupon period's beginning to the settlement date
COUPDAYS	Number of days in the coupon period containing the settlement date
COUPDAYSNC	Number of days to the next coupon date from the settlement date
COUPNCD	Next coupon date after the settlement date
COUPNUM	Number of coupons payable between settlement date and maturity date
COUPPCD	Previous coupon date before the settlement date
CUMIPMT	Cumulative interest paid between the two periods specified
CUMPRINC	Cumulative principal paid on a loan between the two periods specified
DB	Depreciation using the fixed-declining balance method
DDB	Depreciation using the double-declining balance method or other method
DISC	Discount rate for a security
DOLLARDE	Decimal dollar price equivalent of the specified fractional dollar price
DOLLARFR	Fractional dollar price equivalent of the specified decimal dollar price
DURATION	Annual duration of a security that pays interest periodically
EFFECT	Effective annual interest rate
FV	Future value of an investment
FVSCHEDULE	Future value of an investment to which compound interest rates have been applied
INTRATE	Interest rate for a security that is fully vested
IPMT	Interest payments for an investment for a specified period
IRR	Internal rate of return for cash flows
ISPMT	Interest paid for an investment over a specified period

TABLE 7-4   Excel's Financial Functions (*continued*)

Function	What It Returns
MDURATION	Macauley modified duration for a security
MIRR	Modified internal rate of return for cash flows
NOMINAL	Annual nominal interest rate
NPER	Number of periods for an investment
NPV	Net present value of an investment
ODDFPRICE	Price per $100 face value of a security that uses an odd first period
ODDFYIELD	Yield of a security that uses an odd first period
ODDLPRICE	Price per $100 face value of a security that uses an odd last period
ODDLYIELD	Yield of a security that uses an odd last period
PMT	Payment for a loan
PPMT	Payment on the principal for an investment
PRICE	Price per $100 face value of a security that pays interest periodically
PRICEDISC	Price per $100 face value of a discounted security
PRICEMAT	Price per $100 face value of a security that pays interest when it matures
PV	Present value of an investment
RATE	Interest rate per period of an investment
RECEIVED	Value at maturity of a fully invested security
SLN	Straight-line depreciation for an asset
SYD	Sum-of-years' digits depreciation for an asset
TBILLEQ	A treasury bill's bond-equivalent yield
TBILLPRICE	A treasury bill's price per $100 face value
TBILLYIELD	A treasury bill's yield
VDB	Depreciation for an asset using the double-declining balance method or a variable declining balance
XIRR	Internal rate of return (IRR) for a schedule of cash flows
XNPV	Net present value (NPV) for a schedule of cash flows
YIELD	Yield on a security that has periodic interest payments
YIELDDISC	A discounted security's annual yield
YIELDMAT	Annual yield of a security that pays interest when it matures

TABLE 7-4   Excel's Financial Functions (*continued*)

7

Here are two examples of using the financial functions:

- **=PMT(7.25%/12,24,-20000)** calculates the payment required to pay off a $20,000 loan at 7.25 percent APR over 24 payments.

- **=DB(15000,3000,6,3)** calculates the depreciation over the third year of an asset with an initial cost of $15,000, a salvage value of $3,000 at the end of its life, and a life of six years.

- **=TBILLYIELD(DATE(9,30,8),DATE(12,1,8),95.01)** calculates the yield for a treasury bill with a settlement date of September 30, 2008, a maturity date of December 1, 2008, and a price of $95.01 per $100 face value.

Logical Functions

Excel's seven logical functions, explained in Table 7-5, enable you to test logical conditions. By combining these logical functions with other functions, you can make Excel take action that's appropriate to how the condition evaluates.

Here are two examples of using the logical functions:

- **=IF(C21>4000,"More than $4,000","Less than $4,000")** returns *More than $4,000* if C21 contains a number greater than 4000. Otherwise, the function returns *Less than $4,000*.

- **=AND(INFO("system")="pcdos",INFO("osversion")="Windows (32-bit) NT 6.00",INFO("release")="12.0")** returns TRUE if the user is running Excel 2007 (version 12.0) on Windows Vista (which has the internal version number Windows [32-bit] NT 6.00) on a PC.

Often IF is used with the information functions discussed in the next section, which contains further examples.

Function	What It Returns
AND	TRUE if all the specified arguments are TRUE; otherwise FALSE
FALSE	FALSE (always—use to generate a FALSE value)
IF	The first specified value if the condition is TRUE; the second specified value if the condition is FALSE (see the first example before this table.)
IFERROR	The specified error value if the expression results in an error; otherwise, the expression itself.
NOT	FALSE from TRUE; TRUE from FALSE
OR	TRUE if any of the specified arguments is TRUE; FALSE if all arguments are FALSE
TRUE	TRUE (always—use to generate a TRUE value)

TABLE 7-5   Excel's Logical Functions

Information Functions

Excel offers 17 information functions, explained in Table 7-6, for returning information about the contents and formatting of the current cell or range. Some of these information functions are widely useful, whereas others are more specialized.

Here are three examples of using the information functions:

■ **=INFO("osversion")** returns Windows' internal description of the operating system version—for example, *Windows (32-bit) NT 6.00* for Windows Vista, and *Windows (32-bit) NT 5.01* for Windows XP. **=INFO("directory")** returns the current working

7

Function	What It Returns
CELL	Specified details of the contents, location, or formatting of the first cell in the specified range.
ERROR.TYPE	A number representing the error value in the cell: 1 for #NULL!, 2 for #DIV/0!, 3 for #VALUE!, 4 for #REF!, 5 for #NAME?, 6 for #NUM!, and 7 for #N/A.
INFO	Information about Excel, the operating system, or the computer.
ISBLANK	TRUE if the cell is blank; FALSE if it has contents.
ISERR	TRUE if the cell contains any error except #N/A; otherwise FALSE.
ISERROR	TRUE if the cell contains any error; otherwise FALSE.
ISEVEN	TRUE if the cell contains an even number; otherwise FALSE.
ISLOGICAL	TRUE if the cell contains a logical value; otherwise FALSE.
ISNA	TRUE if the cell contains #N/A; otherwise FALSE.
ISNONTEXT	TRUE if the cell contains anything but text—even if it's a blank cell; otherwise FALSE.
ISNUMBER	TRUE if the cell contains a number; otherwise FALSE.
ISODD	TRUE if the cell contains an odd number; otherwise FALSE.
ISREF	TRUE if the cell contains a reference; otherwise FALSE.
ISTEXT	TRUE if the cell contains text; otherwise FALSE.
N	A number derived from the specified value: a number returns that number, a date returns the associated serial date, TRUE returns 1, FALSE returns 0, an error returns its error value (see the ERROR.TYPE entry, earlier in this table), and anything else returns 0.
NA	#N/A (used to enter the error value deliberately in the cell).
TYPE	A number representing the data type in the cell: 1 for a number, 2 for text, 4 for a logical value, 16 for an error value, and 64 for an array.

TABLE 7-6   Excel's Information Functions

directory. **=INFO("numfile")** returns the number of active worksheets in all open workbooks.

- ■ **=IF(ISERROR(Revenue/Price), "Units not available", Revenue/Price)** checks to see whether dividing the cell referenced by the name Revenue by the cell referenced by the name Price will result in an error before it performs the calculation. If the calculation will result in an error, the formula displays a label in the cell instead. If the calculation won't result in an error, the formula performs the calculation and displays its result.

- ■ **=IF(ISBLANK('Amortization Estimates.xls'!Amortization_Rate), "Warning: Base rate not entered","")** displays a warning message if the Amortization_Rate cell in the Amortization Estimates workbook is blank. Otherwise, the formula displays nothing.

Lookup and Reference Functions

Excel includes 18 lookup and reference functions for returning information from lists and tables. Table 7-7 explains these functions.

Here are three examples of the lookup and reference functions:

- ■ **=HLOOKUP("Monitors",A1:E24,5,FALSE)** returns the item in the fifth row of the same column as the "Monitors" label in the first row, searching the range A1:E24.

- ■ **=MATCH("San Francisco",C2:C30,0)** returns the position of the first cell in the range C2:C30 that contains an exact match (specified by 0) for the term "San Francisco."

- ■ **=OFFSET(Start_Cell,10,20)** returns the value in the cell offset 10 rows and 20 columns from the cell named Start_Cell.

Mathematical and Trigonometric Functions

Excel offers 60 mathematical and trigonometric functions. Many of these functions are self-explanatory to anyone who needs to use them in their work. For example, COS returns the cosine of an angle, COSH returns the hyperbolic cosine, ACOS returns the arccosine, and ACOSH returns the inverse hyperbolic cosine. Table 7-8 explains the mathematical and trigonometric functions you might use occasionally for more general purposes.

Here are three examples of using the general-purpose mathematical and trigonometric functions:

- ■ **=SUM(A1:A24)** adds the values in the range A1:A24.

- ■ **=RAND()** enters a random value that changes each time the worksheet is recalculated. (Unless you turn off automatic calculation, Excel recalculates the worksheet each time you enter a change.)

- ■ **=ROMAN(1998)** returns *MCMXCVIII*.

Function	What It Returns
ADDRESS	The cell reference specified by a given row number and a given column number.
AREAS	The number of different areas contained in a reference, where an area is either a single cell or a range of contiguous cells.
CHOOSE	The specified value from a set of values, choosing it based on the specified index number.
COLUMN	The column number of the specified reference.
COLUMNS	The number of columns in the specified reference or array.
GETPIVOTDATA	Data from a PivotTable report.
HLOOKUP	The value from the specified row in the data table. Horizontal lookup searches the top row of the table for the matching value (for example, a field name), and then returns the value from the specified row further down the same column.
HYPERLINK	Contains a hyperlink.
INDEX	A value from within a table or a reference to such a value.
INDIRECT	A reference specified by a text string in a cell. By using INDIRECT, you can change the reference in the cell easily without needing to change the formula.
LOOKUP	A value from either a one-column or one-range row or from an array.
MATCH	The position of a matching item in an array (rather than the contents of the item itself).
OFFSET	A reference to the range the specified number of rows and columns offset from a specified cell or range.
ROW	The row number of the specified reference.
ROWS	The number of rows in the specified reference or array.
RTD	Real-time data via COM automation from another program.
TRANSPOSE	Cells transposed from a vertical range to a horizontal range, or vice versa. You can use TRANSPOSE only as an array formula.
VLOOKUP	The value from the specified column in the data table. Vertical lookup searches the first column of the table for the matching value (for example, a field name), and then returns the value from the specified column further across the same row.

TABLE 7-7   Excel's Lookup and Reference Functions

Statistical Functions

Excel includes a large number of statistical functions that fall into categories such as calculating deviation (including AVEDEV, STDEVA, STDEV, and STDEVP), distributions (BETADIST, CHIDIST, BINOMDIST, EXPONDIST, KURT, POISSON, and WEIBULL), and transformations (FISHER and FISHERINV).

Function	What It Returns
ABS	Absolute value (without the sign) of the specified number
EVEN	Specified positive number rounded up to the next even integer, or the specified negative number rounded down to the next even integer
ODD	Specified positive number rounded up to the next odd integer, or the specified negative number rounded down to the next odd integer
INT	Specified number rounded down to the nearest integer
MOD	Remainder left over after a division operation
RAND	Random number (greater than or equal to 0 and less than 1)
ROMAN	Roman equivalent of the specified Arabic numeral
ROUND	Specified number rounded to the specified number of digits
ROUNDDOWN	Specified number rounded down to the specified number of digits
ROUNDUP	Specified number rounded up to the specified number of digits
SIGN	1 for a positive number, 0 for 0, and -1 for a negative number
SUM	Total of the numbers in the specified range
SUMIF	Total of the numbers in the cells in the specified range that meet the criteria given
TRUNC	Specified number truncated to the specified number of decimal places

TABLE 7-8 Excel's General-Purpose Mathematical and Trigonometric Functions

Unless you're working with statistics, you're not likely to need most of the statistical functions. However, you may need to use some of these functions for more general business purposes; these general statistical functions are listed in Table 7-9.

Function	What It Returns
AVERAGE	Average of the specified cells, ranges, or arrays
MEDIAN	Median (the number in the middle of the given set) of the numbers in the specified cells
MODE	Value that occurs most frequently in the specified range of cells
COUNT	Number of cells in the specified range that either contain numbers or include numbers in their list of arguments
COUNTBLANK	Number of empty cells in the specified range
COUNTIF	Number of cells in the specified range that meet the specified criteria
MAX	Largest value in the specified range
MIN	Lowest value in the specified range

TABLE 7-9 Excel's General-Purpose Statistical Functions

Here are three examples of using the general-purpose statistical functions:

- ◼ **=AVERAGE(Q1Sales)** returns the average value of the entries in the range named Q1Sales.

- ◼ **=COUNTBLANK(BA1:BZ256)** returns the number of blank cells in the specified range.

- ◼ **=COUNTIF(Q2Sales,0)** returns the number of cells with a zero value in the range named Q2Sales.

Text Functions

Excel contains 24 functions for manipulating text, explained in Table 7-10. One of them, BAHTTEXT, is highly esoteric, and another, CONCATENATE, is seldom worth using because the & operator is usually easier for concatenating text strings. You may find the other text functions useful when you need to return a specific part (for example, the first five characters) of a text string, change the case of a text string, or find one string within another string.

Here are three examples of using the text functions:

- ◼ **=EXACT(A1,A2)** compares the text in cells A1 and A2, returning TRUE if they're exactly alike (including case) and FALSE if they're not.

- ◼ **=IF(LEN(H2)>=5, LEFT(H2,5),H2)** returns the first five characters of cell H2 if the length of the cell's contents is five characters or more. If the length is less than five, the formula returns the full contents of the cell.

- ◼ **=TRIM(CLEAN(C2))** strips nonprintable characters from the text string in cell C2, removes extra spaces, and returns the resulting text string.

Function	What It Returns
BAHTTEXT	Number converted to Thai text and with the *Baht* suffix
CHAR	Character represented by the specified character code
CLEAN	Specified text string with all nonprintable characters stripped out (sometimes useful when importing files in other formats)
CODE	Character code for the first character in the specified string
CONCATENATE	Text string consisting of the specified text strings joined together
DOLLAR	Specified number converted to text in the Currency format
EXACT	TRUE if the specified two text strings contain the same characters in the same case; otherwise FALSE
FIND	Starting position of one specified text string within another text string—case-sensitive

TABLE 7-10   Excel's Text Functions

Function	What It Returns
FIXED	Specified number rounded to the specified number of decimals, with or without commas
LEFT	Specified number of characters from the beginning of the specified text string
LEN	Number of characters in the specified text string
LOWER	Text string converted to lowercase
MID	Specified number of characters after the specified starting point in the specified text string
PROPER	Text string converted to "proper case" (first letter capitalized, the rest lowercase)
REPLACE	Specified text string with the specified replacement string inserted in a specified location
REPT	Specified text string repeated the specified number of times
RIGHT	Specified number of characters from the end of the specified text string
SEARCH	Character position at which the specified character is located in the specified string
SUBSTITUTE	Specified text string with the specified new text string substituted for the specified old text string
T	Text string for a text value, empty double quotation marks (a blank string) for a nontext value
TEXT	Text string containing the specified value converted to the specified format
TRIM	Specified text string with spaces removed from the beginning and ends, and extra spaces between words removed to leave one space between words
UPPER	Text string converted to uppercase
VALUE	Value contained in the specified text string

TABLE 7-10   Excel's Text Functions (*continued*)

Chapter 8

Create Formulas to Perform Custom Calculations

How to...

- Understand formula components
- Understand how Excel handles numbers
- Refer to cells, ranges, other worksheets, and other workbooks in formulas
- Enter a sample formula
- Use range names and labels in formulas
- Use absolute, relative, and mixed references in formulas
- Work with array formulas
- Display formulas in worksheets—or hide formulas from other users
- Troubleshoot formulas

In Chapter 7, you learned how to enter Excel's built-in functions to perform calculations. Excel's functions are great for performing a wide variety of standard calculations—as you saw, the functions encompass everything from adding a series of values to testing the logical truth or falsity of conditions to manipulating statistics and text. But often you'll need to perform calculations that the built-in functions don't cover. For such calculations, you create custom formulas.

This chapter describes the basics of formulas in Excel and the components from which formulas are constructed. Then it covers how Excel handles numbers, and how to create both regular formulas and array formulas. Finally, you'll learn how to troubleshoot formulas when they go wrong.

Understand Formula Components

A *formula* is a set of instructions for performing a calculation. Excel enables you to create formulas for performing whatever types of calculations you need. In a formula, you use operands to tell Excel which items to use, and operators to specify which operation or operations to perform on them.

A formula can contain up to 64 nested levels of functions—enough to enable you to perform highly complex calculations.

Each formula begins with an equal sign, so the standard way of starting to enter a formula is to type an equal sign. However, when you start a formula by typing + or − , Excel automatically enters the equal sign when you enter the formula, so you don't always need to type the equal sign yourself.

Operands

The *operands* in a formula specify the data you want to calculate. An operand can be:

- A constant value you enter in the formula itself (for example, **=8*12**) or in a cell (for example, **=B1*8**)
- A cell address, range address, or range name
- A worksheet function

Operators

The *operators* in a formula specify the operation you want to perform on the operands. Excel uses arithmetic operators, comparison operators, reference operators, and one text operator. Table 8-1 explains these operators.

Understand and Change Operator Precedence

When a formula contains only one operator, you don't have to worry about the order in which Excel handles operators. But as soon as you create a formula with two or more different operators, you need to know the order in which they'll be evaluated. For example, consider the formula **=1000-100*5**. Does Excel subtract 100 from 1000 and multiply the result (900) by 5,

Operator	Explanation
Arithmetic Operators	
+	Addition
−	Subtraction
*	Multiplication
/	Division
%	Percent
^	Exponentiation
Comparison Operators	
=	Equal to
<>	Not equal to
>	Greater than
>=	Greater than or equal to
<	Less than
<=	Less than or equal to
Reference Operators	
:	Range of contiguous cells (for example, **A1:C16**)
,	Range of noncontiguous cells (for example, **A1,B2**)
[space]	The cell or range shared by two references. For example, **=SUM(B1: B10 A5:D6)** adds the contents of cells B5 and B6 because these cells are at the intersection of the ranges B1:B10 and A5:D6.
Text Operator	
&	Concatenates (joins) the specified values. For example, if cell A1 contains 50 and cell A2 contains 50, the formula **=A1&A2** returns *5050*—the cell contents joined together rather than added together.

TABLE 8-1 Operators for Formulas

Operator	Explanation
–	Negation (negative numbers)
%	Percentage
^	Exponentiation
*, /	Multiplication, division
+, –	Addition, subtraction
&	Concatenation
=, <>, <, <=, >, >=	Comparison operators

TABLE 8-2   Operator Precedence in Descending Order

giving 4500? Or does Excel multiply 100 by 5 and subtract the result (500) from 1000, giving 500? As you can see, the same calculation gives quite different results depending on the order in which its operations are performed.

In the example, Excel multiplies 100 by 5 and subtracts 500 from 1000 using its default settings, so the result is 500. Table 8-2 shows the order of *operator precedence*—the order in which Excel evaluates the operators—in descending order. When a formula uses two operators that share a precedence, Excel evaluates the operators from left to right, in the same direction as you read.

You can change operator precedence in a formula by using parentheses to indicate which items you want to calculate first. For example, to evaluate the formula **=1000-100*5** the other way, enter **=(1000-100)*5**. Excel then subtracts 100 from 1000 and then multiplies the result (900) by 5.

When you nest multiple items, Excel evaluates the most deeply nested item first. For example, in the formula **=(100-(10*5))/20**, Excel evaluates 10*5 first, because that item is nested within two sets of parentheses. You can use many levels of nested parentheses if necessary.

If you find it hard to remember the order of operator precedence, you can use parentheses even when they're not strictly necessary.

When you're editing a formula, Excel displays differently nested parentheses in different colors to help you keep track of which parenthesis is paired with which. When you use ← and → to move through a formula that you're editing in the active cell or in the Formula bar, Excel flashes the paired parenthesis for each parenthesis you move over. If you omit a parenthesis in a formula, Excel does its best to warn you of the problem and identify where the missing parenthesis should go.

Control Excel's Automatic Calculation

As discussed in "Set Calculation and Formulas Options" in Chapter 2, Excel's default setting is to automatically calculate all formulas every time you make a change. If you're using a worksheet or workbook with enough data and complex calculations to slow down your computer while you're entering data in the workbook, you may prefer to turn off automatic calculation. To do so, follow these steps:

 **Break Down a Complex Formula into Simpler Steps**

Even with Excel's help, formulas with many deeply nested items can be confusing to enter and difficult to troubleshoot when they don't produce the results that you expect.

If math isn't your forte, you may prefer to break a complex calculation down into a sequence of steps that you perform in separate cells. That way, you can trace the steps of the calculation more easily. And you can hide the rows or columns that contain the cells (or use a hidden worksheet) if you prefer not to let other people see them.

1. Click the Office button, and then click Excel Options. Excel displays the Excel Options dialog box.

2. In the left panel, click the Formulas category. Excel displays the Formulas options.

3. In the Calculation Options area, select the Manual option button, and then make sure the Recalculate Workbook Before Saving check box is selected.

4. Click the OK button. Excel closes the Excel Options dialog box and applies the settings.

 You can also switch calculation mode quickly by choosing Formulas | Calculation | Calculation Options, and then choosing Automatic, Automatic Except For Data Tables, or Manual from the panel. However, you can't access the Recalculate Workbook Before Saving setting without opening the Excel Options dialog box.

If you do turn off automatic calculation, Excel displays *Calculate* near the left end of the status bar when the workbook contains uncalculated calculations. You can force calculation manually:

■ To force calculation for the active worksheet, press SHIFT-F9 or choose Formulas | Calculation | Calculate Sheet.

■ To force calculation for the entire active workbook, press F9 or choose Formulas | Calculation | Calculate Now.

Understand How Excel Handles Numbers

Numbers in Excel aren't necessarily as precise as they appear to be. To avoid running into avoidable errors in calculations, you should understand how Excel handles numbers.

The key limitation is that numbers in Excel can be up to 15 digits long. Those 15 digits can appear on either side of the decimal point—for example, 123456789012345, 1234567.89012345, or .123456789012345. Excel changes all digits beyond the 15th to 0. So if you enter **1234567890123456**, Excel actually uses 1234567890123450. For very precise calculations, this truncation can cause problems.

You can format Excel to display up to 30 decimal places, but there's no reason to do so.

Refer to Cells and Ranges in Formulas

To refer to a cell or a range in a formula, enter its address either by typing or by using the mouse. When you use the mouse, Excel displays a flashing border to indicate the selected cell or range. When a formula includes two or more ranges, Excel uses different-colored borders to help you keep them straight.

To refer to a whole column, specify its letter as the beginning and end of the range. For example, to make column K reflect the contents of column C, click the column heading for column K, enter **=C:C**, and then press CTRL-ENTER to enter the formula in all the cells of the selected column.

Similarly, to refer to a whole row, specify its number as the beginning and end of the range: for example, **4:4**. To refer to a set of columns, specify the beginning and ending letters: for example, **A:D**. To refer to a set of rows, specify the beginning and ending numbers: for example, **1:2**.

Refer to Other Worksheets and Other Workbooks in Formulas

To refer to another worksheet in the same workbook in a formula, enter the worksheet name (in single quotes if the name includes one or more spaces) and an exclamation point (!) before the cell address or range address. You can type the name if you choose, but most people find it easier to click the worksheet tab, and then select the cell or range with the mouse. That way, Excel enters the details automatically for you, including single quotes if they're necessary.

This example refers to cell F34 on the worksheet named Computer Equipment:

```
='Computer Equipment'!F34
```

This example refers to cell J17 on the worksheet named Software:

```
=Software!J17
```

 If you rename a worksheet, Excel automatically changes the sheet name in all formulas that reference the worksheet.

A formula can also refer to a worksheet in another workbook, but you need to be careful not to move the referenced workbook—if you do, the formula will stop working unless you change the formula to point to the correct location.

To refer to another workbook, enter the workbook path and filename in brackets ([]) followed by the worksheet name. You can type the reference manually, but the easiest way to enter a reference to a worksheet in another workbook is by opening the workbook. Follow these steps:

1. Open the source workbook (the workbook to which you want to create the reference).
2. Start the formula in the destination workbook.

3. Use the View | Windows | Switch Windows menu to switch to the source workbook. If the source workbook window is visible, you can simply click the window instead.

4. Select the appropriate worksheet and cell.

5. Use the View | Windows | Switch Windows menu to switch back to the destination workbook.

6. Complete the formula. Excel enters the reference automatically for you.

Try Entering a Formula

For practice, try entering a formula. Follow these steps:

1. Enter **2000** in cell A1, **4000** in cell A2, and **2** in cell B1.

2. Select cell B2:

B2		f_x			
A	B	C	D	E	F
1	2000	2			
2	4000				
3					

3. Type =(.

4. Click cell A1. Excel enters it in the formula:

MATCH		X ✓ f_x	=(A1		
A	B	C	D	E	F
1	2000	2			
2	4000	=(A1			
3					

5. Type +.

6. Click cell A2. Excel enters it in the formula:

MATCH		X ✓ f_x	=(A1+A2		
A	B	C	D	E	F
1	2000	2			
2	4000	=(A1+A2			
3					

7. Type)/.

8

8. Click cell B1. Excel enters it in the formula:

MATCH	▼	⊘ ✗ ✓ ƒx	=(A1+A2)/B1			
	A	B	C	D	E	F
1	2000	2				
2	4000	=(A1+A2)/B1				
3						

9. Press ENTER or click the Enter button to enter the formula. Excel completes the formula and displays the result in cell B2:

B2	▼	⊘ ƒx	=(A1+A2)/B1			
	A	B	C	D	E	F
1	2000	2				
2	4000	3000				
3						

TIP

You can quickly copy a formula from one cell to other cells by using the Copy and Paste commands, by using CTRL-drag and drop, by using the options on the Home | Editing | Fill panel, or by dragging the AutoFill handle.

Use Range Names and Table Names in Formulas

An easy way of referring to a cell or a range is to define a name for it. (The section "Assign a Name to a Range" in Chapter 1 discusses how to define range names.) You can then use the range name in formulas instead of specifying the cell address or range address. This technique is particularly useful for simplifying the process of referring to cells and ranges on other worksheets in a workbook. For example, instead of using **='Computer Equipment'!F34** to refer to a cell on another worksheet, you could assign a name (say, **TotalSales**) to it, and then refer to the name: **=TotalSales**.

CAUTION

If you use range names in formulas, be careful when deleting range names. Otherwise, any formula that references the deleted range name will display a #NAME? error.

If you create a table (a named area of a worksheet; see Chapter 9 for details), you can refer to all of it or part of it by name rather than using a cell reference. Even if you change the extent of the table (for example, by adding rows to it or deleting columns from it), Excel gives you the correct part of it.

For example, say you create a table named **Sedona_Sales**. You can refer to it by typing the beginning of its name and then selecting the name from the list of functions and names that Excel displays, as shown here:

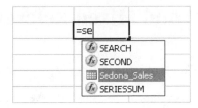

Once you've selected the name, type **[** to display a list of available items in the table, as shown here:

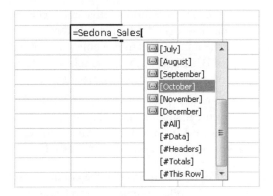

Depending on the item you select, you can type **,** (a comma) to "drill down" further into the table, as shown here:

Here are some examples using the table named **Sedona_Sales**:

- ■ **Sedona_Sales[#Headers]** references the headers in the table.
- ■ **Sedona_Sales[#All]** references the entire table all at once.
- ■ **Sedona_Sales[#Headers],[#Column1]** references the first column's headers in the table.

8

Use Absolute, Relative, and Mixed References in Formulas

Excel distinguishes between three kinds of references for cells and ranges:

- An *absolute reference* always refers to the same cell, even when you move or copy the formula to another cell or range. For example, if you enter in cell A1 a formula that contains an absolute reference to cell B1 and then move the formula to cell C1, the reference will still be to cell B1.

- A *relative reference* refers to a cell's position relative to the cell that contains the formula. For example, if you enter in cell A1 a formula that contains a relative reference to cell B2, Excel notes that the reference is to one column over and one row down. If you move the formula to cell B1, Excel changes the relative reference to refer to cell C2, because C2 is one column over and one row down from the formula's new location.

- A *mixed reference* is a mixture of an absolute reference and a relative reference. A mixed reference can be absolute in column and relative in row, or relative in column and absolute in row. When you move a formula that contains a mixed reference, the relative part of the reference changes, while the absolute part stays the same.

A dollar sign before a column designation means that the column is absolute; no dollar sign means that the column is relative. A dollar sign before a row number means that the row is absolute; no dollar sign means that the row is relative. For example:

- $A$1 is an absolute reference to cell A1.
- A1 is a relative reference to cell A1.
- $A1 is a mixed reference to cell A1 with the column absolute.
- A$1 is a mixed reference to cell A1 with the row absolute.

Excel's default setting is to use relative references, so if you need to use absolute references, you must change them. The easiest way to change the reference type is by selecting the reference in a formula and pressing F4 to cycle through the options: absolute ($A$1), mixed with absolute row (A$1), mixed with absolute column ($A1), and relative. You can also type the necessary dollar signs manually.

 *If you move a formula by using cut and paste, Excel doesn't change any relative references that the formula contains.*

Work with Array Formulas

An *array formula* is a formula that works on an array (a range of cells) to perform multiple calculations that generate either a single result or multiple results.

To enter an array formula, create the formula as explained earlier in this chapter, but press CTRL-SHIFT-ENTER instead of ENTER. Excel displays braces ({ })around an array formula. Excel enters the braces automatically when you create an array formula. You can't achieve the same effect by typing the braces manually.

The example spreadsheet in Figure 8-1 tracks vacation hours used by employees. Each employee starts off (on an unseen area of the worksheet) with a number of accrued vacation hours. The worksheet contains details, in date order, of the vacation hours taken by each employee and a running total showing the number of vacation hours each employee has left.

The array formula in cell D8 is {=SUM(IF($B$2:B8=B8,$C$2:C8))}. The formula first compares each of the previous cells in column B to the current cell in column B. If the IF function returns TRUE, the second argument in the formula adds the contents of the corresponding cell in column C to the running total in column D. The effect is to keep a running total of the vacation hours available by employee.

You can edit an array formula that you've previously created by selecting the cell or the range of cells that contains it. If the array formula is entered in multiple cells, you need to select them all before you can edit the array formula.

Display Formulas in a Worksheet

When editing or troubleshooting formulas, you may benefit from displaying the formulas themselves rather than their results in the cells that contain them. To toggle the display between

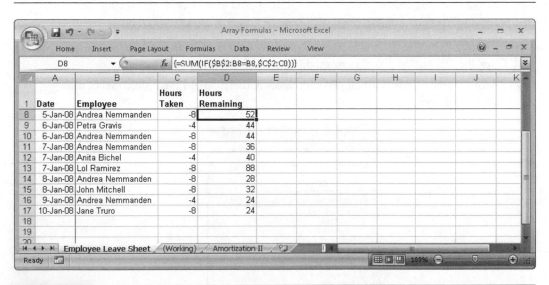

FIGURE 8-1   An array formula works on a range of cells to perform multiple calculations.

formula results and formulas, press CTRL-` (that's the slanted ` character, not the apostrophe) or follow these steps:

1. Activate the worksheet you want to affect.

2. Click the Office button, and then click Excel Options. Excel displays the Excel Options dialog box.

3. In the left panel, click the Advanced category. Excel displays the Advanced options.

4. In the Display Options For This Worksheet area, select the Show Formulas In Cells Instead Of Their Calculated Results check box.

5. Click the OK button. Excel closes the Excel Options dialog box.

When displaying formulas, Excel automatically increases column width so that you can see more of each formula. Excel restores the previous column widths when you redisplay the formula results.

Hide Formulas from Other Users

You can prevent other users from examining or editing your formulas by formatting the relevant cells as hidden and then protecting the worksheet or worksheets. To do so, follow these steps:

1. Select the cell or range of cells that contain the formulas.

2. Choose Home | Cells | Format | Cells. Excel displays the Protection tab of the Format Cells dialog box. (Alternatively, press CTRL-1, and then click the Protection tab.)

3. Select the Hidden check box. Make sure the Locked check box is selected as well (it should be selected by default).

4. Click the OK button. Excel closes the Format Cells dialog box.

5. Choose Home | Cells | Format | Protect Sheet. Excel displays the Protect Sheet dialog box, shown here:

6. Ensure that the Protect Worksheet And Contents Of Locked Cells check box is selected.

7. Type the password for protecting the worksheet in the Password To Unprotect Sheet text box.

8. Click the OK button. Excel closes the Protect Sheet dialog box and displays the Confirm Password dialog box.

9. Type the password again, and then click the OK button. Excel closes the Confirm Password dialog box.

If you forget the password you use for protecting a worksheet, you won't be able to make any changes to the items you protected. However, if you find yourself in this situation, you can find various utilities for cracking Office passwords on the Internet.

Troubleshoot Formulas

No matter how careful you are, many things can go wrong with formulas, so you need to know how to go about troubleshooting them. This section discusses how to deal with the eight common errors that frequently appear in formulas. Then you'll learn how to fix apparent errors caused by formatting, as well as real errors caused by problems with operator precedence and range changes. Finally, you'll see how to use Excel's automatic error-checking features, such as the Formula AutoCorrect feature, and how to supplement or replace this automatic checking with manual checking as needed.

Understand and Fix Basic Errors in Formulas

If you make a mistake while entering a formula, Excel lets you know there's a problem by displaying the dialog box shown here.

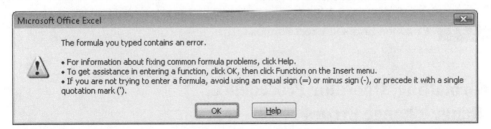

Click the Help button to display help on correcting problems with formulas. If you click the OK button, Excel displays the formula for editing and won't enter it in the cell until you've fixed the problem.

Table 8-3 explains the eight errors you're most likely to see in worksheets, in approximate order of popularity, and how to fix them.

Error	What's Wrong	How to Fix the Problem
####	The formula is fine, but the cell is too narrow to display the formula result.	Widen the column.
#NAME?	The formula contains a misspelled function name or the name of a nonexistent range.	If the problem is a function name or a misspelled range name or table name, correct it. If you've deleted a range name or table name, define it again.
#N/A	No valid value is available.	Enter a valid value if necessary.
#REF!	The formula contains an invalid cell reference or range reference. For example, you may have deleted a cell or range that the formula needs.	Change the formula to remove the invalid reference.
#DIV/0!	The formula is attempting to divide by zero.	If the divisor value is actually 0, change it. If a blank cell is producing the 0 value, add an IF() statement to supply the #N/A value or a usable value.
#VALUE!	The formula contains an invalid argument—for example, text instead of a number.	Correct the argument or change the formula.
#NULL!	The specified two ranges have no intersection.	Correct one or both ranges so that they intersect.
#NUM!	The number specified isn't valid for the function or formula. For example, using a POWER function has generated a number larger than Excel can handle, or SQRT (the square root function) has been fed a negative number.	Correct the number to suit the function.

TABLE 8-3   Common Errors in Excel Formulas

Fix Formatting, Operator Precedence, and Range-Change Errors

Beyond the basic errors explained in the previous section, you may also run into apparent errors caused by formatting, real errors caused by Excel's default order of operator precedence, and real errors caused by the ranges referenced in formulas being changed.

Formatting Makes the Displayed Result Incorrect

If the result that appears in a cell is obviously incorrect but the underlying formula seems to be correct, check that the cell's formatting isn't forcing Excel to round the result for the display.

For example, if you divide 2 by 3 and get the result 1, you might suspect a division error. But if the result cell is formatted to display no decimal places, Excel rounds 0.6667 to 1. There's no error, even though there appears to be—but you may want to change the formatting to remove the apparent error.

Operator Precedence Causes an Incorrect Result

If a formula gives a result that's obviously incorrect, check the operator precedence for errors. Enter parentheses to specify which calculations need to be performed out of the normal order of operator precedence.

Range Changes Introduce Errors in a Formula

Another prime source of errors in a formula is changes to the ranges to which the formula refers. To check whether this has happened, select the formula and press F2 to edit it. Use ← and → to move through the formula, and watch as Excel's Range Finder feature selects each range referenced. When you identify an error, correct the range involved by dragging its borders or by typing in the correct references.

Understand Formula AutoCorrect and How to Use It

Excel's Formula AutoCorrect feature watches as you enter formulas and tries to identify errors as you create them. When Formula AutoCorrect catches a mistake in a formula you're entering, it suggests how to fix it. For example, if you type **A1;B2** in a formula instead of A1:B2, Formula AutoCorrect displays a message box alerting you to the error, suggesting how to fix it, as shown here:

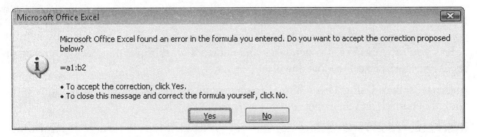

Click the Yes button to accept the suggestion, or click the No button to return to the cell so that you can edit the formula manually.

Configure Error-Checking Options

You can configure how Excel handles errors in worksheets by selecting and clearing the check boxes in the Error Checking area and the Error Checking Rules area of the Formulas category in the Excel Options dialog box (see Figure 8-2). Click the Office button, choose Excel Options, and then click the Formulas category in the left panel.

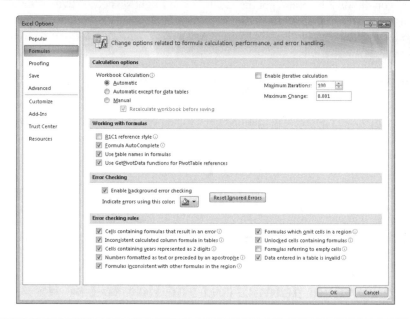

FIGURE 8-2 Configure error-checking options in the Formulas category in the Excel Options dialog box.

You can then choose among the following options in the Error Checking area:

- **Enable Background Error Checking**   Select this check box if you want Excel to check your workbooks for errors as you work. Background error checking is usually helpful, unless you're working with such large and complex workbooks that background error checking causes Excel to slow down.

- **Indicate Errors Using This Color**   To change the color Excel uses for marking errors, click this button, and then choose a color from the panel.

- **Reset Ignored Errors**   Sometimes you may need to tell Excel to ignore an error while you develop a worksheet. You can then click this button to tell Excel to return to the errors and check them again. You may want to use this option when you receive a workbook from someone else and need to make sure it doesn't contain any hidden errors that that person has ignored.

The Error Checking Rules area offers the following options:

- **Cells Containing Formulas That Result In An Error**   Select this check box if you want Excel to display error indicators in cells. Usually, the indicators are helpful, but you may sometimes want to suppress them so that they don't distract you.

- **Inconsistent Calculated Column Formulas In Tables**   Select this check box if you want Excel to flag individual cells that appear to contain the wrong formulas or results compared to the rest of the table column they're in. If all the column cells should contain similar formulas, this option is useful, but you may want to turn it off if you create tables that use different formulas in cells in the same column. For example, if you have three columns showing monthly sales totals and then a column that adds those totals to make a quarterly sales total, Excel flags the quarterly sales total formula as being inconsistent with the other formulas.

■ **Cells Containing Years Represented As 2 Digits**   Select this check box to make Excel flag cells containing dates that show the year as two digits (for example, 2/12/07) rather than four digits (for example, 2/12/2007). This setting helps you avoid getting twentieth century dates instead of twenty-first century dates by mistake.

■ **Numbers Formatted As Text Or Preceded By An Apostrophe**   Select this check box if you want Excel to flag numbers in cells formatted as text or that are preceded by an apostrophe (which makes Excel treat them as labels rather than numbers). This option too is usually helpful.

■ **Formulas Inconsistent With Other Formulas In The Region**   Select this check box if you want Excel to flag formulas that appear not to be correct in their settings. For example, if cell A3 contains the formula **=A1+A2** and cell C3 contains the formula **=C1+C2**, Excel flags the formula **=A1+A2** in cell B3 because the formula **=B1+B2** would be consistent.

■ **Formulas Which Omit Cells In A Region**   Select this check box if you want Excel to double-check that you haven't inadvertently omitted cells when you enter a formula that refers to most of a region but not all of it.

■ **Unlocked Cells Containing Formulas**   Select this check box if you want Excel to flag formulas in unlocked cells when the rest of the worksheet is locked.

■ **Formulas Referring To Empty Cells**   Select this check box if you want Excel to flag formulas that refer to empty cells that may cause problems in calculations.

■ **Data Entered In A Table Is Invalid**   Select this check box if you want Excel to flag cells containing data that's invalid for the column data type. This setting applies to tables connected to SharePoint data.

When Excel identifies an error that contravenes a rule that's selected, it displays a green triangle in the upper-left corner of the affected cell. Select the cell to display a Smart Tag, and then click the Smart Tag to display a menu that explains the problem and offers possible solutions.

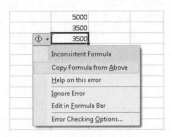

Audit Formulas and Check for Errors Manually

If you turn off Excel's error checking, it's a good idea to check your worksheets manually for errors; if you use error checking, you may still want to check manually to ensure that you haven't ignored any cells flagged with green triangles.

You'll see an example of checking for errors manually in a minute. But first, let's look at the formula auditing commands that Excel offers, because you'll often need to use these to track down errors.

Use the Formula Auditing Commands to Track Down Errors

The commands in the Formula Auditing group on the Formulas tab of the Ribbon (shown here) enable you to track down errors in your formulas more quickly.

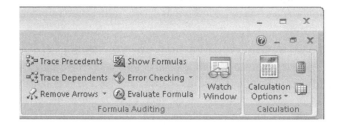

You'll see the Formula Auditing group's controls in action in the next sections, apart from the Watch Window button, which you met in the section "Monitor Calculations with the Watch Window" in Chapter 7.

Trace the Precedents or Dependents of a Cell

To determine which cells a particular value is derived from, you can select the cell and examine its formula in the Formula bar. But checking the derivation of a number of formulas that seem to be giving an incorrect result is tedious and time consuming. To help you, Excel provides tools for tracing a cell's *precedents* (the cells used to make up the value in this cell) and *dependents* (the cells that use this cell in their formulas).

Click the Trace Precedents button in the Formula Auditing group to make Excel display an arrow to show which cells were used to create the value in the active cell. In this illustration, you can see that the range G2:G6 makes up the value in cell G7:

	G7	▾	*fx*	=SUM(G2:G6)				
	A	B	C	D	E	F	G	H
1	Quantity	Item	Description	Price	Subtotal	Tax	Total	
2	1	P14829	WIPER FRONT	$4.99	$4.99	$0.41	$5.40	
3	4	P15083	WIPER BACK	$8.99	$35.96	$2.97	$38.93	
4	1	P15910	SEAT BLADE	$22.99	$22.99	$1.90	$24.89	
5	10	E44493	SEAT BACK	$138.99	$1,389.90	$114.67	$1,504.57	
6	6	E44052	HEAD REST	$84.99	$509.94	$42.07	$552.01	
7					$1,963.78	$162.01	$2,125.79	
8								

Click the Trace Precedents button again to display the precedents of those cells if necessary. In this illustration, the topmost arrow shows that cells E2 and F2 make up the value in cell G2, and the four arrows beneath it show that the next four rows perform corresponding calculations—E3 and F3 make up G3, and so on:

	G7			f_x	=SUM(G2:G6)			
	A	B	C	D	E	F	G	H
1	Quantity	Item	Description	Price	Subtotal	Tax	Total	
2	1	P14829	WIPER FRONT	$4.99	$4.99	$0.41	$5.40	
3	4	P15083	WIPER BACK	$8.99	$35.96	$2.97	$38.93	
4	1	P15910	SEAT BLADE	$22.99	$22.99	$1.90	$24.89	
5	10	E44493	SEAT BACK	$138.99	$1,389.90	$114.67	$1,504.57	
6	6	E44052	HEAD REST	$84.99	$509.94	$42.07	$552.01	
7					$1,963.78	$162.01	$2,125.79	
8								

If your formulas go further, as the ones in the example do, you can pursue them back to their origins by clicking the Trace Precedents button once more for each step. This illustration shows the next (and final) stage of the formula:

	G7			f_x	=SUM(G2:G6)			
	A	B	C	D	E	F	G	H
1	Quantity	Item	Description	Price	Subtotal	Tax	Total	
2	1	P14829	WIPER FRONT	$4.99	$4.99	$0.41	$5.40	
3	4	P15083	WIPER BACK	$8.99	$35.96	$2.97	$38.93	
4	1	P15910	SEAT BLADE	$22.99	$22.99	$1.90	$24.89	
5	10	E44493	SEAT BACK	$138.99	$1,389.90	$114.67	$1,504.57	
6	6	E44052	HEAD REST	$84.99	$509.94	$42.07	$552.01	
7					$1,963.78	$162.01	$2,125.79	
8								

You can remove precedent arrows one set at a time by choosing Remove Arrows | Remove Precedent Arrows. So if Excel is displaying three stages of precedents (as in the example), the first click removes the third stage, the second click removes the second stage, and the third click removes the first stage.

To get rid of all precedent and dependent arrows instantly, click the Remove Arrows button.

Instead of working backward through a formula by tracing precedents, you may need to see which calculations a particular value is used in. To do so, trace its dependents by clicking the Trace Dependents button. Each click displays one stage of calculation. Here's the first stage of the calculation:

	A2			f_x	1			
	A	B	C	D	E	F	G	H
1	Quantity	Item	Description	Price	Subtotal	Tax	Total	
2	1	P14829	WIPER FRONT	$4.99	$4.99	$0.41	$5.40	
3	4	P15083	WIPER BACK	$8.99	$35.96	$2.97	$38.93	
4	1	P15910	SEAT BLADE	$22.99	$22.99	$1.90	$24.89	
5	10	E44493	SEAT BACK	$138.99	$1,389.90	$114.67	$1,504.57	
6	6	E44052	HEAD REST	$84.99	$509.94	$42.07	$552.01	
7					$1,963.78	$162.01	$2,125.79	
8								

8

Here's the second stage:

	A	B	C	D	E	F	G	H
	A2		fx	1				
1	Quantity	Item	Description	Price	Subtotal	Tax	Total	
2	1	P14829	WIPER FRONT	$4.99	$4.99	$0.41	$5.40	
3	4	P15083	WIPER BACK	$8.99	$35.96	$2.97	$38.93	
4	1	P15910	SEAT BLADE	$22.99	$22.99	$1.90	$24.89	
5	10	E44493	SEAT BACK	$138.99	$1,389.90	$114.67	$1,504.57	
6	6	E44052	HEAD REST	$84.99	$509.94	$42.07	$552.01	
7					$1,963.78	$162.01	$2,125.79	
8								

And here's the third stage:

	A	B	C	D	E	F	G	H
	A2		fx	1				
1	Quantity	Item	Description	Price	Subtotal	Tax	Total	
2	1	P14829	WIPER FRONT	$4.99	$4.99	$0.41	$5.40	
3	4	P15083	WIPER BACK	$8.99	$35.	$2.97	$38.93	
4	1	P15910	SEAT BLADE	$22.99	$22.99	$1.90	$24.89	
5	10	E44493	SEAT BACK	$138.99	$1,389.90	$114.67	$1,504.57	
6	6	E44052	HEAD REST	$84.99	$509.94	$42.07	$552.01	
7					$1,963.78	$162.01	$2,125.79	
8								

You can remove dependent arrows one set at a time by clicking the Remove Dependent Arrows button.

If a precedent or dependent cell is on another worksheet in the same workbook or a different workbook, Excel displays an arrow to a small worksheet symbol:

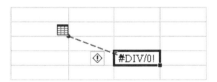

You can't pursue this precedent or dependent trace directly, but you can double-click the arrow to display the Go To dialog box, which provides a reference for displaying the worksheet and accessing the relevant cell or range.

Trace an Error

To trace an error, select a cell that contains an error value, click the drop-down button on the Error Checking button, and then choose Trace Error. Excel displays blue arrows to show the parts of the calculation that are okay (if any are) and red arrows for the parts that produce errors. In this illustration you can't see the colors, but the Smart Tag (the button with the exclamation point) in cell D4 indicates that the problems start in cell E4:

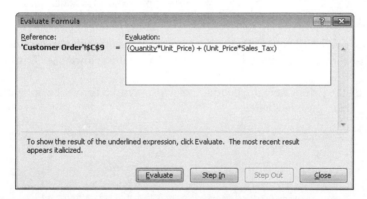

Click the Remove Arrows button to remove the error-tracing arrows from the worksheet.

Evaluate a Formula

To step through a particular formula and determine what's going wrong, select the cell that
contains the formula, and then click the Evaluate Formula button in the Formula Auditing group.
Excel displays the following Evaluate Formula dialog box:

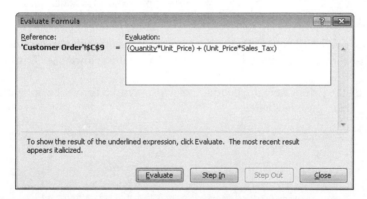

From here, you can click the Evaluate button to evaluate the underlined expression, or click
the Step In button to display the details of the expression. This illustration shows the Evaluate
Formula dialog box after stepping in:

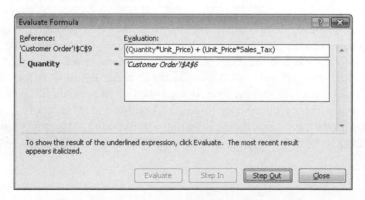

8

After stepping in, click the Step Out button to return to evaluating the formula. Click the Close button when you've finished evaluating the formula.

Check for Errors

To check for errors in the active worksheet, click the Error Checking button in the Formula Auditing group. This spreadsheet contains a straightforward error that's relatively hard to catch by eye because it's visually camouflaged:

	A	B	C	D	E	F	G	H
	F11			fx				
1	Quantity	Item	Description	Price	Subtotal	Tax	Total	
2	1	P14829	WIPER FRONT	$4.99	$4.99	$0.41	$5.40	
3	4	P15083	WIPER BACK	$8.99	$35.96	$2.97	$38.93	
4	1	P15910	SEAT BLADE	$22.99	#VALUE!	#VALUE!	#VALUE!	
5	10	E44493	SEAT BACK	$138.99	$1,389.90	$114.67	$1,504.57	
6	6	E44052	HEAD REST	$84.99	$509.94	$42.07	$552.01	
7					#VALUE!	#VALUE!	#VALUE!	
8								

You can see the six #VALUE! error cells easily enough, but it's difficult to detect immediately that the problem is caused by the entry in cell A4, which contains a lowercase L instead of the number 1.

When you click the Error Checking button, Excel displays the Error Checking dialog box with details of the error, as shown here:

Error Checking	? ✕
Error in cell E4	Help on this error
=D4*A4	Show Calculation Steps...
Error in Value	Ignore Error
A value used in the formula is of the wrong data type.	Edit in Formula Bar
Options...	Previous Next

If the Error Checking dialog box contains the Show Calculation Steps button, you can click it to display the Evaluate Formula dialog box, which provides options for stepping your way through the error to identify where it occurs. This option can be a considerable help in pinning down where an error occurs in the formula. Instead of displaying the Evaluate Formula dialog box, you can click the Ignore Error button to ignore the error, or click the Edit In Formula Bar button to display the formula in the Formula bar while leaving the Error Checking dialog box open.

After dealing with the error, click the Next button to move to the next error or the Previous button to move to the previous error.

Chapter 9

Organize Data with Excel Databases

How to…

- Understand what an Excel table is
- Enter data in a table
- Sort a table
- Find and replace data in a table
- Filter a table to find records that match certain criteria
- Link an Excel worksheet to an external database
- Perform web queries to bring web data into Excel

If you need to organize and manipulate a large amount of data, you can create a table in an Excel worksheet. This chapter discusses how to create Excel tables, enter data in them, and sort and filter the data to find the information you need. You'll also learn how to link an Excel worksheet to an external database (for example, an Access database) so that you can extract data to an Excel worksheet and manipulate it there, and how to perform web queries to bring web data into worksheets.

Understand What an Excel Table Is

A *table* in Excel is an organized collection of data. In a table, each row represents a data *record*—for example, the details of an invoice or the name, address, and contact information for a customer. Each column represents a *field* in the record. In the case of an invoice, one column might contain the field for the invoice number, another the field for the date, another the field for the purchaser's name, and so on; in the case of a customer, separate fields typically contain the last name, first name, middle initial, title, and so on.

Figure 9-1 shows a section of an example table in Excel.

	A	B	C	D	E	F	G	H	I	J	K	
6	Quantity	Stock	Brand	Manufacturer	Category	Description	Color	Price ($)	Horiz. Re	Vert. Res.	Weight (l	More
7	4	SDK848	SkullDam	000348392E	Other	SkullBand monitor decor	Many	$24.99	#N/A	#N/A	2.0	
8	4	LCD001	Elcidee	ED-440-1500J	LCD Monitor	Elcidee 15 inch LCD	Jet	$199.99	1024	768	7.5	Contra
9	2	LCD002	Elcidee	ED-440-1500B	LCD Monitor	Elcidee 15 inch LCD	Beige	$199.99	1024	768	7.5	Contra
10	2 on 4/14/08	LCD003	Elcidee	ED-440-1700J	LCD Monitor	Elcidee 17 inch LCD	Jet	$299.99	1280	1024	10.9	Contra
11	1	LCD004	Elcidee	ED-440-1700B	LCD Monitor	Elcidee 17 inch LCD	Beige	$299.99	1280	1024	10.9	Contra
12	1	LCD005	Elcidee	ED-440-1800J	LCD Monitor	Elcidee 18 inch LCD	Jet	$499.99	1280	1024	15.3	Contra
13	1	LCD006	Elcidee	ED-440-1800B	LCD Monitor	Elcidee 18 inch LCD	Beige	$499.99	1280	1024	15.3	Contra
14	Special order	LCD007	Elcidee	ED-440-2000J	LCD Monitor	Elcidee 20 inch LCD	Jet	$999.99	1600	1200	25.0	Contra
15	Special order	LCD008	Elcidee	ED-440-2000B	LCD Monitor	Elcidee 20 inch LCD	Beige	$999.99	1600	1200	25.0	Contra
16	Special order	LCD009	Elcidee	ED-440-2200J	LCD Monitor	Elcidee 22 inch LCD	Jet	$1,299.99	2048	1536	33.6	Contra
17	Special order	LCD010	Elcidee	ED-440-2200B	LCD Monitor	Elcidee 22 inch LCD	Beige	$1,299.99	2048	1536	33.6	Contra
18	5	MCB121	Elcidee	ED-370-0001	Cable Monito	Elcidee VGA cable 1m	Gray	$9.99	#N/A	#N/A	1.0	
19	4	MCB122	Elcidee	ED-370-0002	Cable Monito	Elcidee DVI cable 1m	Gray	$12.99	#N/A	#N/A	1.0	
20	1	MCB123	Elcidee	ED-370-0003	Cable Monito	Elcidee VGA cable 2m	Gray	$12.99	#N/A	#N/A	1.0	
21	2	MCB124	Elcidee	ED-370-0004	Cable Monito	Elcidee DVI cable 2m	Gray	$14.99	#N/A	#N/A	1.0	
22	0	MCB125	Elcidee	ED-370-0005	Cable Monito	Elcidee VGA cable 3m	Gray	$14.99	#N/A	#N/A	1.2	
23	6	MCB126	Elcidee	ED-370-0006	Cable Monito	Elcidee DVI cable 3m	Gray	$16.99	#N/A	#N/A	1.2	
24	5	MCB127	Elcidee	ED-370-0007	Cable Monito	Elcidee VGA cable 5m	Gray	$16.99	#N/A	#N/A	1.2	
25	4	MCB128	Elcidee	ED-370-0008	Cable Monito	Elcidee DVI cable 5m	Cray	$19.99	#N/A	#N/A	1.2	
26	0	TBX801	Thorbox	THOR801	Computer Sy	Barebones P4 2.4GHz	Beige	$599.99	#N/A	#N/A	22.0	

FIGURE 9-1   The table used for many of this chapter's examples

 **Create Effective Tables**

Follow these tips to create effective tables in Excel:

■ Enter the names of the table's fields in the header row. Technically, a table doesn't have to have a header row. But if you want to use AutoFilter (discussed in "Perform Quick Filtering with AutoFilter," later in this chapter), or if you want to use forms to simplify data entry, your table needs a header row.

■ Make each label in the header row unique so that Excel (and you) can distinguish each field from the other fields. This requirement may seem a no-brainer—but if you extend an existing table by incorporating new fields, you may have to rename existing fields to give each a unique label. For example, if your table contains a field named E-mail for the record's e-mail address and you need to add another e-mail address, you might need to rename the E-mail field to E-mail 1 for uniqueness and clarity.

■ Keep the column labels reasonably concise, because Excel displays them on data entry forms you use for the table. One long label produces an awkwardly wide form and wide gaps between shorter labels and their fields, which can make them slower to read.

■ Make sure the table area doesn't contain any blank rows or columns, because these can interfere with Excel's sorting and searching.

Create a Table

To create a table, follow these steps:

1. Type the headings for the table, together with at least one row of data. You can expand the table as needed later on, so you don't need to select the entire area that the table will occupy.

 While you're developing the table, you may want to use sample data rather than real data, but make sure that it includes items in all the fields the table will use.

2. Select the range that you want to turn into a table.

3. Choose Insert | Tables | Table. Excel displays the Create Table dialog box, shown here:

4. Make sure the Where Is The Data For Your Table? text box shows the correct address. (If you selected the correct range, there should be no problem.) If not, click the Collapse Dialog button, select the correct range, and then click the Collapse Dialog button again.

5. If your table has a header row (as it should for ease of reading), make sure the My Table Has Headers check box is selected.

6. Click the OK button. Excel creates the table, gives it an automatic name, creates headers, and applies banded shading to it (see Figure 9-2). Excel also displays the Table Tools section of the Ribbon whenever the active cell is in the table (or part or all of the table is selected).

- If you selected the My Table Has Headers check box in the Create Table dialog box, Excel turns the top row of the table into headers that you can use to sort the data.

- If you cleared the My Table Has Headers check box, Excel inserts a row above the table and creates headers named Column1, Column2 in the new row.

NOTE *The colors for the shading come from the theme applied to the workbook. You can apply different shading if you find Excel's choice of shading hard to read.*

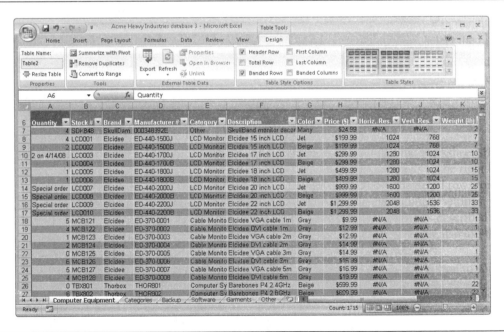

FIGURE 9-2 Excel automatically applies banded shading to tables to help you read along the rows.

Once you've created a table, Excel automatically keeps the column headings visible even when you scroll down the screen. Here are the column headings in their original position:

When you scroll down, Excel moves the headings into the column header row, as shown here:

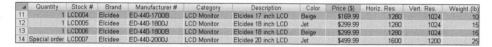

You don't need to freeze the panes to keep the headings visible, which is helpful.

Rename the Table

You can leave the table with its default name (Table1, Table2, or the next unused name), but it's a much better idea to give the table a name that lets you identify it easily—especially if you create several or many tables in the same workbook.

To rename the table, follow these steps:

1. Click anywhere in the table. Excel adds the Table Tools section to the Ribbon and displays the Design tab.

2. Click in the Table Name text box in the Properties group on the Design tab. Excel selects the current table name.

3. Type the new name for the table, following these naming rules:

   ■ Each table name in a workbook must be unique, so that you and Excel can identify the table.

   ■ A table name must start with either a letter or an underscore. After that, you can use any combination of letters, numbers, and underscores.

   ■ Excel doesn't allow you to use spaces in table names, and table names cannot be the same as certain built-in Excel names or the name of another object in the workbook. If you try to use an invalid name, Excel warns you of the problem.

4. Press ENTER. Excel applies the name to the table.

Choose Table Styles and Style Options

If you like the table style that Excel applied automatically to the table, you can simply leave it. If not, you can change the style at any point, as described in this section, applying either one of Excel's built-in styles or a custom style that you create yourself. You can also decide which table elements to display.

Apply a Built-In Table Style

To apply a built-in table style, click anywhere in the table, and then choose the style from the Table Styles panel (see Figure 9-3). Excel displays a preview as you move the mouse pointer over the styles.

Create a Custom Table Style

If none of the built-in table styles appeal to you, you can create your own style. Follow these steps:

1. Click anywhere in the table. Excel adds the Table Tools section to the Ribbon and displays the Design tab.

2. Choose Design | Table Styles | New Table Style. Excel displays the New Table Quick Style dialog box (see Figure 9-4).

3. Type the name for the style in the Name text box. This name appears when you hover the mouse pointer over the style's name in the Table Styles panel.

4. In the Table Element list box, select the element you want to change, and then click the Format button. Excel displays a reduced version of the Format Cells dialog box, containing only the Font tab, Border tab, and Fill tab. Use the controls on these tabs to

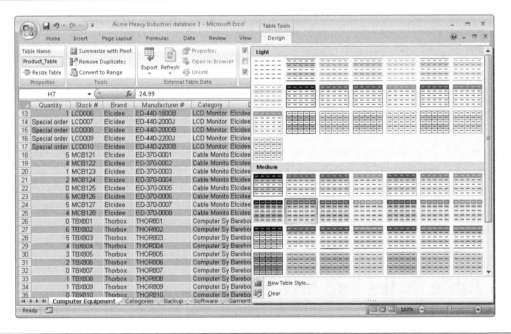

FIGURE 9-3 The Table Styles panel provides a wide range of preset table styles.

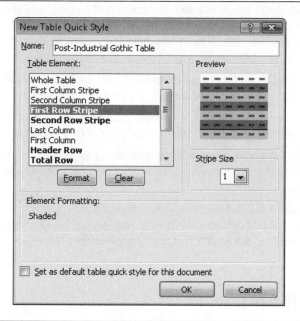

FIGURE 9-4   Use the New Table Quick Style dialog box to set up a custom table style.

specify the formatting for the element, and then click the OK button. For most of the elements, applying shading is most effective, so Excel displays the Fill tab of the Format Cells dialog box first.

5. Repeat step 3 for each element you want to change. The Preview section shows you how the table will look. The Table Element list box shows the names of items you've changed in boldface. You can remove the formatting you've applied by clicking an element in the Table Element list box and then clicking the Clear button.

6. If you want Excel to apply this table style automatically to new tables you create in this workbook, select the Set As Default Table Quick Style For This Document check box.

7. Click the OK button. Excel closes the New Table Quick Style dialog box and adds the table style to the Custom area at the top of the Table Styles panel.

8. To apply your new style, choose it from the Custom area at the top of the Table Styles panel.

Use Table Options to Specify Which Elements to Display

To decide which table elements to display, select or clear the check boxes in the Table Style Options group on the Design tab. These are the options:

- ■ **Header Row**   Select this check box to make Excel display the header row—the row of headings at the top of the columns. Seeing the headers is usually helpful.

- ■ **Total Row**   Select this check box to make Excel add a differently shaded row with a Total label immediately after the last row in the table. Excel puts a SUM formula in the last column, but you can change this formula or insert another formula by using the drop-down list in one of the cells in the Totals row, as shown in Figure 9-5.

- ■ **First Column**   Select this check box to make Excel apply different shading to the first column in the database to help you identify the first column visually.

- ■ **Last Column**   Select this check box to make Excel apply different shading to the last column in the database to help you identify the last column visually.

- ■ **Banded Rows**   Select this check box to make Excel apply different color bands to even rows and odd rows to make them easier to follow. In most table designs, Excel applies banded rows automatically.

- ■ **Banded Columns**   Select this check box to make Excel apply different color bands to even columns and odd columns. Normally, you'll want to use either banded rows or banded columns, but not both. (You *can* apply both, but the results are odd and not usually helpful.)

Enter Data in a Table

You can enter data in a table either by using standard data entry techniques (recapped in the next section, "Enter Data by Using Standard Techniques"), or by using a custom data entry form (discussed in the section after that, "Enter and Edit Data with Data Entry Forms"). Most likely, you'll choose to work with standard techniques while laying out the table and entering the first records. After the table contains more than a few records, a data entry form becomes invaluable.

	A	B	C	D	E
1	Year	U.S.	Canada	Mexico	Venezuela
2	2006	831	1943	1052	167
3	2007	1230	532	1225	477
4	2008	1063	1871	1386	1935
5	2009	1921	1915	119	1946
6	2010	1772	1192	1119	1183
7	2011	593	456	1924	821
8	2012	1072	339	1373	690
9	2013	251	1124	1053	757
10	2014	1461	1994	294	1127
11	Total				9103
12		None			
13		Average			
14		Count			
15		Count Numbers			
16		Max			
17		Min			
18		Sum			
19		StdDev			
		Var			
		More Functions			

FIGURE 9-5   To add formulas quickly to the last row in the table, select the Total Row check box, and then choose formulas from the drop-down lists.

Enter Data by Using Standard Techniques

You can enter data in a table by using standard Excel techniques:

- Type directly into a cell. To enter the same item in each cell in a range, select the range, type, and then press CTRL-ENTER.

- Use copy and paste or CTRL-drag and drop to reuse existing data.

- Use AutoFill to repeat the contents of the current cell or to extend the current table. Depending on the types of data your table contains, you may find it helpful to create custom AutoFill lists. The section "Create Custom AutoFill Lists," in Chapter 3, explains how to do so.

- If a column contains repetitive entries (such as product names or town names), AutoComplete will suggest a matching entry as soon as you type enough letters to distinguish it from all other entries.

- You can also reuse an existing entry by right-clicking the cell, choosing Pick From Drop-Down List, and then selecting the entry from the list that Excel displays. Because of the amount of clicking and scrolling that this technique entails, it's usually slower and clumsier than other methods—especially if the column contains a large number of different entries (rather than fewer repeated entries). However, it may be useful for complex entries that are awkward to type.

All these techniques work fine on a long list, but entering data in a table by moving around a huge worksheet gets old fast. If the columns in the table contain long entries, you'll either need to scroll sideways frequently or display only part of each column's contents. As soon as the table grows beyond a few screens of data, you'll probably want to use forms to make data entry faster and easier.

 When you enter a new record in a table manually, it's usually easier to enter the new record at the end of the table and then sort the table (if necessary) rather than locating the place where the new record should appear and inserting a row there.

Enter and Edit Data with Data Entry Forms

The most effective way of entering data in a table of any size or complexity is to use Excel's data form feature. A *data form* is a custom dialog box that Excel creates and populates with fields that reflect the column headings in the table. Figure 9-6 shows a data form derived from the sample table shown earlier in this chapter. Excel enters the worksheet's name in the title bar of the form, so you can easily see which table you're working on.

To use a data form, you must first add the Form command to the Quick Access Toolbar. Follow these steps:

1. Click the Customize Quick Access Toolbar drop-down button at the right end of the Quick Access Toolbar, and then choose More Commands from the drop-down menu. Excel displays the Customize category of the Excel Options dialog box.

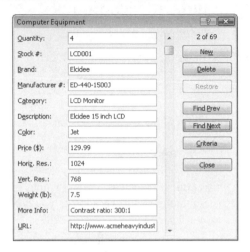

FIGURE 9-6   Excel's data entry forms enable you to view and enter data quickly without scrolling to the remote regions of the table.

2. In the Customize Quick Access Toolbar drop-down list, choose For All Documents if you want to make the Form button available in all workbooks. If you want the Form button to be available only in the current workbook, select the For *Workbook Name* item instead.

3. In the Choose Commands From drop-down list, select the Commands Not In The Ribbon item. Excel displays those commands in the left list box.

4. In the left list box, click the Form command, and then click the Add button. Excel adds the command after the last current item in the Quick Access Toolbar (in the right list box). Use the Move Up button to move it up the list if you want.

5. Click the OK button. Excel closes the Excel Options dialog box and displays the Form button on the Quick Access Toolbar.

To use a data form, activate a cell within the table, and then click the Form button you just added to the Quick Access Toolbar. Excel generates the data form from the table's column headings and displays the data from the first record in the table in it.

To use a data form, follow these steps:

1. Use the Find Prev button and Find Next button to navigate to other records in the table.

2. To change a record, navigate to it, make the changes, and press ENTER. To undo changes you've made to the current record, click the Restore button. This works until you commit the changes by pressing ENTER.

3. To add a new record to the table, click the New button. Enter the data for the new record in the form, then press ENTER. Excel adds the new record at the end of the table.

4. To delete the current record, click the Delete button. Excel displays a message box warning you that the record will be permanently deleted. Click the OK button to delete the record. Note that you won't be able to recover the record (you can't undo the deletion) unless you close the workbook without saving changes; if you do that, you'll lose any other changes you've made to the table since you last saved it.

5. To search for records that match only specific criteria, click the Criteria button. Excel clears the data form and displays *Criteria* above the New button. Specify the criteria in the appropriate boxes and click the Find Next button or Find Prev button.

6. To leave the criteria view, click the Form button to return to the regular form view.

TIP   *To find a particular blank field in a criteria search, enter = and nothing else in that field.*

Resize a Table

You can easily resize a table as needed to accommodate extra rows and columns. Other times, you may need to delete rows or columns from a table when you no longer require them.

Excel automatically expands a table for you when you enter data in a cell in the row immediately after the last row of the table or in the column immediately after the last column, or if you insert rows or columns. Likewise, if you delete one or more rows or columns from the table, Excel automatically reduces the table by that amount.

NOTE   *If Excel automatically adds to the table a row or column you don't want to include, click the AutoCorrect Options button that appears next to the expansion, and then choose Undo Table AutoExpansion from the drop-down menu. You can also choose Stop Automatically Expanding Tables from the drop-down menu to turn off AutoExpansion. To turn it back on, click the Office button, and then click Excel Options. In the Excel Options dialog box, click the Proofing category, and then click the AutoCorrect Options button. In the AutoCorrect dialog box, click the AutoFormat As You Type tab, select the Include New Rows And Columns In Table check box, and then click the OK button to close each dialog box in turn.*

To resize a table manually, drag the triangle in the lower-right corner of the lower-right cell in the table.

When you resize a table, Excel automatically updates any objects that are linked to the table. For example, say you've created a chart using all the data in a table. When you add a column to the table, Excel adds another category to the chart showing the new data.

Select Parts of a Table

You can select part or all of a table by dragging through it, but tables also provide the following selection shortcuts:

■   **Select a column**   Hover the mouse pointer over the column heading until it displays a downward-pointing arrow, and then click.

■ **Select a row**   Hover the mouse pointer over the left part of a cell in the leftmost column so that it displays a right-pointing arrow, and then click.

■ **Select the whole table**   Hover the mouse pointer over the upper-left corner of the upper-left cell in the table so that it displays an arrow pointing down and to the right, and then click.

Sort a Table

After entering data in the table, you'll probably need to sort it so that you can view related records together. For example, you might need to sort a product table by product category or a mailing table by last name.

Excel offers tools for quick sorting, for performing a multifield sort, and for defining custom criteria for sorting. However, before you sort the table at all, you may need to tag the records with the existing sort order.

Prepare to Sort a Table

If for any reason you need to be able to return your table to the order in which you created it, there's an additional step you must perform *before* you sort the table at all. (Or you might need to sort the table at first to get it into the preferred order that you want to be able to return to when necessary.)

Add another column to the table and give it a suitable name, such as Sort Order. Then enter the appropriate number in each cell: for example, enter **1** in the first cell, and then use AutoFill to enter the incremented series of numbers in the other cells. Once you've done this, you'll be able to sort the table by this column to restore its records to the original order.

   *"Use AutoFill to Enter Data Series Quickly," in Chapter 3, explains what AutoFill is and how to use it.*

Sort by a Single Field

The easiest type of sort to perform is a *quick sort,* which sorts data by a single field in ascending order (A to Z, lowest numbers to highest) or descending order (Z to A, highest numbers to lowest). To perform a quick sort, follow these steps:

1.   Activate a cell in the column that contains the field you want to sort.

2.   Choose Data | Sort & Filter | Sort A To Z (the AZ button) or Data | Sort & Filter | Sort Z To A (the ZA button). You can also right-click a cell in the column, and then choose Sort | Sort A To Z or Sort | Sort Z To A from the context menu.

If necessary, you can then perform a further sort by another column, and then another, to sort by other fields. But in most cases, you'll do better to follow the procedure described next.

Sort by Multiple Fields

To sort by multiple fields at once, use the Sort dialog box. Follow these steps:

1. Choose Data | Sort & Filter | Sort. Excel displays the Sort dialog box, shown here with criteria chosen:

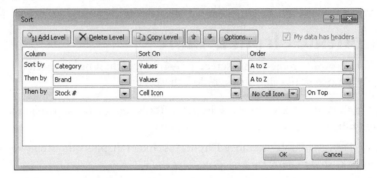

2. In the first row of controls in the list box, set up the first sort criterion:

- In the Sort By drop-down list, select the column by which you want to sort.

- In the Sort On drop-down list, select the item by which you want to sort: Values, Cell Color, Font Color, or Cell Icon. You'll normally want Values, but sorting by Cell Color, Font Color, or Cell Icon can be useful when you're using conditional formatting. (See the section "Use Conditional Formatting with Tables," later in this chapter.)

- In the Order drop-down list, choose the order. The options available depend on your choice in the Sort On list. For Values, choose A To Z for an ascending sort or Z To A for a descending sort; to sort by a custom list, click Custom List, select the list in the Custom Lists dialog box, and then click the OK button. For Cell Color, Font Color, or Cell Icon, you get to choose which icon to put on top.

- To apply case-sensitive sorting, click the Options button. Excel displays the Sort Options dialog box, shown here. Select the Case Sensitive check box, and then click the OK button.

The Sort Options dialog box also lets you choose between sorting from top to bottom and sorting from left to right when you're sorting cells that aren't in a table. In tables, however, you can sort only from top to bottom.

3. To add another level to the sort, click the Add Level icon. Excel adds a new row of controls to the list box. If you need to set up a new sort criterion that's similar to one you've already created, click the row that contains the existing criterion, and then click the Copy Level button. Set up the criterion as described in step 2.

4. Click the OK button. Excel closes the Sort dialog box and performs the sort.

Remove Duplicates from a Table

When your table grows to more than a screen or two in length, it becomes easy to get duplicate entries in it. To remove duplicate entries, follow these steps:

1. Click in the table. Excel displays the Table Tools section of the Ribbon and displays the Design tab.

2. Choose Design | Tools | Remove Duplicates. Excel displays the Remove Duplicates dialog box, shown here:

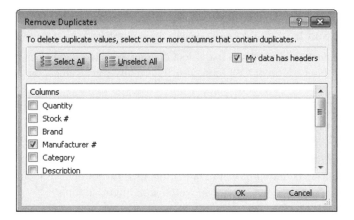

3. Select the check box for each column that you want to check for duplicates. Excel starts you off with all the check boxes selected, but in many cases you'll want to click the Unselect All button to clear them all, and then select only the ones you want.

When removing duplicate rows from a table, be very careful to search only on columns that should contain unique values—for example, a customer reference number or parts number. If you search by a nonunique column, such as price or customer name, removing apparent duplicates will wreck your table. If this happens, click the Undo button immediately to recover your data before you do anything else.

4. Click the OK button. Excel searches for duplicate values, removes them, and then displays a message box telling you what it found, as shown here.

5. Click the OK button. Excel closes the message box.

6. Check that the table still has all the entries that it should have—in other words, that removing the duplicates hasn't caught records you didn't intend to catch.

Find and Replace Data in a Table

You can use Excel's Find functionality (choose Home | Editing | Find & Select | Find or press CTRL-F) to find data in a table as you would in any other worksheet. Likewise, you can use Replace (choose Home | Editing | Find & Select | Replace or press CTRL-H) to replace particular entries—but you need to be careful. This is because in a large table that contains many entries, distinguishing one data record from another similar record can be difficult, and any mistakes made can be hard to track down later. In particular, performing a Replace All operation on a table is fraught with danger.

More often, what you'll need to do in a table is identify all the records that match one or more specified criteria. To do so, you use filtering.

Filter a Table to Find Records That Match Criteria

To find all the records that match one or more specified criteria, you apply logical filters. Filters work by hiding all the records that don't match the criteria, so you see only the records that do match.

You can apply filtering by using Excel's AutoFilter feature or by creating filters manually. AutoFilter is much easier than creating filters manually, so it's best to use AutoFilter unless you actually need the extra control that manual filters can deliver.

Perform Quick Filtering with AutoFilter

AutoFilter lets you quickly apply filters by choosing filter values from drop-down lists. AutoFilter is great for quickly filtering down a table by specific criteria so you can see the matching records, but you can't store the results: when you turn off AutoFilter, the full table is displayed again. So AutoFilter is primarily useful for looking up entries on the fly—for example, in response to a customer inquiry.

To use AutoFilter, follow these steps:

1. Click in the table you want to filter.

2. Click the Data tab, go to the Sort & Filter group, and make sure the Filter button is selected. Excel normally selects the Filter button when you create a table, so it should be selected unless you've clicked it to deselect it. When the Filter button is selected, Excel displays a drop-down arrow at the right side of each column heading when the column heading row is displayed.

3. Click the drop-down arrow on the column by which you want to filter the table. Figure 9-7 shows an example of the AutoFilter list that Excel displays.

4. From the drop-down list, choose the item by which you want to filter the table. Excel offers different choices depending on the column's contents. Your choices should include some of the following:

- **Sort**   Excel offers choices such as Sort A To Z, Sort Z To A, Sort Smallest To Largest, Sort Largest To Smallest, and Sort By Color. Sorting by color is useful when you've applied conditional formatting.

- **Text Filters** *or* **Number Filters**   When you highlight this item, a submenu appears showing types of filters that you can apply. Figure 9-8 shows the Text Filters submenu on the left and the Number Filters submenu on the right. Choosing one of

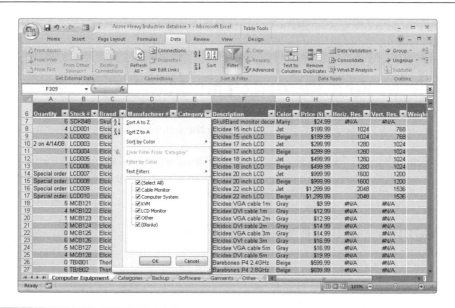

FIGURE 9-7   Click the drop-down arrow on a column heading to display the AutoFilter list for that column. This AutoFilter list is from the Category column.

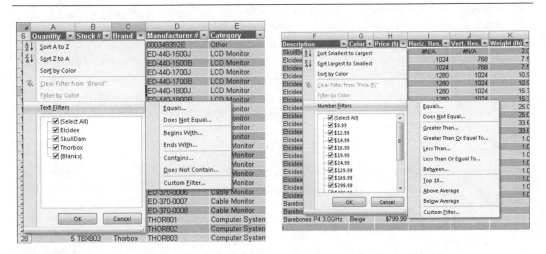

FIGURE 9-8   The Text Filters submenu and the Number Filters submenu provide options relevant to the data in the column you choose.

the menu items without an ellipsis (...) applies that filter. Choosing one of the items with an ellipsis displays the Custom AutoFilter dialog box with the appropriate condition selected for the column, as shown here. Choosing the Custom Filter item also displays the Custom AutoFilter dialog box, but this time with only the Equals item selected in the top drop-down list, so that you can choose a custom condition. The comparison operators are easy to understand, and you can create either AND filters (both conditions must be met for inclusion in the results) or OR conditions (either condition can be met). Make your choices, and then click the OK button.

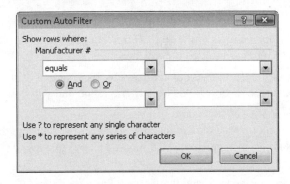

TIP   *For filtering numbers, the Top 10, Above Average, and Below Average items can be particularly useful.*

■ **Items in the List Box**   The list box contains an entry for each unique item in the column. You can filter by selecting the check boxes for only those items you want to display, including blank cells. Such filtering is most effective when a column's contents break down into various categories, but you may occasionally want to use it when each item in the column is unique.

When you apply the filter, Excel displays only the rows that match the filter and displays a filter symbol on the column heading used for the filtering. The Category column heading here has the filter symbol:

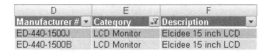

To display all entries in a column again, click the drop-down arrow, and then choose Clear Filter From *Column* in the drop-down list (where *Column* is the name of the column).

To remove all filtering from the table, choose Data | Sort & Filter | Filter (deselecting the Filter button).

Create Custom Filters

AutoFilter lets you apply fairly complex filters to a table, but you may need even finer control over filtering than AutoFilter can deliver. If so, you can create custom filters by using a *criteria range*—a range of rows outside the table that include the criteria for filtering the table.

To create custom filters using a criteria range, follow these steps:

1. Activate the worksheet that contains the table you want to filter.

NOTE *Steps 2 and 3 assume that your table is positioned at the top of the worksheet and that you therefore need to make space for the criteria rows. If you already have five empty rows above the table, skip these steps.*

2. Select cells in the top five rows of the table. (For example, drag from cell A1 to cell A5 to select those cells, or drag through the row headings.)

3. Choose Home | Cells | Insert | Insert Sheet Rows to insert five new blank rows above the selected rows. These rows will be your criteria range and will contain the criteria for filtering.

4. Click the row heading for the column headings to select the row, and then issue a Copy command (for example, choose Home | Clipboard | Copy) to copy the headings to the Clipboard.

5. Click the row heading for row 1, and then issue a Paste command (for example, choose Home | Clipboard | Paste) to paste the headings there, thus creating headings for the criteria range.

6. In row 2, enter the criteria for the first condition you want to implement:

  ▪ Excel treats your entries in the same row as an AND condition: all of the entries must be met for the condition to be true and for a row to be included in the results.

  ▪ If you make multiple entries in different rows of the same column, Excel treats them as OR conditions.

  ▪ To match fields that begin with specific text, enter that text in the cell. For example, enter **Elcid** to find all the Elcidee entries in the sample table.

  ▪ To specify exact text matching, enter an equal sign, opening double quotes, another equal sign, the text, and closing quotes. For example, to find records that have the text *LCD monitor* in a field, enter **="=LCD monitor"**.

  ▪ You can also use the wildcard characters ? and * in filters. The question mark represents a single character, while the asterisk represents any number of characters.

7. Use rows 3 through 5 to specify further conditions, if necessary. If you enter a condition in row 5, insert another blank row below it so that Excel can distinguish the criteria range from the table. This illustration shows two filters applied: one to catch items whose entry in the Category column starts with *LCD*, whose price is less than $600, and whose horizontal resolution is greater than or equal to 1280, and the other to catch items whose Category entry starts with *CRT*, whose price is less than $500, and whose horizontal resolution is greater than or equal to 1600.

	A	B	C	D	E	F	G	H	I	J
1	Quantity	Stock #	Brand	Manufacturer #	Category	Description	Color	Price ($)	Horiz. Res.	Vert. Res.
2					LCD			<600	>=1280	
3					CRT			<500	>=1600	
4										
5										
6	Quantity	Stock #	Brand	Manufacturer #	Category	Description	Color	Price ($)	Horiz. Res.	Vert. Res.
7	6	SDKB48	SkullDam	000348392E	Other	SkullBand monitor decor	Many	$24.99	#N/A	#N/A
8	4	LCD001	Elcidee	ED-440-1500J	LCD Monitor	Elcidee 15 inch LCD	Jet	$129.99	1024	768
9	2	LCD002	Elcidee	ED-440-1500B	LCD Monitor	Elcidee 15 inch LCD	Beige	$129.99	1024	768
10	2 on 4/14/08	LCD003	Elcidee	ED-440-1700J	LCD Monitor	Elcidee 17 inch LCD	Jet	$169.99	1280	1024
11	1	LCD004	Elcidee	ED-440-1700B	LCD Monitor	Elcidee 17 inch LCD	Beige	$169.99	1280	1024

8. After entering criteria, select the criteria range (including the criteria headers) up to the last row you've used—in other words, don't include any blank rows in the criteria range. Then choose Formulas | Named Cells | Name A Range, and create an easy name for the criteria range. (This step isn't essential, but it's helpful.)

9. Click a cell in the table again (so that the criteria range is no longer selected) and choose Data | Sort & Filter | Advanced. Excel displays the Advanced Filter dialog box, as shown here:

10. Excel's default setting in the Action section of the Advanced Filter dialog box is the Filter The List, In-Place option button, which filters the table where it is rather than copying the matching records to another range or worksheet. Select the Copy To Another Location option if you want to export the matching records to another location, and then enter the destination in the Copy To box. You can type the address; type the name of a range; or click the Collapse Dialog button, select the destination, and then click the Collapse Dialog button again.

NOTE   *Copying the records to another location is useful when you need to manipulate them using actions you wouldn't want to use on the table itself. For example, if you need to identify a set of records, and then remove data from each record to produce a report or chart, you'll do best to copy the records to another location, where you can manipulate them without damaging the table.*

11. Check that the List Range box contains the correct range for the table. If necessary, change it by clicking the Collapse Dialog button, selecting the correct range in the worksheet, and then clicking the Collapse Dialog button again. Include the table's header row in the range.

12. Enter the criteria range in the Criteria Range box. If you defined a name for the range, type the name. Otherwise, click the Collapse Dialog button and select the range manually, including the headers for the criteria range but excluding any blank rows in the criteria range.

13. Select the Unique Records Only check box if you want Excel to suppress any duplicate entries in the results.

14. Click the OK button. Excel applies the filter and displays the results.

To remove filtering from the table, choose Data | Sort & Filter | Filter.

Use Conditional Formatting with Tables

Conditional formatting (discussed in the section "Use Conditional Formatting" in Chapter 4) lets you tell Excel to automatically apply formatting to cells that have particular values. Conditional formatting can be especially useful in tables, as it lets you quickly identify values. Here are three examples:

■ You may need to pick out the top 10 values in a table for quick analysis, as in the following illustration, where the reverse-video squares show the top 10 values (of which only some appear here). In practice, you'd probably want to use subtler formatting than this because you'll be seeing the screen in color rather than grayscale.

State	2006	2007	2008
Alabama	22	28	13
Alaska	44	22	16
Alaska	21	50	50
Arizona	17	30	40
Arkansas	31	14	48
California	32	24	26
Colorado	34	23	40

- You may need to highlight atypical values within a table so that they stand out. In the following example, the table of expenses uses a white fill and red text to flag rows whose total cost is over $1,000, and a red fill to flag blank cells in the Authorized By column.

Quantity	Item	Unit Cost	Total Cost	Authorized By
34	CDR spindle	$ 19.99	$ 679.66	PJM
1	Briefcase soft-sided	$ 14.99	$ 14.99	CZS
20	Box Really Useful TM	$ 8.99	$ 179.80	PJM
12	Tray Unit 18 Drawer	$ 89.99	$ 1,079.88	PJM
100	Pull Drawer Fellowes	$ 9.99	$ 999.00	PJM
18	Toner Cartridge Black	$ 116.89	$ 2,104.02	CZS
2	Chair Ergonomic Economic Executive	$ 199.99	$ 399.98	
1	Box King Hippo	$ 399.99	$ 399.99	RTM

- You may need to grade each item in a table according to some form of status. The example in the following illustration uses three colored arrow icons to give a visual indication of stock status: a green, upward-pointing arrow indicates plenty of stock; a yellow, sideways-pointing arrow indicates stock getting low; and a red, downward-pointing arrow indicates low stock or no stock.

	Quantity	Stock #	Brand	Manufacturer #	Category	Description
8 ⇨	4	LCD001	Elcidee	ED-440-1500J	LCD Monitor	Elcidee 15 inch LCD
9 ⇨	2	LCD002	Elcidee	ED-440-1500B	LCD Monitor	Elcidee 15 inch LCD
10 ⇨	2	LCD003	Elcidee	ED-440-1700J	LCD Monitor	Elcidee 17 inch LCD
11 ⬇	1	LCD004	Elcidee	ED-440-1700B	LCD Monitor	Elcidee 17 inch LCD
12 ⬇	1	LCD005	Elcidee	ED-440-1800J	LCD Monitor	Elcidee 18 inch LCD
13 ⬇	1	LCD006	Elcidee	ED-440-1800B	LCD Monitor	Elcidee 18 inch LCD
14 ⬆	8	LCD007	Elcidee	ED-440-2000J	LCD Monitor	Elcidee 20 inch LCD
15 ⬆	6	LCD008	Elcidee	ED-440-2000B	LCD Monitor	Elcidee 20 inch LCD
16 ⬇	1	LCD009	Elcidee	ED-440-2200J	LCD Monitor	Elcidee 22 inch LCD
17 ⬇	0	LCD010	Elcidee	ED-440-2200B	LCD Monitor	Elcidee 22 inch LCD

9

Link an Excel Worksheet to an External Table

If you (or your company) store information in a relational database rather than in an Excel worksheet, you may want to manipulate a subset of that information in Excel. You can do so by performing a query on that database and importing the resulting set of information. (A *relational database* is one that contains multiple tables that are linked to each other, as opposed to a *flat-file* database, which consists of a single table, like those you create in Excel.)

You may also need to get data from another external data source, such as a website, an XML file, or Microsoft Query (which lets you create queries to extract data from a database).

Link to an Access Database

To link an Excel worksheet to an Access database, follow these steps:

1. Open the workbook in which you want to create the link.

2. If you want to place the linked data on an existing worksheet, select it. If you want to use a new worksheet, you can either create one now and select it, or have Excel create one for you automatically as described in step 7.

3. Choose Data | Get External Data | From Access. Excel displays the Select Data Source dialog box, which is a renamed version of the standard Windows Open dialog box.

4. Navigate to the folder that contains the Access database, select the database, and then click the Open button. Excel displays the Select Table dialog box, as shown here, with a list of the database's tables.

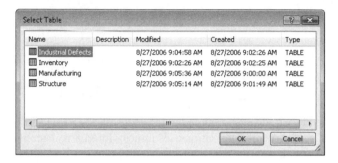

5. Select the table, and then click the OK button. Excel displays the Import Data dialog box, as shown here.

6. In the Select How You Want To View This Data In Your Workbook area, select the Table option button if you want to import the data as a table. Your other options are to create a PivotTable report or both a PivotChart and a PivotTable report. (Chapter 11 discusses PivotTables and PivotCharts.)

7. In the Where Do You Want To Put The Data? area, select the Existing Worksheet button and specify the range in the text box if you want to use the existing worksheet. To have Excel create a new worksheet, select the New Worksheet button.

8. If you want to give the database connection a descriptive name or control how frequently Excel refreshes the data drawn from the database, click the Properties button. Excel displays the Connection Properties dialog box (see Figure 9-9). Choose settings: type a descriptive name in the Connection Name text box, and add a description to the Description text box. You can use the Refresh Control settings to tell Excel how frequently to refresh the data. For example, you might select the Refresh Every check box and specify 30 Minutes.

FIGURE 9-9   The Connection Properties dialog box

9. Click the OK button. Excel establishes the connection and inserts the data in the existing worksheet you specified or in a new worksheet (if you chose that option).

10. Excel gives the table a name starting with **Table_** and ending with the name of the database file. Change this name to a more descriptive name if you want.

Perform Web Queries

Excel can also extract data from tables in web pages by using its built-in Web Query feature. To use Web Query, follow these steps:

1. Open the workbook in which you want to create the link.

2. If you want to place the linked data on an existing worksheet, select it. If you want to use a new worksheet, you can either create one now and select it, or have Excel create one for you automatically as described in step 7.

3. Choose Data | Get External Data | From Web. Excel displays the New Web Query dialog box (see Figure 9-10).

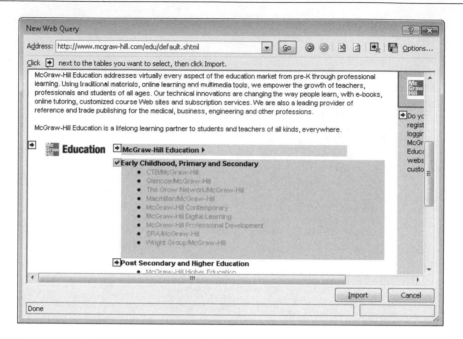

FIGURE 9-10 The New Web Query dialog box resembles a stripped-down version of Internet Explorer.

TIP *You can drag the lower-right corner to expand the New Web Query dialog box.*

4. Browse to the page that contains the table you want.

5. Click the yellow-boxed arrow next to each table to which you want to establish a link.

6. Click the Import button. Excel displays the Import Data dialog box with the Table option button selected.

7. In the Where Do You Want To Put The Data? area, select the Existing Worksheet button and specify the range in the text box if you want to use the existing worksheet. To have Excel create a new worksheet, select the New Worksheet button.

8. Click the Properties button. Excel displays the External Data Range Properties dialog box (see Figure 9-11), in which you can choose settings as follows:

   ■ **Name** Type a descriptive name in the Name text box so that you will be able to identify the query easily.

   ■ **Query Definition area** Normally, you'll want to select the Save Query Definition check box. The Save Password check box is available only if you use a password for the connection; if so, you may want to select it.

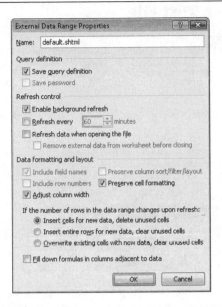

FIGURE 9-11   When setting up a web query, tell Excel how to handle changes to the number of rows in the data range.

9

- **Refresh Control area**   Use the controls to tell Excel whether (and if so, how frequently) to refresh the data. You can use the Refresh Every *NN* Minutes control if you need to update the data periodically. Selecting the Refresh Data When Opening The File check box ensures that the data is up-to-date each time you open the workbook. If you select this check box, you can choose to remove external data from the worksheet before closing it. Usually, it's best to keep the data in the worksheet in case the website isn't available the next time you open the workbook.

- **Data Formatting And Layout Area**   Select the Preserve Cell Formatting check box and the Adjust Column Width check box if you want the table to look approximately the same in Excel as in the web page. In the If The Number Of Rows In The Data Range Changes Upon Refresh area, choose how you want Excel to handle changes in the number of rows in the data range. Normally, the Insert Cells For New Data, Delete Unused Cells option button is the best choice, but you may sometimes want to use the Insert Entire Rows For New Data, Clear Unused Cells option button or the Overwrite Existing Cells With New Data, Clear Unused Cells option button instead. Select the Fill Down Formulas In Columns Adjacent To Data check box only if you want Excel to automatically extend formulas for you, which is normally not a good idea.

9. Click the OK button. Excel inserts the data in the worksheet.

Link a Worksheet to a Text File

Excel also lets you import a text file into a worksheet and have it updated with fresh information if necessary. This capability can be useful when your company receives database information to which Excel can't link directly—for example, because the database belongs to someone who won't let you access it directly or because it runs on a minicomputer so ancient that Excel can't communicate with it.

To link a worksheet to a text file, follow these steps:

1. Open the workbook in which you want to create the link.

2. If you want to place the linked data on an existing worksheet, select it. If you want to use a new worksheet, you can either create one now and select it, or have Excel create one for you automatically as described in step 13.

3. Choose Data | Get External Data | From Text. Excel displays the Import Text File dialog box, which is a standard Windows Open dialog box given a new name.

4. Navigate to the folder that contains the text file, select it, and then click the Open button. Excel launches the Text Import Wizard, which displays its first screen (see Figure 9-12).

5. In the Original Data Type group box, select the Delimited option button if the text file uses commas or tabs to delimit the fields. Select the Fixed Width option button if each field has a fixed width.

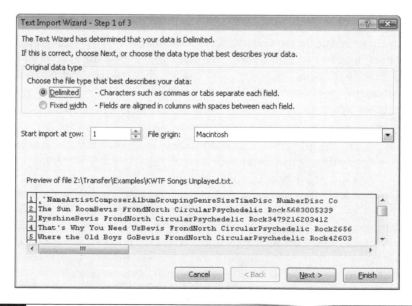

FIGURE 9-12 The first screen of the Text Import Wizard

6. If the contents of the text file start at a row later than row 1, choose that row in the Start Import At Row drop down list.

7. If the preview in the Preview box seems to indicate incorrect characters, you may need to change the setting in the File Origin drop-down list. You can choose from a variety of encodings, including Windows, Macintosh, and MS-DOS.

8. Click the Next button. Excel displays the second screen of the Text Import Wizard (see Figure 9-13).

9. Choose the delimiter or delimiters by selecting the appropriate check box or check boxes in the Delimiters group box. You may need to select the Treat Consecutive Delimiters As One check box if the text file uses delimiters inconsistently. If the text file uses a text qualifier to denote the beginning of a text entry, select it in the Text Qualifier drop-down list.

10. Click the Next button, Excel displays the third screen of the Text Import Wizard (see Figure 9-14).

11. For each column in turn, click in the column, and then choose the data format in the Column Data Format group box. Select the Do Not Import Column (Skip) option

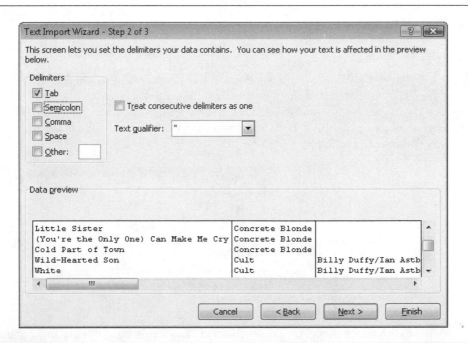

FIGURE 9-13 On the second screen of the Text Import Wizard, choose the correct delimiter for the text you're importing.

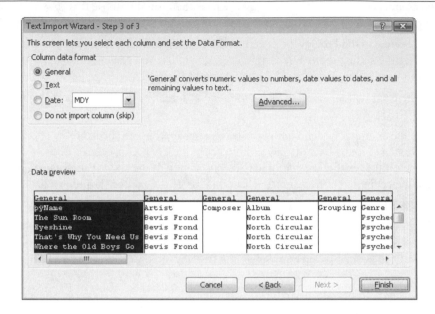

FIGURE 9-14 On the third screen of the Text Import Wizard, select the data format for each column.

button if you want to exclude a column. For columns you include, you can also click the Advanced button, and then use the Advanced Text Import Settings dialog box (shown here) to set the decimal separator and thousands separator for numeric data. Select the Trailing Minus For Negative Numbers check box if you want to add a minus sign at the end of a negative number (for example, $98.45-).

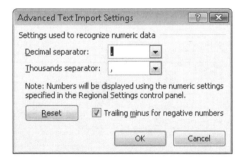

12. Click the Finish button. Excel displays the Import Data dialog box with the Table option button selected.

13. In the Where Do You Want To Put The Data? area, select the Existing Worksheet button and specify the range in the text box if you want to use the existing worksheet. To have Excel create a new worksheet, select the New Worksheet button.

14. If you want to make Excel refresh the data drawn from the text file automatically, click the Properties button. Excel displays the External Data Range Properties dialog box (shown in Figure 9-11, earlier in this chapter), in which you can choose settings as follows:

- ■ **Name**   Type a descriptive name in the Name text box so that you will be able to identify the query easily.

- ■ **Query Definition area**   Normally, you'll want to select the Save Query Definition check box. The Save Password check box is available only if you use a password for the connection; if so, you may want to select it.

- ■ **Refresh Control area**   Use the controls to tell Excel whether (and if so, how frequently) to refresh the data. You can use the Refresh Every *NN* Minutes control if you need to update the data periodically. Selecting the Refresh Data When Opening The File check box ensures that the data is up-to-date each time you open the workbook. If you select this check box, you can choose to remove external data from the worksheet before closing it. Usually, it's best to keep the data in the worksheet in case the website isn't available the next time you open the workbook.

- ■ **Data Formatting And Layout Area**   Select the Preserve Cell Formatting check box and the Adjust Column Width check box if you want the table to look approximately the same in Excel as in the web page. In the If The Number Of Rows In The Data Range Changes Upon Refresh area, choose how you want Excel to handle changes in the number of rows in the data range. Normally, the Insert Cells For New Data, Delete Unused Cells option button is the best choice, but you may sometimes want to use the Insert Entire Rows For New Data, Clear Unused Cells option button or the Overwrite Existing Cells With New Data, Clear Unused Cells option button instead. Select the Fill Down Formulas In Columns Adjacent To Data check box only if you want Excel to automatically extend formulas for you, which is normally not a good idea.

15. Click the OK button. Excel closes the Import Data dialog box and imports the data from the text file.

Connect to Another Kind of Database

The previous sections covered linking an Excel worksheet to an Access database, a web data source, and a text file—the three types of data sources you're arguably most likely to use. But Excel also lets you connect to other types of data sources by using the options on the Data | Get External Data | From Other Sources panel (shown next).

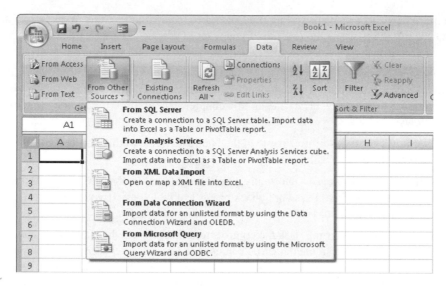

The options on the From Other Sources panel let you do the following:

- **From SQL Server**   Connect to a database running on SQL Server, the big brother of Access. You must provide the server name and credentials for a user authorized to access the database if you yourself are not authorized.

- **From Analysis Services**   Analysis Services can create an Online Analytical Processing (OLAP) cube from data in a SQL Server database. You can bring data from the OLAP cube into an Excel worksheet.

- **From XML Data Import**   If your company uses XML files, you can map an XML schema to an Excel worksheet and bring in the data.

- **From Data Connection Wizard**   The Data Connection Wizard lets you connect an Excel worksheet to a database that uses the OLEDB standard for connecting to databases. For example, you can use OLEDB to access an Oracle database.

- **From Microsoft Query**   The Microsoft Query Wizard lets you connect an Excel worksheet to a database that uses the Open Database Connectivity (ODBC) standard. ODBC is very widely used and provides connectivity to many databases, including those in formats such as Sybase, DB2, and Filemaker.

Refresh the Data in a Table Linked to External Data

If you've set up the table to update automatically, either on a schedule (for example, every 30 minutes) or every time you open the workbook, you may not need to refresh the data manually. Otherwise, you can refresh data from the External Table Data group on the Design tab of the Table Tools section of the Ribbon.

- To refresh a single table, click any cell in it, and then choose Design | External Table Data | Refresh. (Click the top part of the Refresh button, not the drop-down list part. If you open the drop-down list by mistake, choose the Refresh item from it.)

- To refresh all tables in the workbook, choose Design | External Table Data | Refresh | Refresh All. If the refresh operation gets stuck, choose Design | External Table Data | Refresh | Cancel Refresh to cancel it. The Refresh drop-down list also contains a Refresh Status item that you can use during a refresh to see how the refresh is progressing.

NOTE *When you choose to refresh a table linked to a text file, Excel doesn't refresh the data automatically. Instead, Excel displays the Import Text File dialog box for you to select the text file to import.*

Unlink a Table from External Data

Few relationships last forever, even between data tables that are compatible on every discernible level. If you need to unlink a table from an external data source, follow these steps:

1. Choose Data | Connections | Connections. Excel displays the Workbook Connections dialog box, as shown here.

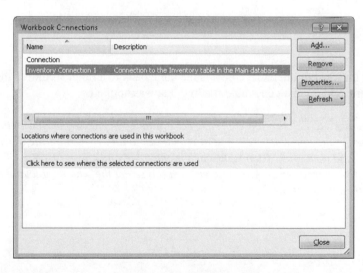

2. In the top list box, select the connection you want to remove.

3. Click the Remove button. Excel displays a dialog box warning you that removing the connection will separate the workbook from its data source and that Refresh operations will no longer work, as shown next.

4. Click the OK button. Excel removes the connection.

5. Click the Close button. Excel closes the Workbook Connections dialog box.

Convert a Table Back to a Range

Sometimes you may find that you no longer need to use table features for the cells in a range. When this happens, you can convert the table back to a range. To do so, follow these steps:

1. Click anywhere in the table. Excel makes the Design section of the Ribbon available and displays the Design tab.

2. Choose Design | Tools | Convert To Range. Excel displays a confirmation message box, as shown here.

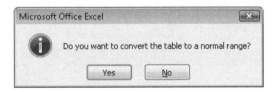

3. Click the Yes button. Excel converts the table back to a range, removes the column headers, and removes any table shading that was applied.

NOTE   *If you need to delete a table, first select it: move the mouse pointer to the upper-left corner of the upper-left cell so that it changes to an arrow pointing down and to the right, and then click. Then right-click in the table and choose Delete | Table Columns from the context menu. Alternatively, drag to select the whole table and cells around it, and then press* DELETE.

Chapter 10

Outline and Consolidate Worksheets

How to...

- Use outlining to create collapsible worksheets
- Create a standard outline automatically
- Create a custom outline manually
- Expand and collapse an outline
- Change an outlined area after adding or deleting material
- Remove an outline from a worksheet
- Consolidate multiple worksheets into one worksheet by position or by category
- Update or change an existing consolidation

Even if you don't create large tables (as described in Chapter 9), Excel worksheets can grow so that they're far longer than will fit on even the highest-resolution display. Working with monster worksheets tends to be awkward and time consuming, especially when you need to scroll frequently to view the relevant parts of the worksheet. In the first part of this chapter, you'll learn how to use Excel's outlining features to create a collapsible worksheet. By defining a hierarchy for a worksheet, you can collapse it to its key areas, which—with any luck—you can fit onscreen at the same time.

Another problem you're likely to run into when using Excel at work is the need to integrate data from multiple similar worksheets into a single worksheet. You may need to do this for a variety of reasons—from turning an archive of workbooks into a single useful resource, to circulating a workbook amongst your colleagues to gather necessary input. Integrating multiple worksheets manually tends to be a long and thankless task, but Excel's tools for consolidating worksheets can save you a great deal of time and effort.

Use Outlining to Create Collapsible Worksheets

For extensive worksheets built around some form of hierarchy, Excel's outlining tools can prove invaluable. For example, the sales worksheet shown in Figure 10-1 tracks the sales of products by reps, groups of reps, and regional offices, and by months, quarters, and years. In its normal state, as shown in the upper part of the figure, the worksheet extends across many columns and down through nearly 30 rows. But when the worksheet has an outline applied to it, you can collapse it to any of various levels to display different amounts of information. The lower part of the figure shows the worksheet with outlining applied and the result partially collapsed.

NOTE   *As you saw in Chapter 4, you can hide columns or rows that you don't want to have displayed by choosing Home | Cells | Format | Hide & Unhide | Hide Columns, or Home | Cells | Format | Hide & Unhide | Hide Rows. You can use hiding to produce a similar effect to collapsing, but doing so is so much slower and clumsier that it is seldom worthwhile.*

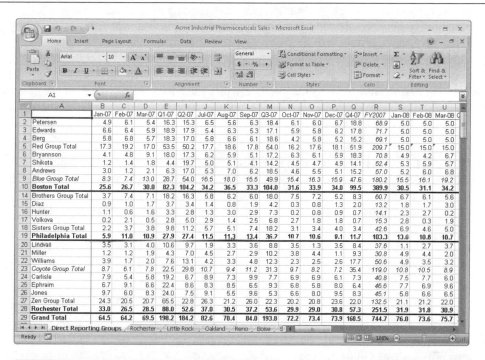

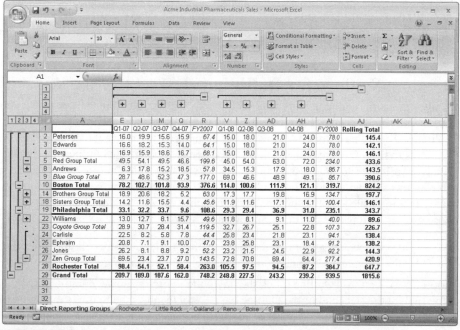

FIGURE 10-1 If a worksheet contains a hierarchy, you can use outlining to collapse it.

An outline can have up to eight outline levels for rows and up to eight outline levels for columns, enabling you to create highly collapsible worksheets. The outline shown in the lower part of Figure 10-1 has four outline levels for rows and four for columns.

You can either create a standard outline automatically from a structured worksheet, or create a custom outline manually. Usually, the best way to proceed is to try creating a standard outline automatically, as described in the next section. If you don't like the results, either choose custom settings for outlining (as described in the section after that) and try again, or create a custom outline manually (as described in the third section).

Create a Standard Outline Automatically

To create a standard outline in an Excel worksheet, follow these general steps:

1. Lay out the basic framework of the outline, and enter the formulas in the appropriate places:

   - Excel creates the outline based on where the formulas are entered in the worksheet, so you must enter the formulas in the worksheet before you can create an outline in it.

   - You don't have to enter all the items within any particular category, because you can insert rows and columns in the data area without disrupting the outline applied. Excel simply expands the outline to accommodate the extra rows or columns.

2. To create a single outline for the whole of the current data area, select a cell in the data area. To create an outline for only a specific part of the current data area, select the range.

3. Choose Data | Outline | Group | Auto Outline (click the Group drop-down button, and then click the Auto Outline item) to create an automatic outline for the whole data area or for the current selection.

Chose Custom Settings for Outlining

Excel's default settings for outlining work well with worksheets laid out like the worksheet shown in Figure 10-1, with summary rows below the detail rows, and summary columns to the right of the detail columns. To outline a worksheet that has its summary rows above the detail rows, or its summary columns to the left of the detail columns, you need to change the outlining settings.

Most likely, you'll need to choose custom settings after using Auto Outline (as described in the previous section) and discovering the results aren't what you need. But you can also use the Settings dialog box to create a custom outline from scratch.

To choose custom settings for outlining, follow these steps:

1. If you've already created an outline and need to change it, click any cell in the outlined area. If you're creating an outline from scratch, select the data range.

2. Choose Data | Outline | Outline (click the tiny button with the arrow pointing down and to the right at the right end of the Outline bar). Excel displays the Settings dialog box, as shown here.

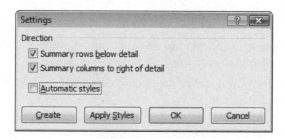

3. Tell Excel where the summary rows and columns are and choose whether to apply styles:

- ■ **Summary Rows Below Detail**   Select this check box if the worksheet has summary rows below the detail rows (for example, rows 1 through 5 contain data, and row 6 summarizes each column). If the summary rows appear above the detail rows, or if there are no summary rows, clear this check box.

- ■ **Summary Columns To Right Of Detail**   Select this check box if the worksheet has summary columns to the right of detail columns (for example, columns A through C contain data, and column D summarizes each row). If the summary columns appear before the detail columns, or if there are no summary columns, clear this check box.

- ■ **Automatic Styles**   Select this check box if you want Excel to automatically apply styles to the outline. Excel uses styles named RowLevel_1, RowLevel_2, ColLevel_1, ColLevel_2, and so on to identify the different row levels and column levels. Click the Apply Styles button to apply the styles to the outline.

4. Click the Create button, the Apply Styles button, or the OK button, as appropriate:

- ■ **Create**   Click this button when you're creating a new outline. Excel closes the Settings dialog box and creates the outline.

- ■ **Apply Styles**   Click this button when you're adjusting an existing outline and have selected the Automatic Styles check box. Excel closes the Settings dialog box and applies the styles.

- ■ **OK**   Click this button when you're adjusting an existing outline and you've changed the Summary Rows Below Detail setting, or the Summary Columns To Right Of Detail setting. Excel closes the Settings dialog box and applies your changes.

Create an Outline Manually

Instead of creating an outline automatically by using the Auto Outline command, you can build an outline manually by using the Group command (and, if necessary, the Ungroup command). Creating an outline manually is far more labor intensive than using Auto Outline, so you'll probably want to do it only when Auto Outline doesn't give you the results you need, or when you need to build an outline at the same time as you create a worksheet.

TIP *You can also use the Group and Ungroup commands to change the grouping of selected rows or columns in an existing outline you've created using the Auto Outline command.*

10

To create an outline manually, follow these steps:

1. Select the detail rows or detail columns that you want to group. The detail rows or detail columns must be adjacent to each other for grouping to work.

2. Choose Data | Outline | Group (click the Group button, not its drop-down button). Excel displays the Group dialog box:

3. Select the Rows option button to group by rows, or the Columns option button to group by columns.

4. Click the OK button. Excel closes the Group dialog box and applies the grouping.

To ungroup grouped columns or rows, follow these steps:

1. Select the cells you want to affect.

2. Choose Data | Outline | Ungroup (click the Ungroup button, not its drop-down button). Excel displays the Ungroup dialog box:

3. Select the Rows option button to ungroup by rows, or select the Columns option button to ungroup by columns.

4. Click the OK button. Excel closes the Ungroup dialog box and ungroups the rows or columns.

Expand and Collapse the Outline

Once you've applied an outline to a worksheet, you can expand and collapse it easily by using the outline symbols that Excel displays (see Figure 10-2):

- ■ Click one of the Column Level buttons to expand or collapse the columns to that level.
- ■ Click one of the Row Level buttons to expand or collapse the rows to that level.
- ■ Click an Expand button to expand a row level or column level, or click a Collapse button to collapse a row level or column level.

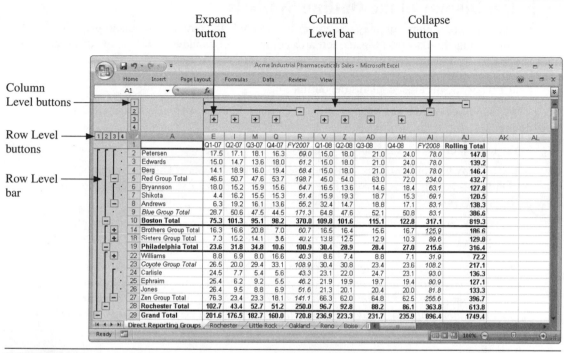

FIGURE 10-2   Use the outline symbols to expand and collapse an outline.

If you have an IntelliMouse with a wheel, you can use it to expand or collapse the outline. Hover the mouse pointer over the summary cell for a row, column, or both, and then SHIFT-scroll backward to collapse the outline or SHIFT-scroll forward to expand the outline.

Change the Outlined Area After Adding or Deleting Material

If you add rows or columns to a worksheet that contains an outline, or delete rows or columns from it, you need to redo the outline. To do so, follow these steps:

1. Click any cell in the outlined area.

2. Choose Data | Outline | Group | Auto Outline. Excel displays a dialog box asking whether you want to modify the existing outline:

3. Click the OK button. Excel modifies the outline to include the changes you made.

10

Toggle the Display of the Outline Symbols

If screen space is at a premium, you may sometimes want to hide the outline symbols to prevent them from consuming chunks of the top and left areas of the Excel window. To toggle the display of outline symbols, follow these steps:

1. Select the worksheet that contains the outline.

2. Click the Office button, and then click Excel Options. Excel displays the Excel Options dialog box.

3. In the left panel, click the Advanced category.

4. In the Display Options For This Worksheet section, clear the Show Outline Symbols If An Outline Is Applied check box to hide the outline symbols, or select this check box to redisplay the symbols.

5. Click the OK button. Excel closes the Excel Options dialog box and toggles the display of the symbols.

If parts of the outline are collapsed when you hide the outline symbols like this, the result can be confusing to anyone who doesn't know that the worksheet contains an outline. At first sight, the collapsed areas of the outline will appear to have rows or columns hidden, but the user won't be able to display these rows or columns by issuing an Unhide command.

If you need to toggle the display of outline symbols frequently, you'll probably find the path through the Options dialog box too slow for comfort. To toggle the display of outline symbols faster, put the Show Outline Symbols command on the Quick Access Toolbar. You'll find the Show Outline Symbols command in the Commands Not In The Ribbon list in the Customization category in the Excel Options dialog box. See "Customize the Quick Access Toolbar" in Chapter 17 for detailed instructions.

Remove an Outline from a Worksheet

To remove an outline from a worksheet, choose Data | Outline | Ungroup | Clear Outline.

Consolidate Multiple Worksheets into One Worksheet

Excel offers powerful features for automatically consolidating multiple worksheets into a single worksheet. Such consolidation can be useful in a variety of situations, such as these:

■ Your predecessor created a workbook containing a single worksheet each week to show the factory's manufacturing output. You need to consolidate those worksheets into a single worksheet to show the total output—and there are nearly a hundred worksheets.

■ You need to retrieve data from the same cell in each of a large number of worksheets in a workbook. You could construct a complex formula or write a macro using Visual Basic for Applications (VBA), but consolidation can take care of the problem more quickly and easily.

Consolidate Worksheets Manually Using 3-D Formulas

If the source worksheets you need to consolidate don't have consistent enough layout or consistent labels to enable Excel to consolidate them automatically, you can consolidate them manually by entering formulas that refer to the appropriate worksheets. This technique works best if all the worksheets are in the same workbook, but it does work when the worksheets are in different workbooks—provided that none of the workbooks gets renamed or moved after you create the formulas. See "Refer to Other Worksheets and Other Workbooks in Formulas," in Chapter 8, for instructions on creating formulas that refer to other worksheets and other workbooks.

This illustration shows a 3-D formula entered in cell B2 on the first worksheet (named FY-2008) that refers to various cells on the next four worksheets:

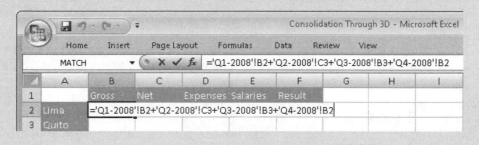

- You need to retrieve data from multiple worksheets that don't have the same cell layout (so you can't specify the exact cell address) but that have the same row labels or column labels. Excel can use the labels as reference points to retrieve the information you need. This capability is especially useful when you've circulated copies of a worksheet to colleagues, and you find they've changed the layout by inserting or deleting rows and columns.

Excel can automatically consolidate up to 255 worksheets (called the *source worksheets*) into a single worksheet (called the *destination worksheet*). You can choose whether to link the destination worksheet to the source worksheets, or to create a destination worksheet that simply contains the data from the source worksheets but no link to them.

When you consolidate worksheets, the workbook that contains the destination worksheet must be open. The workbook or workbooks that contain the source worksheets can be either open or closed—whichever you prefer. Having the source workbooks open tends to be better, for a couple of reasons:

- When you're learning how to consolidate worksheets, you can see at a glance which data Excel places where when you perform the consolidation.
- If the workbooks are closed, you have to type relatively complex references to them; if they're open, you can create the references much more easily.

However, once you understand how consolidation works, you may prefer to leave the source workbooks closed—particularly if you're consolidating so many worksheets at once that having all of their workbooks open on screen would be impractical.

> NOTE *If any source workbooks are open when you consolidate data from them, save them before performing the consolidation.*

Consolidate Worksheets by Their Position

The easiest way of consolidating worksheets automatically is consolidating by position—in other words, retrieving data from the same cell address in each of the source worksheets. Consolidating by position works successfully only if the same cell in each of the source worksheets contains the relevant data. If you or your colleagues have changed the layout of even a single worksheet by a single column, consolidating by position doesn't work correctly and can produce grossly incorrect results.

To consolidate worksheets by position, follow these steps:

1. Open the destination workbook, the workbook that contains the destination worksheet.

2. To make entering the consolidation references as easy as possible, open each workbook that contains one of the source worksheets. If the destination workbook contains the source worksheets, you don't need to take this step.

3. Activate the destination workbook and destination worksheet. For example, if you have multiple workbooks open, use the View | Window | Switch Windows menu to select the destination workbook, and then click the worksheet tab for the destination worksheet to activate it.

4. Select the upper-left cell of the area in which you want to place the consolidated data.

5. Choose Data | Data Tools | Consolidate. Excel displays the Consolidate dialog box (see Figure 10-3).

6. In the Function drop-down list, select the function you want to use for the consolidation. The default function is Sum, which is what you'll need for consolidating many worksheets, but you can choose from Count, Average, Max, Min, Product, Count Numbers, StdDev (standard deviation), StdDevp (standard deviation based on an entire population), Var (variance based on a sample), and Varp (variance based on an entire population).

7. Add the references by taking the following steps:

    ■ Click the Collapse Dialog button in the Reference box if you need to get the Consolidate dialog box out of the way. Otherwise, you can just work around it.

    ■ If necessary, use the View | Window | Switch Windows menu to activate the workbook that contains the worksheet to which you want to refer.

    ■ Click the appropriate worksheet tab to activate it.

    ■ Select the cell or range of cells on the worksheet.

FIGURE 10-3   Use the Consolidate dialog box to add the references for all the worksheets you want to consolidate.

10

- If you collapsed the Consolidate dialog box, click the Collapse Dialog button to restore the dialog box.

- Click the Add button to add the address or range to the All References box.

NOTE   *If the workbook that contains the worksheet isn't open, click the Browse button and use the resulting Browse dialog box to select the workbook. When you click the OK button to close the Browse dialog box, Excel enters the workbook name in the Reference text box for you. You then have to type the worksheet name and cell or range address to enter the rest of the reference—for example, '[May Sales.xlsx]Week1'!$B$16.*

8. Add further references in the same way. Excel's default is to consolidate by position, so Excel automatically suggests the same range when you click the tab of the next worksheet you want to add to the consolidation.

9. In the Use Labels In group box, make sure the Top Row check box and the Left Column check box are cleared.

10. If you want to link the consolidation to the data source (so that Excel automatically updates the consolidation), select the Create Links To Source Data check box. Otherwise, clear this check box.

11. Click the OK button. Excel closes the Consolidate dialog box and consolidates the data into the specified cells.

Consolidate Worksheets by Category

Consolidation by position is straightforward—provided that your colleagues haven't changed the layout of the worksheets by even a single cell. If the worksheets you need to consolidate have even slightly different layouts, consolidation by position won't work. But if the worksheets use the same row labels and column labels, you may be able to consolidate by category instead.

The following illustration shows an example of some worksheets that can't be consolidated by position, but can be consolidated by category. Although the worksheets use the same general layout, the sales assistants' results are sorted in descending order so that they show which sales assistant sold the most meat in that week. However, the labels in column A are consistent, so Excel can use them to identify the cells.

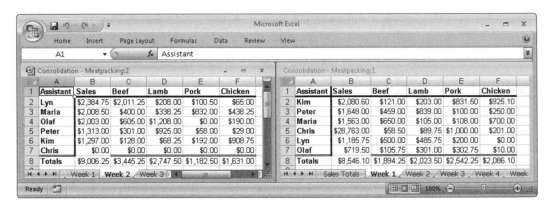

To consolidate workbooks by category, follow these steps:

1. Open the destination workbook, the workbook that contains the destination worksheet.

2. To make entering the consolidation references as easy as possible, open each workbook that contains one of the source worksheets. If the destination workbook contains the source worksheets, you don't need to take this step.

3. Activate the destination workbook and destination worksheet. For example, if you have multiple workbooks open, use the View | Window | Switch Windows menu to select the destination workbook, and then click the worksheet tab for the destination worksheet to activate it.

4. In the destination worksheet, select the cell in which you want to place the upper-left cell of the consolidated data.

5. Choose Data | Data Tools | Consolidate. Excel displays the Consolidate dialog box.

6. In the Use Labels In group box, select the Top Row check box or the Left Column check box as appropriate. In the example, you'd select the Left Column check box, because the names of the sales assistants are in the left column of the data range.

7. In the Function drop-down list, select the function you want to use for the consolidation. In the example, you'd leave the default, Sum, selected.

8. Click in the Reference text box, and then add the references using the techniques explained in step 7 of the previous section, "Consolidate Worksheets by Their Position." You'll need to select the range manually on each source worksheet.

9. If you want to link the consolidation to the data source, select the Create Links To Source Data check box. Otherwise, clear this check box is cleared.

10. Click the OK button. Excel closes the Consolidate dialog box and consolidates the data into the specified cells.

Update an Existing Consolidation

To update an existing consolidation, follow these steps:

1. Select the range containing the consolidation.

2. Choose Data | Data Tools | Consolidate. Excel displays the Consolidate dialog box.

3. Click the OK button. Excel updates the consolidation using the existing references.

Change an Existing Consolidation

If you chose not to create links from the destination worksheet to its source worksheets in a consolidation, you can change the consolidation without redoing it from scratch. To change a consolidation, follow these steps:

1. Select the range containing the consolidation.

2. Choose Data | Data Tools | Consolidate. Excel displays the Consolidate dialog box.

3. Change the details of the consolidation as necessary:

   ■ To add another source range, click in the Reference text box, specify the range as usual, and then click the Add button.

   ■ To remove an existing source range, select it in the All References list box and then click the Delete button.

   ■ To change an existing source range, select it in the All References list. Excel displays the source range's details in the Reference text box. Change the range either by typing corrections, or by using the Collapse Dialog button and standard selection techniques, and then click the Add button to apply the change.

   ■ To link the consolidation to its source data, select the Create Links To Source Data check box. Take this step last, because creating the links prevents you from changing any of the source ranges.

4. Click the OK button. Excel closes the Consolidate dialog box and applies the changes.

NOTE   *If you created your consolidation by entering formulas manually, you'll need to edit those formulas manually to change the consolidation.*

10

Chapter 11

Analyze Data Using PivotTables and PivotCharts

How to...

- Understand PivotTables
- Create a PivotTable framework using the PivotTable and PivotChart Wizard
- Create a PivotTable on a PivotTable framework
- Change, format, and configure a PivotTable
- Create PivotCharts from PivotTables
- Create a conventional chart from PivotTable data

After entering a substantial amount of data in a table (as discussed in Chapter 9), or after consolidating multiple worksheets into a single worksheet (Chapter 10), you may want to manipulate the data to see what conclusions you can draw from it. This chapter and the next introduce you to the tools for drawing those conclusions.

In this chapter, you'll learn how to create and use PivotTables and PivotCharts, two powerful tools for manipulating and analyzing data contained in tables. In the next chapter, you'll see how to solve problems by performing what-if analysis on your data.

Understand PivotTables

A *PivotTable* is a form of report that works by rearranging the fields and records in a table into a different format. You can rotate *(pivot)* the columns in a PivotTable to display data summarized in different ways, easily sort the table in various ways, filter data, and collapse and expand the level of information displayed.

The PivotTable creates a PivotTable field from each field in the table (each column, in the default orientation). Each PivotTable field contains items that summarize the rows of information that contain a particular entry.

Creating and manipulating the PivotTable doesn't change the contents or layout of the table, so you can safely use a PivotTable to experiment with your data without worrying about corrupting the data or needing to restore the table's layout afterwards. A PivotTable also enables you to perform what would otherwise be relatively complex calculations by using its built-in features.

TIP   *If PivotTables seem mysterious, don't worry—that's a normal reaction. The best way to come to grips with PivotTables is by using them to experiment with practice data over which you have control, or with a spare copy of real data that you can reduce to an easily manageable quantity, when you're not under pressure of time to deliver results.*

Until you start using data in a PivotTable, the features and benefits of a PivotTable tend to be hard to grasp. Figure 11-1 shows a section of a table this section uses for examples. The table tracks sales of a microbrewery's products by category (strong ales, standard ales, health products, animal feedstuffs, and so on), item, date (year and month, in separate columns), the sales representative, the sales amount, the customer, and so on. The illustration shows only the most interesting fields for this section's purposes, leaving out various other fields (such as when the order was posted, when it was fulfilled, and when it was paid).

▲	A	B	C	D	E	F	G	H
6	Order #	Year	Month	Rep	Category	Item	Sales	Customer
7	20070045	2007	August	Hickman	Health	Brewer's Yeast	$800	Goods4U
8	20070044	2007	August	Hickman	Feedstuffs	Protein Mix	$400	Winners
9	20070043	2007	August	Velasquez	Str Ale	Boneshaker	$300	Countrywide
10	20070042	2007	August	Hickman	Feedstuffs	Protein Mix	$900	Winners
11	20070041	2007	September	Nilsson	Str Lager	Iron Reserve	$2,384	Extra Continental
12	20070040	2007	July	Hickman	Std Ale	Merry Giant	$3,295	Extra Continental
13	20070039	2007	June	Velasquez	Str Ale	Boneshaker	$400	Countrywide
14	20070038	2007	April	Hickman	Health	Brewer's Yeast	$995	Goods4U
15	20070037	2007	March	Stewart	Std Ale	Corn Circle	$2,500	Moose Pubs

FIGURE 11-1   The example table this chapter uses for demonstrating PivotTables.

You can use a PivotTable to ask the data questions, such as:

■ Which of our categories of product are waxing and which are waning?

■ Who are the key customers we should concentrate on?

■ How do our sales this year compare to our sales in another year?

■ Which rep sells most (or least) of which product? (Depending on your business circumstances, you might formulate the question this way: Should we refocus any particular rep on another product?)

You'll see examples of manipulating the sample table to deliver answers to such questions later in this chapter.

11

Create a PivotTable Framework Using the PivotTable and PivotChart Wizard

You can create a PivotTable either from a named table (see Chapter 9) or from a list of data that you haven't designated as a named table. Usually, it's easiest to start from a named table, as you can then take advantage of table features such as Excel automatically extending the table when you add rows to it.

TIP   *If you've created PivotTables or PivotCharts in earlier versions of Excel, you may be used to working with the PivotTable And PivotChart Wizard, which provides more choices in creating a PivotTable framework than the Create PivotTable dialog box does. Excel 2007 includes the PivotTable And PivotChart Wizard, which you can run by adding it to the Quick Access Toolbar as described in Chapter 17. You'll find the PivotTable And PivotChart Wizard command in the Commands Not In The Ribbon list in the Customize category in the Excel Options dialog box.*

To create a PivotTable framework, follow these steps:

1. Open the workbook that contains the table or data you want to manipulate.

2. Display the worksheet that contains the table or data.

3. Tell Excel which table or data range you want to use:

   ■ To use a named table, click a cell in the table. Excel adds the Table Tools section to the Ribbon and displays the Design tab.

   ■ To use a data range, select that range.

4. Open the Create PivotTable dialog box, shown here.

   ■ If you're using a named table, choose Design | Tools | Summarize With Pivot.

   ■ If you're using a data range, choose Insert | Tables | PivotTable.

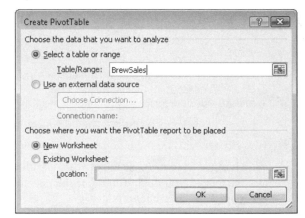

5. Make sure that Excel has selected the Select A Table Or Range option button and identified the table or range correctly in the Table/Range text box. If you need to change the table or range, click the Collapse Dialog button, select the correct item, and then press ENTER or click the Collapse Dialog button again.

> **TIP** *You can also create PivotTable reports (and PivotCharts) from data sources external to Excel—for example, by using MS Query to return data from a database. See "Link an Excel Worksheet to an External Database," in Chapter 9, for information on using external data sources with Excel.*

6. In the Choose Where You Want The PivotTable Report To Be Placed area, select the New Worksheet option button or the Existing Worksheet option button, as appropriate. In most cases, New Worksheet (the default) is the better choice. If you choose Existing Worksheet, specify the location in the text box. Either type the worksheet name or click the Collapse Dialog button to collapse the dialog box, click the appropriate sheet tab, and then click the Collapse Dialog button again to restore the dialog box.

7. Click the OK button. Excel creates the new worksheet or selects the specified existing worksheet (depending on your choice), creates a blank PivotTable, and displays the PivotTable Field List pane together with a blank framework for the PivotTable. Excel also adds the PivotTable Tools section to the Ribbon and displays the Options tab. Figure 11-2 shows these items.

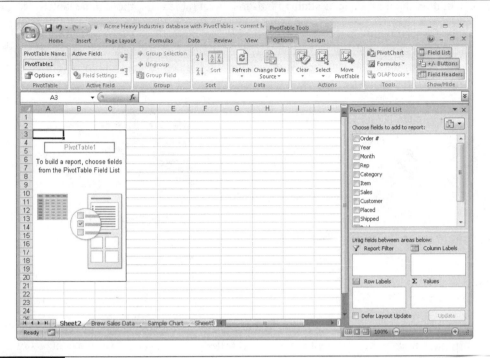

FIGURE 11-2   The PivotTable Tools section of the Ribbon contains an Options tab (shown here) and a Design tab. The PivotTable framework on the left of the document area is where you build your PivotTable.

Now you're ready to create the PivotTable on the framework, as described in the next section.

Create the PivotTable on the Framework

Create your PivotTable by selecting the appropriate check boxes in the Choose Fields To Add To Report list in the PivotTable Field List task pane. When you select a check box, Excel automatically adds the field to the appropriate area of the PivotTable.

NOTE   *In previous versions of Excel, adding fields to a PivotTable framework was the point at which many users became confused and gave up on PivotTables. Microsoft has attempted to simplify the process of adding fields to a PivotTable by making Excel automatically guess in which area of the PivotTable each field you select in the Choose Fields To Add To Report list belongs. As you'll see, Excel's guesses aren't always right—but you can change them quickly when you need to. If you prefer to use the old-style PivotTable layout, choose Options | PivotTable | Options | Options, click the Display tab of the PivotTable Options dialog box, select the Classic PivotTable Layout check box, and then click the OK button.*

Here's an illustrated example of adding fields to a PivotTable using the sample table.

1. In the Choose Fields To Add To Report list box, select the Year check box. Because the data appears to be numeric, Excel adds a Sum Of Year field to the Values area of the PivotTable framework, putting a **Sum of Year** label in cell A3 and adding a Sum of Year drop-down list to the Values box in the PivotTable Field List pane:

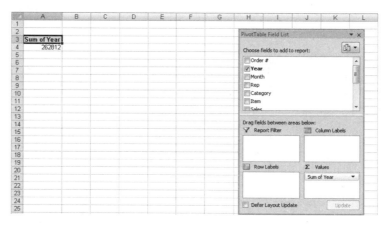

2. Having a sum of the years isn't what you want, so you need to change the field. Click it in the Values box and drag it to the Report Filter box. Excel removes the contents of cell A3, puts a Year label in cell A1, puts in cell B3 a drop-down list for selecting the years, and selects the (All) entry:

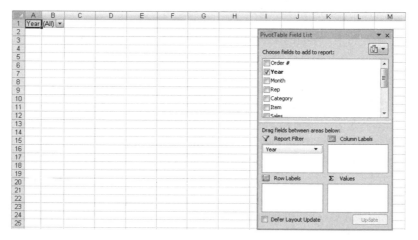

3. In the Choose Fields To Add To Report list box, select the Rep check box. Excel adds the field with a drop-down list button for selecting the rep name, enters the rep names in the cells (again, displaying all items), and adds a Grand Total entry under them:

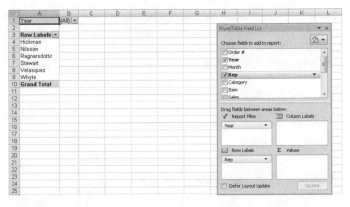

4. In the Choose Fields To Add To Report list box, select the Category check box. Excel adds the field to the list in the Row Labels box in the PivotTable Field List pane, and adds under each rep's name a list of the categories of products he or she has sold:

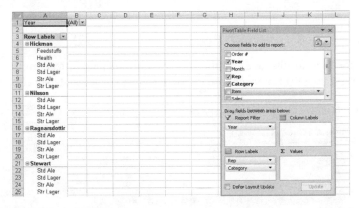

5. Having the categories as row labels isn't what the PivotTable needs, so drag the Category item from the Row Labels box to the Column Labels box. Excel adds the field with a drop-down list button for selecting the category, enters the categories in the cells across the columns, and adds a Grand Total entry immediately to their right:

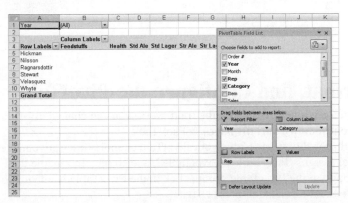

6. In the Choose Field To Add To Report list box, select the Sales check box. Because the data is numeric, Excel adds it to the values area, populating the columns and rows with data and adding a Sum of Sales label at the intersection of the rows and columns. Now you can see which rep has sold how much of each category of product:

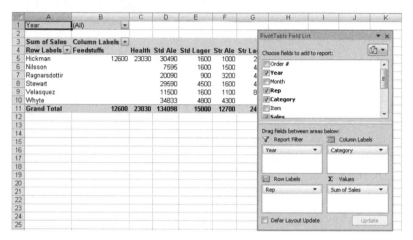

7. To see the reps' results for a specific year (as shown below) instead of for all years, click the Year drop-down list button, choose the year from the panel, and then click the OK button.

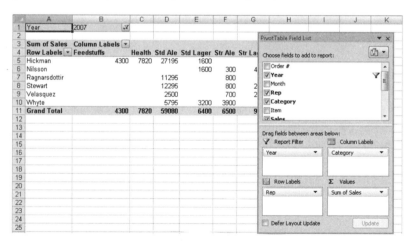

Change, Format, and Configure the PivotTable

Once you've created the PivotTable on the framework, you can change, format, and configure it. You can also control how Excel displays the PivotTable.

First, you'll probably want to give your PivotTable a more descriptive name than the default name that Excel assigns (PivotTable1, PivotTable2, and so on). To rename the PivotTable, click the Options tab, go to the PivotTable group, click in the PivotTable Name text box, type a new name for the PivotTable, and then press ENTER.

Change the PivotTable

You can change a PivotTable by dragging the fields you've placed already to different locations, removing one or more of those fields, or adding other fields. Here are quick examples of manipulating the PivotTable created in the previous section:

- In the Choose Fields To Add To Report list box in the PivotTable Field List pane, click the Item field and drag it to the Column Labels area, dropping it below the Category item. Excel breaks down each category by its components. This illustration shows only some of the categories:

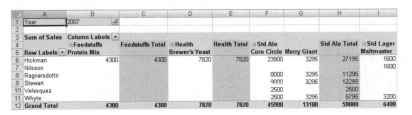

- In the Choose Fields To Add To Report list box in the PivotTable Field List pane, clear the Category check box to remove the Category field. The PivotTable then shows how much of each item each rep sold in the specified year, making it clear which rep is selling most of which item:

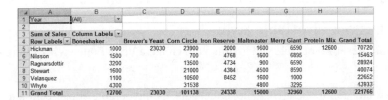

- In the Choose Fields To Add To Report list box in the PivotTable Field List pane, click the Customer item and drag it to the Row Labels area, dropping it below the Rep item. Doing so produces a PivotTable showing which rep sold how much of which item to which customer:

Row Labels	Boneshaker	Brewer's Yeast	Corn Circle	Iron Reserve	Maltmaster	Merry Giant	Protein Mix	Grand Total
Hickman	1000	23030	23900	2000	1600	6590	12600	70720
Countrywide	1000							1000
Extra Continental				2000		6590		8590
Goods4U		23030						23030
IntraBrew			23900					23900
Moose Pubs					1600			1600
Winners							12600	12600
Nilsson	1500		700	4768	1600	6895		15463
Countrywide	1500							1500
Extra Continental				4768		6895		11663
Moose Pubs			700		1600			2300
Ragnarsdottir	3200		13500	4734	900	6590		28924
Countrywide	3200							3200
Extra Continental				4734		6590		11324
IntraBrew			5500					5500
Moose Pubs			8000		900			8900
Stewart	1600		21000	4384	4500	8590		40074
Countrywide	1600							1600
Extra Continental				4384		8590		12974
IntraBrew			14500					14500
Moose Pubs			6500		4500			11000

■ In the PivotTable Field List pane, click the drop-down button on the Rep field, and then choose Remove Field from the menu to remove the Rep field from the PivotTable. The result is a breakdown of which items each customer purchased:

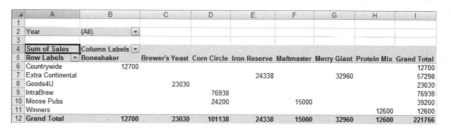

Format a PivotTable

To make a PivotTable look the way you want it, you first apply a PivotTable style—either a built-in style or a custom style of your own. You can then choose PivotTable style options to vary the look within the style.

Apply a PivotTable Style to a PivotTable

When you create a PivotTable, Excel automatically applies a PivotTable style to it. You can apply another PivotTable style from the PivotTable Styles group and panel on the Design tab of the PivotTable Tools section of the toolbar, as shown in Figure 11-3.

Create a Custom PivotTable Style

If none of the preset PivotTable styles suits you, create a PivotTable style of your own. Follow these steps:

1. Click any cell in the PivotTable. Excel adds the PivotTable Tools section to the Ribbon and displays the Options tab.

2. Choose Design | PivotTable Styles | New PivotTable Style. Excel displays the New PivotTable Quick Style dialog box (see Figure 11-4).

3. Type the name for the style in the Name text box. This name appears when you hover the mouse pointer over the style's name in the PivotTable Styles panel.

4. In the Table Element list box, select the element you want to change, and then click the Format button. Excel displays a reduced version of the Format Cells dialog box, containing only the Font tab, Border tab, and Fill tab. Use the controls on these tabs to specify the formatting for the element, and then click the OK button. For most of the elements, applying shading is most effective, so Excel displays the Fill tab of the Format Cells dialog box first.

5. Repeat step 3 for each element you want to change. The Preview section shows you how the table will look. The Table Element list box shows the names of items you've changed in boldface. You can remove the formatting you've applied by clicking an element in the Table Element list box, and then clicking the Clear button.

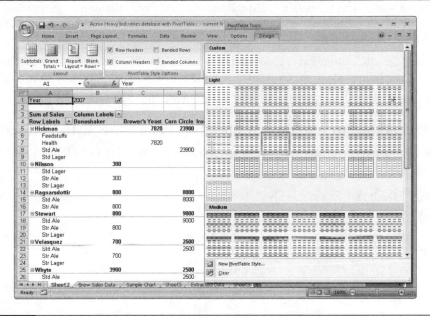

FIGURE 11-3   The PivotTable Styles group and panel on the Design tab provide a wide variety of preset styles for PivotTables, presented in Light, Medium, and Dark categories. Custom PivotTable styles you've created (by using the New PivotTable Style command) appear in a Custom category at the top of the list.

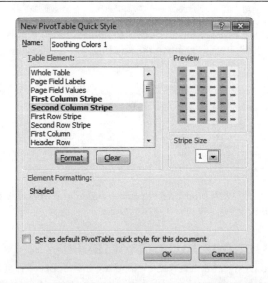

FIGURE 11-4   The New PivotTable Quick Style dialog box works in the same way as the New Table Quick Style box.

6. If you want Excel to apply this PivotTable style automatically to new PivotTables you create in this workbook, select the Set As Default PivotTable Quick Style For This Document check box.

7. Click the OK button. Excel closes the New PivotTable Quick Style dialog box and adds the PivotTable style to the Custom area at the top of the PivotTable Styles panel.

8. To apply your new style, choose it from the PivotTable Styles panel.

Vary a PivotTable Style's Look by Choosing PivotTable Style Options

Once you've chosen a PivotTable style, you can use the options in the PivotTable Style Options group to vary the details:

- **Row Headers**   Select this check box to apply the style's formatting to the row headers. Clear this check box to remove the formatting.

- **Column Headers**   Select this check box to apply the style's formatting to the column headers. Clear this check box to remove the formatting.

- **Banded Rows**   Select this check box to apply shaded bands to rows, as shown here. Clear this check box to remove the shading.

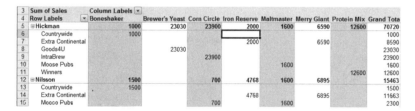

- **Banded Columns**   Select this check box to apply shaded bands to columns, as shown here. Clear this check box to remove the shading.

 NOTE   *Excel lets you apply both banded rows and banded columns, but the results tend not to be visually helpful.*

Choose Layout Options for a PivotTable

The Layout group on the Design tab lets you change the layout of a PivotTable by choosing whether to display subtotals and grand totals, switch among three types of layouts, and insert a blank row after each item to make the PivotTable easier to read:

■ **Subtotals**   Click this button, and then choose Do Not Show Subtotals, Show All Subtotals At Bottom Of Group, or Show All Subtotals At Top Of Group, as appropriate. Subtotals at the top of the group appear on the same line as the group's label. Subtotals at the bottom of the group appear on a separate row marked with the label name and **Totals**.

■ **Grand Totals**   Click this button, and then choose Off For Rows And Columns, On For Rows And Columns, On For Rows Only, or On For Columns Only to tell Excel which grand total columns and rows to display.

■ **Report Layout**   Click this button, and then choose Show In Compact Form, Show In Outline Form, or Show In Tabular Form, as appropriate. Figure 11-5 shows the differences in these layouts. Compact Form is the default and is useful for packing large amounts of data into a small area on screen.

■ **Blank Rows**   Click this button, and then choose Insert Blank Line After Each Item if you want to add blank lines between items to make the PivotTable less dense. To remove existing blank lines, choose Remove Blank Line After Each Item.

Change Which Parts of the PivotTable Excel Displays

The Show/Hide group on the Options tab of the PivotTable Tools section of the Ribbon lets you control which parts of the PivotTable Excel displays:

■ **Field List**   Click this button to toggle the display of the Field List pane. You can also toggle the display of the Field List pane by right-clicking in the PivotTable and choosing Show Field List or Hide Field List from the context menu (only one of these commands appears at a time), or simply click the Close button (the × button) to close the Field List pane.

■ **+/– Buttons**   Click this button to toggle the + and – buttons (for expanding and collapsing data) on and off. Once you've collapsed the PivotTable to show exactly what you want, you may want to hide the buttons to make the PivotTable easier to read or give it a cleaner look when you print it.

■ **Show Field Headers**   Click this button to turn the display of field headers on or off. Usually, having field headers displayed makes your PivotTable easier to read, but you may sometimes want to suppress them.

Change a Field to a Different Function

To change the function used for summarizing the data area in a PivotTable, follow these steps:

1. In the PivotTable, click the field itself or data that belongs to a cell containing the field. The Active Field text box in the Active Field group on the Options tab shows the field's name, as shown on the right.

11

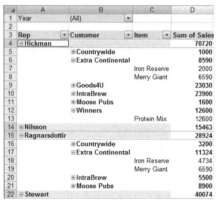

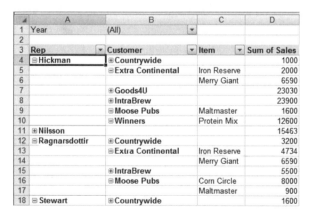

FIGURE 11-5 Excel offers three layouts for PivotTables: Compact (top), Outline (middle), and Tabular (bottom).

FIGURE 11-6   In the Field Settings dialog box, you can change the subtotals used for the PivotTable. You can also assign the field a custom name if you want.

2. Click the Field Settings button in the Active Field group. Excel displays the Field Settings dialog box (see Figure 11-6).

3. On the Subtotals & Filters tab, select the Custom option button, and then choose the function in the Select One Or More Functions list box.

   ■ You can select multiple functions by clicking each one in turn—you don't need to SHIFT-click or CTRL-click.

   ■ To deselect a selected function, click it again.

4. Click the OK button. Excel closes the Field Settings dialog box and applies the function to the field.

Choose PivotTable Options to Configure a PivotTable

Once you've got your PivotTable looking mostly as you want it to look, you can adjust it further by choosing PivotTable options. To choose options, choose Options | PivotTable | Options (click the Options button, not its drop-down button), and then work in the PivotTable Options dialog box (see Figure 11-7).

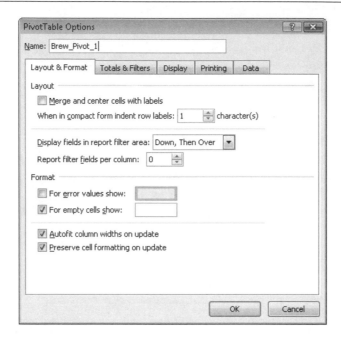

FIGURE 11-7   The PivotTable Options dialog box provides five tabs' worth of settings for configuring a PivotTable. Start by choosing options on the Layout & Format tab.

The Layout & Format tab of the PivotTable Options dialog box contains the following settings:

- **Merge And Center Cells With Labels**   Select this check box if you want Excel to merge and center the items in outer rows and columns. You may find the merged and centered look helps make PivotTables more readable. Clear this check box to keep the labels left-aligned.

- **When In Compact Form Indent Row Labels *NN* Characters**   Adjust the number in the spinner box to tell Excel how far to indent row labels when you're using Compact Form for the PivotTable. You can set any value from 0 characters to 127 characters.

- **Display Fields In Report Filter Area**   Choose Down, Then Over to display fields from top to bottom before moving to another column. Choose Over, Then Down to display fields from left to right before moving to another row.

- **Report Filter Fields Per Column**   Enter the number of fields you want Excel to display in a row or column (depending on your Display Fields In Report Filter Area drop-down list) before starting another row or column.

- **For Error Values Show**   To force Excel to display a specific value (for example, an error message) in each cell that contains an error value, select this check box, and then type the value you want.

■ **For Empty Cells Show**   To force Excel to display a specific value in each empty cell, select this check box, and then type the value you want.

■ **Autofit Column Widths On Update**   Select this check box to make Excel automatically adjust column widths to accommodate data after you update the PivotTable. This behavior is normally helpful.

■ **Preserve Cell Formatting On Update**   Select this check box to make Excel retain formatting that is applied to the PivotTable when you change the PivotTable's layout or refresh its data. You'll almost always want to keep this check box selected so that you don't need to reapply formatting to a PivotTable after you change its layout or update its contents.

The Totals & Filters tab of the PivotTable Options dialog box (see Figure 11-8) contains the following settings:

■ **Show Grand Totals for Rows**   Select this check box to make the PivotTable display grand totals for rows.

■ **Show Grand Totals For Columns**   Select this check box to make the PivotTable display grand totals for columns.

FIGURE 11-8   The Totals & Filters tab of the PivotTable Options dialog box lets you choose which grand totals to show, how to filter fields, and whether to use custom lists for sorting.

- **Subtotal Filtered Page Items** Select this check box to include items filtered from a report in subtotals. This option is available only when you're working with an OLAP (Online Analytical Processing) data source.

- **Allow Multiple Filters Per Field** Select this check box if you want to include any values hidden by filtering with the other values in subtotals and grand totals. Clear this check box to make subtotals and grand totals include only the items displayed. This option is not available for an OLAP data source.

- **Use Custom Lists When Sorting** Select this check box if you want to allow Excel to use custom lists for sorting data. (See the section "Create Custom AutoFill Lists" in Chapter 3 for details on creating custom lists.)

The Display tab of the PivotTable Options dialog box (see Figure 11-9) contains the following options:

- **Show Expand/Collapse Buttons** Select this check box to display the + and − buttons for expanding and collapsing data. Usually, it's easier to choose Options | Show/Hide | +/− Buttons if this is the only setting you want to change.

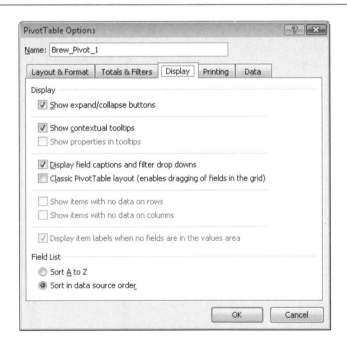

FIGURE 11 9   The Display tab of the PivotTable Options dialog box lets you choose which display items to include in the PivotTable.

■ **Show Contextual Tooltips**   Select this check box to make Excel display a tooltip containing the row or column label and value when you hover the mouse pointer. Here's an example:

3	Rep	▼	Customer	▼	Item	▼	Sum of Sales		
4	⊟Hickman		⊞Countrywide				1000		
5			⊞Extra Continental				859	Sum of Sales	
6			⊞Goods4U				2303	Value: 1000	
7			⊞IntraBrew				2390	Row: Hickman - Countrywide	

■ **Show Properties In Tooltips**   Select this check box to make Excel display a tooltip containing the property information for an item over which you hover the mouse pointer. This check box is available only when you're using an OLAP data source.

■ **Display Field Captions And Filter Drop Downs**   Select this check box to display the captions at the top of the PivotTable and drop-down arrows on column labels and row labels. Clear this check box to hide these items.

■ **Classic PivotTable Layout**   Select this check box if you want to lay out your PivotTables using the techniques for Excel 2003 and earlier versions.

■ **Show Items With No Data On Rows**   Select this check box if you want the PivotTable to include rows that contain no data. This setting is available only when you're using an OLAP data source.

■ **Show Items With No Data On Columns**   Select this check box if you want the PivotTable to include columns that contain no data. This setting is available only when you're using an OLAP data source.

■ **Display Item Labels When No Fields Are In The Values Area**   Select this check box if you want the PivotTable to displays labels when the value area contains no fields. This setting works only for PivotTables created in earlier versions of Excel than Excel 2007.

■ **Field List option buttons**   Select the Sort A To Z option button if you want to sort the fields alphabetically. Otherwise, select the Sort In Data Source Order option button to keep the fields in the order in which the data source provides them. These option buttons aren't available when you're using an OLAP data source.

The Printing tab of the PivotTable Options dialog box (see Figure 11-10) contains the following options:

■ **Print Expand/Collapse Buttons When Displayed On PivotTable**   Select this check box if you want to print the + and − buttons on a printout if they're displayed in the PivotTable. If the buttons are hidden already, they won't print even if you select this check box.

■ **Repeat Row Labels On Each Printed Page**   Select this check box to make Excel repeat the outer row field item labels at the top of each page in a printout. Usually, repeating the labels like this makes a PivotTable easier to read.

11

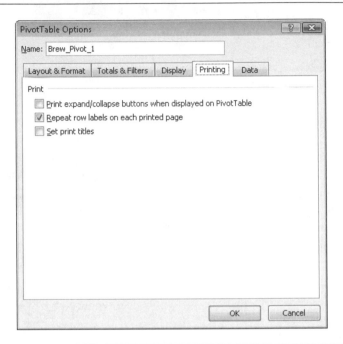

The Printing tab of the PivotTable Options dialog box lets you choose whether to include + and − buttons, repeat row labels, and print titles on printouts of PivotTables.

- **Set Print Titles**   Select this check box to make Excel print the field and item labels as row and column titles. To specify which rows or columns to print, close the PivotTable Options dialog box, choose Page Layout | Page Setup | Print Titles, and then enter the rows in the Rows To Repeat At Top text box, or the columns in the Columns To Repeat At Left text box on the Sheet tab of the Page Setup dialog box.

The Data tab of the PivotTable Options dialog box (see Figure 11-11) contains the following options:

- **Save Source Data With File**   Select this check box if you want Excel to save a copy of the PivotTable's data in the workbook. Saving the copy enables you to reopen the workbook and work with the PivotTable without refreshing the data, but it makes the workbook file substantially larger than it would be otherwise. If you need to keep the workbook file as small as possible, clear this check box. This option doesn't work with an OLAP data source.
- **Enable Expand To Detail**   Select this check box if you want Excel to let you double-click a cell in the PivotTable's data area to create and display a new worksheet showing

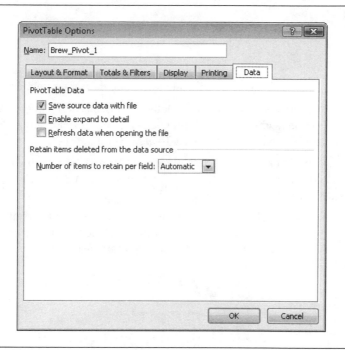

FIGURE 11-11   The Data tab of the PivotTable Options dialog box lets you choose whether to cache PivotTable data in the workbook, and whether to refresh the data each time you open the workbook.

the data behind that cell. This option is on by default, and can help you understand from which data a particular figure is being derived. Expanding to detail doesn't work with an OLAP data source.

- **Refresh Data When Opening The File**   Select this check box if you want Excel to refresh the PivotTable data when you reopen the workbook. This option doesn't work with an OLAP data source.

- **Number Of Items To Retain Per Field**   In this drop-down list, choose the number of items for each field you want Excel to cache in the workbook. The best choice is usually Automatic, which lets Excel cache the default number of unique items contained in each field. You can choose None to turn off caching, or choose Max to make Excel cache the maximum number of unique items contained in each field. (With Max selected, Excel will cache up to 1,048,576 items.)

Sort a PivotTable

To sort a PivotTable, follow these steps:

1. Click the field by which you want to sort.

2. Go to the Sort group on the Options tab, and then click the appropriate button:

   ■ For a quick sort in ascending order, click the AZ button. (The button's name varies depending on the field's data type—for example, Sort A To Z for text, Sort Smallest To Largest for numbers, or Sort Oldest To Newest for dates.)

   ■ For a quick sort in descending order, click the ZA button. Again, the button's name depends on the field's data type—for example, Sort Z To A, Sort Largest To Smallest, or Sort Newest To Oldest.

   ■ For any other sort, click the Sort button, and then follow the other steps in this list. Excel displays the Sort dialog box with the name of the field in the title bar—for example, Sort (Customer) when you've selected the Customer field, as shown here:

3. Choose the appropriate option button in the Sort Options area. The options available depend on which type of data you're sorting—text, numbers, or dates.

   ■ **Manual**   (Text fields; date fields) Select this option button if you want to be able to drag the items into the order you want.

   ■ **Ascending (A To Z) By**   (Text fields; date fields) Select this option button to sort in ascending order, and then choose the item in the drop-down list—either the field's name or a function used to calculate the field.

   ■ **Descending (Z To A) By**   (Text fields; date fields) Select this option button to sort in descending order, and then choose the item in the drop-down list—either the field's name or a function used to calculate the field.

■ **Smallest To Largest**   (Number fields) Select this option button to sort in ascending order.

■ **Largest To Smallest**   (Number fields) Select this option button to sort in descending order.

4. If you need further sort options, click the More Options button. (The More Options button isn't available for number fields.) Excel displays the More Sort Options dialog box, as shown here. Choose from the following options, and then click the OK button to return to the Sort dialog box.

■ **Sort Automatically Every Time The Report Is Updated**   Select this check box if you want to use automatic sorting. Normally, when you open the More Sort Options dialog box, you'll want to clear this check box so that you can use the other options (which are disabled when the check box is selected.)

■ **First Key Sort Order**   In this drop-down list, select Normal for a normal sort, or select one of your custom lists to sort by that list.

■ **Sort By area**   When these controls are available, you can select the Grand Total option button or the Values In Selected Row option button. If you select the Values In Selected Row option button, click the Collapse Dialog button, click a cell in the row, and then press ENTER or click the Collapse Dialog button again.

5. Click the OK button. Excel closes the Sort dialog box and performs the sort.

TIP   *You can apply conditional formatting to PivotTables to highlight particular values or emphasize the relationship among values in a set of data. For example, you might apply data bars to make values easier to compare with each other.*

Filter a PivotTable

You can filter the items in a PivotTable by using much the same techniques described in the section "Perform Quick Filtering with AutoFilter" in Chapter 9. For example, click one of the field drop-down buttons to produce a panel of options, as in the two examples shown here:

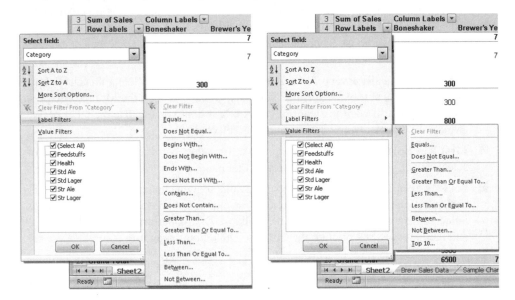

You can then do the following:

■ Select a means of filtering by label from the Label Filters submenu.

■ Select a means of filtering by value from the Value Filters submenu.

■ Select or clear the check boxes in the list box to specify which items to include and which to exclude.

■ Once you've applied a filter to the field, select the Clear Filter item to remove it.

Group and Ungroup Items

To help identify the data you need to work with, you can group items.

Group Items in a Numeric Field

To group the items in a numeric field, follow these steps:

1. In the PivotTable, click the numeric field whose items you want to group.

2. Choose Options | Group | Group Field. Excel displays the Grouping dialog box shown here:

3. Select the Starting At check box, and enter the starting number for the grouping in the text box.

4. Select the Ending At check box, and enter the ending number for the grouping in the text box.

5. In the By text box, type how many items you want to group together.

6. Click the OK button. Excel closes the Grouping dialog box and groups the items as specified.

Group Items in a Date or Time Field

To group the items in a date or time field, follow these steps:

1. In the PivotTable, click the date or time field whose items you want to group.

2. Choose Options | Group | Group Field. Excel displays the Grouping dialog box shown here:

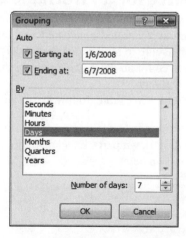

3. Select the Starting At check box, and enter the starting date for the grouping in the text box.

4. Select the Ending At check box, and enter the ending date for the grouping in the text box.

5. In the By list box, select the time period or periods by which you want to group the dates: Seconds, Minutes, Hours, Days, Months, Quarters, or Years. You can select

multiple items by clicking each in turn (you don't need to SHIFT-click or CTRL-click). To group by weeks, select only the Days item, and then choose 7 in the Number Of Days text box.

6. Click the OK button. Excel closes the Grouping dialog box and groups the items as specified.

Group Selected Items

To group selected items, follow these steps:

1. Select the items you want to group:

   - Click and drag to select a contiguous range of items.

   - Click the first item, and then SHIFT-click another item to select all items between the two.

   - Click the first item, and then CTRL-click each other item to select noncontiguous items.

2. Choose Options | Group | Group Selection. Excel groups the items.

Ungroup Items

To ungroup grouped items, select the items, and then choose Options | Group | Ungroup.

Change the Data Source for a PivotTable

Getting a PivotTable set up to your satisfaction can take a fair amount of time and effort that you'd probably prefer not to repeat if you don't have to. Excel lets you easily change the data source for a PivotTable without having to reconstruct the PivotTable itself. This capability lets you swap in an updated data source for an older one, or create the PivotTable using sample data and then switch it to using the real data.

To change the data source for a PivotTable, follow these steps:

1. Choose Options | Data | Change Data Source (click the top part of the Change Data Source button, not the drop-down part). Excel displays the Change PivotTable Data Source dialog box, as shown here.

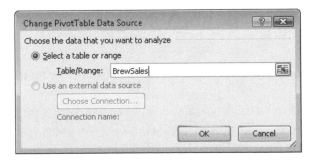

2. If the data source is a table or range, click the Collapse Dialog button, select the new data source, and then press ENTER or click the Collapse Dialog button again. If the table uses an external data source, click the Choose Connection button, and then use the resulting dialog box to specify the data source.

3. Click the OK button. Excel switches the PivotTable to the new data source and snaps the data into place.

Move a PivotTable to Another Location

If you need to move a PivotTable to a different location, follow these steps:

1. Click anywhere in the PivotTable. Excel adds the PivotTable Tools section to the Ribbon and displays the Options tab.

2. Choose Options | PivotTable Options | Move PivotTable. Excel displays the Move PivotTable dialog box, as shown here.

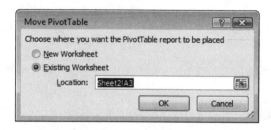

3. To move the PivotTable to a new worksheet, select the New Worksheet option button. To move it to an existing worksheet, select the Existing Worksheet option button, click the Collapse Dialog button, choose the sheet and the upper-left cell, and then press ENTER or click the Collapse Dialog button again.

4. Click the OK button. Excel moves the PivotTable to the new location.

Create PivotCharts from PivotTables

A PivotChart is a chart derived from a PivotTable. The advantage of a PivotChart over a regular chart is that you can drag fields to different locations in the chart layout to display different levels of detail or different views of the data. This flexibility makes PivotCharts great for analyzing data.

This section shows you how to create a PivotChart from a PivotTable.

Create a PivotChart from a PivotTable

To create a PivotChart, follow these steps:

1. Create a PivotTable as described earlier in this chapter.

2. Click anywhere in the PivotTable. Excel adds the PivotTable Tools section to the Ribbon.

11

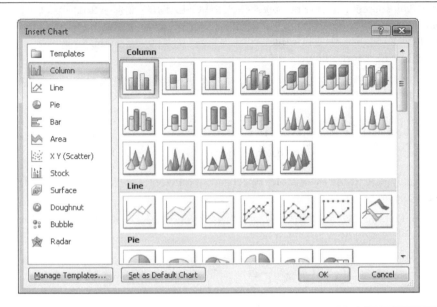

FIGURE 11-12 In the Insert Chart dialog box, select the type of PivotChart you want to create.

3. Choose Options | Tools | PivotChart. Excel displays the Insert Chart dialog box (see Figure 11-12).

4. Select the type of PivotChart you want to create.

5. Click the OK button. Excel closes the Insert Chart dialog box and creates a PivotChart as an object in the worksheet that contains the PivotTable. Excel also adds the PivotChart Tools section to the Ribbon and displays the PivotChart Filter Pane task pane (see Figure 11-13).

NOTE *The first three tabs on the PivotChart Tools section of the Ribbon—the Design tab, the Layout tab, and the Format tab—are the same as the tabs on the Chart Tools section of the Ribbon. Chapter 13 shows you how to use these tabs to design, lay out, and format charts.*

Move the PivotChart to Its Own Worksheet

Excel creates the PivotChart on the same worksheet as the PivotTable, but it's usually a good idea to move the PivotChart to its own sheet immediately so that you have plenty of space to work with it. To move the PivotChart, follow these steps:

1. With the PivotChart selected, choose Design | Location | Move Chart. Excel displays the Move Chart dialog box, as shown here.

2. Select the New Sheet option button.

3. Instead of the default name that Excel suggests for the new chart sheet (Chart1, Chart2, or the next unused name), type a descriptive name that enables you to identify the PivotChart sheet easily. As with any sheet name, the name can be up to 31 characters long.

4. Click the OK button. Excel closes the Move Chart dialog box, creates the new sheet, gives the sheet the name you specified, and moves the PivotChart to it.

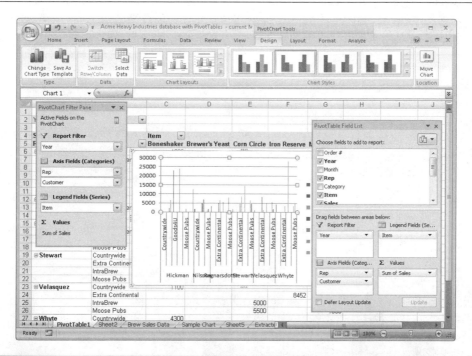

FIGURE 11-13 A PivotChart created as an object in a worksheet, the PivotChart Tools section of the Ribbon, and the PivotChart Filter Pane tend to make the Excel window cluttered.

Arrange the Data on the PivotChart

When you create a PivotChart, Excel places the fields on it according to where you had them on the PivotTable and some algorithmic guesswork. Sometimes the guesswork is inspired, and you get a PivotChart that shows what you want. More often, you get a PivotChart that only Excel could love and that needs immediate rearranging to make any sense.

To arrange the data on the PivotChart, drag the fields to the appropriate places in the PivotTable Field List pane in the same way you did to adjust a PivotTable. Figure 11-14 shows a PivotChart that displays sales by the Customer field. You can use any of the drop-down lists in the PivotChart Filter Pane to change the displayed data. In this example, you can change the year, the customer, and the item. For example, you could change the chart so that it showed only certain years, only some customers, or only particular items.

Similarly, you can add or remove fields to pivot the chart. To change the fields, select or clear the check boxes in the Choose Fields To Add To Report list box in the PivotTable Field List pane, or drag the current fields from one box to another at the bottom of the PivotTable Field List pane. Figure 11-15 shows the chart rearranged to show product sales by rep.

> TIP
>
> *You can create a PivotChart instantly with the default settings by selecting a PivotTable and pressing F11. If you customize the default setting to the type of PivotChart you usually need to create, you may find this option useful. To customize the default setting, click the Set As Default Chart button in the Chart Type dialog box.*

FIGURE 11-14 The PivotChart Filter Pane lets you filter any of the fields displayed on the PivotChart.

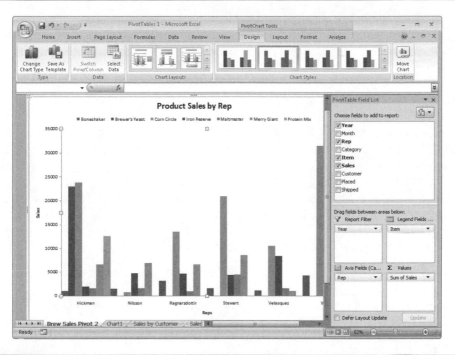

FIGURE 11-15   Here's the same PivotChart rearranged to show product sales by rep.

Create a Conventional Chart from PivotTable Data

Sometimes you may want to create a conventional chart from data in a PivotTable rather than create
an interactive PivotChart. To create a conventional chart, you must extract the values from the data
in the PivotTable and then use the Chart Wizard to create the chart. To do so, follow these steps:

1.   Select the data in the PivotTable. If you need to include field buttons and any data contained
     in the first column and row of the report, drag upwards and across from the lower-right corner
     of the data range rather than dragging down and across from the upper-left corner.

2.   Issue a Copy command (for example, press CTRL-C).

3.   Select a cell in a blank area of the same worksheet or a different worksheet that will
     contain the data values.

4.   Right-click in the cell, and then choose Paste Special from the context menu to display
     the Paste Special dialog box.

5.   Select the Values option button.

6.   Click the OK button. Excel pastes the values from the PivotTable data into the range that
     starts with the cell you selected.

7.   Choose Insert | Charts, click the button for the chart category you want, and then choose
     the chart type from the resulting panel. See Chapter 13 for instructions on creating charts.

11

Chapter 12

Solve Problems by Performing What-If Analysis

How to...

- ■ Create data tables to assess the impact of variables
- ■ Explore alternative data sets with scenarios
- ■ Solve problems using Goal Seek
- ■ Use the Solver to manipulate two or more values

In Chapter 11, you learned how to create PivotTables and PivotCharts to manipulate and analyze data in a table so that it yielded the answers to particular questions. In this chapter, you'll learn how to perform a what-if analysis to examine what will given particular results or circumstances.

First, you'll learn how to create data tables that enable you to assess what impact one or two variables have on a calculation. Then you'll learn how to use Excel's scenarios to explore the effects of alternative data sets within the same worksheet. At the end of the chapter, you'll see how to solve one-variable problems using Goal Seek, and how to use the Solver to solve multivariable problems.

Create Data Tables to Assess the Impact of Variables

If you need to assess the impact of a single variable or two variables on a calculation, the tool to use is a *data table*. A data table is an automated way of entering an array formula in a range of cells so as to display the results of using different values in one formula or multiple formulas.

NOTE   *Data tables are sometimes also called* sensitivity *tables.*

Create a Single-Variable Data Table

The easiest type of data table to create is a single-variable data table. You must lay out a single-variable data table so that its input values (the values you want to test) either run down a column or run across a row. In other words, you can't place the input values in a range of cells that spans multiple rows *and* multiple columns.

Excel feeds input values to a data table through a cell called the *input cell*. You enter the input cell in the formula (or formulas) in place of one of the values or references for which you want to test the input values. The input cell must be blank (otherwise, Excel uses the cell's value in the formula, which defeats the point of the exercise), and can be anywhere on the worksheet. In most cases, using a cell adjacent to the range that contains the input values is clearest and least confusing.

Following is an illustrated example of creating a single-variable data table. The example uses the =DB() function, which (as you saw in "Financial Functions," in Chapter 7) calculates the depreciation of an asset over a specified year in its life by using the fixed-declining balance method. The example uses a data table to display the depreciation for each year of the asset's life, instead of displaying only one year.

To create the single-variable data table, follow these steps:

1. Enter the supporting data for the calculation in the range B1:B4, together with identifying labels in the range A1:A4:

	A	B	C
1	Initial Cost	$25,000.00	
2	Salvage Value	$3,000.00	
3	Asset Life (Years)	6	
4	Period	2	
5			

2. Enter the input values down one column or across one row:

■ Leave at least one blank row before the first input value in a column. (This example leaves row 5 blank.) Leave at least one blank column before the first input value in a row.

■ Entering the input values down a column creates a *column-oriented* data table. Entering the input values across a row creates a *row-oriented* data table. This example creates a column-oriented data table.

■ You can type or paste the values as usual, but if the values vary by a consistent amount, you may also be able to use AutoFill instead to enter them quickly.

	A	B	C
1	Initial Cost	$25,000.00	
2	Salvage Value	$3,000.00	
3	Asset Life (Years)	6	
4	Period	2	
5			
6	Input Values		
7		1	
8		2	
9		3	
10		4	
11		5	
12		6	

3. Enter the formula in the appropriate cell:

■ For a column-oriented data table, enter the formula in the row immediately above the first input value and in the next column to the right:

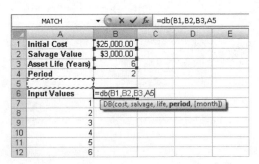

MATCH	▼	× ✓ ƒx	=db(B1,B2,B3,A5)		
	A	B	C	D	E
1	Initial Cost	$25,000.00			
2	Salvage Value	$3,000.00			
3	Asset Life (Years)	6			
4	Period	2			
5					
6	Input Values	=db(B1,B2,B3,A5			
7		1	DB(cost, salvage, life, **period**, [month])		
8		2			
9		3			
10		4			
11		5			
12		6			

12

- For a row-oriented data table, enter the formula in the column to the left of the first input value and the next row down.

- Enter the input cell in place of the appropriate argument in the formula. Be warned that the formula will likely display an error value (as in this example) or an obviously incorrect value. This is because the input cell is blank and, therefore, receives a zero value. As you'll see in a moment, the data table works fine even with an error value appearing as the formula result.

	B6		f_x	=DB(B1,B2,B3,A5)	
	A	B	C	D	E
1	Initial Cost	$25,000.00			
2	Salvage Value	$3,000.00			
3	Asset Life (Years)	6			
4	Period	2			
5					
6	Input Values	#NUM!			
7		1			
8		2			
9		3			
10		4			
11		5			
12		6			

4. Select the range of cells that contains the formula (or formulas) and the input values:

	A6		f_x	Input Values	
	A	B	C	D	E
1	Initial Cost	$25,000.00			
2	Salvage Value	$3,000.00			
3	Asset Life (Years)	6			
4	Period	2			
5					
6	Input Values	#NUM!			
7		1			
8		2			
9		3			
10		4			
11		5			
12		6			
13					

5. Choose Data | Data Tools | What-If Analysis | Data Table. Excel displays the Data Table dialog box, as shown here:

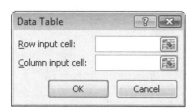

6. Enter the cell reference for the input cell by typing or by selecting the cell in the worksheet:

   ■ For a column-oriented data table, enter the cell reference in the Column Input Cell text box. In this example, you would enter the cell reference **$A$5** by clicking cell A5.

   ■ For a row-oriented data table, enter the cell reference in the Row Input Cell text box.

7. Click the OK button. Excel closes the Table dialog box and creates the data table, entering the array formula **{=TABLE(,A5)}** in each results cell:

	A6	▼	f_x	Input Values	
▲	A	B	C	D	E
1	Initial Cost	$25,000.00			
2	Salvage Value	$3,000.00			
3	Asset Life (Years)	6			
4	Period	2			
5					
6	Input Values	#NUM!			
7	1	$7,450.00			
8	2	$5,229.90			
9	3	$3,671.39			
10	4	$2,577.32			
11	5	$1,809.28			
12	6	$1,270.11			
13					
14					

Notice that, in this example, the cell that contains the formula still displays the #NUM! error because the input cell is blank. However, the range B7:B12 displays the correct output.

Add Further Formulas to a Data Table

If necessary, you can use two or more formulas in a single-variable data table. If you need to use more than one formula in a data table, place them as follows:

■ For a column-oriented data table, enter the formulas in the cells to the right of the first formula.

■ For a row-oriented data table, enter the formulas in the cells below the first formula.

Here's an example of adding a second formula, DDB, to the data table created in the previous section. As you'll remember from "Financial Functions," in Chapter 7, DDB calculates depreciation using the double-declining balance method, so the resulting data table lets you compare the depreciation in each year of the asset's life using each depreciation method.

To add the second formula to the data table, follow these steps:

1. Enter the formula **=DDB(B1,B2,B3,A5)** in cell C6, the cell to the right of the first formula:

	A	B	C	D	E	F
1	Initial Cost	$25,000.00				
2	Salvage Value	$3,000.00				
3	Asset Life (Years)	6				
4	Period	2				
5						
6	Input Values	#NUM!	=ddb(B1,B2,B3,A5			
7		1	$ 7,450.00			
8		2	$ 5,229.90			
9		3	$ 3,671.39			
10		4	$ 2,577.32			
11		5	$ 1,809.28			
12		6	$ 1,270.11			

MATCH — X ✓ fx =ddb(B1,B2,B3,A5)

DDB(cost, salvage, life, **period**, [factor])

2. Select the range that contains the input range and the two formulas. In this case, select the range A6:C12:

A6 — fx Input Values

	A	B	C	D	E
1	Initial Cost	$25,000.00			
2	Salvage Value	$3,000.00			
3	Asset Life (Years)	6			
4	Period	2			
5					
6	Input Values	#NUM!	#NUM!		
7		1	$7,450.00		
8		2	$5,229.90		
9		3	$3,671.39		
10		4	$2,577.32		
11		5	$1,809.28		
12		6	$1,270.11		
13					

3. Choose Data | Data Tools | What-If Analysis | Data Table. Excel displays the Data Table dialog box.

4. Enter the cell reference for the same input cell as for the previous formula—in this case, **$A$5**—in the Column Input Cell text box.

5. Click the OK button. Excel closes the Table dialog box and adds the second formula to the data table, entering the array formula **{=TABLE(,A5)}** in each results cell:

C12 — fx {=TABLE(,A5)}

	A	B	C	D	E
1	Initial Cost	$25,000.00			
2	Salvage Value	$3,000.00			
3	Asset Life (Years)	6			
4	Period	2			
5					
6	Input Values	#NUM!	#NUM!		
7		1	$7,450.00	$8,333.33	
8		2	$5,229.90	$5,555.56	
9		3	$3,671.39	$3,703.70	
10		4	$2,577.32	$2,469.14	
11		5	$1,809.28	$1,646.09	
12		6	$1,270.11	$292.18	
13					

Create a Two-Variable Data Table

Single-variable data tables can help you assess what happens when a single piece of information in a calculation changes. But often you'll need to assess what happens when two pieces of information change. For example, when calculating the depreciation of an asset, you might need to assess what happens not only for different periods of its life but also for different salvage values of the asset at the end of its life.

To create a two-variable data table, you enter the second set of input data in the other dimension from the first set: if the first set of input data is in a column, you enter the second set of input data in a row across the top of the results area, and vice versa. You place the formula at the intersection of the input data row and the input data column.

Here's an example of creating a two-variable data table along the same lines as the single-variable data table created earlier in this chapter. The table is rearranged and formatted so it's easier to read, but the principle is the same:

	I7		f_x	{=TABLE(B6,B7)}					
	A	B	C D	E	F	G	H	I	J
1	Initial Cost	$25,000							
2	Salvage Value	$3,000		SALVAGE VALUES					
3	Asset Life (Years)	6	#NUM!	$1,000	$2,000	$3,000	$4,000	$5,000	$6,000
4	Period	3	P 1	$10,375	$8,600	$7,450	$6,575	$5,875	$5,300
5			E 2	$6,069	$5,642	$5,230	$4,846	$4,494	$4,176
6	Row Input		R 3	$3,551	$3,701	$3,671	$3,571	$3,438	$3,291
7	Column Input		I 4	$2,077	$2,428	$2,577	$2,632	$2,630	$2,593
8			O 5	$1,215	$1,593	$1,809	$1,940	$2,012	$2,044
9			D 6	$711	$1,045	$1,270	$1,430	$1,539	$1,610

To create this two-variable data table (without all the formatting and labels), follow these steps:

1. Enter the first series of input data (**1, 2, 3, 4, 5, 6**) in the range D4:D9. This range will be linked to the column input cell.

2. Enter the second series of input data (**$1000, $2000, $3000, $4000, $5000, $6000**) in the range E3:J3. This range will be linked to the row input cell.

3. Enter the formula **=DB(B1,B6,B3,B7)** in cell D3, at the intersection of the input column and the input row. B6 is the row input cell, and B7 is the column input cell. As before, the formula produces an error result (#NUM!) in its cell because it receives zero values from the two input cells.

4. Choose Data | Data Tools | What-If Analysis | Data Table. Excel displays the Data Table dialog box.

5. Enter **B6** in the Row Input Cell text box.

6. Enter **B7** in the Column Input Cell text box.

7. Click the OK button. Excel closes the Table dialog box and creates the data table, entering the array formula **{=TABLE(B6,B7)}** in each results cell.

12

Change, Copy, or Move a Data Table

Once you've created a data table, you can manipulate its contents only by changing the input values or the formula. You can't directly change the contents of any results cell, because Excel implements the data table as an array formula. So to change the contents of a data table, you need to clear the data table (as described in "Clear a Data Table," next) and then create it again from scratch.

However, you can copy the results of the data table to a different location by using Copy and Paste. When you do so, Excel copies not the array formulas themselves but the results of the formulas.

You can move a data table in its entirety by selecting it and using drag and drop. When you move a data table, Excel changes the references in the formulas but otherwise leaves the array formulas intact.

Clear a Data Table

Because a data table consists of an array formula, you have to clear the whole of it at once rather than just part of it. (See "Work with Array Formulas," in Chapter 8, for an explanation of array formulas.) If you try to clear just part of the data table, Excel displays this error message box:

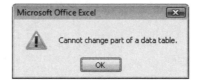

To clear the values from the data table, select the range of cells that contains the values, and then choose Home | Editing | Clear | Clear Contents or press DELETE. Make sure you don't select any formula cells.

To clear a data table entirely, select every cell in the range it occupies, including all cells that contain formulas, and then choose Home | Editing | Clear | Clear All.

Explore Alternative Data Sets with Scenarios

Excel's scenarios feature lets you define and use alternative data sets within the same workbook. Instead of creating a separate version of a workbook and using it to experiment with different values or different formulas, you can use scenarios to experiment more comfortably without damaging your main workbook. Better yet, you can create a what-if model in a workbook, share it with your colleagues so that they can admire your scenarios and perhaps create their own, and track the results of the changes your colleagues make to the scenarios.

Create the Worksheet You Want to Manipulate with Scenarios

The first step in using scenarios is to create the worksheet you want to manipulate and to define names for the cells whose values will be manipulable in the scenarios. Defining names isn't necessary, because you can refer to cells by their references instead, but names make the process so much clearer that you'll almost always want to define them.

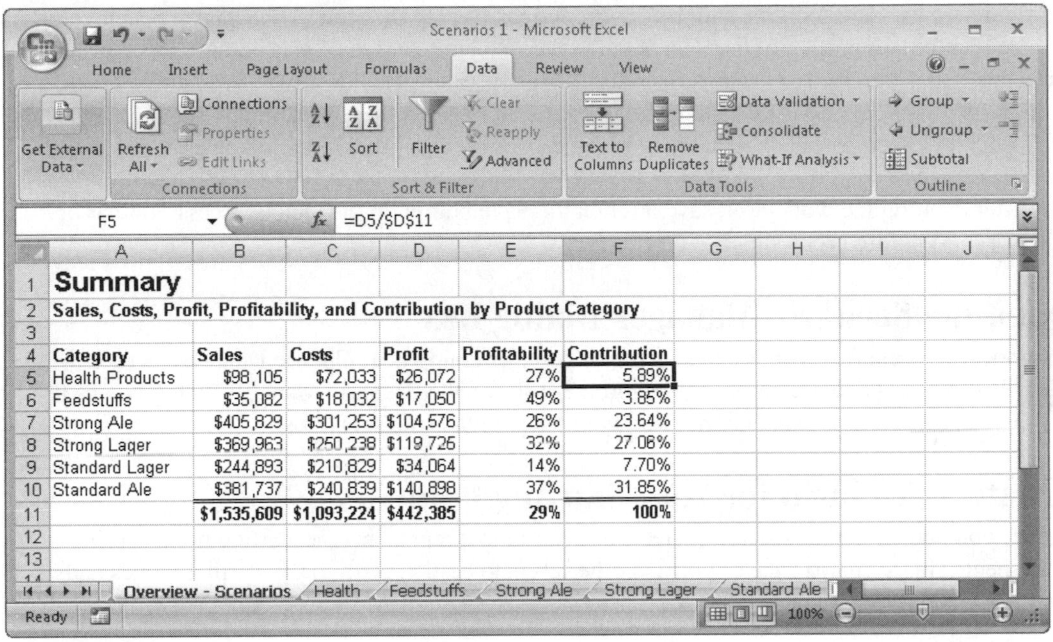

FIGURE 12-1 The sample worksheet used for scenarios

Create the worksheet by using the methods you've learned so far in this book. Figure 12-1 shows the worksheet used for examples in the following sections. It summarizes the sales, costs, profit, profitability, and contribution to profitability of the six categories of products that a microbrewery makes.

The worksheet is easy to grasp:

- The figures in the Sales column are total sales figures drawn from the underlying worksheets. The total at the bottom of the column adds the sales figures together.

- The figures in the Costs column are total costs figures (production and distribution costs) drawn from the underlying worksheets. The total at the bottom of the column adds the costs figures together.

- The figures in the Profit column are calculated by subtracting each product's costs from its sales. The total at the bottom of the column adds the profit figures together.

- The percentages in the Profitability column are calculated by dividing each product's profit by its total sales. The figure at the bottom of the column is the overall profitability, calculated by dividing the total profit by the total sales.

- The percentages in the Contribution column are calculated by dividing each product's profit by the company's total profit (cell D11). The total at the bottom of the column adds the contribution figures to confirm that they represent 100 percent and that nothing is missing.

12

The brewery's management team will use scenarios to examine what happens when they change the figures in the Sales column and the Costs column. To help the team see instantly which value they're manipulating, each of the figures in the Sales column and the Costs column (apart from the totals) has a descriptive name defined for it: Health_Sales, Health_Costs, Feedstuffs_Sales, Feedstuffs_Costs, and so on. The longer names are shortened a little (Health instead of Health Products, Std Lager instead of Standard Lager, and so on) because the Scenario Values dialog box truncates longer labels.

After creating the worksheet, save it (click the Save button on the Quick Access Toolbar or press CTRL-S) before proceeding.

Open the Scenario Manager Dialog Box

To work with scenarios, you use the Scenario Manager dialog box. Choose Data | Data Tools | What-If Analysis | Scenario Manager. Figure 12-2 shows the Scenario Manager dialog box as it first appears when you display it in a workbook that contains no scenarios.

Create a Scenario for Your Starting Point

Before you add any other scenarios, create a scenario that represents the starting point for the worksheet. This scenario enables you and other users to easily return to the starting values and assumptions for the worksheet.

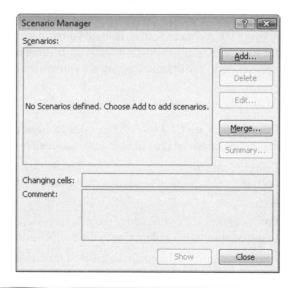

FIGURE 12-2 Use the Scenario Manager dialog box to create and manipulate scenarios.

To create a scenario for your starting point, follow these steps:

1. If the Scenario Manager dialog box isn't already displayed, choose Data | Data Tools | What-If Analysis | Scenario Manager to display it.

2. Click the Add button. Excel displays the Add Scenario dialog box (see Figure 12-3).

3. Type the name (for example, *Starting Scenario*) in the Scenario Name text box.

4. Click in the Changing Cells text box, and then select the cells in the spreadsheet that will be changeable in the scenario:

   ■ Click and drag to select contiguous cells. CTRL-click to add noncontiguous cells to the current selection.

   ■ Excel automatically collapses the Add Scenario dialog box while you select cells in the worksheet, so you don't need to click the Collapse Dialog button to collapse the dialog box manually. Excel restores the dialog box after you finish making a selection.

   ■ After you make a selection, Excel changes the dialog box's title from Add Scenario to Edit Scenario. Otherwise, the dialog box remains the same.

5. Type a comment (if appropriate) in the Comment text box. Excel starts you off with a comment saying that the scenario was created by you (whatever Office thinks your name is) and the date.

6. Select or clear the Prevent Changes check box and the Hide check box as necessary. See the next section, "Add Further Scenarios," for details on these check boxes.

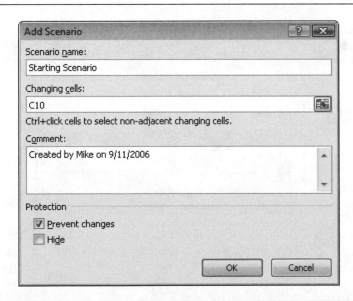

FIGURE 12-3   Start by using the Add Scenario dialog box to create a scenario that represents the starting point for the worksheet.

7. Click the OK button. Excel closes the Edit Scenario dialog box and displays the Scenario Values dialog box, which contains the current values for each of the changeable cells:

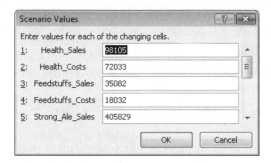

8. For the starting scenario, you don't need to change the existing values. Click the OK button. Excel closes the Scenario Values dialog box and returns you to the Scenario Manager dialog box.

Add Further Scenarios

To add another scenario, repeat the steps you took to create the starting scenario, but with these differences:

■ Type a different (and descriptive) name for the scenario in the Add Scenario dialog box.

■ Change the selection of changeable cells only if necessary. Excel automatically suggests those cells that are defined in the first scenario you defined.

■ Change the appropriate values in the Scenario Values dialog box to effect changes in the worksheet. As well as typing values, you can enter formulas in the Scenario Values dialog box to change the existing cell contents. For example, to see what effect a 25 percent decrease in costs would look like, enter **=.75*** before the existing value. Excel displays this message box to tell you that it has converted the formula result to a value; click the OK button:

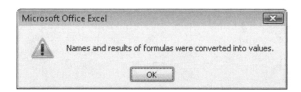

■ Select the Prevent Changes check box if you want to prevent changes to the scenario. After selecting this check box, you need to implement protection by using a Review | Changes | Protect Sheet command, and then working in the Protect Sheet dialog box.

NOTE   *See "Protect Cells, a Worksheet, or a Workbook," in Chapter 14, for an explanation of protecting worksheets and workbooks.*

■   Select the Hide check box if you want to hide the scenario from other users. After selecting this check box, you need to implement protection by using a Review | Changes | Protect Sheet command, and then working in the Protect Sheet dialog box.

Edit and Delete Existing Scenarios

To edit an existing scenario, select its entry in the Scenarios list box in the Scenario Manager dialog box, click the Edit button, and then work in the Edit Scenario dialog box. Excel automatically adds details of the modification to the comment attached to the scenario—for example, *Modified by Jason Acme on 11/22/2007*. After making such edits as are needed, click the OK button.

To delete a scenario, select its entry in the Scenarios list box in the Scenario Manager dialog box, and then click the Delete button. Excel deletes the scenario without confirmation.

Switch from One Scenario to Another

To switch from one scenario to another, follow these steps:

1.   Choose Data | Data Tools | What-If Analysis | Scenario Manager. Excel displays the Scenario Manager dialog box.

2.   Select the scenario in the Scenarios list box.

3.   Click the Show button to display the scenario in the workbook.

4.   Click the Close button to close the Scenario Manager dialog box.

That's easy enough, but it takes a handful of clicks or keystrokes. If you need to switch more easily from one scenario to another, add the Scenario drop-down list to the Quick Access Toolbar. You'll find the Scenario drop-down list in the Commands Not In The Ribbon list in the Customize category in the Excel Options dialog box. You can then switch instantly from one scenario to another by using the Scenario drop-down list, as shown here:

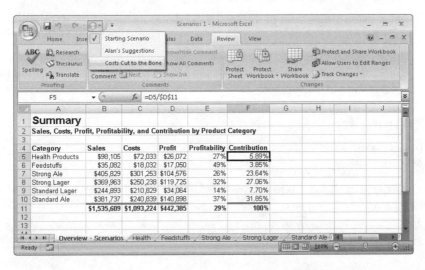

12

Merge Scenarios into a Single Worksheet

Often, you'll need to share workbooks containing scenarios with your colleagues so that they can create new scenarios. When you receive the workbooks back, you can merge the scenarios they contain back into your master workbook. You can also use Excel's scenario-merging capability to merge scenarios from one worksheet into another worksheet.

To merge scenarios, follow these steps:

1. Open each workbook that contains scenarios you want to merge.

2. Activate the workbook and worksheet into which you want to merge the scenarios.

3. Choose Data | Data Tools | What-If Analysis | Scenario Manager. Excel displays the Scenario Manager dialog box.

4. Click the Merge button. Excel displays the Merge Scenarios dialog box:

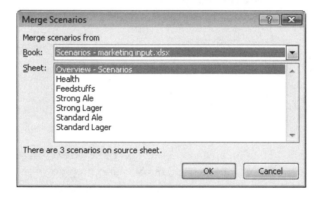

5. Select the source workbook in the Book drop-down list. Excel lists the workbook's worksheets in the Sheet list box.

6. In the Sheet list box, select the worksheet that contains the scenarios. Excel displays the number of scenarios on the worksheet in the readout below the Sheet list box.

7. Click the OK button to merge the scenarios. If any scenario you're merging has the same name as a scenario in the destination workbook, Excel adds the creator's name and date to the scenario name to distinguish it.

Create Reports from Scenarios

Excel can create either a summary report or a PivotTable report from scenarios. To create a report, follow these steps:

1. Choose Data | Data Tools | What-If Analysis | Scenario Manager. Excel displays the Scenario Manager dialog box.

2. Click the Summary button. Excel displays the Scenario Summary dialog box:

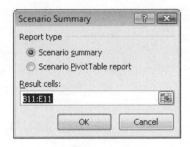

3. Select the Scenario Summary option button or the Scenario PivotTable Report option button, as appropriate.

4. In the Result Cells text box, enter references for the cells that you want the report to contain. Either type the references (separating them with commas) or select the cells in the worksheet by clicking, dragging, or CTRL-clicking. If necessary, click the Collapse Dialog button to reduce the Scenario Summary dialog box to its essentials and get it out of the way.

5. Click the OK button. Excel closes the Scenario Summary dialog box and creates the report.

If you chose to create the summary report, Excel adds a new worksheet named Scenario Summary before the active worksheet and places the summary report on it (see Figure 12-4).

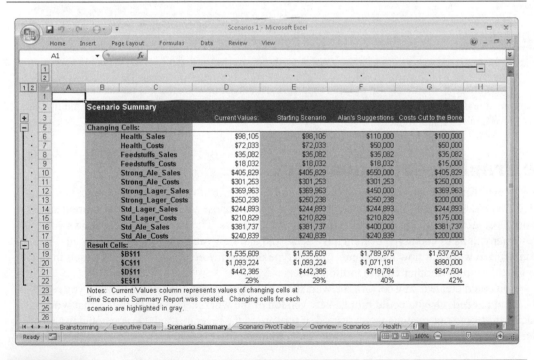

FIGURE 12-4   A summary report created from three scenarios

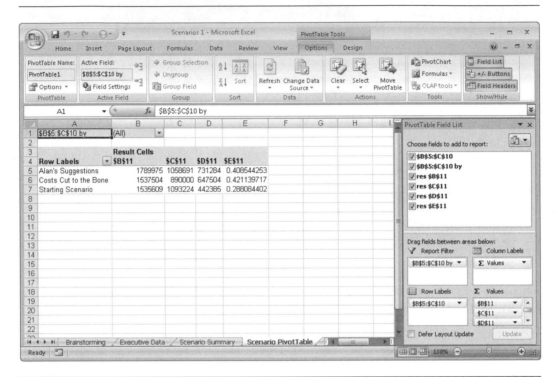

FIGURE 12-5 A PivotTable report created from three scenarios

If you chose to create the PivotTable report, Excel adds a new worksheet before the active worksheet and places the PivotTable on it (see Figure 12-5). You may need to format or manipulate the PivotTable to make it useful.

Solve Problems with Goal Seek

If you ever find yourself trying to work backward from the result you want to achieve, you may well find the Goal Seek feature valuable. For example, suppose you're using your current sales worksheet as the basis for next year's planning spreadsheets. The sales worksheet shows you how many units of each type of item have been sold and how much money that brings in—but you want to work out how many units of each type of item the company will need to sell in order to get sales up by another couple million dollars.

You could create a new copy of the worksheet and try increasing the numbers until you reach the level needed. Or you could build a new version of the worksheet with formulas that work backward from your revenue target instead of forward to the revenue total. Or you could use Goal Seek, which can give you the information you need much more quickly.

To use Goal Seek, follow these steps:

1. Open the workbook if it's not already open.

2. Select the cell that contains the formula you're interested in.

3. Choose Data | Data Tools | What-If Analysis | Goal Seek. Excel displays the Goal Seek dialog box, shown in this illustration. The cell you selected in step 2 appears in the Set Cell box. (If you chose the wrong cell, type the reference for the correct cell, or click the Collapse Dialog button and then select it.)

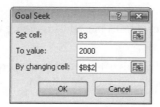

4. In the To Value text box, enter the target value for the formula.

5. In the By Changing Cell text box, type the reference for the cell whose value you want Goal Seek to manipulate. Alternatively, click the cell in the worksheet. If necessary, click the Collapse Dialog button to collapse the Goal Seek dialog box so that you can access the cell.

6. Click the OK button. Goal Seek computes the problem and then displays the Goal Seek Status dialog box:

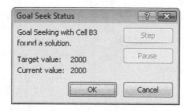

7. Goal Seek automatically enters the target value it achieved and the By Changing Cell value it found in the worksheet. Click the OK button to accept these values, or click the Cancel button to reject them.

Use the Solver to Manipulate Two or More Values

As you saw in the previous section, Goal Seek is a powerful tool for working backward from a conclusion by manipulating a single value. But if you need to work backward by manipulating two or more values, Goal Seek can't help. Instead, you need to use the Solver, one of the add-ins that comes with Excel.

The Solver is an add-in rather than a built-in component of Excel, so you need to load it before you can use it. To load the Solver, follow these steps:

1. Click the Office button, and then click Excel Options. Excel displays the Excel Options dialog box.

2. In the left panel, click the Add-Ins category. Excel displays the Add-Ins controls.

3. In the Manage drop-down list, select the Excel Add-Ins item, and then click the Go button. Excel displays the Add-Ins dialog box.

4. Select the Solver Add-in check box.

5. Click the OK button. Excel closes the Add-Ins dialog box and returns you to the Excel Options dialog box.

6. Click the OK button. Excel closes the Excel Options dialog box and adds the Solver to the Analysis group on the Data tab of the Ribbon.

To use the Solver, follow these steps:

1. Open the workbook and activate the appropriate worksheet.

2. Select the cell that contains the formula you're interested in.

3. Choose Data | Analysis | Solver. Excel displays the Solver Parameters dialog box, shown here with data entered. The cell you selected in step 2 appears in the Set Target Cell box. (If you chose the wrong cell, type the reference for the correct cell, or click the Collapse Dialog button and select it.)

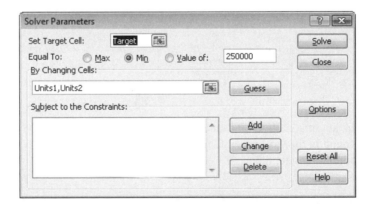

4. In the Equal To area, select the Max option button, the Min option button, or the Value Of option button, as appropriate, and then type the value in the text box.

5. In the By Changing Cells text box, enter the references for the cells whose value you want the Solver to manipulate. Alternatively, click the Collapse Dialog button and enter the cell references by selecting them in the worksheet. In most cases, you won't want to use the Guess button unless you're seeking entertainment rather than answers.

6. If you want to apply constraints to the Solver, use the controls beside the Subject To The Constraints box to add, change, and delete constraints. The basic procedure is to click the Add button; use the controls in the Add Constraint dialog box (shown next) to specify the cell reference, the operator, and the constraint; and click the OK button. Use the other controls to change or delete any constraints you've already applied.

7. Click the Solve button to start computing the solution. When the Solver has finished, it displays the Solver Results dialog box:

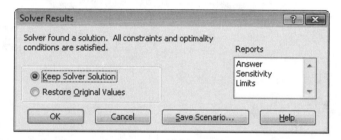

8. Select the Keep Solver Solution option button or the Restore Original Values option button as appropriate.

9. To generate one or more reports, select the ones you want in the Reports list. (Click an item to select it; click again if you need to deselect it.) The Solver inserts each report on a fresh worksheet.

10. Click the OK button. Excel closes the Solver Results dialog box and creates those reports you requested.

12

Part III

Share, Publish, and Present Data

Chapter 13

Create Effective Charts to Present Data Visually

How to...

- Understand the basics of Excel charts
- Create a chart
- Choose the right type of chart for your data
- Edit charts to produce the best effect
- Format charts
- Copy formatting from one chart to another
- Unlink a chart from its data source
- Print charts
- Create custom chart types for easy reuse

Often in business, and sometimes at home, entering data in worksheets and performing suitable calculations with the data is only half the battle. The other half is using the data to create charts that convey a particular message effectively enough to convince your readers or your audience of your point of view.

This chapter shows you how to use Excel's chart features to create charts that illustrate the points you're trying to make. You'll learn how to create charts, how to choose which type of chart to use for which data, and how to edit and format charts to give them the effect you need. You'll also learn how to copy formatting you've applied to one chart to another chart, how to unlink a chart from its data source, how to print charts, and how to add custom chart types to Excel's existing types so that you can reuse them quickly and easily.

Understand the Basics of Excel Charts

Excel can create two types of charts:

- **Embedded chart**   A chart positioned on a worksheet page alongside other data. Embedded charts are useful for charting smaller amounts of data and for experimenting with the best ways to chart data that you need to edit while creating the chart.

- **Chart on chart sheet**   A chart sheet is a separate sheet that appears in the workbook. Using a chart sheet gives you more space to create a detailed chart, but it means that you can't see the source data for the chart on the same sheet.

You can switch a chart from one type to another. For example, you can create an embedded chart and then move it to a chart sheet if you find you need more space for it.

Typical charts consist of the components described in Table 13-1.

Figure 13-1 shows a straightforward chart with its components labeled.

Component	Explanation
X-axis	The category axis of the chart. Usually horizontal, but some charts have a vertical X-axis.
Y-axis	The series axis (the vertical axis).
Z-axis	The value axis (the depth axis of the chart; 3D charts only).
Axis titles	A title (name) for each of the axes used.
Chart title	The name of the chart.
Data series	The set or sets of data from which the chart is created. Some charts, such as pie charts, use only one data series. Other charts use two or more data series. The chart represents the data series as data markers.
Data marker	The chart's representation of a point in a data series. You may want to display data markers in different data series as differently shaped points to distinguish them from one another.
Data labels	Text that appears on or near points in the data series to identify them.
Legend	Notes on the color, pattern, or other identification used to distinguish each data series.
Gridlines	Reference lines drawn across the chart from the axes so that you can see the values of the data series.
Categories	The distinct items in the data series. For example, in a chart showing the sales performance for each of a company's regions, each region would be a category.
Chart area	The area occupied by the entire chart, including legend, labels, and so on.
Plot area	The area occupied by the data plotted in the chart (not including legend, labels, and so on).

TABLE 13-1   Components of a Typical Excel Chart

13

Create a Chart

To create a chart, follow these three general steps:

1. Select the range of data from which you want to create the chart.

NOTE   *You can adjust any of the parameters for the chart after creating the chart, so mistakes matter little. Alternatively, you can delete the chart and start again.*

2. Choose the chart type you want. Excel inserts a chart of that type on the worksheet.

3. Use the controls on the Ribbon to format and arrange the chart.

The following sections go through the details of these steps.

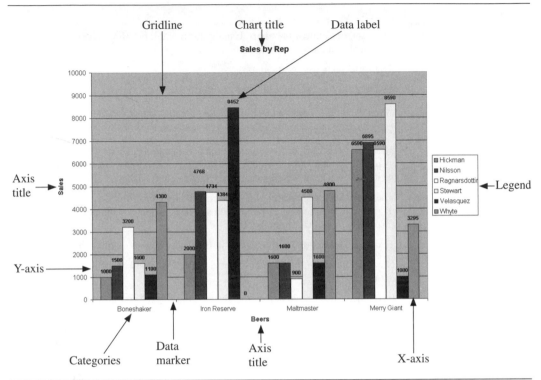

FIGURE 13-1   One of the many types of charts you can create in Excel.

Select the Range of Data for the Chart

You can use any means of selection to select the range of data for the chart. For example, drag from the beginning cell in the range to the last cell; or click the first cell, hold down SHIFT, and then click the last cell in the range.

You can select either a contiguous range or a noncontiguous range. To select a noncontiguous range, hold down CTRL while you add further cells or ranges to the current selection.

Include in the range any headings you want to use as labels for the data.

Choose the Chart Type You Want

To choose the chart type for your chart, click the Insert tab of the Ribbon, go to the Charts group, click one of the chart-type buttons, and then select the chart subtype you want from the panel. Figure 13-2 shows the Column panel (column charts are very widely used) and the Other Charts panel (which provides a selection of chart types whose categories don't appear in the Charts group).

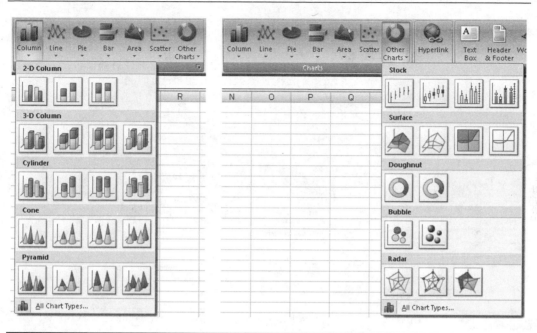

FIGURE 13-2   Click the chart type button in the Charts group to display the chart subtypes, and then click the subtype you want.

The chart-type panels are handy if you know roughly which type of chart you want, as they let you browse visually; and if you know exactly which type you want, you can go right to it. But if you want to see the full range of charts, click the Create Chart button, the tiny button at the right end of the Charts group bearing an arrow pointing down and to the right. Excel displays the Insert Chart dialog box (see Figure 13-3). You can also display the Insert Chart dialog box by clicking the All Chart Types item at the bottom of one of the charts panels.

The right pane in the Insert Chart dialog box contains a scrolling list showing all the chart subtypes broken up by chart type: the list starts with the Column section, showing the column chart subtypes; continues with the Line section, showing the line chart subtypes; and so on down to the Radar section, which shows the few types of radar charts. If you know which chart type you want, click it in the left pane to display that section of the list. Otherwise, scroll the list until you find the chart type you want.

To see the name of a chart subtype, hover the mouse pointer over it for a moment so that Excel displays a ScreenTip.

13

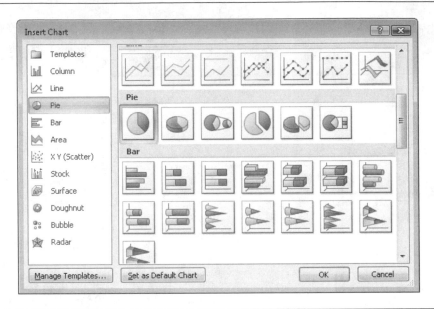

FIGURE 13-3   The Insert Chart dialog box lets you see all the chart types that Excel offers.

Click the chart subtype you want, and then click the OK button. Excel closes the Insert Chart dialog box, creates a chart of the type you chose, and then inserts it as an object on the worksheet that contains the cells you selected.

If you've chosen a suitable chart type, that may be all you need to do. But more likely, you'll need to format the chart and add elements to it, as described in the following sections.

TIP   *If you often need to create the same type of chart, set it as your default chart type in Excel. In the Insert Chart dialog box, click the chart subtype, and then click the Set As Default Chart button. Windows then selects that chart subtype when you display the Insert Chart dialog box. You can also create a chart of the default type instantly on a new chart sheet by selecting the data and pressing F11 or ALT-F1.*

Find Excel's Chart Tools

Excel's tools for working with charts appear on the Chart Tools section of the Ribbon. Excel adds the Chart Tools section to the Ribbon automatically whenever you've selected a chart or a component of a chart. The Chart Tools section has three tabs: the Design tab, the Layout tab, and the Format tab. You'll see the groups and controls these tabs offer later throughout the rest of this chapter.

Excel also makes many tools available through the context menus. For example, when you right-click a chart itself, the context menu offers commands for working with the chart as a whole. When you right-click an individual element within the chart, the context menu offers commands for working with that element.

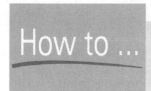

Choose the Right Type of Chart for Your Data

Excel offers 11 chart types (Column, Line, Pie, Bar, Area, XY or Scatter, Stock, Surface, Doughnut, Bubble, and Radar), each with two or more subtypes. You can also add your own custom chart types if Excel's built-in chart types don't meet your needs. (The section "Create Custom Chart Types for Easy Reuse," later in this chapter, discusses how to do this.)

Such a wide choice of chart types can make it difficult to decide which type to use. Should you use a conventional bar chart or line chart; go for an area chart, a doughnut, or radar; try a Piece Of Pie; or go for glory with an Exploded Pie? In general, you should use the simplest type of chart that can present your data satisfactorily. Don't feel you must use an unusual type of chart just because Excel makes doing so easy or because the standard chart type seems boring or conventional. As a rule of thumb, if you don't know what a chart type is for, try applying it to your data, and see if it's easy to understand. If not, leave that chart type alone.

Many of the more esoteric chart types are designed for highly specific needs. For example, stock charts are designed for tracking the opening, closing, and high and low prices of a stock over a given time period. If you use a stock chart for your sales results or your staffing forecasts, the result will be of little use. Similarly, the 100% Stacked chart types are designed for showing the contribution of constituent parts over time. If you use such types to chart your company's output of widgets, the results will be meaningless.

Beyond using the simplest type of chart that can present the data satisfactorily, keep the chart itself as simple and legible as possible. Excel's wide variety of options may tempt you to indulge in unnecessary complications; resist this temptation. Always ask yourself: Is the chart as clear as you can make it? Does it need titles on each axis, plus the legend, *and* its underlying data table? Are those frills you added necessary, or are they distractions?

In business, you may sometimes need to use a chart to obscure the facts rather than highlight them. For example, you might need to use a chart creatively to mask deficient sales results or to put the best possible spin on a drastic budget overrun. In such a situation, an esoteric chart type might seem a good idea—but it's not.

If you need to use a chart to make your audience overlook some inconvenient data, choosing an unusual or complex chart type is almost always a bad move. An unusual or incomprehensible chart type will make your audience scrutinize it much more closely than an apparently straightforward chart on which you've subtly manipulated the axis values. For example, you might be able to change the timescale on a column chart to obscure a decline in sales. Such sleight of mouse is much more likely to pass unnoticed because the chart itself is unremarkable. That said, if the situation is really bad, and you find that you "can't get there from here" with your current data set, you may need to base the chart on a different data set to achieve an acceptable result.

13

Name the Chart

When you create a chart, Excel automatically assigns it a name that's unique on its worksheet or chart sheet—for example, Chart 1 or Chart 2. If you create more than one chart on a worksheet, you may find it helpful to give each chart a descriptive name so that you can identify them more easily. Descriptive names are especially helpful if you start working with charts using VBA, when you can't see which chart you're manipulating.

To name a chart, follow these steps:

1. Select the chart. Excel adds the Chart Tools section to the Ribbon.

2. Choose Layout | Properties | Chart Name, type the name for the chart, and then press ENTER.

Toggle a Chart Between Embedded and Chart Sheet

Given that Excel automatically creates the chart on the same sheet as its data, what you'll often want to do first is move the chart to its own chart sheet so that you have more space for it. If you decide you want to have the chart with its source data after all, or if you create a chart on its own chart sheet by pressing F11 or ALT-F1 and then decide you want to have it on the same sheet as its data, you can move it back.

To change a chart from embedded to being on its own chart sheet, follow these steps:

1. Select the chart. Excel displays the Chart Tools section of the Ribbon.

2. Choose Design | Location | Move Chart. Excel displays the Move Chart dialog box, as shown here:

3. Choose the appropriate option button:

   ■ To move the chart to a new sheet, select the New Sheet option button, and then type a name for the new sheet in the text box.

   ■ To change the chart to an embedded chart, select the Object In option button, and then select the appropriate worksheet in the drop-down list.

4. Click the OK button. Excel closes the Move Chart dialog box and moves the choice to where you indicated.

Move or Resize the Chart

If you decide to leave the chart on a worksheet (or you move the chart to a worksheet), you may want to resize it or move it:

■ To resize the chart, move the mouse pointer over one of the dotted handles in the chart's border so that the pointer changes to a double-headed arrow, and then drag the border to resize the chart. Drag a side handle to resize the chart in only one dimension—for example, drag the bottom handle down to make the chart deeper without affecting its width. Drag a corner handle to resize the chart in both dimensions at once. SHIFT-drag a corner handle to resize the chart proportionally in both dimensions.

■ To move the chart, move the mouse pointer over an area of the border that's not one of the dotted handles, and then drag the chart to where you want it.

Select Objects in a Chart

You can select objects in a chart in any of the following ways:

■ Click with the mouse. This technique is easiest for larger objects and those that aren't obscured by other objects.

■ Click the Layout tab or the Format tab, go to the Current Selection group, open the Chart Elements drop-down list, and then choose the object, as shown here. This technique is useful for selecting smaller objects or objects that are obscured by other objects.

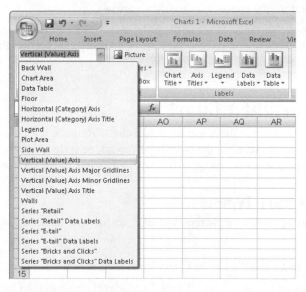

■ Use the arrow keys (↑, ↓, ←, and →) to select the next element in the appropriate direction.

■ When you're working on a worksheet that contains text boxes, shapes, or pictures as well as a chart, you may need to use the Selection And Visibility pane to turn off objects that are in the way. Follow these steps:

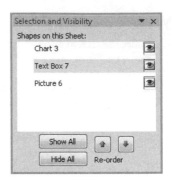

1. Select the chart. Excel adds the Chart Tools section to the Ribbon.

2. Choose Format | Arrange | Selection Pane. Excel displays the Selection And Visibility pane, shown here.

3. Choose what you want to do:

   ■ **Select an item**   Click the item in the Shapes On This Sheet list.

   ■ **Hide an item**   Clear the item's visibility box (the check box containing an eye symbol).

   ■ **Display an item again**   Select the item's visibility box.

   ■ **Hide all items**   Click the Hide All button. (Hiding all items allows you to see the worksheet contents.)

   ■ **Show all items**   Click the Show All button.

   ■ **Reorder the items in the front-to-back stack**   Click an item, and then click the Bring Forward button (the button with the up arrow) or the Send Backward button (the button with the down arrow).

4. When you've finished using the Selection And Visibility pane, click its Close button (the × button) or choose Format | Arrange | Selection Pane again. Excel closes the pane.

Lay Out and Format a Chart

By this point, you should have the beginnings of a chart. To make it look exactly the way you need it to, you may need to change the chart type, layout, or style—or even the source data. You'll almost certainly also want to apply formatting to some of the elements in the chart.

Change the Chart Type

If you find that you've chosen the wrong type of chart for your data, follow these steps to change the chart type:

1. Select the chart. Excel adds the Chart Tools section to the Ribbon.

2. Choose Design | Type | Change Chart Type. Excel displays the Change Chart Type dialog box, which is the same as the Insert Chart dialog box, except for the name.

3. Choose the chart type and subtype, and then click the OK button. Excel closes the dialog box and changes the chart to the type you chose.

Troubleshooting: Excel Doesn't Display ScreenTips for Chart Elements

To help you work with charts, Excel normally displays a ScreenTip showing the name of a chart element when you hover the mouse over that element for a second or two. Similarly, Excel displays the value for a data point when you hover the mouse pointer over it, which is handy if you haven't included data labels in a chart.

If you find Excel doesn't display these ScreenTips, you'll need to turn them on. Follow these steps:

1. Click the Office button, and then click Excel Options. Excel displays the Excel Options dialog box.

2. In the left panel, click the Advanced Category. Excel displays its contents.

3. Scroll down to the Display section (about halfway down).

4. Select the Show Chart Element Names On Hover check box if you want to see the element names.

5. Select the Show Data Point Values On Hover check box if you want to see the values for data points.

6. Click the OK button. Excel closes the Excel Options dialog box.

Change the Chart's Layout

Even when you've chosen the chart type, you may need to change the chart's layout.

To do so, follow these steps:

1. Select the chart. Excel adds the Chart Tools section to the Ribbon.

2. Choose Design | Chart Layouts | More (in other words, click the small button with the line and downward arrow in the lower-right corner of the Chart Layouts group). Excel displays the Chart Layouts panel, showing all the layouts available for the current chart type. Here is an example:

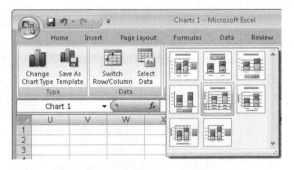

3. Click the layout you want. Excel closes the Chart Layouts panel and applies the layout to the chart.

13

Change the Chart's Style

With the chart type and layout decided, you can change the chart's style. To do so, follow these steps:

1. Select the chart. Excel adds the Chart Tools section to the Ribbon.

2. Choose Design | Chart Styles | More (in other words, click the small button with the line and downward arrow in the lower-right corner of the Chart Styles group). Excel displays the Chart Styles panel, showing all the styles available for the chart in its current state. Here is an example.

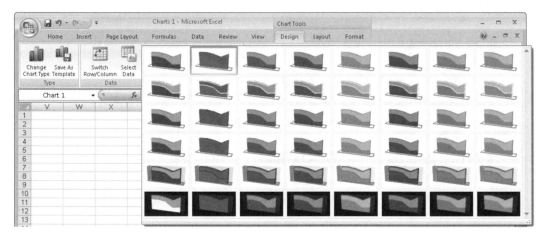

3. Click the style you want (the styles look better in color than in grayscale). Excel closes the Chart Styles panel and applies the style to the chart.

Change the Chart's Source Data

To change the source data from which a chart is drawn, follow these steps:

1. Select the chart. Excel adds the Chart Tools section to the Ribbon.

2. Choose Design | Data | Select Data. Excel selects the current source data in the worksheet and displays the Select Data Source dialog box (see Figure 13-4).

3. If the Select Data Source dialog box is in the way of the data you need to select, click the Collapse Dialog button to collapse it, drag in the worksheet to select the data range you want to use, and then click the Collapse Dialog button again. If the dialog box isn't in the way, simply drag in the worksheet to select the data range. Excel collapses the dialog box automatically as you drag and then restores it.

4. Click the OK button. Excel closes the Select Data Source dialog box and changes the chart to reflect the data in the range you selected.

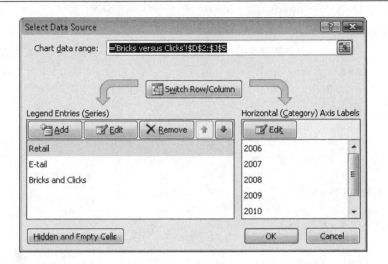

FIGURE 13-4   The Select Data Source dialog box lets you change the source data for the chart or switch the rows and columns around.

Switch the Rows and Columns, or Include Hidden and Empty Cells

What you'll often find when you create a chart is that the chart type you need draws the data from the rows rather than the columns (or vice versa). In the bad old days of spreadsheets, when you ran into this problem, you had to go back to the spreadsheet and rearrange the data. With Excel 2007, you can simply choose Design | Data | Switch Row/Column. If you're making other changes in the Select Data Source dialog box, you can also click the Switch Row/Column button in this dialog box to switch the rows and columns.

Another change you may need to make is changing whether Excel shows hidden and empty cells in the chart or suppresses them. To change Excel's handling of these cells, follow these steps:

1. Click the Hidden And Empty Cells button in the Select Data Source dialog box. Excel displays the Hidden And Empty Cell Settings dialog box, as shown here:

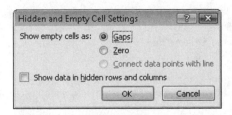

2. In the Show Empty Cells As area, select the appropriate option button:

- **Gaps**   Select this option button if you want to show a gap for each empty cell.

- **Zero**   Select this option button if you want to show each empty cell as a zero value.

- **Connect Data Points With Line**   In some chart types, you can select this option button to connect the data points with a line instead. Many chart types don't offer this option.

3. If you want Excel to include in the chart data contained in hidden rows and columns, select the Show Data In Hidden Rows And Columns check box. This option can be useful when you're preparing warts-and-all charts that need to show all possibilities. Normally, though, if you've hidden data so that it doesn't appear in the source area, you will want to suppress the data in the chart as well.

4. Click the OK button. Excel closes the Hidden And Empty Cell Settings dialog box and returns you to the Select Data Source dialog box.

Change the Data Series' Contents or Plotting Order

Sometimes you may need to change the order in which the data series in a chart are plotted. You can do this by changing the data source for the chart, but in some cases making such a change may cause more problems in the worksheet than it solves in the chart. Other times, you may need to remove one or more data series from the chart without removing them from the data source.

To change the data series in the chart but not in the data source, follow these steps:

1. Choose Design | Data | Select Data. Excel displays the Select Data Source dialog box.

2. In the Legend Entries (Series) list box, select the column you want to affect.

3. Click the appropriate action button:

- **Add**   To add a data series to the chart, click this button. Excel displays the Edit Series dialog box, as shown here. Click in the Series Name box, and then select the range in the worksheet. The Series Values box shows the values of the data series you've selected. You can also set a specific value by clicking in the Series Value box, and then selecting the cell in the worksheet. Click the OK button. Excel closes the Edit Series dialog box and returns you to the Select Data Source dialog box.

- **Edit**   To edit an existing data series, select it in the list box, and then click this button. Excel displays the Edit Series dialog box, this time containing the current data and values. Click in the box you want to change, and then select the appropriate cells in the worksheet. Click the OK button. Excel closes the Edit Series dialog box and returns you to the Select Data Source dialog box.

- **Remove**   To remove an existing data series, select it in the list box, and then click this button.

- **Move Up and Move Down**   To change the order of the series, select the series you want to move, and then click the Move Up button to move it up the list or the Move Down button to move it down the list.

NOTE   *For an XY (scatter) chart or a bubble chart, the Edit Series dialog box contains a Series X Values box and a Series Y Values box. For a bubble chart, the Edit Series dialog box also contains a Series Bubble Size box.*

4.   Click the OK button. Excel closes the Select Data Source dialog box and applies the changes to the chart.

Add Labels to a Chart

To be visually effective and easy to read, different charts need different elements:

- Most charts benefit from a chart title announcing what the chart is about and axis titles showing what each axis represents.

- Many charts are clearer with a legend that shows which color or pattern represents which data series.

- When the viewer should be able to tell how much a data point represents, including data labels showing the values is a good idea.

- Some charts even need a data table showing all the data from which the chart is drawn.

To add these elements, select the chart, click the Layout tab, and then work with the controls in the Labels group. For example, to add a chart title, click the Chart Title button, and then choose Centered Overlay Title or Above Chart from the panel as shown here:

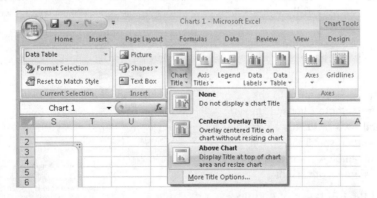

For each of these elements, you can also choose the More *Object* Options item (for example, the More Title Options item or the More Data Label Options item) from the bottom of the panel, and then work in the resulting Format dialog box. For example, you can apply a border, shadow, or 3-D format to many elements. Figure 13-5 shows the Format Data Labels dialog box.

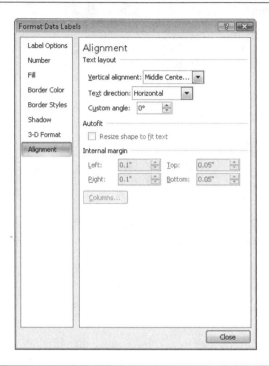

FIGURE 13-5   For fine control over a chart element, display its Format dialog box, and then work with the options the dialog box offers.

Configure and Change the Scale of an Axis

One trick that can be very effective is changing the scale of an axis from its default settings. To change the scale of an axis, follow these steps:

1. Select the chart. Excel adds the Chart Tools section to the Ribbon.

2. Choose Layout | Axes | Axes, choose the axis from the Axes panel (for example, choose Primary Horizontal Axis or Primary Vertical Axis), and then select the option you want. can be seen on a sample of the axis options the right.

3. To get at the full range of options that Excel offers for the axis, choose the More *Axis* Options item at the bottom of the panel. Excel displays the Format

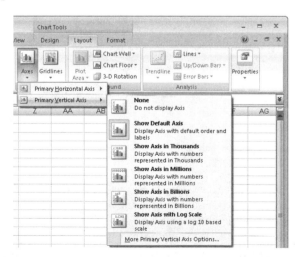

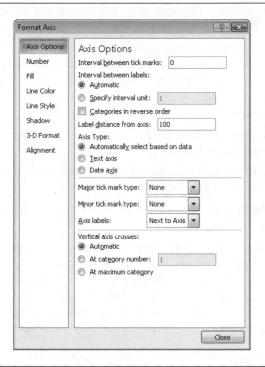

FIGURE 13-6   You can change the scale of an axis in the Axis Options category in the Format Axis dialog box.

Axis dialog box, in which the Axis Options category shows the available options for the axis. Figure 13-6 shows an example of the Axis Options category in the Format Axis dialog box.

4. Choose the options you want (see the discussion after these steps), and then click the Close button. Excel closes the dialog box and applies your choices.

The options available for an axis depend on the chart type. This list explains what you can do in the Format Axis dialog box for a horizontal axis:

■ **Interval Between Tick Marks**   This setting controls the number of categories that appear between each pair of tick marks.

■ **Interval Between Labels**   This setting controls the number of category items that appear between each tick-mark label. Select the Automatic option button to label each category. To label only some categories, select the Specify Interval Unit option button, and then type the number in the text box: To label every other category, type **2**; to label every third category, type **3**; and so on.

■ **Categories In Reverse Order**   Select this check box if you need to reverse the order of your categories. On occasion, reversing the order can produce a better chart.

■ **Label Distance From Axis** The number (in pixels) controls the distance between the axis and the labels. Increase or decrease the number to increase or decrease the distance.

■ **Axis Type** Select the Automatically Select Based On Data option button to have Excel determine the appropriate type of axis based on the data it finds in the cells. Otherwise, select the Text Axis option button to make the axis a text axis, or the Date Axis option button to make the axis a date axis. See the sidebar "Understand Date Axes and Text Axes" for an explanation of the difference between the two.

■ **Major Tick Mark Type** In this drop-down list, choose the type of major tick marks to use: None, Inside, Outside, or Cross.

■ **Minor Tick Mark Type** In this drop-down list, choose the type of minor tick marks to use: None, Inside, Outside, or Cross.

■ **Axis Labels** In this drop-down list, choose whether and where to display the labels: Next To Axis, High, Low, or None.

■ **Vertical Axis Crosses** Choose where the vertical axis crosses the horizontal axis. Select the Automatic option button to have Excel decide. To make the axis cross at a particular category number, select the At Category Number option button, and then type the number in the text box. To make the axis cross at the last category, select the At Maximum Category option button. For example, on a column chart, selecting the At Maximum Category option button places the vertical axis on the right of the chart instead of the left.

Figure 13-7 shows an example of the Axis Options category of the Format Axis dialog box for a vertical axis. These are the options available:

■ **Minimum** Select the Auto option button to have Excel choose the minimum value based on the data set. To specify the minimum value yourself, select the Fixed option button, and then type the value in the text box.

■ **Maximum** Select the Auto option button to have Excel choose the maximum value based on the data set. To specify the maximum value yourself, select the Fixed option button, and then type the value in the text box.

■ **Major Unit** Select the Auto option button to have Excel choose the major unit value (the value for major tick marks) based on the data set. To specify the major unit value yourself, select the Fixed option button, and then type the value in the text box.

■ **Minor Unit** Select the Auto option button to have Excel choose the minor unit value (the value for minor tick marks) based on the data set. To specify the minor unit value yourself, select the Fixed option button, and then type the value in the text box.

■ **Values In Reverse Order** Select this check box if you want to reverse the order. This can be useful for some charts.

■ **Logarithmic Scale** To use a logarithmic scale for the axis, select this check box, and then type the base in the text box. (The default base value is 10.)

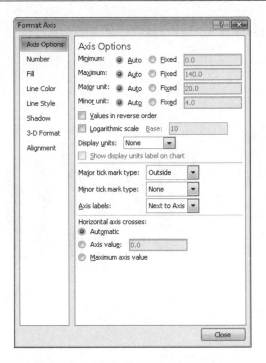

FIGURE 13-7   The Axis Options category of the Format Axis dialog box for a vertical axis.

- ■ **Display Units**   In this drop-down list, select the units you want to display: None, Hundreds, Thousands, 10000, 100000, Millions, 10000000, 100000000, Billions, or Trillions.

- ■ **Major Tick Mark Type**   In this drop-down list, select the major tick marks you want: None, Inside, Outside, or Cross.

- ■ **Minor Tick Mark Type**   In this drop-down list, select the minor tick marks you want: None, Inside, Outside, or Cross.

- ■ **Axis Labels**   In this drop-down list, choose whether and where to display the labels: Next To Axis, High, Low, or None.

- ■ **Horizontal Axis Crosses**   Choose where the horizontal axis crosses the vertical axis. Select the Automatic option button to have Excel decide. To make the axis cross at a particular value number, select the Axis Value option button, and then type the number in the text box. To make the axis cross at the maximum value, select the Maximum Axis Value option button. For example, in a column chart, selecting this check box puts the X-axis at the top of the chart instead of the bottom.

Understand Date Axes and Text Axes

A *text axis* is an axis that has the data points evenly spaced out, whereas a *date axis* is an axis that has the dates arranged in chronological order according to standard intervals (such as years, months, or days).

For example, if you have a chart showing rainfall data for 1960, 1970, 1980, 1990, 2000, 2003, 2004, 2005, and 2006, using a text axis creates a chart as shown on the right.

Needs vary, but this is the kind of look you'd normally want if you intend to give equal weight to each year. By contrast, using a date axis emphasizes the distribution of the dates along the timeline, as shown here:

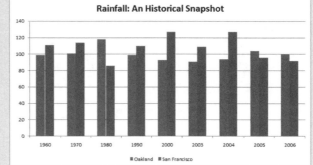

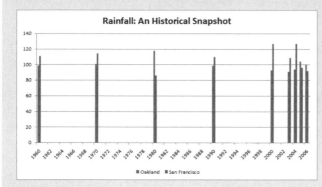

The date axis doesn't work well for the rainfall, because there's no link between one year's rainfall and the next, and the chart type leaves large gaps for the missing years. But for data such as population figures and a chart type such as a line chart, a date axis makes much more sense, as in this example:

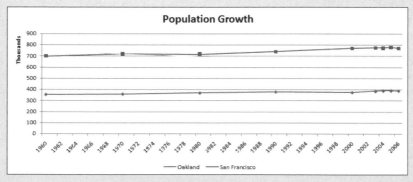

Liven Up Charts with Fills Consisting of Colors, Gradients, Textures, or Pictures

To make a chart more lively or individual, you can apply a fill consisting of a color, a gradient, a picture, or a texture. In a two-dimensional chart, you can apply the fill to the entire plot area, while in a three-dimensional chart, you can apply fills to the chart wall and chart floor. In either type of chart, you can also apply a fill to an individual item, such as a data series or the legend.

To apply a fill, follow these steps:

1. Select the chart. Excel adds the Chart Tools section to the Ribbon.

2. Choose the object to which you want to apply the fill, making Excel display the Fill category in the Format dialog box (see Figure 13-8) for the object:

   - To fill the plot area, choose Layout | Background | Plot Area | More Plot Area Options.

   - To fill the chart wall, choose Layout | Background | Chart Wall | More Walls Options.

   - To fill the chart floor, choose Layout | Background | Chart Floor | More Floor Options.

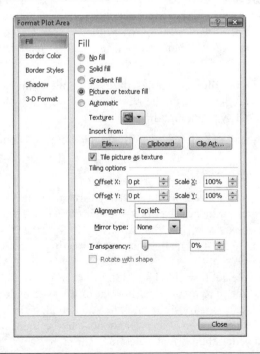

FIGURE 13-8   The Fill category of the Format dialog box.

13

For the plot area, chart wall, and chart floor, you can apply a default fill by choosing the Show item (for example, Show Plot Area) from the panel, or remove the current fill by choosing the None item.

■ To format an individual object, either click it in the chart, or choose Format | Current Selection | Chart Elements, and then choose the obj*ct* from the drop-down list. Then choose Format | Current Selection | Format Selection.

3. Choose the fill type you want:

■ **Remove the existing fill**   Select the No Fill option button.

■ **Apply a solid fill**   Select the Solid Fill option button, click the Color drop-down button, and then select a color from the panel. The Theme Colors area offers colors that coordinate with the workbook's current theme; the Standard Colors area offers standard colors, such as red, blue, and green; and the More Colors item lets you choose exactly the color you want.

■ **Apply a gradient fill**   Select the Gradient Fill option button, and then use the controls that appear in the lower part of the Format dialog box to specify the gradient.

■ **Apply a picture or texture fill**   Select the Picture Or Texture Fill option button. Click the Texture drop-down button to select a texture from a panel, click the File button to insert a picture from a file, click the Clipboard button to insert a picture from the Clipboard, or click the Clip Art button to insert a picture from the Select Picture dialog box. You can then choose tiling and transparency options for the texture or picture.

■ **Apply the automatic fill**   Select the Automatic option button. The automatic fill gives you a fill coordinated with the workbook's look, but without the contrast or individuality you may be looking for.

4. Click the Close button. Excel closes the Format dialog box and applies the fill to the item.

Format the Chart Area

When formatting a chart, typically you'll want to start by formatting the chart area, because the chart area exercises the greatest influence over how the chart looks as a whole. For example, you can set a background color or pattern for the chart area, specify a border for it, and set overall font formatting for the chart. You can then apply further formatting to the elements of the chart as necessary to pick them out.

To format the chart area, select it so that its handles appear, right-click, and choose Format Chart Area from the context menu to display the Format Chart Area dialog box. If the chart area is obscured so that you can't easily right-click it, you can also click anywhere in the chart; choose Format | Current Selection | Chart Elements, choose the Chart Area item from the drop-down list, and then click the Format Selection button.

Once you've opened the Format Chart Area dialog box, you can use the controls in the Fill, Border Color, Border Styles, Shadow, and 3-D Format categories to apply the formatting you want.

Apply Analysis Lines and Bars to a Chart

When you're using a chart to analyze data, you may want to apply analysis bars to it. Excel provides trendlines, drop lines, high-low lines, up/down bars, and error bars.

Apply Trendlines to a Chart

Excel lets you apply the types of trendlines explained in Table 13-2.

To apply trendlines to a chart, follow these steps:

1. Select the chart. Excel adds the Chart Tools section to the Ribbon.

2. Choose Layout | Analysis | Trendline, and then either choose the type of trendline from the Trendline panel (shown below); or choose More Trendline Options, use the controls in the Trendline Options category in the Format Trendline dialog box (see Figure 13-9) to apply the trendline, and then click the Close button.

13

Trendline Type	Explanation
Linear Trendline	A straight-line trendline derived by applying a best fit to the existing data points. Use a linear trendline when your data shows a steady increase or decrease. Excel's Linear Forecast Trendline type applies a linear trendline.
Logarithmic Trendline	A curved trendline derived by applying a best fit to the existing data points. Use a logarithmic trendline when your data shows a rapid increase or decrease followed by a leveling out.
Exponential Trendline	A curved trendline used for data sets in which values increase or decrease at increasingly rapid rates.
Power Trendline	A curved trendline used for data sets that have measurements that increase at a constant rate.
Polynomial Trendline	A curved trendline used for analyzing data that fluctuates considerably.
Moving Average	A trendline that smoothes out fluctuations in the data set so that you can see the underlying pattern more easily. You choose the number of periods to use for the average. For example, if you use two periods (creating a Two Period Moving Average Trendline, one of Excel's standard types), Excel uses the average of the first two data points to create the first point in the trendline, and the average of the second and third data points to create the second point. The greater the number of periods, the smoother the trendline is, but the farther it diverges from the actual data points.

TABLE 13-2   Excel's Trendline Types

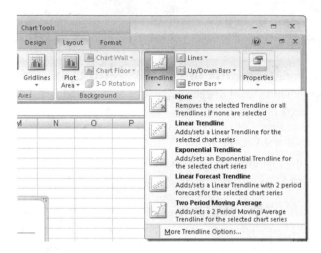

3. Excel applies the trendline to the chart.

To remove a trendline from a chart, click the trendline, and then choose Layout | Analysis | Trendline | None.

FIGURE 13-9   The Trendline Options category in the Format Trendline dialog box lets you create exactly the type of trendline you need.

Apply Drop Lines

To make an area chart or a line chart easier to read, you can apply the following drop lines or high-low lines:

■ **Drop lines**   Excel applies a vertical line from each data point in the topmost data series down through all other data series to the horizontal axis. Drop lines let you see the values on the horizontal axis more easily.

■ **High-low lines**   Excel applies a vertical line from each data point in the topmost data series down to the corresponding data point in the bottommost data series. High-low lines allow you to compare high and low values more easily.

To apply drop lines or high-low lines, follow these steps:

1. Select the chart. Excel adds the Chart Tools section to the Ribbon.

2. Choose Layout | Analysis | Lines, and then choose Drop Lines or High-Low Lines, as appropriate. To remove the lines, choose None.

Apply Up/Down Bars

Up/down bars are bars that show the difference between data points in the first series and the last series. To add up/down bars, follow these steps:

1. Select the chart. Excel adds the Chart Tools section to the Ribbon.

2. Choose Layout | Analysis | Up/Down Bars | Up/Down Bars. Excel adds the bars.

To remove up/down bars, choose Layout | Analysis | Up/Down Bars | None.

Apply Error Bars

If the data in your chart may contain some margin of error, you can apply error bars to the chart to indicate the margin of error. To apply error bars, follow these steps:

1. Select the chart. Excel adds the Chart Tools section to the Ribbon.

2. Choose Layout | Analysis | Error Bars, and then either choose Error Bars With Standard Error, Error Bars With Percentage, or Error Bars With Standard Deviation from the panel, or choose More Error Bars Options to make Excel display the Format Error Bars dialog box (see Figure 13-10).

3. In the Display group box, select the appropriate Direction option button (for vertical error bars, you can choose Both, Minus, or Plus), and then select the No Cap option button or the Cap option button in the End Style area.

4. In the Error Amount group box, select the option button for the type of error (Fixed Value, Percentage, Standard Deviation, Standard Error, or Custom). If appropriate, use the text box or the Specify Value button to specify the value.

13

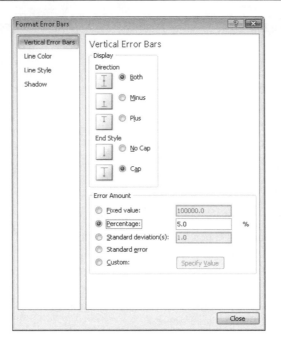

FIGURE 13-10 In the Error Bars category in the Format Error Bars dialog box, choose the type of error bars you want and define the error amount.

5. Click the Close button. Excel closes the Format Error Bars dialog box and applies the error bars to the chart. Here's an example:

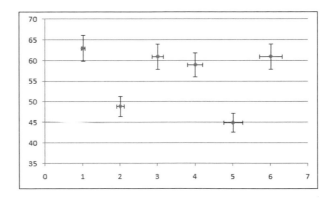

Format Different Data Series Using Different Chart Types

If you need to differentiate two data series strongly, try using a different chart type for each series. Figure 13-11 shows an example that uses a column chart for one data series and a line chart for the other.

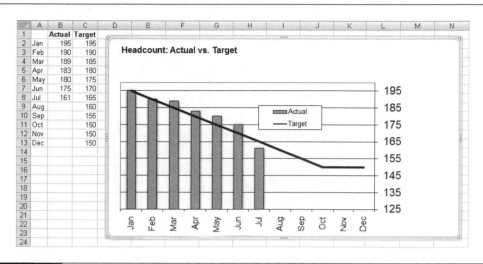

FIGURE 13-11   You can use different chart types for different data series to compare and contrast information.

You'll need to experiment with this technique to get striking and comprehensible results. You'll quickly find that some chart types work well with others, while other combinations create a truly horrible chart that will confuse most sentient beings.

To use two different chart types in the same chart, follow these steps:

1. Create the chart as usual, and format it using the chart type that you want to have applied to most of the chart.

2. Right-click the data series you want to affect, and then choose Change Series Chart Type from the context menu. Excel displays the Change Chart Type dialog box.

3. Select the chart type and subtype as usual.

4. Click the OK button. Excel closes the Change Chart Type dialog box and applies the chart type to this data series.

Show Future Projections with Different Formatting

If your charts include projections of the future as well as analyses of the past, you may want to use different formatting on your future projections to indicate the cut-off between real figures and projected (or fantasy) figures. To do so, plot one data series for the real figures and another data series for the projected figures. Make the data series meet at the end of the real figures and the start of the projected figures. Figure 13-12 shows an example of a chart that uses two sets of projected figures to show different outcomes.

13

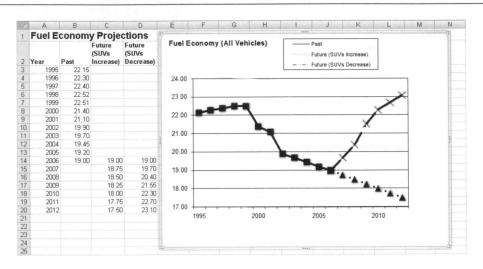

FIGURE 13-12 Plot separate data series that share a data point when you need to use different formatting on future projections.

Copy Formatting from One Chart to Another

Once you've applied custom formatting to a chart, you can quickly copy it to another chart. Follow these steps:

1. Select the chart area of the source chart.

2. Issue a Copy command (for example, press CTRL-C).

3. Select the destination chart.

4. Choose Home | Clipboard | Paste | Paste Special. Excel displays the Paste Special dialog box.

5. Select the Formats option button.

6. Click the OK button. Excel closes the Paste Special dialog box and applies the formatting.

Print Charts

To print a chart, select it, click the Office button, and then choose Print. Alternatively, press CTRL-P. Excel displays the Print dialog box. Bear these considerations in mind:

■ Before printing a chart, use Print Preview to see how it will look.

■ To print a chart in draft quality (saving ink), choose Page Layout | Page Setup | Size, More Paper Sizes, click the Charts tab, and then select the Draft Quality check box in the Printing Quality area. To print a chart in black and white instead of color, select the Print In Black And White check box in the Printing Quality area.

■ If you're using a color printer, you shouldn't worry about how the colors will look. But if you're using a black-and-white printer, check how the chart will look in grayscale. Select the Print In Black And White check box in the Printing Quality area, and then display the chart in Print Preview. You may need to adjust the colors—or substitute patterns for colors—to get enough differentiation between data markers in grayscale.

Create Custom Chart Types for Easy Reuse

You can add custom chart types you create to the Custom Types list in the Chart Type dialog box. By doing so, you can reuse the chart type quickly and easily.

To add a custom chart type, follow these steps:

1. Create the chart and apply formatting as needed.

2. Select the chart, so that Excel adds the Chart Tools section to the Ribbon:

   ■ Click an embedded chart to select it.

   ■ Click the tab for a chart sheet to select it.

3. Choose Design | Type | Save As Template. Excel displays the Save Chart Template dialog box, which is the Save As dialog box by another name.

4. If necessary, change the folder. Excel saves chart templates in the Templates\Charts folder in your user profile by default. This folder works well if the template is for your use only, but if you will need to share the template with your colleagues, you will need to save the template in a shared folder.

5. In the File Name text box, type the name for the chart template.

6. Click the Save button. Excel closes the Save Chart Template dialog box and saves the chart template.

To use a custom chart template, select it in the Templates list in the Insert Chart dialog box.

13

NOTE *To delete a custom chart template you've added, click the Manage Templates button in the Insert Chart dialog box. Excel opens a Windows Explorer window to your Templates\Charts folder, where you can delete (or rename) a custom chart template.*

Chapter 14

Share Workbooks and Collaborate with Colleagues

How to...

- Share a workbook by placing it on a shared drive
- Configure sharing on a workbook
- Restrict data and protect workbooks
- Work with comments
- Send workbooks via e-mail
- Track changes to a workbook

Unless you work entirely on your own, you're likely to need to share the workbooks you develop and use with your colleagues. In this chapter, you'll learn about the range of features that Excel provides for sharing workbooks, protecting them from types of changes you don't want others to make, and collecting and reviewing input from your colleagues to produce a final version of a workbook.

Share a Workbook by Placing It on a Shared Drive

The simplest way to share an Excel workbook with your colleagues is to place the workbook file in a shared folder or drive that each of your colleagues' computers can access. Each user can then open the workbook file, make changes to it, and save them. However, only one user can open the workbook file at a time for editing—a limitation that may cause problems. If you try to open the workbook file while another user has it open, Excel displays the File In Use dialog box to warn you of the problem:

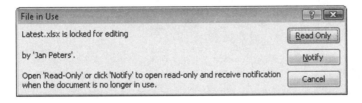

NOTE *The user name that Excel displays in the File In Use dialog box comes from the User Name text box in the Popular category in the Excel Options dialog box (click the Office button, and then click Excel Options). So if Excel announces that a file is locked for editing by "Authorized User" or something equally unhelpful, you may have to tour the office to find out which of your colleagues actually has the file open. But if you see the user identified as "another user" (in lowercase like that), it usually means that another user is just opening the file and that Excel hasn't yet transferred the details of who they are. Click the Cancel button, wait a second or two, and then try opening the file again. This time, Excel should be able to tell you the user's name.*

When you run into the File In Use dialog box, you have three choices:

◼ Click the Cancel button to give up on opening the file for the time being, go and do something else (you're probably not short of work), and try again later to open the file.

◼ Click the Read Only button to open the file in what Windows calls a "read-only" state. Excel displays "[Read-Only]" after the file's name in the title bar to remind you that the file is read-only. This state doesn't actually mean you can't make changes to the file; you just can't save any changes under the file's current path and name (because the other user has the original file locked). But you can use a Save As command to save the file under a different name in the same location or under either the same name or a different name with a different path. You can issue a Save As command either by clicking the Office button and choosing Save As or by issuing a Save command (for example, press CTRL-S) and then clicking the OK button in the warning message box that Excel displays to tell you that the file is read-only.

NOTE   *The problem with creating a new file containing your changes is that you'll probably need to integrate them with the original version of the file later. But in a pinch (for example, if you need to print out a changed version of a worksheet by the deadline for an imminent meeting), saving changes to a new file may be your best choice.*

◼ Click the Notify button to open the file in the read-only state and have Excel notify you when the user who has the file open finally closes it. In the meantime, you can work on the file, but you may have to integrate any changes you make into the original file. Excel checks the original file every few seconds to see if it is still locked. When Excel discovers that your colleague has closed the file, or has just shared it, Excel displays the File Now Available dialog box (as shown here), and you can click the Read-Write button to open the file for editing.

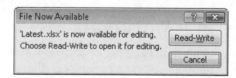

At this point, things get a little complex:

◼ If your colleague closed the file without making any changes since you opened it, Excel automatically integrates the changes you've made to the read-only version into the original file without consulting you. Excel then closes the read-only version, leaving you with the original file open and containing the changes you've made. Excel performs these changes without advertising them, so all you'll see is that the "[Read-Only]" designation has vanished from the title bar. Otherwise, you appear to be working in the same workbook, even though in fact you're not.

14

■ If your colleague made and saved changes since you opened the file, Excel displays
the File Changed dialog box (shown here). You can click the Discard button to discard
the changes you made to the read-only version, click the Save As button to save your
changes to a different file (for example, so that you can integrate them later), or click the
Cancel button to cancel opening the original file.

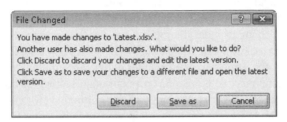

 *Excel doesn't keep a waiting list of notifications requested for a file. If two or more people
ask to be notified when the same file is available, Excel notifies them both (or all) when it
discovers the file is available. So if you're competing with your colleagues for a workbook,
act quickly when Excel displays the File Now Available dialog box.*

As you can see from this description, sharing a file by placing it on a shared drive is tolerable
for small or informal workgroups but is unlikely to work well in large or busy offices. However,
sharing a file this way does have one significant advantage that you should be aware of: each
user who opens it (separately) can take any action that Excel supports (unless you restrict what
they can do, as discussed in "Restrict Data and Protect Workbooks," later in this chapter)—
anything from entering data in cells to inserting cells to inserting worksheets to recording
macros. By contrast, when you share a workbook using Excel's sharing feature, Excel clamps
right down on what users can do in the workbook.

Configure Sharing on a Workbook

To get around the problems discussed in the previous section, Excel lets you configure a
workbook for sharing so that multiple users can have it open for editing at the same time.

To configure a workbook for sharing, follow these steps:

1. Choose Review | Changes | Share Workbook. Excel displays the Share Workbook dialog box.

2. On the Editing tab (shown on the left in Figure 14-1), select the Allow Changes By More
Than One User At The Same Time check box.

*The Who Has This Workbook Open Now list box shows the users who currently have the
workbook open. When you're enabling sharing on a workbook, only your name should
be listed here, and it should be marked Exclusive. After you share the workbook, you
may need to revisit the Editing tab and use the Remove User button to remove users who
have the workbook open when you need exclusive access to it.*

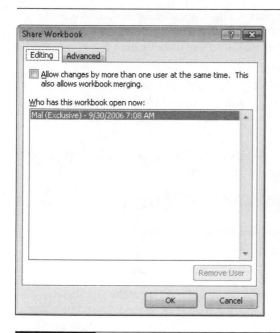

FIGURE 14-1 On the Editing tab (left) of the Share Workbook dialog box, turn on sharing. On the Advanced tab (right), choose settings for tracking and handling changes in the workbook.

3. On the Advanced tab (shown on the right in Figure 14-1), choose the appropriate options for sharing this workbook:

■ **Track Changes section** Select the Keep Change History For *NN* Days option button or the Don't Keep Change History option button as appropriate. Excel's default setting is to keep the change history for 30 days. Your company might prefer to keep the change history for longer to track changes to important workbooks. Or you might prefer not to keep the change history in order to reduce the file size of the workbook.

■ **Update Changes section** Select the When File Is Saved option button (the default) or the Automatically Every *NN* Minutes option button, as appropriate. If you select the latter, specify the number of minutes (the default is 15 minutes) and select the Save My Changes And See Others' Changes option button or the Just See Other Users' Changes option button as needed. You can set any interval between 5 minutes and 1440 minutes (which is 24 hours).

■ **Conflicting Changes Between Users section** Select the Ask Me Which Changes Win option button (the default) if you want to decide which changes to keep when

14

different users have made conflicting changes. This is usually the best choice, as it lets you reduce the likelihood of unsuitable changes occurring. The alternative is to select the The Changes Being Saved Win option button, which makes Excel save the latest changes even when there's a conflict.

■ **Include In Personal View section** Select or clear the Print Settings check box and the Filter Settings check box to specify whether to include print settings and filter settings in your view of the shared workbook. Both check boxes are selected by default.

4. Click the OK button. Excel closes the Share Workbook dialog box and displays this message box, warning you that it will save the workbook now:

5. Click the OK button. Excel applies the sharing to the workbook, saves the workbook, and adds "[Shared]" to the title bar to indicate that the workbook is shared.

Each user of a shared workbook can set the settings on the Advanced tab of the Share Workbook dialog box for themselves.

Resolve Conflicts in Shared Workbooks

If you set Excel to ask you which changes win in a workbook, Excel displays the Resolve Conflicts dialog box when it detects conflicts between the version you're saving and a version that another user has already saved. The Resolve Conflicts dialog box presents your changes that conflict with another user's changes:

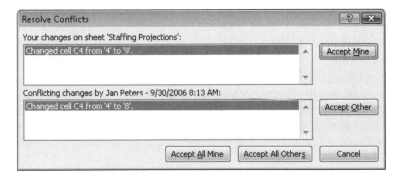

Which Editing Actions You Can and Can't Take in a Shared Workbook

If you think for even a minute about two or more people editing a workbook at the same time, plenty of complexities will come to mind. For example, what happens when your colleague decides to delete the worksheet you've spent the last hour perfecting? Could you protect your worksheet with a password to stop them trashing it inadvertently (or otherwise)?

The answer to both questions is—Not Applicable. To make shared editing work at all, Excel severely restricts the actions that users can take in a shared workbook. You can't:

- Insert or delete blocks of cells (as opposed to rows and columns, which you *can* insert or delete), or merge cells.
- Insert charts, diagrams, hyperlinks, or other objects.
- Assign passwords to worksheets or workbooks.
- Record macros in the shared workbook.
- Add conditional formatting, data validation, or scenarios to the shared workbook.
- Outline the workbook.

Reading that little list, you might find yourself wondering which actions you *can* perform in a shared workbook. Here are the details:

- Enter new cell values or modify existing ones.
- Apply formatting to or remove formatting from cells.
- Insert rows, columns, or worksheets.
- Enter new formulas and edit existing ones.
- Cut, copy, and paste data.
- Move data by using drag and drop.

These restrictions mean that you should design and lay out a worksheet as fully as possible before sharing it with colleagues so that they can enter or adjust data in it.

14

For each change, you can click the Accept Mine button to accept your change or click the Accept Other button to accept the other user's change. Alternatively, you can click the Accept All Mine button to accept all your remaining changes without reviewing them one by one, or click the Accept All Others button to accept the other user's changes without reviewing them further. Excel then displays this message box:

You can also click the Cancel button to cancel the Save operation (for example, so that you can consult your colleague before accepting or overwriting their changes). Excel displays a message box warning you that the workbook wasn't saved. Click the OK button.

After updating the workbook, Excel displays an outline around each cell that has been changed in the update, together with a shaded triangle in the upper-left corner of the cell. Hover the mouse pointer over such a cell to display a comment that details the change made:

3	Emeryville	215	Jan Peters, 9/30/2006 8:13 AM:
4	San Diego	6	Changed cell B4 from '4' to '6'.
5	Little Rock	2	
6	Boston	29	
7	Montreal	8	
8	Vancouver	2	3

Turn Off Sharing and Remove a User from a Shared Workbook

You may sometimes need to either turn off sharing or remove a user from a shared workbook. For example, you might need to turn off sharing so that you can change the design or layout of the workbook in ways that shared editing doesn't support.

Unless it's absolutely necessary, don't turn off sharing when another user has the workbook open, and don't remove a user forcibly from a shared workbook. This is because unsharing the workbook or removing the user prevents the user from saving any unsaved changes to the workbook, which means that they lose those changes. Worse, they receive no warning until they try to save the workbook, so they may waste further time and effort on editing the workbook.

To turn off sharing or remove a user, follow these steps:

1. Choose Review | Changes | Share Workbook. Excel displays the Share Workbook dialog box.

2. On the Editing tab, select the user in the Who Has This Workbook Open Now check box, and then click the Remove User button. Excel displays this warning dialog box to make sure you understand the consequences of removing the user:

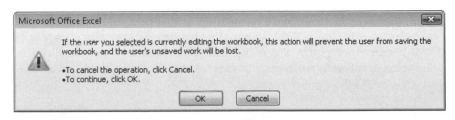

3. Click the OK button. Excel removes the user from the Who Has This Workbook Open Now list box.

4. If you want to turn off sharing, clear the Allow Changes By More Than One User At The Same Time check box.

5. Click the OK button. Excel closes the Share Workbook dialog box and displays the confirmation message box shown here.

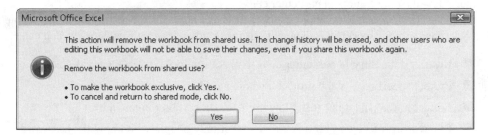

6. Click the Yes button. Excel removes the sharing from the workbook.

If you've left the workbook shared, when the user you've removed tries to save the workbook, Excel displays the dialog box shown here. The user can use the OK button and use the Save As dialog box (which Excel displays automatically) to save their changes to the previously shared file under a different file name in the hope of later merging those changes with the previously shared workbook.

If you removed the user and turned off sharing, when the user you've removed tries to save the workbook, Excel displays the message box shown here, warning the user that the file is no longer shared. After clicking the OK button, the user can use the Save As dialog box (which Excel displays automatically) to save their changes under a different file name.

14

Restrict Data and Protect Workbooks

By default, Excel workbooks are open for editing: any user who can access an Excel workbook in their computer' file system can open it and change it or simply delete it. Such openness makes for easy work, but chances are that you won't want colleagues you barely know manipulating your valuable data or poking subtle alterations into your formulas. And you may want to restrict even your trusted colleagues from changing the design of your worksheets when they're supposed only to enter a few missing figures in particular cells.

In this section, you'll learn about the options Excel provides for restricting other people's ability to change your workbooks. The options break down into four categories. You can:

- Restrict data entry in particular cells to make sure nobody enters invalid data.
- Protect specific cells and protect a whole workbook against change.
- Protect a worksheet but still allow users to edit certain ranges in it.
- Password-protect a workbook either so that only people who know the password can open it or so that only people who know the password can modify it.

NOTE *Your first line of defense for your Excel workbooks (and any other important files) should be to store them where people you don't want to access them can't get at them. Depending on your situation, such a location might be on your hard disk, on a USB key drive that you carry with you, or in a network folder to which access is tightly controlled.*

Check Data Entry for Invalid Entries

You can greatly reduce data-entry problems in your workbooks by making Excel check entries before entering them in specific cells. To do so, you define restrictions and data-validation rules for those cells.

For example, often you'll need to make sure that a number the user enters is within a certain range, to prevent the user from accidentally entering a different order of magnitude with a misplaced finger. Similarly, on an application form for permission to travel to an affiliate office, you could use a drop-down list of the possible destinations to prevent the user from typing in any other destination.

To make Excel check data entry for invalid entries, follow these steps:

1. Select the cell or range you want Excel to check.

2. Choose Data | Data Tools | Data Validation (click the Data Validation button, not its drop-down button). Excel displays the Data Validation dialog box.

3. On the Settings tab (shown here), specify the validation criteria to use. Select the appropriate type (see the following list) in the Allow drop-down list, and then set parameters accordingly.

■ **Any Value**   Accepts any input (Excel's default setting for cells). This setting effectively turns off validation, so you normally select it only when you need to remove validation from a cell or range. But you can also use this setting to display an informational message for a cell or range. To do so, enter the title and message on the Input Message tab, as discussed in step 5.

■ **Whole Number**   Lets you specify a comparison operator (see the Note) and appropriate values. The user must not enter a decimal point.

NOTE   *The validation criteria use these self-explanatory comparison operators: Between, Not Between, Equal To, Not Equal To, Greater Than, Less Than, Greater Than Or Equal To, and Less Than Or Equal To.*

■ **Decimal**   Lets you specify a comparison operator and appropriate values. The user must include a decimal point and at least one decimal place (even if it's **.0**).

■ **List**   Lets you specify a list of valid entries for the cell. You can type in entries in the Source text box, separating them with commas, but the best form of source is a range on a worksheet in this workbook. If you hide the worksheet, the users won't trip over it. Usually, you'll want to select the In-Cell Drop-down option to produce a drop-down list in the cell. Otherwise, users have to know the entries (or enter them from the help message).

■ **Date**   Lets you specify a comparison operator and appropriate dates (including formulas).

■ **Time**   Lets you specify a comparison operator and appropriate times (including formulas).

■ **Text Length**   Lets you specify a comparison operator and appropriate values (including formulas).

■ **Custom**   Lets you specify a formula that returns a logical TRUE or a logical FALSE value.

14

4. Select or clear the Ignore Blank check box as appropriate. If you clear this check box, the user must fill in the cell.

5. On the Input Message tab (shown here), choose whether to have Excel display an input message when the cell is selected. If you leave the Show Input Message When Cell Is Selected check box selected (as it is by default), enter the title and input message in the text boxes.

6. On the Error Alert tab (shown here), choose whether to have Excel display an error alert after the user enters invalid data in the cell. If you leave the Show Error Alert After Invalid Data Is Entered check box selected (as it is by default), choose the style (Stop, Warning, or Information) in the Style drop-down list, and enter the title and error message in the text boxes. Stop alerts prevent the user from continuing until they enter a valid value for the cell. Warning alerts and Information alerts display the message but allow the user to continue after entering an invalid value in the cell.

7. Click the OK button. Excel closes the Data Validation dialog box and applies the validation to the cell or range.

When a user selects a restricted cell, Excel displays the information message (unless you chose not to display one):

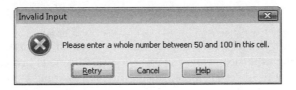

If the user enters an invalid value, Excel displays the appropriate alert message box:

CAUTION   *A user can bypass validation by pasting data into the cell.*

Protect Cells, a Worksheet, or a Workbook

The next stage in preventing users from mangling your workbooks is to prevent them from accessing cells they're not supposed to change. Excel offers several means of doing this; you can:

- Lock cells so that users can't change them.
- Lock a workbook or a worksheet with a password to prevent changes.
- Password-protect a workbook against being opened or modified by people who don't know the password.

Lock a Cell or Range

To lock a cell or range, follow these steps:

1. Select the cell or range.
2. Choose Home | Cells | Format | Lock.
3. To make the locking take effect, protect the workbook as described in "Protect a Workbook," next.

NOTE   *You can also lock cells from the Format Cells dialog box. Press CTRL-1, click the Protection tab, select the Locked check box, and then click the OK button.*

14

Protect a Workbook

To prevent other users from changing a workbook, protect it. To do so, follow these steps:

1. Choose Review | Changes | Protect Workbook | Protect Structure And Windows. Excel displays the Protect Structure And Windows dialog box:

2. Leave the Structure check box selected (as it is by default) if you want to protect the structure of the worksheet. Doing so prevents users from making changes to the worksheets—inserting, deleting, hiding, displaying, or renaming worksheets.

3. Select the Windows check box if you want to protect the current layout of windows in the worksheet. This more specialized form of protection is useful for some workbooks, but you won't normally need it.

4. Type a password. The password is optional, but the protection is worthless without one. With a weak password, the protection is worth little, so use a strong password (see the next Tip).

5. Click the OK button. If you used a password, Excel displays the Confirm Password dialog box:

6. Enter the password in the Reenter Password To Proceed text box, and then click the OK button. Excel closes the Confirm Password dialog box and the Protect Workbook dialog box, leaving your workbook protected.

To create a strong password, follow these basic rules: Use six characters minimum; don't use a real word in any language; don't use a name, least of all one that can be associated with you; mix letters, numbers, and symbols in the password; and use both uppercase and lowercase (passwords are case sensitive). Make sure you memorize the password so that you don't lose access to the workbook.

Unprotect a Workbook

To unprotect a workbook, follow these steps:

1. Choose Review | Changes | Protect Workbook | Protect Structure And Windows. Excel displays the Unprotect Workbook dialog box:

2. Type your password, and then click the OK button. Excel closes the Unprotect Workbook dialog box and removes the protection.

Protect a Worksheet

Instead of protecting an entire workbook, Excel also enables you to protect one or more worksheets in a workbook. To do so, follow these steps:

1. Choose Review | Changes | Protect Sheet. Excel displays the Protect Sheet dialog box:

2. Ensure that the Protect Worksheet And Contents Of Locked Cells check box is selected.

3. Type a strong password in the Password To Unprotect Sheet text box.

4. Select or clear the Allow All Users Of This Worksheet To check boxes to specify which actions all users may take with this worksheet. For example, if you want users to be able to format cells, select the Format Cells check box; if you want users to be able to edit scenarios, select the Edit Scenarios check box.

TIP   *You'll get better protection by limiting the number of actions users can take to the absolute minimum necessary.*

14

5. Click the OK button.

6. If you used a password, Excel displays the Confirm Password dialog box on top of the Protect Sheet dialog box. Enter the password in the Reenter Password To Proceed text box, and then click the OK button. Excel closes the Confirm Password dialog box and the Protect Sheet dialog box.

Unprotect a Worksheet

When a worksheet no longer needs protection, unprotect it again. Follow these steps:

1. Choose Review | Changes | Unprotect Worksheet. Excel displays the Unprotect Sheet dialog box:

2. Type the password, and then click the OK button. Excel closes the Unprotect Sheet dialog box and removes the protection.

Allow Users to Edit Ranges in a Protected Worksheet

When you protect a worksheet, you may want to allow users to edit specific ranges—for example, so they can fill in certain data (perhaps in validated cells) without changing other parts of the worksheet. Excel enables you to:

- Leave a range unprotected so that any user can edit it.
- Password-protect a range so that only users who can supply the password can edit the range.
- Password-protect a range (as above) but exempt specific users from having to supply the password. For example, you might exempt yourself from the password so you can edit the worksheet easily.
- Protect different ranges with different passwords to implement different levels of access to different groups of users with whom you share the passwords. For example, you might allow a group to edit most ranges but reserve other ranges for administrators.

To allow users to edit ranges in a protected worksheet, follow these steps:

1. Choose Review | Changes | Allow Users To Edit Ranges. Excel displays the Allow Users To Edit Ranges dialog box:

2. Create as many ranges as necessary by clicking the New button and working in the New Range dialog box:

- ■ Name each range and specify which cells it refers to. Use a descriptive name so that you can easily identify the range by name.

- ■ Enter a password if you want to use a password to restrict access to the range. You may want to leave the range open so anyone can edit it without a password.

- ■ If you use a password, click Permissions and use the Permissions dialog box (see Figure 14-2) to specify which users are permitted to edit the range without a password. To add a user or group, click the Add button, and then work in the Select Users Or Groups dialog box. Remember to add yourself if appropriate.

3. If necessary, select an existing range and modify or delete it:

- ■ Click the Modify button to modify the range using the Modify Range dialog box, which contains the same controls as the New Range dialog box.

- ■ Click the Delete button to delete the range.

- ■ Click the Permissions button to change the permissions on the range. Excel displays the Permissions dialog box.

4. Click the Protect Sheet button to make Excel display the Protect Sheet dialog box, and then proceed as described in the previous section, "Protect a Worksheet." (Alternatively, click the OK button to close the Allow Users To Edit Ranges dialog box, and then protect your worksheet manually later.)

14

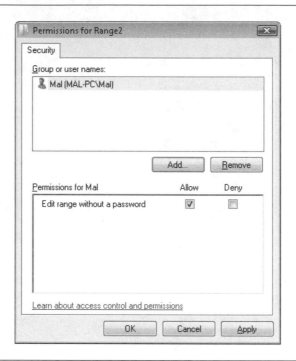

FIGURE 14-2 Use the Permissions dialog box to build a list of groups or users who are allowed to edit a range without a password.

NOTE *To track the ranges' titles, locations, password protection, and password-exempt users, select the Paste Permissions Information Into A New Workbook check box. When you close the Allow Users To Edit Ranges dialog box, Excel creates a new workbook and enters details of the ranges in its top sheet. Save this somewhere convenient for reference, or move the top worksheet to a workbook in which you store details of all your shared workbooks.*

5. Press CTRL-S or click the Office button, and then click Save. Excel saves the workbook that contains the worksheet.

When a user tries to make an entry in a protected cell, Excel displays the Unlock Range dialog box (shown next) demanding the password. If the user can't supply the password, Excel doesn't enter the entry in the cell.

Protect a Workbook with Passwords

To keep users out of your workbooks without authorization, you can apply Open passwords and Modify passwords to them:

- **Open password**   The user must enter the password to open the workbook at all.
- **Modify password**   The user can open the workbook in read-only format without a password. To open the workbook for editing, the user must supply the password.

To protect a workbook with a password, follow these steps:

1. Click the Office button, and then click Save As. Excel displays the Save As dialog box.

2. Click the Tools button (to the left of the Save button), and then choose General Options from the pop-up menu. Excel displays the General Options dialog box:

3. To apply an Open password, type it in the Password To Open text box.

4. To apply a Modify password, type it in the Password To Modify text box.

5. Click the OK button. Excel displays the Confirm Password dialog box.

6. Type the password in the Reenter Password To Proceed text box or the Reenter Password To Modify text box, and then click the OK button. Excel closes the Confirm Password dialog box and the General Options dialog box.

7. Click the Save button. Excel displays the Confirm Save As dialog box, warning you that you are overwriting an existing file.

8. Click the Yes button. Excel closes the Confirm Save As dialog box and the Save As dialog box, and saves the workbook with the password you specified.

14

The next time you open the workbook, Excel displays the Password dialog box, prompting you for the password. The next illustration shows the Password dialog box for an Open password on the left and the Password dialog box for a Modify password on the right. As you can see, for a Modify password, the Password dialog box includes a Read Only button that you can click to open the workbook in read-only mode. You can then change the workbook (depending on other forms of protection used) and save the results under a new name. You can't save changes to the original workbook.

To remove the password, open the General Options dialog box again, delete the password, and then save the workbook again. As before, you'll need to overwrite the existing file.

Protect a Workbook with Encryption

An Open password or a Modify password offers only weak protection, because you (or anyone else) can easily find password-cracking utilities on the Internet. To protect a workbook more securely, you can encrypt it. To do so, follow these steps:

1. Click the Office button, and then choose Prepare | Encrypt Document. Excel displays the Encrypt Document dialog box:

2. Type a strong password in the Password text box.

3. Click the OK button. Excel displays a Confirm Password dialog box:

4. Click the OK button. Excel closes the Confirm Password dialog box and applies the encryption.

5. Click the Office button, and then click Save. Alternatively, press CTRL-S. Excel saves the workbook.

Work with Comments

A *comment* is a text tag that you add to a cell. Comments can be very useful for helping you produce powerful and effective worksheets. Most people find comments primarily useful for adding extra information to worksheets that may help their colleagues use the worksheets or add suitable input to them. But you may also find that comments are valuable for worksheets that you alone use. For example, you can add comments to cells explaining what you're trying to achieve with a particular formula, noting where you need to add extra cells, or jotting down suggestions about how the design of the worksheet should evolve from the point you're currently struggling with.

Add a Comment to a Cell

You can add a comment to the selected cell in either of the following ways:

■ Choose Review | Comments | New Comment.

■ Right-click the cell and choose Insert Comment from the shortcut menu.

Excel adds a comment box attached to the cell and enters your user name (the name in the User Name text box on the General tab of the Options dialog box) in boldface at the top of the comment box:

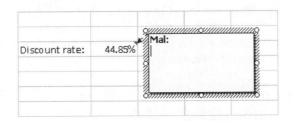

Type the text of the comment, and then click a cell in the worksheet to exit the comment. Depending on your comments settings, the comment will probably then disappear, leaving just a red triangle marker in the cell.

NOTE   *If you don't want your user name to appear in the comment box, select it and press DELETE.*

14

Display and Hide the Comments in a Worksheet

You can control Excel's overall display settings for comments by using the Excel Options dialog box. Follow these steps:

1. Click the Office button, and then click Excel Options. Excel displays the Excel Options dialog box.

2. In the left panel, click the Advanced category. Excel displays the Advanced options.

3. In the Display section, select the appropriate option button in the For Cells With Comments, Show list: the No Comments Or Indicators option button; the Indicators Only, And Comments On Hover option button; or the Comments And Indicators option button.

4. Click the OK button. Excel closes the Excel Options dialog box and applies your choices.

The default setting is Indicators Only, And Comments On Hover, which makes Excel display a small red triangle in the upper-right corner to indicate that a cell has a comment attached to it. You can display the comment by hovering the mouse pointer over a cell with a comment indicator:

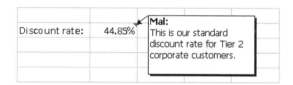

To toggle the display of a particular comment, right-click its cell and choose Show/Hide Comments from the shortcut menu. Alternatively, choose Review | Comments |Show/Hide Comment.

To display all comments, choose Review | Comments | Show All Comments button. To hide all comments, choose Review | Comments | Show All Comments again.

To move to the next comment, choose Review | Comments | Next. To move to the previous comment, choose Review | Comments | Previous.

Edit and Format Comments

After inserting a comment, you can edit and format it easily:

■ To edit a comment, right-click the cell, and then choose Edit Comment from the shortcut menu. Alternatively, click the cell, and then choose Review | Comments | Edit Comment. You can also display the comment in one of the ways mentioned in the previous section, and then simply click in the comment's text to start editing it.

■ To format a comment, right-click the comment box and choose Format Comment, then work on the tabs of the Format Comment dialog box (see Figure 14-3). A comment is a rectangular AutoShape, so you can format it in many of the ways that you can format most AutoShapes. For example, you can change the orientation of text in a comment by working on the Alignment tab of the Format Comment dialog box.

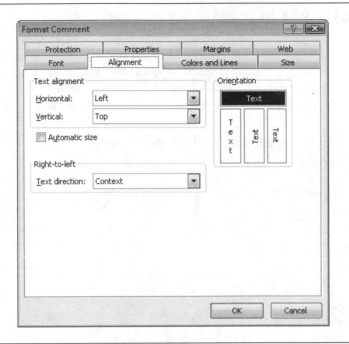

FIGURE 14-3   Use the eight tabs of the Format Comment dialog box to format a comment the way you want it to look and behave.

■ You can also use many of the drawing commands discussed in Chapter 5 to manipulate comments. In normal use, you'll seldom need to do so, but occasionally you may find this capability useful. For example, you can group a comment with other AutoShapes, and you can use the Order submenu on the shortcut menu to change the comment's position within the sublayers of the drawing layer. (See the section "Understand How Excel Handles Graphical Objects," in Chapter 5, for an explanation of the drawing layer.)

Delete a Comment

You can remove a comment from a cell in any of the following ways:

■ Right-click the cell and choose Delete Comment from the shortcut menu. This technique is most useful if you have only comment indicators displayed.

■ If you have comments displayed, click the comment's frame to select it, and then press DELETE.

■ Select the cell, and then choose Review | Comments | Delete.

Send Workbooks via E-mail

Depending on the type of company or organization you work for, you may need to send documents to your colleagues via e-mail. Excel provides one easy-to-reach command for sending an Excel workbook via e-mail as an attachment to an Outlook message; you'll learn about this command in this section. Excel also has two hidden commands for sending workbooks and worksheets in different ways; you'll learn about these ways briefly at the end of this section.

Send a Workbook as an E-mail Attachment

To send a workbook as an e-mail attachment, follow these steps:

1. Open the workbook and make sure it's ready for distribution.

2. Click the Office button, and then choose Send | E-mail. Excel activates Outlook (if it's running) or launches it (if it isn't running), creates a new message, enters the workbook's name in the Subject field, and attaches the workbook to the message. Here's an example:

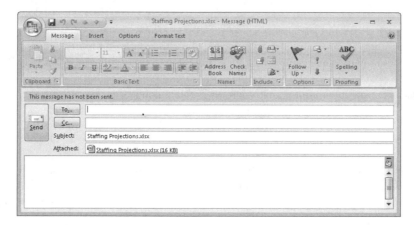

3. Enter the names of the recipient or recipients and any cc recipients.

4. Adjust the Subject line if necessary (the workbook's name on its own isn't very informative).

5. Enter any further information required in the body of the document. For example, you might tell the recipient what the workbook contains, why you're sending it, and what action you're expecting them to take with it.

6. Choose any further options for the message, as you would for any other message. For example, you might choose Options | Tracking | Request A Read Receipt so that you receive a notice when the recipient opens the message.

7. Click the Send button. Outlook sends the message with the workbook as an attachment.

Receive a Workbook Sent As an Attachment

When you receive a workbook sent as an attachment, simply save it to the appropriate folder. You can then work with it as you would any other workbook.

Make the Send To Mail Recipient and Mail Recipient (For Review) Commands Available

In addition to the Send | E-mail command that appears on the Office Button menu, Excel also offers two other commands for sending workbooks:

- **Send To Mail Recipient**   This command lets you send either the current (active) worksheet in the current workbook as part of an e-mail message, or send the entire current workbook as an attachment to a message.

- **Mail Recipient (For Review)**   This command lets you send a shared workbook to other people so that they can review it. Usually, they'll return the workbook to you after reviewing it—for example, so that you can integrate their suggestions into a master version. You can send the workbook either as a "regular attachment," so that each recipient gets a separate copy, or as a "shared attachment," in which each recipient gets a separate copy but Office also creates a copy in a document workspace. The copy in the document workspace can be automatically updated with the changes the recipients make to their individual copies of the workbook.

To make the Send To Mail Recipient command or the Mail Recipient (For Review) command available, follow these steps:

1. Click the Customize Quick Access Toolbar button (the small button at the right end of the Quick Access Toolbar), and then choose More Commands from the drop-down menu. Excel displays the Customize category in the Excel Options dialog box.

2. In the Choose Commands From drop-down list, select the Commands Not In The Ribbon item.

3. To add the Send To Mail Recipient command, select the Send To Mail Recipient item in the left list box, and then click the Add button. Excel adds the command to the right list box.

4. To add the Mail Recipient (For Review) command, select the Send For Review command in the left list box, and then click the Add button. Excel adds the command to the right list box.

5. Click the OK button. Excel closes the Excel Options dialog box and adds the command or commands to the Quick Access Toolbar. You can then click the appropriate button to issue one of the commands.

14

Track Changes to a Workbook

Excel lets you track changes made to a workbook so that you can see who changed what when. Normally, people use change tracking on shared workbooks, so to streamline this process, Excel automatically shares a workbook when you turn on change tracking.

Turn On and Configure Change Tracking

To turn on and configure change tracking, follow these steps:

1. Choose Review | Changes | Track Changes | Highlight Changes. Excel displays the Highlight Changes dialog box:

2. Select the Track Changes While Editing check box. When you select this check box, Excel makes all the other controls in the dialog box available.

3. In the Highlight Which Changes section, specify which changes you want to track by selecting the appropriate check boxes and choosing suitable options:

   ■ The When drop-down list offers the choices Since I Last Saved, All, Not Yet Reviewed (changes you haven't reviewed yet), and Since Date (you specify the date).

   ■ The Who drop-down list offers the choices Everyone, Everyone But Me, and each user by name (including you). For example, you might choose to see only the changes that your supervisor makes.

   ■ The Where text box lets you restrict change tracking to a specific range (or multiple ranges) instead of the whole workbook. Select the check box, and then drag in the worksheet to select the range or ranges.

4. Leave the Highlight Changes On Screen check box selected (as it is by default) if you want to see the tracked changes on screen. Clear this check box to hide the tracked changes. Hiding the tracked changes can help keep your worksheets easy to read.

5. Select the List Changes On A New Sheet check box if you want Excel to create a list of the tracked changes on a separate worksheet called History. This overview lets you quickly scan the list of changes without having to examine each worksheet separately, but it includes only the changes made in the current editing session. If the workbook isn't yet shared, Excel makes this check box unavailable.

NOTE *You may be wondering what happens if your workbook already contains a worksheet named History—but it can't. Excel reserves the name History for change tracking and prevents you from changing a worksheet's name to History.*

6. Click the OK button. Excel closes the Highlight Changes dialog box. If the workbook wasn't already shared, Excel shares it now and displays a message box warning you that it will save the workbook. Click the OK button.

Work with Change Tracking On

When change tracking is on, you can work as you would in any shared workbook—which is to say, you can perform basic editing, apply formatting, and work with formulas, but you can't make major changes to the design or layout of the workbook. (See "Which Editing Actions You Can and Can't Take in a Shared Workbook," earlier in this chapter, for a discussion of the limitations that sharing imposes.)

If Excel is set to display changes on screen, any cell that you change is marked with a border and a triangle in its upper-left corner. Hover the mouse pointer over the cell to display a comment box containing details of the change:

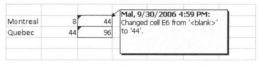

If Excel is set not to display changes on screen, you won't see any visual indication of the tracking of the changes you make.

If Excel is set to list changes on a new worksheet, you'll notice that a worksheet named History appears at the end of the workbook.

Review Tracked Changes

If Excel is set to display changes on screen, you can use the technique of hovering the mouse pointer over a cell to see the change made. This technique tends to be useful only when you've tracked changes to just a handful of cells.

To work through the tracked changes in a workbook, follow these steps:

1. Choose Review | Changes | Track Changes | Accept/Reject Changes. Excel prompts you to save the workbook if it contains unsaved changes, and then displays the Select Changes To Accept Or Reject dialog box:

2. Select or clear the When check box, the Who check box, and the Where check box, as appropriate, and use their options to specify which changes you want to review. (See step 3 in "Turn On and Configure Change Tracking," earlier in this chapter, for details of these options.)

14

3. Click the OK button. Excel closes the Select Changes To Accept Or Reject dialog box, displays the Accept Or Reject Changes dialog box, and selects the first cell that contains a change that matches the details you specified:

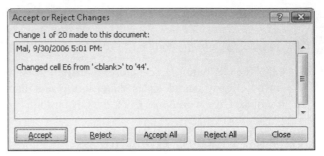

4. Click the Accept button to accept this change or the Reject button to reject this change, and move on to the next change. Alternatively, click the Accept All button to accept all the remaining changes, or click the Reject All button to reject all the remaining changes, without reviewing them further.

5. After reviewing the changes, click the Close button. Excel closes the Accept Or Reject Changes dialog box.

If you set Excel to log the changes on a separate worksheet, display the History worksheet to get an overview of the changes to the workbook in the current editing session. Figure 14-4 shows an example of the History worksheet, which you can filter by using the column headings.

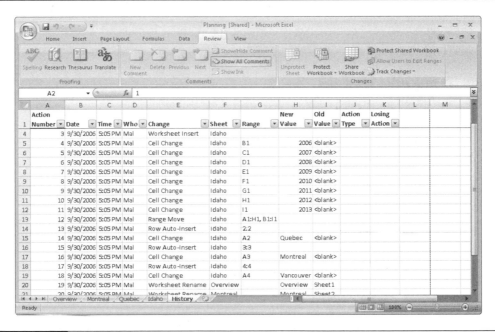

FIGURE 14-4 Display the History worksheet to get an overview of the changes to the workbook in the current editing session.

Chapter 15

Using Excel's Web Capabilities

How to...

- Understand saving directly to an intranet site or Internet server
- Choose Web Options to control how Excel creates web pages
- Understand HTML, round tripping, and web file formats
- Save a worksheet or workbook as a web page
- Work in an interactive web workbook
- Understand and use Excel's XML capabilities

In this chapter, you'll learn how to use Excel's web capabilities—everything from understanding the considerations involved in saving files directly to an intranet site or Internet server, to creating web pages from workbooks and using Excel's powerful XML capabilities.

Depending on the type of work you do, only some of this chapter may be relevant to you. For example, while many home and small businesses can benefit directly and immediately from publishing some worksheets on the Web for their customers, typically only larger businesses use XML documents widely.

Understand Saving Directly to an Intranet Site or Internet Server

Excel can store files directly on a web server, a File Transfer Protocol (FTP) server, or a server running Microsoft's SharePoint Services. This capability can be very useful for working with intranet sites, because you can open a page on an intranet server directly in Excel, edit or update the page, and then save it. To open a file from a server, you need what's called *read permission;* to save a file to a server, you need *write permission.*

The technology for opening files from and saving files to web servers is called Web Digital Authoring and Versioning, or WebDAV. Sometimes it's also called Web Sharing.

If you have a fast and reliable Internet connection, you can work with files on Internet servers (as opposed to intranet sites) as well. You *can* also work with files on Internet servers across slower or less reliable connections, but the results tend to be less satisfactory. The problem is that if Excel is unable even temporarily to write data to the server, it may be unable to save a file. If worse comes to worst, you may lose any unsaved changes in the file.

For this reason, it's usually best not to work directly with files on Internet servers; even fast and usually reliable Internet connections can suffer glitches severe enough to cost you work. Instead, use Windows Explorer or another tool to download a copy of any file you need to open in Excel. Then work with the file on your local disk, where you can save changes instantly as often as necessary. When you've finished making changes to the file, or when you've created a new file that you want to place on the Internet server, upload the file. This way, you keep a copy of the file on your local disk at all times, which will help you avoid losing any data.

You can access an intranet server or Internet server via Internet Explorer or another web browser, a third-party graphical FTP client (or even the command-line FTP client built into Windows Vista and Windows XP), or a common dialog box (for example, the Open dialog box or the Save As dialog box). But the most convenient way to access a server is to create a network place using a wizard.

To launch the wizard:

- ■ **Windows Vista**   Use the Add Network Location Wizard. Follow these steps:

    1. Choose Start | Computer. Windows displays a Computer window.

    2. Click the Map Network Drive button on the toolbar. Windows displays the Map Network Drive dialog box.

    3. Click the Connect To A Web Site That You Can Use To Store Your Documents Or Pictures link. Windows launches the Add Network Location Wizard.

- ■ **Windows XP**   Use the Add Network Place Wizard. Follow these steps:

    1. Choose Start | My Network Places. Windows displays the My Network Places folder.

    2. Click the Add A Network Place link in the Network Tasks pane.

Once you've launched the wizard, follow its steps to create the network. Choose the Custom Network Location option (in Windows Vista) or the Choose Another Network Location (in Windows XP) that allows you to specify the address of a website or FTP site.

Choose Web Options to Control How Excel Creates Web Pages

To control how Excel creates web pages, choose options in its Web Options dialog box. (The other Office applications have their own Web Options dialog boxes, but the settings you choose in one application don't affect the other applications.)

To display the Web Options dialog box, follow these steps:

1. Click the Office button, and then click Excel Options. Excel displays the Excel Options dialog box.

2. In the left panel, click the Advanced category, and then scroll down to the General area.

3. Click the Web Options button. Excel displays the Web Options dialog box.

15

Choose Options on the General Tab

The General tab of the Web Options dialog box contains the following two compatibility options:

- **Save Any Additional Hidden Data Necessary To Maintain Formulas**   This check box controls whether Excel includes in web spreadsheets any hidden data that's needed to make the formulas work. You'll almost always want to select this check box.

- **Load Pictures From Web Pages Not Created in Excel**   This check box controls whether Excel loads pictures in web pages created by other applications. This feature is usually helpful.

Choose Options on the Browsers Tab

The Browsers tab of the Web Options dialog box (see Figure 15-1) lets you specify the types of browsers for which you want to make the web page work properly.

Select the lowest expected version of browser in the People Who View This Web Page Will Be Using drop-down list. (The default setting is Microsoft Internet Explorer 4 or later, which plays safe.) Excel automatically selects and deselects the options in the Options box to match that browser's needs. You can also select and deselect check boxes manually to suit your needs:

- **Allow PNG As A Graphics Format**   Select this check box to allow web pages to use the Portable Network Graphics (PNG) format. PNG is a new format, and Internet Explorer versions before version 6 can't display it.

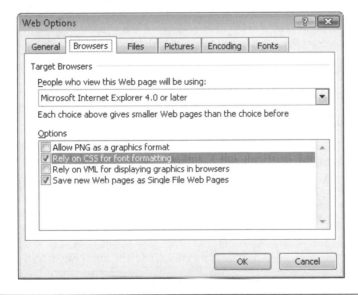

FIGURE 15-1   On the Browsers tab of the Web Options dialog box, specify the types of browsers for which you want to make the web page work.

- **Rely On CSS For Font Formatting**   Select this check box to use Cascading Style Sheets (CSS) for font formatting.

- **Rely On VML For Displaying Graphics in Browsers**   Select this check box to use Vector Markup Language (VML; a text-based format for vector graphics) for displaying graphics.

- **Save New Web Pages As Single File Web Pages**   Select this check box to make Excel save new web pages using the Single File Web Page format by default. (You can override this setting manually.)

Choose Options on the Files Tab

The Files tab of the Web Options dialog box (see Figure 15-2) includes the following check boxes:

- **Organize Supporting Files In A Folder**   Select this check box to make Excel place the supporting files in a subfolder of the folder that contains the page rather than in the same folder as the page. Using a subfolder tends to be neater and easier, especially when you need to move the page.

- **Use Long File Names Whenever Possible**   Select this check box to make Excel use long file names if possible when saving files to a web server. You may want to clear this check box to force the application to use short (eight-character) names.

- **Update Links On Save**   Select this check box to make Excel automatically update hyperlinks in the page when you save it. Updating the links helps prevent the page containing broken links.

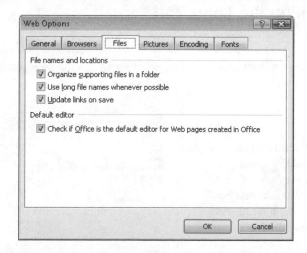

15

FIGURE 15-2   On the Files tab of the Web Options dialog box, specify how Excel should handle file names and locations.

■ **Check If Office Is the Default Editor For Web Pages Created In Office**   Select this check box to make Excel see if it's the default editor for web pages that Office applications create. If you use the Office applications to create most of your web pages, you'll probably want to select this check box. This check box is selected by default but is a matter of preference. If you prefer to use another web editor than Excel, clear this check box to prevent Excel constantly warning you about a choice you know you've made.

Choose Options on the Pictures Tab

On the Pictures tab of the Web Options dialog box, you can select the screen resolution of the monitor on which your web pages will be viewed. The default is 800 × 600 resolution, which is a good choice for making sure that anybody on the Internet can view the pictures. If you're creating web pages for a specific audience—for example, cutting-edge computer professionals, or your colleagues in an office equipped with new computer hardware—you may want to choose a higher resolution, such as 1024 × 768 or 1280 × 1024.

You can also specify the number of pixels per inch on that monitor. The default is 96 pixels per inch and is normally the best choice; the other available settings are 72 pixels per inch and 120 pixels per inch.

Choose Options on the Encoding Tab

On the Encoding tab of the Web Options dialog box, you can select the type of encoding to use for the web page—for example, Western European (Windows) or Unicode (UTF-8)—and whether to always save web pages in the default encoding.

Choose Options on the Fonts Tab

On the Fonts tab of the Web Options dialog box (shown here), you can choose the character set, proportional font, and fixed-width font for your web pages. The default character set for a U.S. English installation of Office is English/Western European/Other Latin Script, and you'll seldom need to change it unless you need to create, say, Arabic or Japanese pages. On the other hand, you may want to change the fonts in the Proportional Font drop-down list and the Fixed-Width Font drop-down list for visual effect.

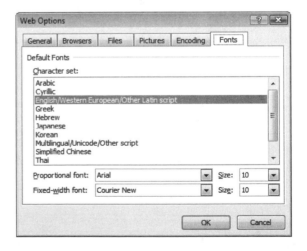

After choosing options, click the OK button. Excel closes the Web Options dialog box, returning you to the Excel Options dialog box. Click the OK button to close this dialog box as well.

Understand HTML, Round Tripping, and Web File Formats

For creating web content, Excel and the other Office applications use Hypertext Markup Language (HTML), a formatting language that's extensively used and that's understood more or less perfectly by all modern web browsers. HTML uses *tags,* or codes, to specify how an item should be displayed. For example, if you apply an <H2> tag to indicate that some text is a level-two heading, any browser should recognize the tag and apply the appropriate formatting to the heading.

Excel automatically applies all necessary tags when you save a worksheet or workbook in one of the HTML formats. Roughly speaking, the tags break down into two separate categories:

- ■ Standard HTML tags for coding those parts of the file—the text and its formatting—that a web browser will display.

- ■ Custom, Office-specific HTML tags for storing document information and application information. For example, when you save a workbook in Single File Web Page format or Web Page format, Excel saves items such as the author's name and the last author's name, creation date, and VBA projects using custom HTML tags.

Excel's custom tags should be ignored by web browsers, which don't care about document items such as name of the person who last modified the document or the application that created the file. These tags are used for *round tripping*—saving a workbook or worksheet with all its contents, formatting, and extra items (such as VBA code) so that Excel can reopen the file with exactly the same information and formatting as when it saved the file.

Saving files without losing the information they contain is something that any well-designed application should normally do as a matter of course, but in most cases, applications that create rich content (as opposed to, say, basic text) have historically used proprietary formats for saving their contents rather than HTML. For example, Excel used to be able to save its workbooks only in the Excel Workbook format. When Excel first gained the capability to create HTML files, it wasn't able to round-trip fully: the HTML files Excel produced contained only a subset of the data saved in the Excel Workbook format, and if you reopened such an HTML file in Excel, most of the noncontent items would be missing.

But Excel 2007 and the other Office 2007 applications support HTML as a native format alongside their previous native formats. This means that, should you need to, you can save workbooks in HTML instead of the Excel Spreadsheet format, without losing any parts of those workbooks.

Excel can save web pages in two file formats: Single File Web Page and Web Page. Both file types use Office-specific HTML tags to preserve all of the information the file contains in an HTML format. In most cases, you'll find the Single File Web Page format the better choice, because it creates files that you can easily distribute.

15

The Single File Web Page format creates a web archive file that contains all the information required for the web page. This doesn't seem like much of an innovation until you know that the Web Page format (discussed next) creates a separate folder to contain graphics. Files in the Single File Web Page format use the .mht and .mhtml file extensions.

The Web Page format creates an HTML file that contains the text contents of the document, together with a separate folder that contains the graphics for the document. This makes the web page's HTML file itself smaller, but the page as a whole is more awkward to distribute, because you need to distribute the graphics folder as well. The folder is created automatically and assigned the web page's name followed by _files. For example, a web page named Web1.htm has a folder named Web1_files. Files in the Web Page format use the .htm and .html file extensions.

Save a Worksheet or Workbook As a Web Page

After choosing the appropriate web options for Excel and learning the essentials of HTML and the available file formats, you're ready to save an existing worksheet or workbook as a web page.

Put the Web Page Preview Command on the Quick Access Toolbar

Before you save a worksheet or workbook as a web page, it's a good idea to use Web Page Preview to make sure the page will look okay. Microsoft chose not to include Web Page Preview on the Office button menu or on the Ribbon, so you need to add it to the Quick Access Toolbar before you can use it. To do so, follow these steps:

1. Click the Customize Quick Access Toolbar button (the small button at the right end of the Quick Access Toolbar), and then choose More Commands from the drop-down menu. Excel displays the Customize category in the Excel Options dialog box.

2. In the Choose Commands From drop-down list, select the Commands Not In The Ribbon item.

3. In the left list box, select the Web Page Preview command, and then click the Add button. Excel adds the command to the right list box.

4. Click the OK button. Excel closes the Excel Options dialog box and adds the command or commands to the Quick Access Toolbar. You can then click the button to issue the command.

Use Web Page Preview to Preview the Workbook

To preview the workbook, click the Web Page Preview button on the Quick Access Toolbar. Excel creates a temporary file in your *%userprofile%*\AppData\Local\Temporary Internet Files\Content.MSO\ExcelWebPagePreview\ folder, and then displays the page in your default browser (for example, Internet Explorer). Figure 15-3 shows an example of Web Page Preview.

Check the web page, and then close the browser tab or window. If the page needs changing, make the changes, and then use Web Page Preview again to verify them.

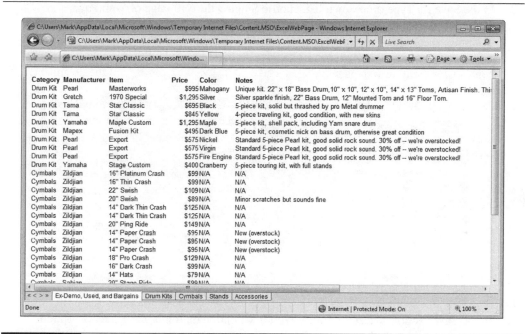

FIGURE 15-3 Use Web Page Preview to check how a page will look before you save it.

Choose Whether to Create a Save or to Publish

Excel offers you the choice between merely saving the workbook (or a part of it) as a web page and *publishing* a copy of the workbook (or the specified part of it). When you publish a copy of the workbook (or a part of it), Excel creates a copy of the workbook or part and saves it under the specified file name, but doesn't save the workbook itself. So you can publish a copy of an unsaved workbook if you choose.

Save As a Web Page

To save an Excel workbook, worksheet, or part of a worksheet as a web page, follow these steps:

1. To save a worksheet rather than a workbook, make that worksheet active. To save a range from a worksheet, select that range.

2. Click the Office button, and then click Save As. Excel displays the Save As dialog box.

15

3. In the Save As Type drop-down list, choose Single File Web Page or Web Page, depending on which type of file you want to create. (See "Understand HTML, Round Tripping, and Web File Formats," earlier in this chapter, for an explanation of the differences between the file types.) The Save As dialog box changes to include extra controls for creating web pages:

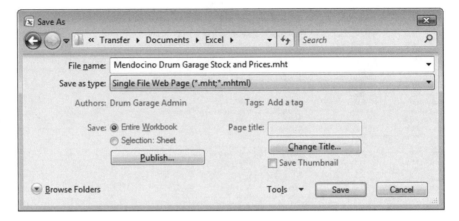

4. In the Save section, select the Entire Workbook option button or the Selection option button to specify whether to save the whole workbook, the active worksheet, or the specified range. If you made a selection before displaying the Save As dialog box, the Selection option button shows that selection (for example, Selection: $C$6:$E$10). If not, the Selection option button appears as Selection: Sheet.

5. Check the title (if any) assigned to the web page:

   ■ If there is a title, it appears in the Page Title text box.

   ■ The title is displayed in the browser's title bar when the browser loads the page.

   ■ To change the title, click the Change Title button. Excel displays the Set Page Title dialog box (shown here). Type the text for the title, and then click the OK button.

6. If you're saving the workbook for the first time, follow these steps:

   ■ Type the file name in the File Name text box.

   ■ Click the Save button to save the workbook.

   ■ Click the Office button, and then click Save As again to display the Save As dialog box once more so that you can publish the web page.

7. Click the Publish button. Excel displays the Publish As Web Page dialog box (see Figure 15-4).

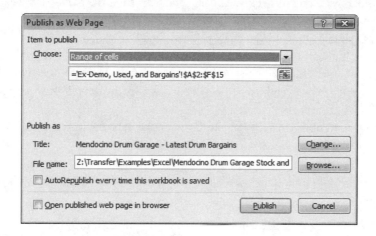

FIGURE 15-4 Choose publication options for an Excel workbook, worksheet, or range in the Publish As Web Page dialog box.

8. If necessary, change the item selected in the Choose drop-down list:

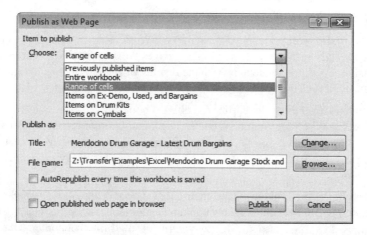

■ The choices are Previously Published Items, Entire Workbook, Range Of Cells, or the items on any of the worksheets in the workbook. For example, select Items On Drum Kits to have Excel publish all the cells that have contents on the worksheet named Drum Kits.

■ If you selected the appropriate worksheet or range in step 1, the selection here should be correct.

■ If you select the Range Of Cells item, Excel displays a Collapse Dialog button that allows you to select a range in the appropriate worksheet manually.

9. In the Publish As section, check and change the page title, file name, and location, as necessary.

10. Select the AutoRepublish Every Time This Workbook Is Saved check box if you want Excel to automatically publish this web page again each time you save the file. This option is convenient for making sure the web page is always up-to-date, but use it only if you have a permanent and fast connection to the site on which you're publishing the web page.

11. Leave the Open Published Web Page In Browser check box selected (as it is by default) if you want Excel to display the web page in your browser so that you can check it after Excel has published it.

12. Click the Publish button. Excel publishes the page and (if appropriate) displays it in your browser.

Your colleagues or your audience can now view the page using a browser.

Understand and Use Excel's XML Capabilities

Excel 2007's new file format is based on XML—so if you use that file format, you're using XML in a way every time you work with Excel. The file format is named Excel Workbook, just as the previous file format was, but there are several major differences:

- **.xlsx file extension** The XML-based Excel Workbook file format uses the .xlsx file extension, whereas the previous (binary) Excel Workbook file format used the .xls file extension. So if you've switched on the display of file extensions (Windows keeps them hidden by default), and you see the .xlsx file extension, you know that's an XML file.

- **No macros** Whereas the earlier Excel Workbook file format could contain macros, the Excel 2007 Excel Workbook file format cannot contain macros. (This limitation is for safety reasons.) If you need to store macros in a workbook, you must use a different file format, the Excel Macro-Enabled Workbook file format (which takes the .xlsm file extension).

- **Underlying zipped folder** The XML-based format is actually a zipped folder containing individual files and subfolders that contain the components of the workbook. For example, if you dig down inside an XLSX file, you find a small file that contains theme information for the workbook. By contrast, the earlier Excel Workbook format really was a single file that contained all the workbook's information. Having the zipped folder of separate files offers several advantages over a single file, including that you can edit or replace a component file without having to open the workbook as a whole. (These are specialized behaviors normally performed only by administrators. Normally, if you want to change a workbook, you open it in Excel, and Excel handles all the details for you.)

Excel 2007 brings a similar change for templates, which are slightly mutated workbook files. A standard Excel 2007 template has the .xltx file extension, is XML, and can contain no macros, whereas its predecessor Excel Template format had the .xlt file extension, was binary, and could contain macros. Excel 2007 introduces a new Excel Macro-Enabled Template file format (with the .xltm file extension) for templates that must include macros.

But while these new XML-based file formats mean that you're "using" XML when you're doing just about anything with Excel 2007 files, the actions that you can take using XML in Excel 2007 are rather different. Read on.

What XML Is

XML is the abbreviation for *Extensible Markup Language.* As its name states, XML is a markup language—a language that uses tags to identify different parts of a document, like HTML does.

HTML is a formatting language: by using HTML tags, you can specify more or less how a document appears on screen (there's some variation depending on how the browser used displays the document, plus some variation caused by any overrides the user has programmed to take effect—for example, large font sizes). By contrast, XML uses tags to describe not only formatting but also the contents of a document. XML can be used to create machine-readable documents attached to an external *schema* (a specification) that explains what the contents of the document are and the types of data they should contain. This allows XML documents to be used for data transfer among disparate computer systems using XML-compatible applications. (If you want to be fully buzzword-compliant, XML is *platform independent*—it can be used across different computer platforms. For example, XML can be used by Unix, Linux, and Macintosh applications as well as by Windows applications.)

XML is a simplified form of the Standard Generalized Markup Language (SGML) that has long been used for government and corporate documents. SGML provides rigid definitions of all the items an SGML document can contain. By contrast, XML is extensible in that XML documents can define custom tags to identify information rather than having to stick strictly with a predefined set of tags.

> NOTE   *Like HTML files, XML files—and that includes XML schema files—are plain text. So anyone expert in XML can create or edit a schema in a text editor such as Notepad or vi. For normal users, it makes much more sense to use an XML editor that automates as much of creating the schema for you as possible.*

What XML Is For

XML is for data exchange. Data exchange may sound like more of a priority for a company's IT department and developers than for end users of applications, but in fact XML can greatly benefit end users as well as developers:

- End users can access their company's information-management system directly through the familiar interfaces of Excel and Word. For example, you can fill in an XML spreadsheet (say, a complex invoice) by using Excel or an XML document (say, a travel-request form) by using Word, without having to learn to use a new application or new features.

- Developers can create documents and forms that can be deployed easily across different computing platforms and read by any XML-capable application. Various tools are available for creating such documents and forms. Microsoft's main entry in the field is InfoPath, which enables administrators, developers, or power users to create XML-based templates. These templates can provide built-in help and extra commands to assist the user in completing and using them correctly.

- The IT department can extract the relevant details from such forms by using server-based tools. (For example, Microsoft's BizTalk Server has extensive capabilities for processing XML documents.)

- The company can share data with other companies without having to worry about operating-system or application compatibility. For example, another company can open spreadsheet data saved in XML format, or even a complete workbook saved in the XML spreadsheet format, without using Excel.

The Benefits XML Offers

At this writing, each typical company produces many files in separate and proprietary formats: Excel or Lotus 1-2-3 spreadsheets, Word or WordPerfect documents, PowerPoint or Keynote presentations, and so on. These files tend to behave as discrete islands of information rather than as a cohesive and accessible whole that can act as the company's knowledge base. This raises these problems:

- Searching for specific content in these files tends to be a slow and unwieldy process unless the company successfully enforces strict policies on file naming, folder locations, and keywords. Windows and Office provide tools for searching for files by specific information, but such searches tend to produce multiple results that the searcher has to examine to find the right file.

- Extracting specific information from a file typically involves opening it manually in the associated application, locating the information by eye or by using the search feature, and copying the information out of the file. In some cases, developers can automate the extraction of information by creating VBA solutions for extracting specific parts of files. For example, a procedure might extract the contents of specific ranges from worksheets in an Excel workbook or of specific bookmarks from a Word document. (Such workbooks and documents would have been designed to allow the relevant parts of data to be extracted.) But in general, such automation tends to be labor intensive.

XML offers a neat solution to these problems for Excel spreadsheets and Word documents. By using spreadsheets and documents saved in XML formats and linked to external schemas, a company can automatically extract key information that would otherwise be stored in discrete documents.

Another strong component of XML's appeal is the validation it offers, which can provide a solution to the problems of formatting documents consistently and filling them in correctly. An XML document can validate its contents and formatting against the set of rules contained in the schema attached to it. For example, the schema attached to an invoice spreadsheet can ensure that cells mapped to specific elements contain data (rather than being empty) and that the data is of the required type. Likewise, the schema for a text document might require each table to be followed by a caption; validation can identify tables missing their captions.

What You're Likely to Do with XML Files

Depending on the type of work you do, you're likely to work with XML documents in one of two very different ways:

- ■ **As a user** Most people who use XML documents will fill in documents and create new documents by using existing schemas that developers in their company or organization created. To fill in existing XML documents and to create new XML documents based on existing schemas, you need only add a few skills to the core Excel and Word skills you probably already possess.

- ■ **As a developer** Someone needs to develop the XML documents and related schemas that the other users will work with. If you're a developer of XML documents and schemas, you'll need a much wider set of skills than if you just need to fill in the documents.

Work with XML Files in Excel

For opening, editing, and saving XML files, you use many of the same commands as for working with regular Excel worksheets and workbooks.

XML data files contain XML data, typically including references to external schemas. When you open an XML data file, you get to decide whether to import all of its data into an Excel worksheet, whether to open the file as a read-only list, or whether to perform a custom mapping of elements in the file's attached schema to specify exactly which data you want to extract from the file.

Open an XML Spreadsheet File in Excel

You can open an XML spreadsheet in Excel by using standard Excel commands:

- ■ Click the Office button, and then click Open. Excel displays the Open dialog box. Navigate to and select the XML file, and then click the Open button. If you want to restrict the list of files to only XML files, click the Files Of Type button (the button above the Open button and the Cancel button), and then choose XML Files in the drop-down list.

- ■ Click the Office button, and then choose an XML file from the Recent Documents list.

Right-click an XML file in a Windows Explorer window (or on the desktop) and choose Open With | Microsoft Office Excel from the context menu. If Microsoft Office Excel doesn't appear on the Open With submenu, follow these steps:

1. Choose Open With | Choose Default Program from the context menu. Windows displays the Open With dialog box.

2. If Microsoft Office Excel appears in the Recommended Programs list or in the Other Programs list, select it. Otherwise, click the Browse button, navigate to the EXCEL.EXE file in the %ProgramFiles%\Microsoft Office\Office12 folder, and then click the Open button.

3. Clear the Always Use The Selected Program To Open This Kind Of File check box.

4. Click the OK button. Windows closes the Open With dialog box and starts opening the file in Excel.

Open an XML Data File in Excel

You can open an existing XML data file in Excel by using the standard Excel commands mentioned in the previous section. What's different is that, when you take any of these actions, Excel displays the Open XML dialog box:

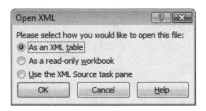

Choose the appropriate option button for your needs, and then click the OK button:

- **As An XML Table** Excel imports the data from the XML file into a new workbook containing one worksheet and displays the schema for the XML file in the XML Source task pane.

- **As A Read-Only Workbook** Excel opens the XML file as a spreadsheet under its own name and doesn't create a schema. The file is read-only, so you can't save changes to it under its own name, but you can save changes to it under a different name.

- **Use The XML Source Task Pane** Excel displays the schema for the XML file in the XML Source Task pane. From here, you can map the elements contained in the schema to cells or ranges in the worksheet.

If you open the file as an XML list or using the XML Source task pane, and the XML file doesn't contain a reference to a schema, Excel displays a message box informing you that it will create a schema based on the XML source data, as shown here.

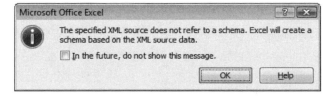

Select the In The Future, Do Not Show This Message check box if you want to suppress the display of this message box in the future. Click the OK button. Excel closes the message box.

Save Excel Files in XML Data Format

Excel can save your data in XML data format, retaining just the data mapped to the elements in the XML schema attached to the workbook.

To save a workbook in XML, follow these steps:

1. Click the Save button on the Quick Access Toolbar, or click the Office button, and then click Save. Excel displays the Save As dialog box. (If the file has already been saved in a different format, click the Office button, and then click Save As. Excel displays the Save As dialog box.)

2. In the Save As Type drop-down list, select the XML Data item.

3. Specify where to save the file as usual, and enter the file name.

4. Click the Save button. Excel closes the Save As dialog box and saves the workbook as XML data.

Create XML Files in Excel

The second and more difficult stage of using XML with Excel is creating your own XML files attached to an external schema and mapping the appropriate elements so as to be able to extract the relevant pieces of information from the files.

First, you attach an XML schema to a workbook. This creates what's called an *XML map*— a relationship between the schema and the workbook. You use this map to link elements in the schema to cells and ranges in worksheets in the workbook to define which element in the schema is represented by which cell. For example, you can map cells in a schema to specify which output from your manufacturing database you want to analyze in a worksheet containing custom calculations.

 *A workbook can contain a single XML map or multiple XML maps. When a workbook contains multiple XML maps, each can refer to a different schema, or two or more maps can refer to the same schema.*

Once you've performed the mapping, you can export data from the mapped cells and ranges—for example, so you can use the data with another application. You can also import an XML data file into an existing XML mapping, so that the relevant parts of the data file snap into place. For example, you can import different months' output from your manufacturing database so that you can analyze them.

You can also use XML mapping to import XML-formatted data from a web source into a worksheet.

Add the Developer Tab to the Ribbon

Before you can use the XML controls in Excel, you must add the Developer tab to the Ribbon. To do so, follow these steps:

1. Click the Office button, and then click Excel Options. Excel displays the Excel Options dialog box.

2. In the Popular category, select the Show Developer Tab In The Ribbon check box.

3. Click the OK button. Excel closes the Excel Options dialog box and adds the Developer tab to the Ribbon, as shown here.

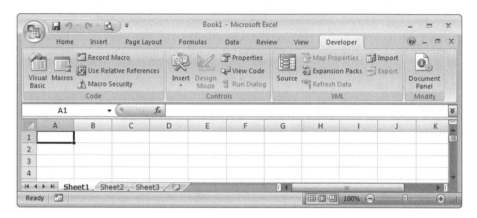

Attach an XML Schema to a Workbook

To attach an XML schema to a workbook, follow these steps:

1. Choose Developer | XML | Source. Excel displays the XML Source task pane, which at first indicates that the workbook doesn't contain any XML maps. This is normal.

2. Click the XML Maps button. Excel displays the XML Maps dialog box, as shown here. Again, there's no map yet, but this is still normal.

3. Click the Add button. Excel displays the Select XML Source dialog box (which is a renamed Open dialog box).

4. Navigate to and then select the XML schema you want to use.

5. Click the Open button. If the schema you specified contains more than one root element, Excel displays the Multiple Roots dialog box (shown here) so that you can choose which root element to use for the XML map. Select the root element, and then click the OK button.

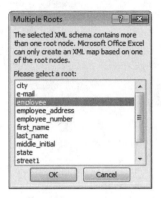

6. Excel adds the XML map to the XML Maps dialog box, as shown here:

7. If necessary, rename the map from its default name by clicking the Rename button (or clicking the Name entry for the map twice in slow succession—not double-clicking), typing the new name, and then pressing ENTER.

8. Click the OK button. Excel closes the XML Maps dialog box. The XML Source task pane displays the XML map you've added, showing the elements in the schema (or partial schema) as a hierarchical list.

You can now map elements to cells in the workbook by using the XML Source task pane.

15

Understand the Icons in the XML Source Task Pane

The XML Source task pane uses different icons to represent the different elements in an XML schema. The following list explains what the icons mean:

Icon	Meaning
	Parent element
	Repeating parent element
	Required parent element
	Required repeating parent element
	Child element
	Repeating child element
	Required child element
	Required repeating child element
	Attribute
	Required attribute
	Simple content in a complex structure

Map XML Elements to an Excel Worksheet

To map XML elements from a schema to a worksheet, follow these steps:

1. If the XML Source task pane isn't displayed, choose Developer | XML | Source to make Excel display it.

2. If you've added multiple maps to the workbook, select the appropriate map in the XML Maps In This Workbook drop-down list.

3. Select one or more elements in the schema:

   ■ Click a parent element to select it and all its child elements.

   ■ Click to select a single element.

   ■ CTRL-click to select multiple elements.

4. Drag the element or elements to the appropriate cell or range in the worksheet and drop it there. Excel adds the element as a drop-down list.

   ■ In the example spreadsheet shown here, the first_name and middle_initial elements have been added to the cells below their corresponding headings.

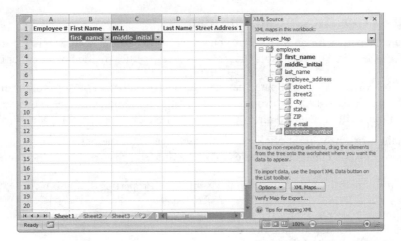

■ You can also map an element to a cell by right-clicking it in the XML Maps In This Workbook list and choosing Map Element from the shortcut menu, using the Map XML Elements dialog box to specify the cell or range, and clicking the OK button:

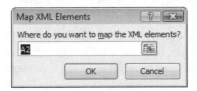

■ The XML Source task pane displays mapped elements in boldface and unmapped elements in regular font.

■ If Excel displays a Smart Tag when you map the field, you can choose the appropriate heading option from the Smart Tag's menu. The choices are My Data Already Has A Heading, Place XML Heading To The Left, and Place XML Heading Above:

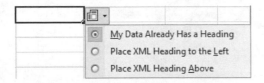

■ When you map an element declared as having two or more values, Excel creates a drop-down list named after the element. The drop-down list offers the Sort A To Z, Sort Z To A, and other filters that you'll recognize from using AutoFilter (see "Perform Quick Filtering with AutoFilter," in Chapter 9).

To remove an element you've mapped, right-click it in the XML Source task pane, and then choose Remove Element from the context menu.

15

Configure Properties for an XML Map

To configure properties for an XML map, you set the options in the XML Map Properties dialog box (see Figure 15-5). You can display the XML Map Properties dialog box in either of two ways:

- In the XML Source task pane, activate the appropriate map by selecting it in the XML Maps In This Workbook drop-down list. (If the workbook contains only one XML map, that map will be selected already.) Then choose Developer | XML | Map Properties.

- In the worksheet, right-click a cell to which one of the elements from the appropriate map is mapped, and then choose XML | XML Map Properties from the context menu.

You can set the following options in the XML Map Properties dialog box:

- **Name**   You can change the name assigned to the mapping. However, changing the name via the XML Maps dialog box is usually easier.

- **XML Schema Validation**   In this section, select or clear the Validate Data Against Schema For Import And Export check box to control whether Excel validates the data in this mapping against the schema when you import or export data. Validation helps avoid unsuitable data being entered, but you may want to turn validation off while you're learning to use XML.

- **Data Source**   In this section, selecting the Save Data Source Definition In Workbook check box saves the XML binding in the workbook. Clear this check box to remove the XML binding from the workbook. This option is sometimes unavailable.

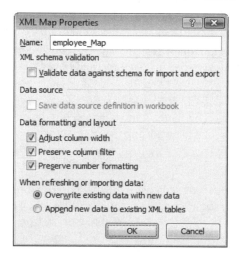

FIGURE 15-5   Use the XML Map Properties dialog box to configure properties for an XML map.

- **Date Formatting And Layout** In this section, select or clear the three check boxes to specify whether or not to adjust column width; preserve column filtering; and preserve number formatting.

- **When Refreshing Or Importing Data** In this section, choose between the Overwrite Existing Data With New Data option button (the default setting) and the Append New Data To Existing XML Tables option button. In most cases, you'll want to overwrite the existing data with the new data.

Choose XML Options

To configure how XML behaves in Excel, click the Options button near the bottom of the XML Source task pane and choose the appropriate menu item:

- **Preview Data In Task Pane** Controls whether the XML Source task pane displays sample data next to each mapped element in the element list. By default, this check box is cleared. Previewing the data can help you identify problems in the mappings.

- **Hide Help Text in the Task Pane** Controls whether Excel hides the help text that it normally displays below the element list in the XML Source task pane. Displaying the help text is useful when you're learning to use XML. After that, you'll probably begrudge the help text the space it occupies.

- **Automatically Merge Elements When Mapping** Controls whether Excel automatically expands an XML list when you drop an element in the cell adjacent to the list.

- **My Data Has Headings** Controls whether Excel uses your existing data as column headings when you map repeating elements to a worksheet.

Import an XML Data File into an Existing XML Mapping

Once you've mapped the appropriate XML elements to cells or ranges in a workbook, you can import an XML data file into the mapping you've created. This creates what's called an *XML data binding* between the XML data file and the XML map. Each XML map can have only a single XML data binding. That binding is bound to each mapping created from the XML map.

Importing XML data in this way enables you to use Excel as a front end for manipulating data saved in XML format using the schema you've mapped to the workbook. This XML data can come from any XML-compliant source using the same schema. Using Excel like this helps companies avoid having to retrain users with XML applications, instead leveraging the users' existing Excel skills and keeping the users within their comfort zone.

To import an XML data file into an existing XML mapping, follow these steps:

1. Select a cell in the mapped range into which you want to import the data from the XML data file.

2. Choose Developer | XML | Import. Excel displays the Import XML dialog box.

3. Navigate to and select the file you want to import, and then click the Import button.

4. Excel checks the data and raises any issues:

- ■ If the XML data file doesn't refer to a schema, Excel displays a dialog box to notify you that it will create a schema based on the source data. You can choose to suppress this warning in the future by selecting the In The Future, Do Not Show This Message check box before dismissing the dialog box.

- ■ If Excel encounters a problem with the XML data file you're trying to import, Excel displays the XML Import Error dialog box, which lists the errors encountered. You can select an error and click the Details button to display a dialog box giving more information on the error and where it occurred. This information may help you fix problems in the XML data file so that you can subsequently import it without errors.

5. Excel displays the Import Data dialog box to let you specify where to import the data:

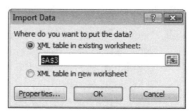

6. Choose whether to import the list to the active worksheet (and if so, specify a location), or to a new worksheet. You can also set properties for the XML map by clicking the Properties button, and then working in the XML Map Properties dialog box.

7. Click the OK button. Excel closes the Import Data dialog box and imports the data.

If Excel discovers noncritical errors that allow it to import some or all of the data, it imports the data and displays the XML Import Error dialog box to notify you of the errors. For example, Excel may need to truncate data that's too long for worksheet cells.

Refresh an XML Data Binding

To refresh the data in an XML data binding by importing the latest data available in the data source, choose Developer | XML | Refresh Data.

Verify a Map for Export

To verify an XML map for export before exporting it, click the Verify Map For Export link at the bottom of the XML Source task pane. Excel checks the map and displays a message box indicating whether all is well or you need to make changes.

Export XML Data

To export XML data from a workbook, follow these steps:

1. Choose Developer | XML | Export. Excel displays the Export XML dialog box.

2. Specify the file name and location for the file to which you want to export the data.

3. Click the Export button. Excel closes the Export XML dialog box and exports the data.

Chapter 16

Use Excel with the Other Office Applications

How to...

- Transfer data using the Clipboard and Office Clipboard
- Embed and link objects
- Insert Excel objects in Word documents
- Insert Excel objects in PowerPoint presentations
- Insert Word objects in worksheets
- Insert PowerPoint objects in worksheets

As its full name suggests, Office Excel 2007 is thoroughly integrated with the other applications in Office—Office Word, Office PowerPoint, Office Outlook, and Office Access. In this chapter, you'll learn how to make Excel share data with and receive data from the other Office applications, focusing mainly on Word and PowerPoint.

The primary tools for passing information from one application to another are the Windows Clipboard and the Office Clipboard. For example, you can copy cells from an Excel worksheet, and then paste them into a table in a Word document or onto a PowerPoint slide. Similarly, you can copy data from a Word document or an Outlook message, and then paste it into an Excel worksheet.

You can also use the Clipboard and the Office Clipboard to embed or link data from a file created in one application in a file created in another application. For greater control over the objects you embed and link, you can use the Object dialog box.

Because you're likely to want to transfer data both to and from Excel, this chapter discusses not just Excel but also the other Office applications to some extent. It discusses the methods for transferring, embedding, and linking data in general, and then gives specific examples of integrating Excel with Word and PowerPoint.

For heavier-duty data sharing in a corporate environment, you can use Excel's XML features to manipulate XML data files and to save data in a machine-readable format, as discussed in Chapter 15.

Transfer Data Using the Clipboard and Office Clipboard

As you saw in Chapter 3, the Windows Clipboard and the Office Clipboard provide an easy means of copying and moving data, either within an application or between applications. From the source application, you issue a Copy command or a Cut command to place the appropriate data on the Windows Clipboard or the Office Clipboard, switch to the destination file in the appropriate application, and then issue a Paste or Paste Special command to insert the information.

These are the main points you need to remember when transferring data via the Windows or Office Clipboards:

- The Windows Clipboard can hold several different types of data, including text and graphics, but it can hold only one item of each type at once. When you issue another Cut or Copy command, Windows overwrites the contents of the Clipboard for that data type with the new information.

- The Office Clipboard can contain up to 24 items of the same or different types. You can display the Office Clipboard task pane at any time by choosing Home | Clipboard | Clipboard (click the tiny Clipboard button at the right end of the bar) in most of the Office applications.

- You can choose Home | Clipboard | Paste | Paste Special (in most of the Office applications), and then use the Paste Special dialog box to control the format in which the object is pasted.

- You can also simply issue a Paste command to paste the object in the default format. (The default format varies depending on the type of object you're pasting and the destination application into which you're pasting it.) If you don't get the result you want, you can use the Paste Options Smart Tag to change the format in which the object was pasted. (Alternatively, you can undo the Paste operation and then use the Paste Special dialog box instead.)

Embed and Link Objects

Excel and the other Office applications support three different ways of including an object created in one application in a file created in another application: embedding, linking, and inserting. An *object* is a component of a file that can be handled separately. Examples of objects include charts and ranges in Excel, tables in Word, and slides in PowerPoint. Embedding, linking, and inserting are different ways of including an object created in one application in a file created in another application.

You'll read about embedding and linking at some length in this chapter. Inserting is relatively straightforward, and if you've worked your way through this book, you'll already have inserted objects such as graphics (see Chapter 5) in your worksheets. When you insert an object in a file, the file contains neither the information for editing the object in place nor a link to the source file that contains the object: the object simply appears in the file in the place you specify. Graphics are typically inserted in another file (for example, a document, workbook, or presentation) rather than being embedded or linked.

Before using embedding or linking, you should understand the differences between the two, the effects they produce, and when to use which technique.

Understand the Differences Between Embedding and Linking

Embedding is the basic means of inserting an object created in another application into a file. For example, if you need to create PowerPoint slides that contain charts or WordArt objects, you use embedding. When you embed an object in a file, the file contains a full copy of that object. For example, if you embed an Excel chart in a Word document, that document contains a full copy of the chart together with the workbook that contains it. Depending on the type of object involved, embedding can greatly increase the file size.

The copy is independent of the original chart in the Excel workbook, and you can edit it separately. You can't update the copy directly from the original chart. Instead, you can replace

16

the copy with a new copy of the updated original. Manual updating like this is too slow and clumsy to make sense in most cases, but for some purposes (for example, version control of documentation) it can sometimes prove a better option than linking.

Linking is the more complex method of inserting an object created in another application into a file. When you link an object to a file, the file displays the current information for that object but stores only a link that describes the object, where it's located, and other relevant information. Storing the information about the link is much more compact than storing the actual data for even the smallest object, so the size of the file that contains the link hardly changes. When you need to edit a linked object, you do so at the source.

When you link an object, you can update the link by issuing an Update command. The application reads the latest data from the source of the link and displays it in the file. However, the application can't update the link if either the source or the destination is offline relative to the other, or if the source file has moved or been renamed so that the application and Windows can't identify it.

Understand the Advantages and Disadvantages of Embedding and Linking

The advantage of embedding is that, because the object is saved in the file, the object remains available even if you move the file or disconnect the computer so that the object source file is no longer available. The disadvantages are that embedding an object significantly increases the file's size (because the object's data must be saved in it, either in the original format or in a modified format) and that there's no easy way to update the object if the source file changes: instead, you need to manually replace the embedded object with the latest version of the object from the source file.

Linking has two advantages. First, because only the link is saved in the file, not the object itself, the file's size increases by only a tiny amount. Linking can greatly reduce the file size of a file that includes many large or complex objects. Second, you can make the file display the latest version of the object by updating the link.

The disadvantage of linking is that if the source file isn't available, the object doesn't appear. So if, for example, you need to distribute a worksheet that includes PowerPoint slides, embedding is a better choice than linking, even though the file size of the workbook with the embedded slides is far larger than that of the workbook with links to those same slides.

Choose When to Embed and When to Link

To decide whether to embed or link objects, consider the following:

- Will you need to edit the object in the destination file? If so, embed it.
- Do you need to keep file size down? If so, link the objects.
- Will the destination file and the source files stay in the same place as when you create the destination file, or do the files need to be able to move independently of each other?

If you need to be able to move the destination file to another computer that won't be able to access the source files, embed the objects rather than link them.

■ Will different people need to work on different components of the same project at the same time? Even with Excel's support for a single file to be opened for editing by multiple people at the same time, it's best to keep shared editing to a minimum (or avoid it altogether). By linking objects rather than embedding them, you can enable different people to work on different components without the possibility of confusion or corruption. For example, you may continue to edit the Word report while Annie improves the slides linked to it and Bill manipulates the latest data in the Excel spreadsheet that provides the linked charts.

Verify Whether an Object Is Linked or Embedded

By looking at an object in a document, you can't immediately tell whether it's linked or embedded. The easiest way to find out in Excel is to select the object and check the readout in the reference area. If the readout starts with *=EMBED* (for example, =EMBED("Document","")), the object is embedded. If the readout contains a reference to a file by name (for example, = Word.Document.12|'C:\Temp\Doc1.doc'!'!OLE_LINK1'), the object is linked.

In Word, PowerPoint, and Outlook, right-click the object and see whether the shortcut menu contains an Update Link command. If so, the object is linked; if not, the object is embedded.

Embed or Link an Object

You can embed or link an object by using the Paste Special dialog box or the Object dialog box. In some cases, you can also choose to display the embedded or linked object as an icon rather than as itself.

Embed or Link an Object by Using the Paste Special Dialog Box

In most cases, the easiest way to embed or link an existing object is to use the Paste Special dialog box. Follow these steps:

1. In the object's source application, select the object, and then issue a Copy command (for example, press CTRL-C or choose Home | Clipboard | Copy).

2. Activate the destination application, and then select the location in which you want to embed or link the object.

3. Choose Home | Clipboard | Paste | Paste Special (click the lower part of the Paste button, and then choose Paste Special from the panel). Excel displays the Paste Special dialog box. The following illustration shows the Paste Special dialog box for Excel with a Word object (a table) on the Clipboard.

16

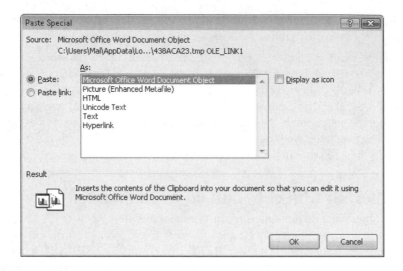

4. Choose the format in which you want to embed or link the object. The choices available depend on the type of object you copied and the destination application.

5. Select the Paste option button to embed the object. Select the Paste Link option button to link the object.

6. If the Display As Icon check box is available, you can select it to make the application display not the object itself but an icon representing it. See "Display an Embedded or Linked Object As an Icon," later in this chapter, for a discussion of why you may want to do this and how the icon appears.

7. Click the OK button. The application closes the Paste Special dialog box and embeds or links the object, depending on the choice you made.

Embed or Link an Object by Using the Object Dialog Box

You can also embed a new object that you create and embed in the same process. To do so, follow these steps:

1. In the destination application, position the insertion point or selection where you want the new object to appear.

2. Choose Insert | Text | Object. The application displays the Object dialog box. The next illustration shows the Object dialog box for Excel. (In PowerPoint, the dialog box is called Insert Object and is configured a little differently than the Object dialog box.)

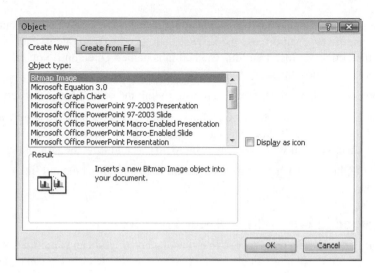

3. Click the Create New tab if it isn't already displayed.

4. Select the type of object you want to create and embed.

5. Click the OK button. The application closes the Object dialog box and inserts the object.

By using the Create From File tab of the Object dialog box, you can embed or link an object that consists of the entire contents of an already existing file. To do so, follow these steps:

1. In the destination application, position the insertion point or selection where you want the new object to appear.

2. Choose Insert | Text | Object. The application displays the Object dialog box (or, for PowerPoint, the Insert Object dialog box).

3. Click the Create From File tab (shown here) if it isn't already displayed.

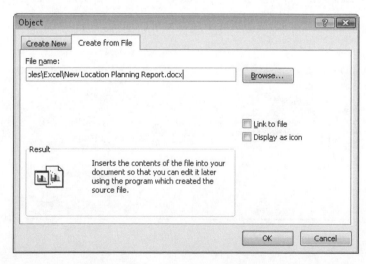

16

4. Enter the path and file name in the File Name text box. (The easiest way to enter this is to click the Browse button, use the Browse dialog box to navigate to and select the file, and then click the Insert button. The button is named Open until you select a file, at which point its name changes to Insert.)

5. Select the Link To File check box if you want to link the object rather than embed it.

6. Select the Display As Icon check box (if it's available) if you want to display an icon instead of the object itself. See "Display an Embedded or Linked Object As an Icon," next, for a discussion of why you may want to do this and how the icon appears.

7. Click the OK button. The application closes the Object dialog box and links or embeds the object.

Display an Embedded or Linked Object As an Icon

Instead of embedding or linking an object so that it is displayed, you can sometimes make the object appear as an icon. Displaying an object as an icon is available only for some paste and paste-link formats.

Displaying the icon can be useful when you want to make extra information available to the user of a file but you don't want that information to overshadow the file's primary content. For example, if you display a large worksheet on a PowerPoint slide, it will tend to dominate the slide. So instead, you might choose to display an icon that lets the user open the worksheet in a separate window where they can examine it comfortably.

To display an object as an icon, select the Display As Icon check box in the Paste Special dialog box or the Object dialog box (or Insert Object dialog box). When you select this check box, the dialog box displays the current icon and caption for the object, together with the Change Icon button:

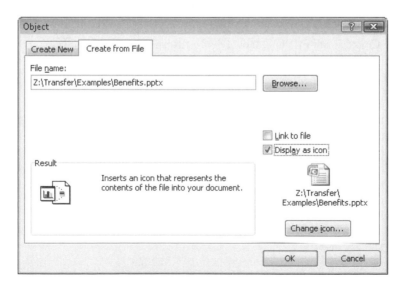

To change the icon or caption, click the Change Icon button, use the options in the Change
Icon dialog box (shown here) to specify the icon or the caption, and then click the OK button.

*Most applications have a limited selection of icons, but Windows library files such
as MORICONS.DLL and SHELL32.DLL (in the System32 folder in your %Windir%
folder—for example, the Windows folder) offer some colorful and entertaining icons.
You may also have icons of your own that you prefer to use.*

Edit an Embedded Object

How you edit an embedded object depends on the object type and the application whose
document you've embedded it in. Normally, when you right-click the object and then select
the Object | Edit command from the context menu, the destination application either adds the
relevant section of the Ribbon from the source application to its own Ribbon, or displays a
stripped-down version of the Ribbon that provides only controls for the source application.
The Object command varies depending on the object—for example, the command is named
Document Object for a Word document object and Presentation Object for a PowerPoint
presentation object.

Figure 16-1 shows an example of the former behavior. In this figure, an embedded Excel chart
is being edited in a Word document. Word has added Excel's Chart Tools section of the Ribbon to
its own Ribbon, making the controls on the Design tab, the Layout tab, and the Format tab available
just as if you were working in Excel.

Figure 16-2 shows an example of the latter behavior. In this figure, Excel has reduced the
Ribbon to the controls needed for Word, hiding its own parts of the Ribbon.

You can then edit the object as if you were working in the other application (which, in effect,
you are). The source object remains unchanged, because there's no link between the embedded
object and the source.

16

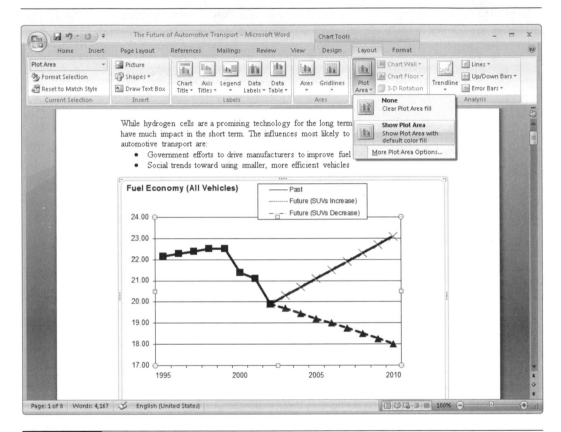

FIGURE 16-1   Editing an embedded Excel chart in a Word window.

For you to be able to edit an embedded object, the application that created the object must be installed on the computer you're using. This can cause problems when you move a document to a different computer. For example, suppose you create a Word document that contains a couple of PowerPoint slides on your work computer. If you take this document home and open it on your home computer, which has Word and Microsoft Works installed, you'll be able to edit the Word parts of the document but not the embedded PowerPoint objects.

Edit a Linked Object

You edit a linked object in its source application rather than in place in the destination application. Right-click the object and issue an Edit command (for example, choose Document Object | Edit for a Word document object) from the shortcut menu to open the object for editing in the source application. You can then edit the object as usual. When you close the object in the source application, the linked object in the destination application is updated.

Embedding and Linking Terminology You May Need to Know

It's worth knowing the terminology used for embedding and linking, even if you choose not to use the terminology yourself:

- **Compound document**   A document that contains data of two or more different types (for example, a Word document that contains an Excel chart).

- **ActiveX object or COM object**   An object that can be embedded in or linked to a file in another application. Unless you're programming, it's usually easier to describe each embedded or linked item simply as an *object* rather than worrying about exactly which type of object it is.

- **ActiveX container or COM container**   A document that can contain objects such as ActiveX objects or COM objects.

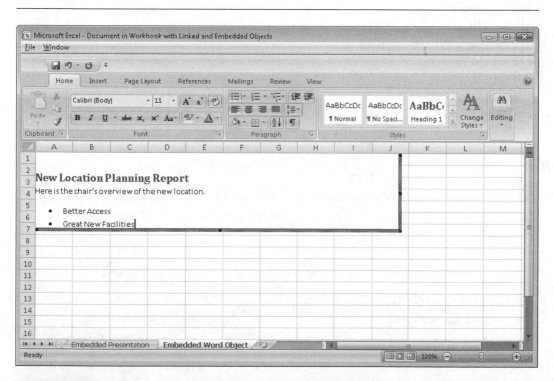

FIGURE 16-2   Editing an embedded Word object in an Excel window. Excel is showing only Word's Ribbon.

Edit, Update, and Break Links

To work with links in an Excel workbook, choose Data | Connections | Edit Links. Excel displays the Edit Links dialog box:

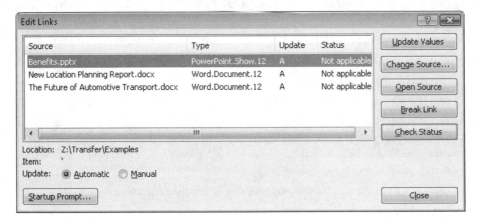

From the Edit Links dialog box, you can take these actions to a selected link:

- Click the Update Values button to force an update of the link.

- Click the Change Source button and use the resulting Change Links dialog box to change the link to a different file:

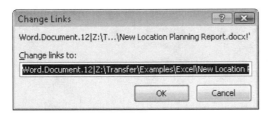

- Click the Open Source button to open the source file for the link in the source application.

- Click the Break Link button to break the link. Click the Break Links button in the warning dialog box that the application displays:

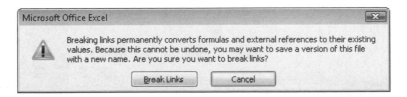

◼ Click the Check Status button to check the status of the link.

◼ Switch the link between automatic updating and manual updating by selecting the Automatic option button or the Manual option button as appropriate. For example, you might switch to manual updating before taking a file offline from the sources of its linked objects.

Control Whether Excel Prompts the User to Update Links at Startup

Excel provides two ways for you to control what happens when the user opens a file that contains links. First, the Ask To Update Automatic Links check box in the General area of the Advanced category in the Excel Options dialog box (click the Office button, and then click Excel Options) controls whether Excel prompts the user to update automatic links. If you clear this check box, Excel updates automatic links without prompting the user. Second, the Edit Links dialog box lets you specify for any given file that contains links what Excel does when the user opens that file. To use this feature, follow these steps:

1. Click the Startup Prompt button in the Edit Links dialog box. Excel displays the Startup Prompt dialog box:

2. Choose the appropriate option button:

◼ The Let Users Choose To Display The Alert Or Not option button causes Excel prompt the user about updates when they open the workbook.

◼ The Don't Display The Alert And Don't Update Automatic Links option button causes Excel to suppress both the alert and the updating of links. This option can be useful when you're distributing a workbook to users who don't have access to the source files for the links and so won't be able to update them.

◼ The Don't Display The Alert And Update Links option button causes Excel to suppress the alert but to update the links automatically. This option is useful when you don't want the user to be able to avoid updating links (for example, because they might then waste time by working with out-of-date data).

3. Click the OK button. Excel closes the Startup Prompt dialog box.

Deal with Security Warnings About Automatic Updates of Links

If an application displays a Security Warning bar such as the one shown here, saying that "Automatic update of links has been disabled," click the Options button.

16

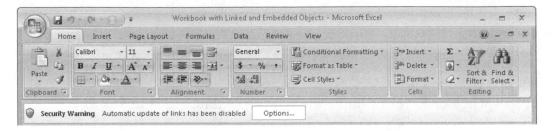

The application displays a Microsoft Office Security Options dialog box like this:

If you want to have links updated automatically, select the Enable This Content option button, and then click the OK button. The application closes the Microsoft Office Security Options dialog box and enables the content.

Insert Excel Objects in Word Documents

If you keep much data in Excel (for example, in a database), chances are that you'll often need to use some of that data in your Word documents. For example, you may need to insert a chart from an Excel workbook in a report you're creating in Word, perhaps together with parts of the data table that underlie the chart. You may also need to use an Excel database as the data source for a mail merge in Word.

Insert a Chart in a Word Document

When you paste an Excel chart into a Word document, Word's default settings are to paste it as a chart linked to Excel data. In most cases, this is the best way of handling the chart: You can resize the chart easily, edit it from within Word (for example, apply a different chart type), and update it from the latest version of the chart in Excel when necessary.

Sometimes, however, you may want to handle the chart differently. When you do, paste the chart in as usual, but then click the Paste Options button that appears after pasting the chart, and then choose a different option from the pop-up menu:

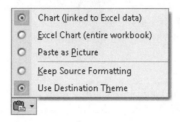

- ■ **Chart (Linked To Excel Data)**   This is the default paste format, so you'll need to choose it only if you've chosen one of the other options and decided that you don't like the results.

- ■ **Excel Chart (Entire Workbook)**   This option pastes the entire workbook into the Word document. The advantage of this arrangement is that you can edit the Excel chart even when you don't have access to the original source file. The primary disadvantage is that because the chart in the Word document isn't linked to the original workbook, you can't update the chart with a new version in the workbook. (Instead, you can paste in a new version of the chart or workbook.) The secondary disadvantage is that the Word document can become much bigger (depending on how big the Excel workbook is).

- ■ **Paste As Picture**   This option pastes the chart in as a picture rather than as a chart object. You can format the picture, but you can't edit the chart. The picture isn't linked to the workbook.

NOTE   *The Paste Options pop-up menu also lets you choose between maintaining the original formatting of the pasted object (select the Keep Source Formatting option button) and applying formatting based on the destination document's theme to the pasted object (select the Use Destination Theme option button).*

These options handle most normal needs. For special needs, however, you can choose Home | Clipboard | Paste | Paste Special, and then use the Paste Special dialog box to specify exactly how you want Word to enter the chart in the document. These are your choices:

- ■ With the Paste option button selected, the Microsoft Office Excel Chart Object item embeds the chart and its workbook in the document. You can then edit the chart in place, but the document's file size will increase substantially. This is the same as Excel Chart (Entire Workbook) in the Paste Options pop-up menu.

16

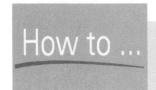

Choose Among Picture Formats When Pasting

Depending on the object on the Clipboard, the Paste Special dialog box may offer you a variety of graphics formats: Picture (Windows Metafile), Bitmap, Picture (Enhanced Metafile), and Device Independent Bitmap, and sometimes Picture (PNG), Picture (JPEG), and Picture (GIF). Here's what you need to know in order to choose sensibly among these options:

- *Windows Metafile (WMF)* is a standard graphical format used by Windows. WMF is a 16-bit vector graphics format, which means that the picture details are stored as a series of drawn lines, polygons, and text. Vector graphics files can be resized smoothly to any size without suffering from blurriness or blockiness.

- *Enhanced Metafile (EMF)* is a 32-bit vector graphics format that offers more commands and flexibility than the WMF format. EMF is device independent, but some applications don't support it.

- *Bitmap* is a standard format that stores the details of the information contained in each pixel of the picture. Bitmaps are uncompressed, so they take up more space than other graphics formats. Bitmaps do not resize smoothly and suffer from blurriness or blockiness when displayed at a size that doesn't allow all their pixels to be displayed. Generally, it's not a good idea to insert objects as bitmaps unless you need to be able to extract the picture from the file later and manipulate it as a graphic. Technically, this "bitmap" format is a *Device Dependent Bitmap (DDB)*—a bitmap whose sequence and depth of pixels is specifically designed for output on a particular device.

- *Device Independent Bitmap (DIB)* is a bitmap that's not designed specifically for output on any particular device. A DIB may give better image quality than a DDB, but it will typically take longer to display.

- *Portable Network Graphics (PNG)* is a relatively new graphics format developed for Internet usage. PNG supports *lossless compression*—compressing graphics without discarding any of the detail they contain. When this format is available, it's a good option to choose.

- *Joint Photographic Experts Group (JPEG)* is a graphics format widely used on the Web. JPEG uses *lossy compression,* compressing graphics by discarding some of their detail.

- *Graphics Interchange Format (GIF)* is a standard format very widely used on the Web. GIF offers lossless compression but has larger file sizes than PNG.

To keep file size down and allow the picture to be resized smoothly, your best bet is usually to choose EMF or WMF format. But if you need to store an exact picture of the object you're pasting, use bitmap or DIB format instead.

- With the Paste Link option button selected, the Microsoft Office Excel Chart Object item links the chart and its workbook to the document.

- With the Paste Link option button selected, the Microsoft Office Graphic Object item gives the same effect as Chart (Linked To Excel Data) in the Paste Options pop-up menu.

- With the Paste option button selected, you can paste the chart in Windows Metafile, bitmap, Enhanced Metafile format, GIF, PNG, or JPG. See "Choose Among Picture Formats When Pasting," How to… box, for an explanation of these formats.

- With the Paste Link option button selected, you can link a picture of the chart in either Windows Metafile format or bitmap format.

Insert Cells in a Word Document

When you paste a range of cells from an Excel worksheet into a Word document, by default Word pastes them as a Word table, retaining as much formatting as possible—everything from font formatting to column widths and row heights. The Paste Options pop-up menu offers these choices:

- **Keep Source Formatting**   This option (the default) retains the cells' formatting.

- **Match Destination Table Style**   This option applies Word's default table style to the table created from the cells.

- **Paste As Picture**   This option inserts a picture showing the contents of the cells in a noneditable format. You might want to use this option when creating Word documents explaining how to use custom Excel documents.

- **Keep Text Only**   This option pastes only the text from the cells, separating the contents of cells with tabs.

- **Keep Source Formatting And Link To Excel**   This option retains the cells' formatting and links the table to its source cells in the Excel worksheet.

- **Match Destination Table Style And Link To Excel**   This option applies Word's default table style to the table and links it to its source cells in the Excel worksheet.

The Paste Special dialog box offers a wide range of choices (discussed next) for pasting a range of cells. Except as noted here, all the options are available for both pasting and paste-linking.

- **Microsoft Office Excel Binary Worksheet Object**   This option pastes or links the entire workbook. If you paste (rather than paste-link), Word embeds the workbook so that you can edit it in place.

- **Formatted Text (RTF)**   This option pastes or links the text and table cells with rich-text formatting. Typically, this option gives almost, but not quite, the same result as the default HTML Format option.

16

■ **Unformatted Text**   This option pastes or links only the text from the cells, separating the contents of cells with tabs. The text is pasted using ASCII. Depending on the text in the cells, this option can have exactly the same effect as the Unformatted Unicode Text option.

ASCII (American Standard Code for Information Interchange) and Unicode are two different methods of coding plain text. ASCII is an old standard; Unicode is newer and more capable. ASCII uses 1 byte of data to represent each character, which restricts it to representing 256 characters. Unicode uses 2 bytes of data to represent each character and so can represent 65,536 character combinations. ASCII works fine for plain text but may substitute different characters for unusual characters and symbols. When ASCII gives you incorrect results, use Unicode instead.

■ **Picture (Windows Metafile)**   This option pastes or links the cells as a WMF picture. You can format the picture but not edit it.

■ **Bitmap**   This option pastes or links the cells as a bitmap picture. You can format the picture but not edit it.

■ **Picture (Enhanced Metafile)**   This option pastes the cells as an EMF picture. Again, you can format the picture but not edit it. This option is available only for pasting, not for paste-linking.

■ **Word Hyperlink**   This option paste-links the cells and creates hyperlinks from each table cell that has contents to the corresponding cells in the source workbook. This option is available only for paste-linking.

■ **HTML Format**   This option pastes the cells as a table, retaining all font and table formatting. This option is Word's default behavior when you issue the Paste command with a range of cells on the Clipboard.

■ **Unformatted Unicode Text**   This option pastes or links only the text from the cells, separating the contents of cells with tabs. Depending on the text in the cells, this option can have exactly the same effect as the Unformatted Text option.

When you link a range in an Excel worksheet to a Word document or PowerPoint slide, use a range name or a table name rather than a range reference. The range name or table name will tolerate changes to the worksheet that contains it, whereas a range reference remains tied to the specific cells it references. For example, if somebody deletes a few rows from the worksheet, a range reference will deliver the wrong data, but a range name or table name will deliver the right data.

Use an Excel Table As the Data Source for a Word Mail Merge

If you keep a table of names and addresses in an Excel workbook, you may want to use that database as a data source for a mail-merge operation in Word. You can do so easily by using Word's Mail Merge Wizard. Follow the general steps given on the next page:

1. Set up the table as discussed in Chapter 9, with each item of data that you need to use separately allotted to a separate field:

   ■ In the table, keep each element of a typical name and address in a separate field—first name, middle initial, last name, first address item, second address item, city, state, zip, and so on.

   ■ Place field names as the first row of your table. Format this row using different formatting than the rest of the table. (For example, apply boldface to the first row.)

   ■ Make sure that each field name (in other words, each column heading in a default layout) is unique, because duplicate field names will confuse the Mail Merge Wizard.

2. In Word, choose Mailings | Start Mail Merge | Start Mail Merge | Step By Step Mail Merge Wizard. Word displays the Mail Merge task pane. Work your way through the steps of defining the merge until you reach the Select Recipients stage.

3. Select the Use An Existing List option button, and then click the Browse link. Excel displays the Select Data Source dialog box.

4. Navigate to the folder that contains the workbook, select it, and click the Open button. Word displays the Select Table dialog box:

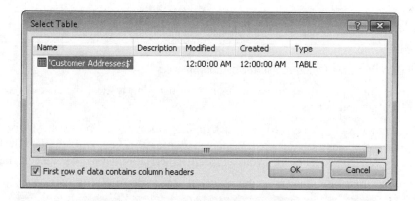

5. Make sure the First Row Of Data Contains Column Headers check box is selected.

6. Select the name of the worksheet that contains your mailing list.

16

7. Click the OK button. Word closes the Select Table dialog box and displays the Mail Merge Recipients dialog box:

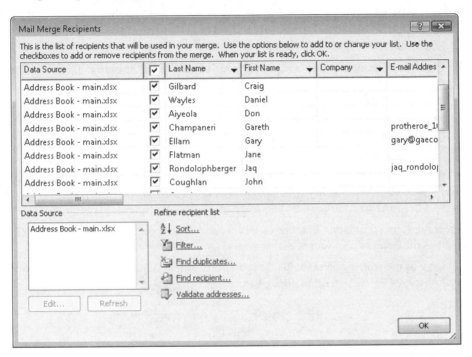

8. Select the entries you want to use for the mail merge:

- ■ If you want to use most of the entries in your list, simply clear the check boxes for the entries you don't want to use.

- ■ To filter the list by one of the fields, click the drop-down button and select All (the default), Blanks, Nonblanks, or Advanced. When you choose Advanced, Word displays the Filter And Sort dialog box, in which you can specify criteria for filtering or sorting the fields:

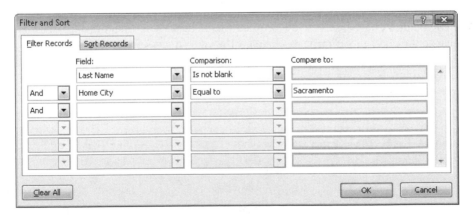

9. After selecting the appropriate entries, click the OK button. Word closes the Mail Merge Recipients dialog box.

10. Proceed with the remaining steps in the Mail Merge task pane as usual.

Insert Excel Objects in PowerPoint Presentations

If you create presentations, you may frequently need to include data and charts from Excel worksheets on slides. To do so, you can use either the Clipboard or the Insert Object dialog box as discussed earlier in this chapter.

Insert a Chart in a PowerPoint Slide

When you paste a chart into a slide, PowerPoint pastes the chart linked to Excel data. As with pasting into a Word document, this is usually the neatest solution, because you get a chart that you can edit in PowerPoint (for example, you can change the chart type), resize, and update from the original data in Excel.

To change the format, click the Paste Options button, and then choose from the pop-up menu, as shown here:

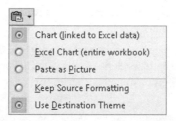

- **Chart (Linked To Excel Data)**   This is the default paste format, so you'll need to choose it only if you've chosen one of the other options and decided that you don't like the results.

- **Excel Chart (Entire Workbook)**   This option pastes the entire workbook into the presentation. The advantage of this arrangement is that you can edit the Excel chart even when you don't have access to the original source file. The primary disadvantage is that because the chart in the presentation isn't linked to the original workbook, you can't update the chart with a new version in the workbook. (Instead, you can paste in a new version of the chart or workbook.) The secondary disadvantage is that the presentation can become much bigger (depending on how big the Excel workbook is).

- **Paste As Picture**   This option pastes the chart in as a picture rather than as a chart object. You can format the picture, but you can't edit the chart. The picture isn't linked to the workbook. Provided that the chart is final, a picture can be a good option for a presentation, because its file size is small and you can't change its contents inadvertently.

16

When you choose Paste As Picture, PowerPoint inserts the chart as a Microsoft Office Graphic Object. If you want to use a different graphics format, follow these steps:

1. Choose Home | Clipboard | Paste | Paste Special. PowerPoint displays the Paste Special dialog box:

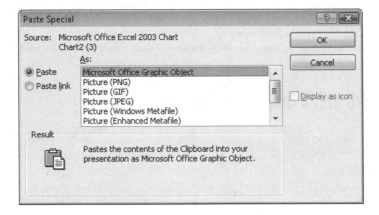

2. Make sure the Paste option button is selected. (Selecting the Paste Link option button eliminates all the picture options.)

3. In the As list box, select the picture format you want: PNG, GIF, JPEG, Windows Metafile, Enhanced Metafile, Device Independent Bitmap, or Bitmap. (See the sidebar "Choose Among Picture Formats When Pasting," earlier in this chapter, for an explanation of the different picture formats.)

4. Click the OK button. PowerPoint closes the Paste Special dialog box and inserts the picture on the slide in the format you chose.

Insert a Range of Cells in a PowerPoint Slide

When you paste a range of cells from an Excel worksheet onto a PowerPoint slide, PowerPoint creates a PowerPoint table using HTML formatting that's supposed to retain the formatting applied to the range. (Sometimes this retention works. Other times, the results range from entertaining to disastrous.) You can edit the table as a PowerPoint object, but you can't double-click the table to edit it as an Excel object.

If the table doesn't meet your needs, click the Undo button to remove the table, and then choose Home | Clipboard | Paste | Paste Special. PowerPoint displays the Paste Special dialog box. Choose one of the items:

■ **Microsoft Office Excel Worksheet Object** This option pastes the range as a table, including the entire worksheet, so that you can edit the range in place as an Excel object.

■ **HTML Format** This option pastes the range as a PowerPoint table (like a standard Paste operation), supposedly retaining the formatting, as discussed earlier in this section.

- ■ **Picture (Windows Metafile), Picture (Enhanced Metafile), Device Independent Bitmap, Bitmap**   These options paste the range as a picture that you can format but not edit in PowerPoint. Enhanced Metafile is usually the best format for printing to high-resolution printers.

- ■ **Formatted Text (RTF)**   This option pastes the text with rich-text formatting. This option can be effective for retaining the look of the text but not the formatting of the cells that contain the text (unlike the HTML Format item).

- ■ **Unformatted Text**   This option pastes the text without any formatting. This option gives the cleanest result, provided you're prepared to apply such formatting as necessary in PowerPoint.

Insert Word Objects in Worksheets

Depending on the type of work you do, you may often need to insert part of a Word document— a sentence, a paragraph, or more—in an Excel worksheet. On occasion, you may need to insert an entire Word document.

When inserting Word items, it's best *not* to simply paste the copied part of the Word document into the worksheet. This is because Excel pastes in data from Word in the HTML format by default rather than creating an embedded object. After you paste data, the Paste Options pop-up menu offers only two choices: Keep Source Formatting (the default) or Match Destination Formatting.

Instead, choose Home | Clipboard | Paste | Paste Special (or right-click and choose Paste Special from the context menu) to display the Paste Special dialog box, and then specify how you want to paste or paste-link the data. These are your choices:

- ■ **Microsoft Word Document Object**   This option embeds (with the Paste option button selected) or links (with the Paste Link option button selected) the Word object with its upper-left corner anchored in the active cell. If you embed the object, you can edit it in place.

- ■ **Picture (Enhanced Metafile)**   This option embeds or links a picture of the object in the EMF format.

- ■ **HTML**   This option embeds or links the text with formatting. HTML is the default paste format.

- ■ **Unicode Text**   This option embeds or links the text in Unicode format without formatting.

- ■ **Text**   This option embeds or links the text in ASCII format without formatting.

- ■ **Hyperlink**   This option creates a hyperlink to the object in the Word document.

16

NOTE   *Instead of using the Paste Special dialog box, you can use the Paste Link item, the Paste As Hyperlink item, or the As Picture submenu on the Paste panel. Often, using the Paste Special dialog box is easier because it gives you access to all the available options.*

Insert PowerPoint Objects in Worksheets

Sometimes, you may also need to insert a PowerPoint object in a worksheet. For example, you might need to paste-link a slide to the part in a planning worksheet that provides the information for the slide, so that a colleague reviewing the worksheet can easily review the slide as well.

The Paste Special dialog box lets you paste or paste-link a slide as a Microsoft PowerPoint Slide Object or as a picture in any of five formats (PNG, JPEG, GIF, EMF, or Bitmap). With the Paste option button selected, the Microsoft PowerPoint Slide Object option inserts the whole slide into the worksheet, so that you can edit it in place.

By using the Create From File tab of the Object dialog box, you can insert an entire presentation into an Excel worksheet so that you can run the presentation directly from the worksheet. This capability is occasionally useful, but because the presentation's data is saved in the workbook, the workbook's file size can increase greatly. Double-click the embedded presentation to start it running.

Part IV

Customize and Program Excel

Chapter 17

Customize Excel's Interface

How to...

- Change the position of the Quick Access Toolbar
- Add items to or remove items from the Quick Access Toolbar
- Customize the status bar

In Chapter 2, you learned how to configure the most important of Excel's many settings to suit the way you work and make Excel as easy to use as possible. In this chapter, you'll learn how to customize Excel's Quick Access Toolbar to put the commands you need at your fingertips.

If you've worked with earlier versions of Excel, you may have been reluctant to customize the interface because of the drastic nature of the changes you could make. For example, Excel 2003 makes it trivially easy to remove one or more of the main menus—which can make the program hard to use.

With the Ribbon, Excel 2007 makes customization far simpler but greatly reduces your options. You can change the position of the Quick Access Toolbar, and you can add controls to it and remove them from it. You can decide which items to display on the status bar. And that's about it. While there *is* a way of changing the Ribbon—for example, you can add a new tab to it containing custom commands, or suppress some or all of the built-in tabs—it's highly complex and suitable for developers only.

Change the Position of the Quick Access Toolbar

At first, the Quick Access Toolbar appears in its upper position, to the right of the Microsoft Office Button and taking up part of the title bar, as shown here:

When the Quick Access Toolbar has only a few buttons on it, as it does to start with, this is the best position for it, as it takes up a minimal amount of space. But if you add many controls to the Quick Access Toolbar (as described next), it starts taking up too much of the title bar for comfort. When this happens, click the Customize Quick Access Toolbar button at the right end of the toolbar, and then choose Show Below The Ribbon from the drop-down menu, as shown here.

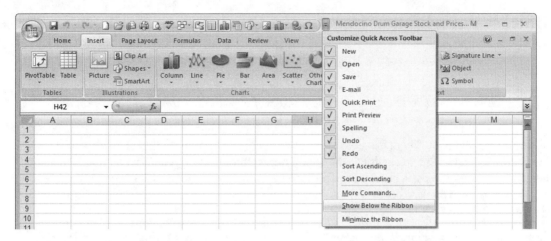

Excel moves the Quick Access Toolbar to its lower position, below the Ribbon, as shown here:

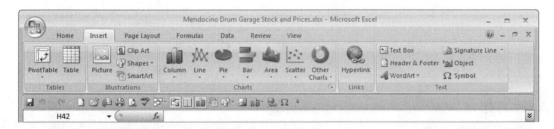

NOTE *You can also move the Quick Access Toolbar from one position to another by selecting or clearing the Show Quick Access Toolbar Below The Ribbon check box in the Customize category in the Excel Options dialog box—but using the drop-down menu is faster and more convenient.*

To move the Quick Access Toolbar back to its position in the title bar, click the Customize Quick Access Toolbar button at the right end of the toolbar, and then choose Show Above The Ribbon from the drop-down menu.

Customize the Items on the Quick Access Toolbar

Excel lets you add pretty much any command or interface item to the Quick Access Toolbar, so you can put all the commands and groups you use most frequently on the Quick Access Toolbar.

17

Quickly Put a Ribbon Item on the Quick Access Toolbar

To add an item that appears on the Ribbon to the Quick Access Toolbar, right-click the item, and then choose Add To Quick Access Toolbar from the drop-down menu.

When you add an item to the Quick Access Toolbar by right-clicking the item and then choosing Add To Quick Access Toolbar, Excel applies the change to all workbooks. You can't customize only one workbook using this technique. Instead, use the next technique.

When you add a single control to the Quick Access Toolbar, it appears as a button. When you add a group, it appears as a panel that pops out when you click it. Figure 17-1 shows an example of a group on the Quick Access Toolbar.

If you add so many controls that the Quick Access Toolbar is too long to fit in either the upper position or the lower position, Excel displays a More Controls button at the right end of the Quick Access Toolbar. Click this button to display a panel containing the remaining controls.

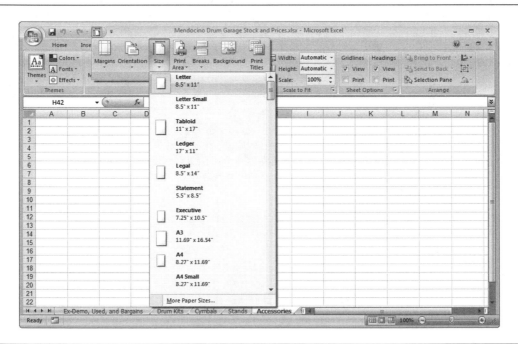

FIGURE 17-1   By putting an entire group on the Quick Access Toolbar, you get instant access to all its controls from a single toolbar button.

Put Any Command on the Quick Access Toolbar or Rearrange Items

To put any command on the Quick Access Toolbar, or to rearrange the items on the Quick Access Toolbar, follow these steps:

1. Right-click anywhere on the Quick Access Toolbar, and then choose Customize Quick Access Toolbar from the context menu. Alternatively, click the Customize Quick Access Toolbar button at the right end of the toolbar, and then choose More Commands from the drop-down menu. Excel displays the Customize category in the Excel Options dialog box (see Figure 17-2).

2. In the Customize Quick Access Toolbar drop-down list, select For All Documents if you want to apply the changes to Excel itself, so that the commands are available for any workbook that you open. If you want to apply the changes to only an open document, select it in the drop-down list.

3. In the Choose Commands From drop-down list, select the category of command. The commands in the category appear in the list box.

■ The Office menu category contains the commands on the Office Button menu.

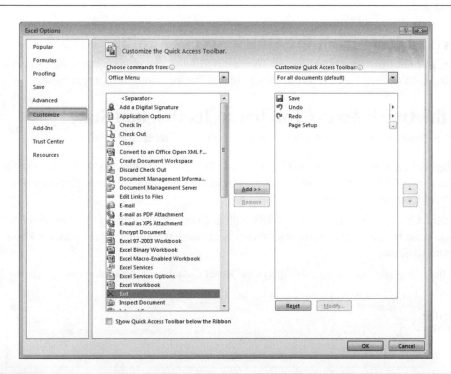

FIGURE 17-2   The Customize category in the Excel Options dialog box lets you add any command to either Excel itself or to just an open workbook.

■ The Home Tab, Insert Tab, Page Layout Tab, and other categories include the commands from those tabs in the Ribbon.

■ The Popular Commands category includes a selection of widely used commands. The Commands Not In The Ribbon category contains mostly specialized commands. The All Commands list is extremely long, but if you know the name of the command you want, it can be a handy way of finding a command.

4. In the left list box, select the command you want to add.

5. In the right list box, select the command after which you want to add the new command. (You can rearrange the commands later, but you might as well place the command where you want it when adding it.)

6. Click the Add button. Excel adds the command to the right list box.

7. If you need to remove an item from the Quick Access Toolbar, click it in the right list box, and then click the Remove button.

8. To rearrange the items on the Quick Access Toolbar, click an item in the list box, and then click the Up button or the Down button.

9. When you've finished customizing the Quick Access Toolbar, click the OK button. Excel closes the Excel Options dialog box, and the Quick Access Toolbar takes on the items you added.

Remove an Item from the Quick Access Toolbar

To remove an item from the Quick Access Toolbar, right-click the item on the Quick Access Toolbar, and then choose Remove From Quick Access Toolbar from the context menu.

Reset the Quick Access Toolbar to Its Original State

To reset the Quick Access Toolbar to its original selection of items, follow these steps:

1. Right-click any control on the Quick Access Toolbar, and then choose Customize Quick Access Toolbar from the context menu. Excel displays the Customize category of the Excel Options dialog box.

2. In the Customize Quick Access Toolbar drop-down list, choose For All Documents if you want to affect all documents. Otherwise, choose the name of the open workbook you want to affect.

3. Click the Reset button. Excel displays the Reset Customizations dialog box, as shown here:

4. Click the Yes button. Excel resets the customizations.

5. Click the OK button. Excel closes the Excel Options dialog box.

Customize the Status Bar

Excel also lets you decide which items appear on the status bar, the bar that appears along the bottom of the Excel window.

To customize the status bar, follow these steps:

1. Right-click anywhere in the status bar. Excel displays the Customize Status Bar menu (see Figure 17-3).

2. The check marks indicate which items will appear, either permanently or when they're active. Click an item to toggle its check mark on or off. Table 17-1 explains what the items are.

3. Click the status bar or click anywhere in your worksheet. Excel closes the Customize Status Bar menu.

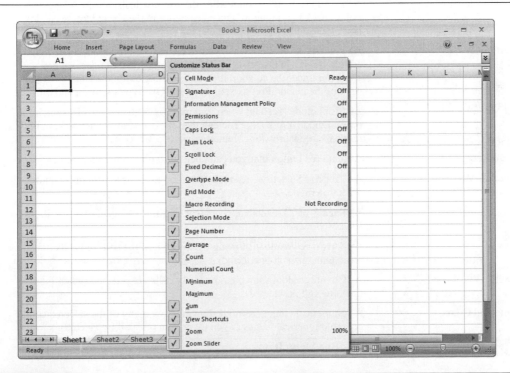

FIGURE 17-3   Use the Customize Status Bar menu to choose which items appear on the status bar.

17

Status Bar Item	What It Displays When Turned On
Cell Mode	The indicator that says "Edit" when you're editing a cell and "Ready" when you're not.
Signatures	An indicator near the left end of the status bar showing that the workbook has a digital signature applied to it.
Information Management Policy	An indicator near the left end of the status bar showing that the workbook has information management policy applied to it (for example, to meet auditing or retention requirements).
Permissions	An indicator near the left end of the status bar showing that the workbook has permission restrictions applied (for example, to prevent unauthorized distribution).
Caps Lock	A "Caps Lock" readout when the Caps Lock key on the keyboard is switched on.
Num Lock	A "Num Lock" readout when the Num Lock key on the keyboard is switched on.
Scroll Lock	A "Scroll Lock" readout when the Scroll Lock key on the keyboard is switched on.
Fixed Decimal	A "Fixed Decimal" readout when the Automatically Insert A Decimal Point check box in the Advanced category in the Excel Options dialog box is selected.
Overtype Mode	An "Overtype" readout when you're using Overtype mode when editing a cell. (In Overtype mode, typing a character replaces the character under the cursor rather than pushing along the character to the right of the cursor. Press INSERT to toggle Overtype mode on and off.)
End Mode	An "End mode" readout when End mode is switched on. (To switch on End mode, press END. You can then press one of the arrow keys to move to the last row or column in that direction.)
Macro Recording	A round red button that you can click to start recording a macro.
Selection Mode	An "Extend Selection" readout when you press F8 to turn on Extend Selection mode.
Page Number	A "Page X of Y" readout appears (for example, "Page 2 of 5") in Page Layout view.
Average	An "Average" readout showing the average of the selected cells (when more than one cell is selected).
Count	A "Count" readout showing how many cells are selected (when more than one cell is selected).
Numerical Count	A "Numerical Count" readout showing how many of the selected cells contain numerical values (when more than one cell is selected).

TABLE 17-1   Customize Status Bar Menu Items

Status Bar Item	What It Displays When Turned On
Minimum	A "Min" readout showing the minimum value in a selected cell (when more than one cell is selected).
Maximum	A "Max" readout showing the maximum value in a selected cell (when more than one cell is selected).
Sum	A "Sum" readout showing the sum of the values in all the numerical cells selected (when more than one cell is selected).
View Shortcuts	The three View buttons—Normal View, Page Layout View, and Page Break Preview.
Zoom	The Zoom Level readout.
Zoom Slider	The Zoom slider and its control buttons.

TABLE 17-1   Customize Status Bar Menu Items (*continued*)

17

Chapter 18

Use Macros to Automate Tasks

How to...

■ Understand what macros are and what they're for

■ Configure Excel's macro virus-protection features

■ Set trusted locations and publishers

■ Use the Macro Recorder to record a macro

■ Test and run a macro

■ Create a toolbar button or menu item for running a macro

■ Assign a macro to an object in a worksheet

■ Delete a macro

If you find yourself performing the same task over and over in Excel, consider automating that task as much as possible. To automate a task, you can record a macro, as described in this chapter, or program in Visual Basic for Applications (VBA), a subject beyond the reach of this book. (You can also combine the two approaches by recording a macro and then enhancing it by programming in VBA.)

This chapter begins by explaining what macros are and what you should use them for. Then you'll see the macro virus-protection features that Excel uses, because they can prevent you from running even the simplest macro. After that, you'll learn where Excel stores macros; how to record macros in Excel; and how to test, run, and (if necessary) delete macros.

Understand What Macros Are and What They're For

A *macro* in Excel is a sequence of commands, either recorded (by using the built-in Macro Recorder) or written down in the Visual Basic Editor. For example, you could record a macro to format certain parts of a worksheet in a specific way. To do this, you switch on the Macro Recorder, perform the series of formatting actions, and then turn off the Macro Recorder.

After you record the macro, it can then be run when necessary, either by a user (such as you) or by another macro or piece of code. (*Code* is the generic term for the program lines and program objects, such as custom dialog boxes, that you create with a programming language.) You can run your Excel macro manually to format a worksheet, or you can call the macro from another macro—for example, to perform the formatting as part of a series of tasks.

In Excel, macros are recorded or written in VBA, a programming language developed by Microsoft. VBA is implemented in all the other major Office applications (Word, PowerPoint, Outlook, and Access) as well, and it has become such a standard that many third-party companies have added it to their applications. By using VBA, you can make one application access another application; so you can create, for example, a macro in Excel that accesses Word, Visio, AutoCAD, WordPerfect, or another VBA-enabled application.

Configure Excel's Macro Virus-Protection Features

VBA and the Macro Recorder greatly increase Excel's power, flexibility, and usefulness. Unfortunately, VBA and macros also expose Excel (and other VBA-enabled applications) to the attentions of malefactors who create *macro viruses*—harmful code built using a macro language.

Macro viruses can be contained in frequently exchanged files—such as Excel workbooks, Word documents, or PowerPoint presentations—and can be triggered when the file is opened, closed, or otherwise manipulated. So whenever anyone sends you a file, you should check it for macro viruses.

Macro viruses can spread themselves in several ways. Some automatically add themselves surreptitiously to your existing documents and insert themselves into new documents you create. When you share a document with another user, that user's computer becomes infected with the virus as well and can spread it further. Other macro viruses take a more aggressive approach, using a programmable e-mail application such as Outlook to send themselves to as many people as possible as an apparently normal or attractive document attached to a suitable e-mail message. For example, a macro virus designed to spread in a corporate environment might disguise itself as a routine document such as a memo or spreadsheet. A macro designed to spread anywhere might appeal to recipients' curiosity by pretending to contain—or actually containing—jokes or pornography.

VBA is by no means the only macro language that can be exploited by virus writers, but because Office and VBA are so widely used, they're the most popular targets for malefactors. In particular, because Outlook can be controlled via VBA, it's one of the easiest ways for a malefactor to spread a virus: Outlook (or one of the other VBA-enabled applications) can be programmed to automatically send messages to every entry in its address book. This can generate enough e-mail to crash even powerful corporate mail servers in short order.

To protect its users against macro viruses, Office includes antivirus features. To use macros and VBA, you need to understand what these features are and how they work.

Office's antivirus features provide some protection against macros written in VBA, but there are plenty of non-VBA types of viruses, scripts, and other malware *(malicious software) that can damage your software or hardware. So even with Office's antivirus measures on, you should use third-party antivirus software to protect your computer.*

Understand and Set Security Levels

Office uses a four-part security mechanism for preventing harmful code from being run by an Office application:

- **Security level**   You can set security levels to specify whether an installation of Office may or may not run code that might be harmful. You can set a different security level in each Office application, if you wish. For example, you might set Excel to use the Medium security level but set Word to use the High security level.

- **Digital signature**   You can sign a VBA project (a unit of VBA code) with a digital signature derived from a digital certificate to prove that you were the last person who changed that VBA project. This digital signature tells other people the source of the VBA project. If other people have reason to trust you, they may trust the code you've signed.

- **Trusted locations**   You can designate certain folders as being *trusted locations*— folders that you guarantee will never contain unsafe code. Excel allows you to run code in documents contained in trusted locations.

- **Trusted publishers**   You can designate certain digital certificates as being *trusted publishers*, telling the Office security mechanism to trust any code signed with one of those digital certificates.

As you can see, these security measures are intertwined. The following sections discuss how you work with them.

Set the Security Level for Running VBA Code

To set the security level that Excel uses for macros, follow these steps:

1. Click the Office button, and then click Excel Options. Excel displays the Excel Options dialog box.

2. In the left panel, click the Trust Center category, and then click the Trust Center Settings button. Excel displays the Macro Settings category in the Trust Center dialog box, shown here:

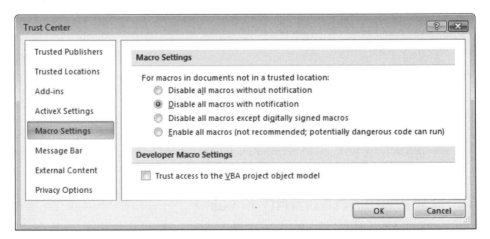

3. In the Macro Settings area, select an option button to tell Excel how to handle macros contained in documents stored in folders that are not trusted locations.

- Usually, the best choice for someone who uses macros is the Disable All Macros With Notification option button, which disables all macros and displays a Security Alert bar to let you know that it has done so. (The sidebar "Enable Blocked Macros" shows an example of the Security Alert bar.) You can choose to enable the macros or leave them disabled.

■   The Disable All Macros Without Notification option button makes Excel disable the macros but give you no indication that it has done so. This setting is useful for users who should not receive documents containing macros and, even if they do, should certainly not run such macros.

■   In a corporate environment, an administrator may set up Excel using the Disable All Macros Except Digitally Signed Macros option button to ensure that you can run only macros that have been tested, approved, and signed.

■   The Enable All Macros option button is a setting that only security researchers working on cordoned-off computers should use.

4.   In the Developer Macro Settings area, clear the Trust Access To The VBA Project Object Model check box unless you're creating your own macros in the Visual Basic Editor (as opposed to using the Macro Recorder, as described in this chapter).

5.   Leave the Trust Center dialog box open so that you can verify your trusted locations, as described in the next section.

Verify Your List of Trusted Locations

Before you start creating macros or other code, verify the folders that Excel is set to regard as trusted locations. You may need to add other folders to the list, or even remove existing folders that you no longer want to trust.

NOTE   *In a corporate environment, an administrator is likely to prevent you from adding or changing trusted locations and trusted publishers.*

To verify your trusted locations, follow these steps:

1.   In the Trust Center dialog box, click the Trusted Locations category in the left panel. Excel displays the Trusted Locations list (see Figure 18-1).

2.   Look through the folders to make sure that you want to trust all of them. If the Path readout in the list doesn't show the full path to the folder, click the entry to select it, and then look at the Path readout below the list box. Excel normally trusts the following folders, but an administrator may have added further trusted locations to this list:

■   **User Templates folder**   This folder contains your user templates—the templates you create or download. In a corporate environment, an administrator may have removed this folder from the list of trusted locations.

■   **User Startup folder**   This folder contains your personal items to be loaded when Excel starts—for example, your Personal Macro Workbook (explained later in this chapter). In a corporate environment, an administrator may have removed this folder from the list of trusted locations.

■   **Application Templates folder**   This folder contains the templates installed automatically by Office.

18

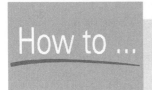

Enable Blocked Macros

If you choose the Disable All Macros With Notification option button in the Macro Settings category in the Trust Center dialog box, Excel displays a Security Warning bar below the Ribbon when it disables macros. Here's an example:

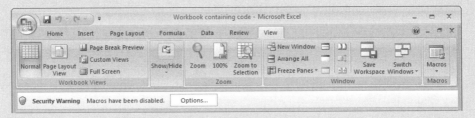

If you don't need to use the macros (or if you don't know what they are), you can leave them blocked by simply clicking the Close button (the × button) on the Security Warning bar. But if you want to enable the macros, click the Options button. Excel displays the Microsoft Office Security Options: Security Alert – Macro dialog box shown here. If the document is signed with a digital signature, but the digital signature is invalid, the dialog box looks like this, with only the Help Protect Me From Unknown Content option button available:

If the digital signature is valid, but it's from a publisher that you haven't yet specified you trust, the Microsoft Office Security Options: Security Alert – Macro dialog box looks like this:

If the document doesn't have a digital signature, the Microsoft Office Security Options: Security Alert – Macro dialog box contains the Help Protect Me From Unknown Content option button and the Enable This Content option button, but not the Signature box or the Trust All Documents From This Publisher option button.

If the Signature box appears (as in the example here), examine the details of the digital certificate, and then decide whether this is a person or company you can trust. To see the details of the digital certificate, click the Show Signature Details link. Excel displays the Digital Signature Details dialog box.

For either a signed document with a valid signature or an unsigned document, select the Enable This Content option button if you want to enable the content for this document. If the document has a digital signature, you can also select the Trust All Documents From This Publisher option button to tell Excel to add the holder of this digital certificate to your list of trusted publishers.

Click the OK button. If you chose to enable the macros, Excel enables them.

- In the Path text box, enter the path to the folder. If you wish, you can type the path, but it's usually easier to click the Browse button, use the Browse dialog box to select the folder, and then click the OK button.

- If you want Excel to trust the contents of any subfolders this folder contains, select the Subfolders Of This Location Are Also Trusted check box. If you keep workbooks that contain macros in a hierarchy of folders, you will either need to select this check box for the parent (topmost) folder, or designate each folder in the hierarchy as a trusted location.

18

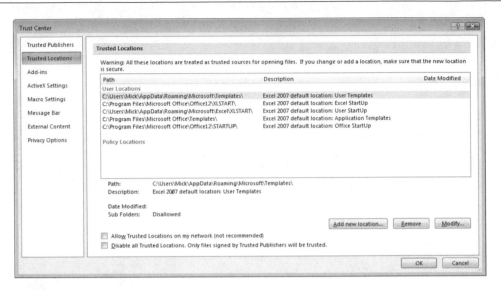

FIGURE 18-1 The Trusted Locations category in the Trust Center dialog box lets you tell Excel which folders contain trustworthy code.

- **Excel Startup folder** This folder contains items for Excel to load at startup, such as add-ins.

- **Office Startup folder** This folder contains items for the Office programs to load at startup, such as templates or add-ins. Some software manufacturers use this folder for all their Office startup items rather than the program-specific folders (such as the Excel startup folder).

3. To add a trusted location to the list, follow these steps:

- Click the Add New Location button. Excel displays the Microsoft Office Trusted Location dialog box, shown here with choices made.

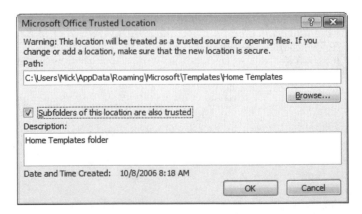

■ In the Description text box, type a description of the trusted location. This description appears in the Trusted Locations list to help you identify the trusted location.

■ Click the OK button. Excel closes the Microsoft Office Trusted Location dialog box and adds the trusted location to the Trusted Locations list.

4. To remove a trusted location, select it in the Trusted Locations list, and then click the Remove button.

5. To modify a trusted location, select it in the Trusted Locations list, and then click the Modify button. Excel displays the Microsoft Office Trusted Location box, in which you can change the folder or its description. The change you'll most often want to make is selecting the Subfolders Of This Location Are Also Trusted check box for the folder. For example, you might need to trust the subfolders of your User Templates folder.

6. If you need to work with workbooks containing code that are stored in folders on your network, select the Allow Trusted Locations On My Network check box. Unless you control your entire network (for example, it's your home network), this setting may expose your computer to code that others create. If you can keep all your code in folders on your hard drive, leave this check box cleared.

7. Clear the Disable All Trusted Locations, Only Files Signed By Trusted Publishers Will Be Trusted check box if you need to work with your own code.

8. Leave the Trust Center dialog box open so that you can verify your trusted publishers, as described in the next section.

Designate Trusted Publishers for VBA Code

The Trusted Publishers category in the Trust Center dialog box (see Figure 18-2) lists the publishers you or your administrator have specified as being trusted. In this context, a *publisher* means the holder of a particular digital certificate. Click the View button to display the details of a selected publisher, or click the Remove button to remove a selected publisher you no longer want to trust.

   You can add trusted publishers to your Windows installation by selecting the Trust All Documents From This Publisher option button in the Microsoft Office Security Options: Security Alert – Macro dialog box, as discussed earlier in this chapter.

The list of trusted publishers is applied across all Windows applications and features that use digital certificates. So if you add a trusted publisher in Excel, Word and PowerPoint trust that publisher too.

Understand Digital Signatures

As you just saw, the Office security mechanism uses a digital signature on a macro project to determine whether the source of the project is trusted (and, therefore, whether you can use the project or not). In this section, you'll learn what a digital signature is and how you get a digital certificate for applying a digital signature.

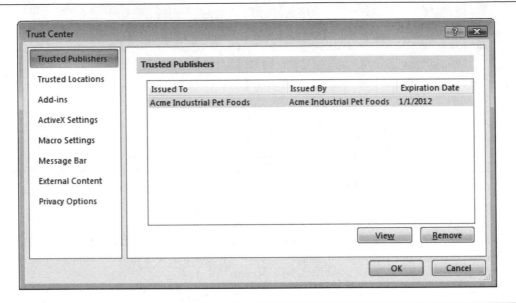

Use the Trusted Publishers category in the Trust Center dialog box to examine, manage, and remove trusted publishers.

Understand What Digital Certificates Are and What They're For

A digital signature is derived from a *digital certificate*, an encrypted piece of code intended to identify its holder. That holder may be an individual, a group of individuals, a department, or an entire company. Different types of digital certificates are available, including the following:

- **Personal certificates**   For signing and encrypting e-mail messages
- **Software developer certificates**   For signing macros and software
- **Corporate certificates**   For identifying companies or parts of them

Digital certificates aren't foolproof, but they provide reasonably effective security. Digital certificates are issued by *certification authorities* (CAs) and are only as reliable as the CAs choose to make them. For example, some CAs let you buy a personal digital certificate over the Web without providing any more verification than a credit card number and its current expiry date. This standard of verification is satisfactory for telephone and Internet mail order because the physical address to which the goods are delivered corroborates the information on the credit card (assuming the goods are delivered to the card's billing address). But for proving identity via the Internet, this standard of verification is woefully unsatisfactory.

Create Your Own Digital Certificate for Office

Office includes a tool called Digital Certificate For VBA Projects for creating your own digital certificates for practicing signing code. This is a useful practice tool, but the certificate is useless in the real world, because your identity isn't authenticated. As a result, Office trusts a certificate created with Digital Certificate For VBA Projects only on the computer that created the certificate.

Digital Certificate For VBA Projects is included in Complete installations of Office. For other installations, you may need to install it by rerunning the Office installation program. Expand the Office Shared Features category, click the drop-down button on the Digital Signature For VBA Projects item, and then choose Run From My Computer from the menu.

Once Digital Certificate For VBA Projects is installed, you can run it by choosing Start | All Programs | Microsoft Office | Microsoft Office Tools | Digital Certificate For VBA Projects. In the Create Digital Certificate dialog box (shown here), type the name you want to assign to the certificate, and then click the OK button.

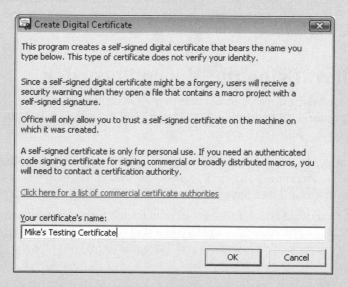

The Digital Certificate For VBA Projects displays a SelfCert Success dialog box (the application's filename is SelfCert.exe) telling you that the certificate was created. The application also installs the certificate automatically for you, so you don't need to install it manually.

18

Software developer certificates and corporate certificates typically require better proof of identity than this, but again they usually leverage existing means of identification (for example, passports or other identity cards for individuals, business listings such as Dun & Bradstreet for companies, and so on) rather than checking rigorously from scratch. Another problem is that a digital certificate can be stolen from its holder, used by someone else without the holder's permission, applied inadvertently by its holder, or applied by *malware* (hostile software) running on the holder's computer.

Get and Install a Digital Certificate

The three main public sources of digital certificates at the time of this writing are:

- VeriSign (www.verisign.com)
- Thawte (www.thawte.com; a VeriSign company)
- GlobalSign (www.globalsign.net)

If your company requires that you use a digital certificate in your work, it may well run a CA of its own. For example, Windows 2003 Server provides CA features.

When you acquire a digital certificate, you'll need to install it on your computer before you can use it. The certificate-issuing routines that some CAs use automatically install the certificate for you. To install the certificate manually, double-click the certificate's file and follow the steps in the Certificate Import Wizard, which Windows launches.

Record a Macro Using the Macro Recorder

The easiest way to create a macro in Excel is to use Office's built-in Macro Recorder tool. (The Macro Recorder works with Word and PowerPoint as well as with Excel.)

To record a macro, follow these steps:

1. Decide what the macro will do. If necessary, write down the main points so you don't forget them. Planning the macro's sequence of actions will help you avoid making mistakes that you'll then have to edit out of the macro for it to work properly.

2. Launch or activate Excel, and then set it up for the actions you're about to perform. For example, if you're recording a macro that will format a particular type of workbook, open a workbook of that type. As creating a macro may involve the possibility of damaging or destroying data, it's best to use a copy of a workbook rather than data you actually care about.

3. Choose View | Macros | Record Macro. Excel displays the Record Macro dialog box, shown here with settings chosen:

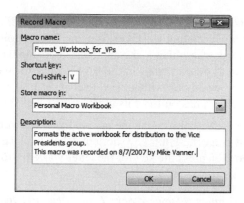

4. The Macro Recorder enters a default name (such as Macro1) in the Macro Name box. You can accept this default name, but it's a much better idea to type a descriptive name of your own.

   - Macro names must start with a letter, after which they can be your choice of mix of letters, numbers, and underscores. They can't contain spaces, symbols, or punctuation marks.

   - The maximum length for a macro name is 80 characters.

   - Shorter names tend to be more practical, because you can see them in full in the Macro dialog box.

5. Type a description of the macro's contents and purpose in the Description box. Either replace the Macro Recorder's default description or add to it. This description helps you (or others) identify the macro when the name isn't sufficiently descriptive.

6. Choose where to store the macro. You must store your macros in a suitable location; otherwise, you won't be able to use them when you need them. Your choices are as follows:

   - **Personal Macro Workbook** This is Excel's central repository for macros you create. Macros in the Personal Macro Workbook are available whenever Excel is running. The Personal Macro Workbook is the \Application Data\Microsoft\Excel\ XLSTART\PERSONAL.XLSB file. Excel automatically creates this file when you first choose to store a macro in the Personal Macro Workbook.

   - **This workbook** Stores the macro in the active workbook. Macros stored in a workbook are available only when that workbook is open. This option is good for macros that apply only to a particular workbook. Use this option if you're creating a macro-enabled workbook that you plan to distribute to your colleagues.

NOTE *If you store the macro in a workbook, you must save the workbook using the Excel Macro-Enabled Workbook format rather than the Excel Workbook format. The Excel Macro-Enabled Workbook format takes the .xlsm file extension, instead of the .xlsx file extension.*

18

■ **New workbook** Creates a new workbook and stores the macro in it. The macro is available only when that workbook is open. This option is primarily useful for recording a quick macro that you want to use to manipulate a workbook but which you don't want to store in that workbook or in the Personal Macro Workbook. By closing the new workbook without saving changes to it, you can dispose of the new macro easily after it has outlived its usefulness.

7. Optionally, specify a way of running the macro. Excel lets you assign the macro to a CTRL key shortcut or a CTRL-SHIFT key shortcut. Click to place the focus in the Shortcut Key text box, and then press the key for the letter you want to assign. To create a CTRL-SHIFT key shortcut, press SHIFT and the letter.

Assign a way of running the macro only if you intend to leave the macro in the location in which the Macro Recorder places it. If you intend to move the macro to a better location by using the Visual Basic Editor, don't assign a way of running the macro now—assign it manually later instead. Also, be aware that if the shortcut you create is already used in Excel, your macro shortcut will override the existing setting when the workbook that contains the shortcut is open.

8. Click the OK button. Excel closes the Record Macro dialog box, displays the Stop Recording button (a blue square) on the status bar, and starts the Macro Recorder.

9. Take the actions that you want the macro to record:

   ■ You can use either the keyboard or the mouse to choose menu commands.

   ■ For selecting objects, you can use the mouse only for maneuvers that unambiguously identify the object. This means most objects, because cells and ranges have fixed addresses.

   ■ To switch between using relative references and absolute references, choose View | Macros | Use Relative References.

10. Click the Stop Recording button on the status bar, or choose View | Macros | Stop Recording.

After you stop recording a macro, Excel changes the Stop Recording button on the status bar to a Record Macro button. You can click this button to open the Record Macro dialog box so that you can start recording a new macro.

Test and Run a Macro

After recording a macro, test it immediately to make sure it works as it should. If so, you're all set to use it in the future; if not, decide whether to edit the macro (a topic beyond this book) to fix its problems, or to delete it and record it again in the hope of getting it right.

Remember that you may need to restore the Excel environment or a workbook to conditions suitable for the macro to run, because when recording the macro, you may have created conditions in which the macro won't run. For example, if the macro searches for a particular value in a cell, changes the value, and then applies formatting, you'll need to restore the original value before the macro will run successfully again.

Run a Macro from the Macro Dialog Box

The most straightforward way of running a macro is to use the Macro dialog box. Follow these steps:

1. Click the Play Macro button on the status bar, or choose View | Macros | View Macros, or press ALT-F8. Excel displays the Macro dialog box (see Figure 18-3).

2. Select the macro either by scrolling to it or by typing down (typing the first letters) to identify the name.

   ■ Macros in workbooks other than the active workbook appear with the filename and an exclamation point before their name. For example, macros in the Personal Macro Workbook are listed with PERSONAL.XLSB! (the Personal Macro Workbook's filename) as their prefix.

   ■ Macros in the active workbook appear without a prefix.

   TIP *If you can't locate a macro, it's probably because the Macros In drop-down list is set to display the wrong location. Change to the right location—for example, you might need to choose the All Open Workbooks entry or the Personal Macro Workbook entry rather than the This Workbook entry.*

3. Click the Run button. Excel closes the Macro dialog box and runs the macro.

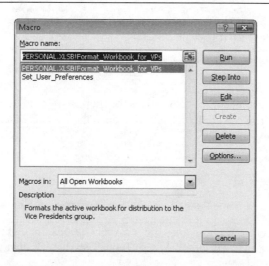

FIGURE 18-3   In the Macro dialog box, select the macro you want to run, and then click the Run button.

18

This way of running macros is most suitable for macros you don't need to run frequently. For any macro you need to run frequently, create a button on the Quick Access Toolbar, as described next.

Create a Quick Access Toolbar Button to Run a Macro

If you assigned a key combination to a macro when you recorded it, you can run the macro by pressing that key combination. If not, you can create a button on the Quick Access Toolbar that runs the macro. Follow these steps:

1. Click the Customize Quick Access Toolbar button (the drop-down button at the right end of the Quick Access Toolbar), and then choose More Commands from the drop-down menu. Excel displays the Customize category in the Excel Options dialog box (shown in Figure 18-4 with choices made).

2. In the Choose Commands From drop-down list, choose Macros. Excel displays the list of macros in the left list box.

3. Click the macro you want to add to the Quick Access Toolbar, and then click the Add button. Excel adds the macro to the bottom of the list in the right list box.

4. If you want to move the macro to a different position on the Quick Access Toolbar, click the Up button.

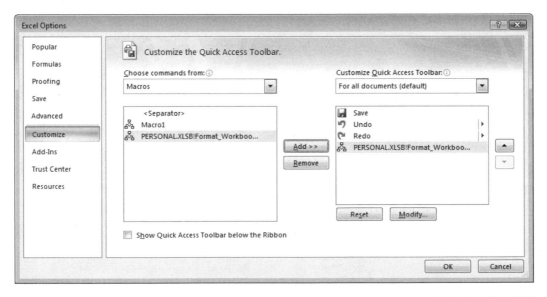

FIGURE 18-4 The Customization category of the Excel Options dialog box lets you add a macro button to the Quick Access Toolbar so that it's always available.

5. With the macro still selected in the right list box, click the Modify button. Excel displays the Modify Button dialog box, shown here:

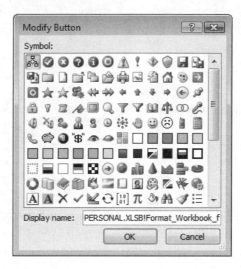

6. In the Symbol list box, select the symbol you want to use for the button.

7. In the Display Name text box, edit the macro's name to something short and easy to understand.

8. Click the OK button. Excel closes the Modify Button dialog box and returns you to the Excel Options dialog box.

9. Click the OK button. Excel closes the Excel Options dialog box and adds the button to the Quick Access Toolbar.

If you find you no longer need a particular button on the Quick Access Toolbar, right-click the button, and then choose Remove From Quick Access Toolbar from the pop-up menu.

Assign a Key Combination or Description to a Macro

If you chose not to assign a key combination or description to a macro while recording it, you can assign a key combination or change the key combination or description afterward. Follow these steps:

1. Choose View | Macros | View Macros, or press ALT-F8. Excel displays the Macro dialog box.

2. Select the macro in the Macro Name list box. If necessary, use the Macros In drop-down list to select the location that contains the macro.

18

3. Click the Options button. Excel displays the Macro Options dialog box, shown here:

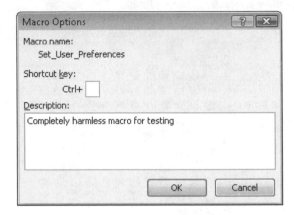

4. To change the key combination, click in the Shortcut Key text box, and then press the key. To create a CTRL-SHIFT combination, press SHIFT and the key.

5. To change the description, type or edit in the Description text box.

6. Click the OK button. Excel closes the Macro Options dialog box.

7. Click the Cancel button. Excel closes the Macro dialog box.

Assigning a Macro to an Object

Excel also offers another way of running a macro: assigning the macro to an object, such as a picture, chart, or shape. To do so, follow these steps:

1. Right-click the object, and then choose Assign Macro from the shortcut menu. Excel displays the Assign Macro dialog box.

2. Select the macro to associate with the object. If necessary, change the selection in the Macros In drop-down list so that the macro you need is displayed.

3. Click the OK button. Excel closes the Assign Macro dialog box and assigns the macro.

You can then run the macro by clicking the object in the worksheet.

Delete a Macro

When you no longer need a macro, delete it. Follow these steps:

1. If the macro is in the Personal Macro Workbook, unhide the Personal Macro Workbook: choose View | Window | Unhide, select PERSONAL.XLSB, and then click the OK button. (You also need to take this step if you've hidden the workbook that contains the macro.)

2. Choose View | Macros | View Macros, or press ALT-F8. Excel displays the Macro dialog box.

3. Select the macro in the Macro Name list box. If necessary, use the Macros In drop-down list to select the location that contains the macro.

4. Click the Delete button. Excel closes the Macro dialog box and displays a confirmation dialog box.

5. Click the Yes button. Excel deletes the macro.

Sign a Workbook with a Digital Signature

If you've recorded some useful macros that make a workbook easier to use, you may want to distribute it to your colleagues. By signing the project with a digital certificate issued by or approved by your company, you can make Excel treat your macros as trusted rather than as suspicious.

To sign a workbook with a digital signature, follow these steps:

1. Open the workbook and make it the active workbook.

2. Press ALT-F11. Excel opens the Visual Basic Editor and selects the active workbook in the Project Explorer window in the upper-left corner of the Visual Basic Editor window.

3. Choose Tools | Digital Signature. The Visual Basic Editor displays the Digital Signature dialog box, shown here:

18

4. Click the Choose button. The Visual Basic Editor displays the Select Certificate dialog box, shown here:

5. Click the certificate you want, and then click the OK button. The Visual Basic Editor closes the Select Certificate dialog box and returns you to the Digital Signature dialog box, which now shows the certificate you chose.

6. Click the OK button. The Visual Basic Editor closes the Digital Signature dialog box.

7. Choose File | Close And Return To Microsoft Excel. The Visual Basic Editor closes, and the Excel window becomes active.

8. Press CTRL+S or click the Save button on the Quick Access Toolbar.

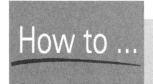

Display the Developer Tab of the Ribbon and the Status-Bar Macro Controls

When you pressed ALT-F11 to display the Visual Basic Editor, you may have wondered why the Ribbon doesn't have a control for opening the Visual Basic Editor. In fact, the Ribbon *does* have a control, but it's hidden to prevent people from stumbling across the Visual Basic Editor unintentionally the way they did in earlier versions of Excel (in which the Visual Basic Editor appeared on the Tools | Macros submenu).

If you want to be able to access the Visual Basic Editor from the Ribbon, add the Developer tab to the Ribbon. Follow these steps:

1. Click the Office button, and then click Excel Options. Excel displays the Excel Options dialog box.

2. In the Popular category, go to the Top Options For Working With Excel area, and then select the Show Developer Tab In The Ribbon check box.

3. Click the OK button. Excel adds the Developer tab to the Ribbon, as shown here.

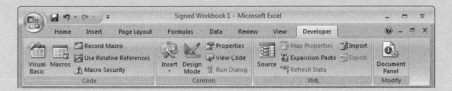

Now you can click the Visual Basic button in the Code group to display the Visual Basic Editor, or click the Macro Security button to display the Macro Settings category in the Trust Center dialog box.

Appendix

Keyboard Shortcuts

As you've seen throughout the book, Excel supports many keyboard shortcuts for invoking commands from the keyboard rather than using the menus. You can save a lot of time and effort in your work by memorizing and using the keyboard shortcuts for the actions you take frequently, but unless your job is wildly varied, you won't need to learn all the keyboard shortcuts—there'll be many shortcuts you use so seldom that they'd save you hardly any time even if you memorized them.

This appendix presents Excel's keyboard shortcuts by category.

■ This list contains most of the keyboard shortcuts that are widely useful. It omits some esoteric keyboard shortcuts. For example, the keyboard shortcut for inserting a new macro sheet isn't widely useful.

■ Some of the keyboard shortcuts have the same effect in the other Office applications as well, but others have different effects—so don't apply Excel's shortcuts rashly to vital documents in other applications.

■ For a quick-reference list of essential keyboard shortcuts, see the inside back cover of the book.

NOTE   *Some actions have multiple keyboard shortcuts for historical reasons: Microsoft introduced new keyboard shortcuts for actions but didn't remove key combinations that users knew from older versions of the software. Some keyboard shortcuts cater to users with different keyboard layouts. For example, most keyboard shortcuts that use F11 or F12 are duplicated with shortcuts that don't use F11 or F12, because some keyboards don't have the F11 and F12 keys.*

Action	Keyboard Shortcut
Creating and Displaying Workbooks	
Create a new default workbook	CTRL-N
Minimize the active workbook window	CTRL-F9
Restore or maximize the selected minimized workbook window	CTRL-F10
Opening and Saving Workbooks	
Display the Open dialog box	CTRL-O, CTRL-F12, CTRL-ALT-F2
Display the Save As dialog box	F12
Save the active workbook	CTRL-S, SHIFT-F12, ALT-SHIFT-F2
Display the Print dialog box	CTRL-P, CTRL-SHIFT-F12
Moving and Resizing Windows	
Maximize the active workbook window	CTRL-F10
Restore the active workbook window	CTRL-F5

Action	Keyboard Shortcut
Resize the active workbook window	CTRL-F8 (and then press arrow keys)
Close the active window or exit the application	ALT-F4
Close the active workbook window	CTRL-F4, CTRL-W
Switch to the next application window	ALT-TAB
Switch to the previous application window	ALT-SHIFT-TAB

Navigating Worksheets

Action	Keyboard Shortcut
Insert a new worksheet in the active workbook	SHIFT-F11, ALT-SHIFT-F1
Move to the next worksheet	CTRL-PAGE DOWN
Move to the previous worksheet	CTRL-PAGE UP
Select the current worksheet and the next worksheet	CTRL-SHIFT-PAGE DOWN
Select the current worksheet and the previous worksheet	CTRL-SHIFT-PAGE UP
Move to the specified edge of the data region	CTRL-$\uparrow$, $\downarrow$, $\leftarrow$, or $\rightarrow$,
Move to the first cell in the row	HOME
Move to the first cell in the worksheet	CTRL-HOME
Move to the last used cell in the worksheet	CTRL-END
Move down one screen	PAGE DOWN
Move up one screen	PAGE UP
Move to the right by one screen	ALT-PAGE DOWN
Move to the left by one screen	ALT-PAGE UP
Scroll the workbook to display the active cell	CTRL-BACKSPACE
Display the Go To dialog box	CTRL-G

Selecting Items

Action	Keyboard Shortcut
Select the current column	CTRL-SPACEBAR
Select the current row	SHIFT-SPACEBAR
Select all cells on the current worksheet	CTRL-A
Reduce the selection to the active cell	SHIFT-BACKSPACE
Select all the objects on the current worksheet while retaining the current selection	CTRL-SHIFT-SPACEBAR
Enter the time in the active cell	CTRL-SHIFT-:
Enter the date in the active cell	CTRL-SHIFT-;
Fill the selected cells with the current entry	CTRL-ENTER

A

Action	Keyboard Shortcut
Formatting Items	
Toggle boldface	CTRL-B
Toggle italic	CTRL-I
Toggle underline	CTRL-U
Display the Style dialog box	ALT-'
Display the Format Cells dialog box	CTRL-1
Apply the General number format	CTRL-SHIFT-~
Apply the two-decimal-place Currency format	CTRL-SHIFT-$
Apply the Percentage format (no decimal places)	CTRL-SHIFT-%
Apply the *DD-MMM-YY* date format	CTRL-SHIFT-#
Apply the HH:MM AM/PM time format	CTRL-SHIFT-@
Apply the two-decimal-place number format with the thousands separator	CTRL-SHIFT-!
Toggle strikethrough	CTRL-5
Apply an outline border	CTRL-SHIFT-&
Remove the outline border	CTRL-SHIFT-_
Hiding and Unhiding Rows and Columns	
Hide all selected rows	CTRL-9
Hide all selected columns	CTRL-0
Unhide hidden rows in the selection	CTRL-SHIFT-(
Unhide hidden columns in the selection	CTRL-SHIFT-)
Cutting, Copying, and Pasting	
Copy the current selection to the Clipboard	CTRL-C, CTRL-INSERT
Paste the current contents of the Clipboard	CTRL-V, SHIFT-INSERT
Cut the current selection to the Clipboard	CTRL-X, SHIFT-DELETE
Copy the screen to the Clipboard as a picture	PRTSCR
Copy the active window to the Clipboard as a picture	ALT-PRTSCR
Display the contents of the current or next smart tag	ALT-SHIFT-F10
Repeating Actions and Invoking Tools	
Undo the previous action	CTRL-Z, ALT-BACKSPACE
Display the Find tab of the Find And Replace dialog box	CTRL-F, SHIFT+F5
Display the Replace tab of the Find And Replace dialog box	CTRL-H
Find the next instance of the search term (after closing the Find And Replace dialog box)	F4

Action	Keyboard Shortcut
Display the Insert Hyperlink dialog box	CTRL-K
Run the Spell Checker	F7
Display the Research pane with information about the clicked word	ALT-CLICK
Repeat the previous action	CTRL-Y
Working in PivotTables	
Select the entire PivotTable	CTRL-SHIFT-*
Group the selected items	ALT-SHIFT-→
Ungroup the grouped items	ALT-SHIFT-←
Creating a Chart	
Create a chart from the selected range	F11, ALT-F1
Creating a Table	
Display the Create Table dialog box	CTRL-L
Launching Help and the Visual Basic Editor	
Launch Help	F1
Display the Visual Basic Editor	ALT-F11
Display the Macro dialog box	ALT-F8

A

Index